# NEW
# DECORATING
# BOOK

# Better Homes and Gardens®

# NEW DECORATING BOOK

**BETTER HOMES AND GARDENS® BOOKS**
Editor: Gerald M. Knox
Art Director: Ernest Shelton

Furnishings and Design Editor: Shirley Van Zante
Senior Furnishings Editor, Books: Pamela Wilson Cullison

Associate Art Directors: Neoma Alt West,
Randall Yontz
Copy and Production Editors: David Kirchner,
Lamont Olson, David A. Walsh
Assistant Art Director: Harijs Priekulis
Senior Graphic Designer: Faith Berven
Graphic Designers: Alisann Dixon, Linda Ford,
Lyne Neymeyer, Lynda Haupert, Tom Wegner

Editor in Chief: Neil Kuehnl
Group Editorial Services Director: Duane Gregg
Executive Art Director: William J. Yates

General Manager: Fred Stines
Director of Publishing: Robert B. Nelson
Director of Retail Marketing: Jamie Martin
Director of Direct Marketing: Arthur Heydendael

**New Decorating Book**
Editor: Pamela Wilson Cullison
Copy and Production Editor: David A. Walsh
Graphic Designer: Faith Berven
Contributing Writers: Rose Gilbert, Jean LemMon,
Jane Cornell, Ola M. Pfeifer, Mary Bryson

Decorating means creating an environment that is as nice to live in as it is to look at. Mere embellishment is not enough. Today, for a home to be truly livable, it must be as practical as it is pretty—flexible and functional enough to meet all your family's needs. The aim of Better Homes and Gardens® **New Decorating Book** is to help and inspire you to achieve this end as easily and effectively as possible.

Twenty-five years have elapsed since the first Better Homes and Gardens® **Decorating Book** was published in 1956. Through the years, the original book has undergone numerous changes and reprintings—and has sold nearly 2,250,000 copies.

This latest, completely new edition departs from the familiar old looseleaf version; the new format provides a larger page size with bigger pictures and more information.

The **New Decorating Book** deals with good design in a straightforward way that is easy to understand and use. The book's 20 chapters cover all the elements of decorating a room—furniture selection; room arrangement; window, wall, and floor treatments; lighting; accessories; and much more. Hundreds of color photographs, plus helpful charts and how-to instructions, provide both practical information and inspirational ideas to help you make your home more beautiful, more comfortable, and more personal.

# CONTENTS

# BEGINNINGS

**D**ecorating a home is a rewarding experience, and not necessarily a costly one. However, few of us embark on a decorating project with total and absolute confidence. We may know in our mind's eye what we want our home (or a particular room) to look like, but turning this vision into a reality is often easier said than done. The difficulty, usually, is simply not knowing where or how to begin. Sometimes it's not being sure how to best express our tastes in a personal way. With so many options available, so many directions to go, it's no wonder we need help getting started on a decorating project. The best way to get over the initial hurdle is to spend some time making a realistic appraisal of your own and your family's living needs, your house and the space within it, and, of course, your budget. Make this appraisal and you will be well on your way to creating a home that not only looks good, but is truly right for you.

# BEGINNINGS

The process of decorating a home begins long before the first piece of furniture is purchased, or the first stroke of a paintbrush touches the wall. Actually, the process begins in childhood. Consciously or subconsciously, we take note of our own and other people's surroundings, and form an image of what for us constitutes beauty and comfort in a home. If our fondest memories include curling up with a good book in an overstuffed easy chair, it's likely we'll want to have a similar chair in our own homes. We can know and appreciate only the things we've been exposed to.

To expand our awareness of good design, it's necessary for most of us to study and observe. We can do this by making a concerted effort to expose ourselves to as many design influences as possible (books, magazines, museums, high-quality furniture stores, decorator showhouses), and by learning what we can about basic design principles, such as scale, balance, and contrast. One of the most important things to be learned from an increased awareness and sensitivity to good design is that good taste is not dependent on the size of one's bankbook. Quite the contrary. What matters most is expressing a sense of personal style—something that money can't buy. Here's another tenet of good design: Don't overdecorate. The secret of success is knowing when to stop.

Not only do personal concepts of design influence how we decorate our homes; much also depends on what's happening to society as a whole. Changing social patterns and economic trends invariably are reflected in our attitudes toward our homes. Take, for instance, the unparalleled rise of women in the work force during the past decade. Due in part to the movement for equal rights, and in part to economic pressures caused by high inflation and the need for two incomes, it is now the exception—not the rule—for a woman to be a full-time homemaker. It wasn't long ago that women—theoretically at least—could devote most of their time and energies toward home-related activities.

Now that this is no longer the case, one might think that interest in decorating would have decreased. But it hasn't. If anything, the interest is stronger. What has changed is our attitude toward furnishings for the home. Most homemakers today simply won't tolerate products that demand excessive time and effort to keep them looking and functioning well. It is no longer enough for, say, a floor covering to be merely beautiful. Now it must be beautiful, well-made, and most of all, easy to maintain. These demands extend to virtually all home furnishings products available today.

Another change that's occurring is the trend toward smaller living spaces. Increasing costs of land, labor, and building materials are not

likely to abate in the near future. New homes will continue to be built, but on a much smaller scale than in the past. The paradox involved here is that as homes decrease in size, the demands we put on them will increase proportionately. It is one thing to give up square footage, but another to sacrifice comfort and convenience. Only by adopting a flexible approach to decorating will our high expectations be met.

# BEGINNINGS

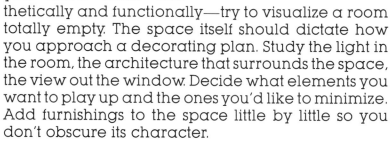

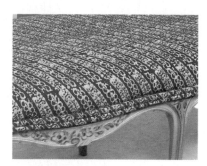

The space inside your home is your own little slice of the universe. It's where you do what you want, where you shut out the rest of the world if you choose, or invite others in to share your surroundings and hospitality. When you think of it like this, the space that is your home takes on new meaning and importance. How you use this space should, too.

To best use the space you have—both aesthetically and functionally—try to visualize a room totally empty. The space itself should dictate how you approach a decorating plan. Study the light in the room, the architecture that surrounds the space, the view out the window. Decide what elements you want to play up and the ones you'd like to minimize. Add furnishings to the space little by little so you don't obscure its character.

It isn't necessary—or even wise—to decorate an entire room all at once. To do so is hard on the budget. More importantly, additions to a room need to "settle in" before you can accurately assess what other furnishings are necessary. Only when several pieces are assimilated into the space around them should you think about adding more.

Be open-minded about your space. No longer should you allow a floor plan to dictate how you put various rooms to work. Forget labels. If you'd rather the dining room be a living room or vice versa, then by all means make the switch. The important thing is to make your space function in a way that will best suit you and your family's needs. If this means turning an extra bedroom into a den or a dining room, then so be it.

And don't overlook the possibilities that remodeling changes offer. Add divider "walls" where you want them, or, where structurally practical, consider removing unneeded walls that simply confine space in small-room cubicles. Open up these tightly strictured areas into one larger space and you immediately increase the options for function, comfort, and livability.

Remember, too, that it isn't the size of the space you have but how you use it that counts. Don't let small space intimidate you. Even the smallest home can be given the illusion of spaciousness. Start by paring down. For some reason, many people feel compelled to fill every square inch with things and more things. All too often the end effect is downright claustrophobic. Any room can be made to look considerably larger than it is simply by stripping it of unnecessary furniture and extraneous accessories.

In the pages that follow we'll demonstrate just how easily some sound decorating principles can help you visually expand your space. You'll see how low furniture arrangements tend to give a room an open, uncrowded feeling, and how small-scale furniture creates a light, open effect in a room. There's the illusion that more space exists for people and activities when less of the space is taken up by furniture.

Color can visually alter how large an area appears. To make a room look larger than it is, use a light color on the walls and ceiling. Reflective surfaces such as foil paper or mirrored walls make the illusion of spaciousness still greater, as do dimensional effects such as scenic murals.

And to make the space you have work even harder, do not settle for furniture that performs only a single function. Choose versatile dual-purpose pieces. And try to build more than one function into each room. Combine day and night uses for bedrooms so they are sleeping quarters by night, but when the sun comes up, they easily convert to office, playroom, or den.

# BEGINNINGS

B efore a decorating dream can become a reality, certain practicalities must be attended to. First of all, you must be honest with yourself. Is the project you have in mind realistic? Have you figured out approximately how much it's going to cost and whether your pocketbook can afford it? Is it a project you can do yourself, or will outside help be required? Is it a project you are willing to do yourself? If not, you might consider hiring the services of an interior designer. If you're not sure of your talents, paying for professional help might well save you money in the long run. Once you've established whether your dream is within the realm of possibility, your next step is to develop a game plan that will see the project through to completion. You'll want to do this whether your project involves a total redo, or simply sprucing up an existing scheme. The objective is to work out your plan in attainable increments of both time and money. Begin by listing your priorities in terms of needs and wants. Some expenditures should take precedence. For instance, a comfortable bed is a must, but the bedroom wallpaper—or even the bedspread—can wait. Once your priorities are in order, you can determine how quickly you can afford to proceed. And don't be discouraged if your decorating plan is going to take longer than you'd hoped. The best decorating schemes develop very slowly over a period of time.

You'll get a lot more mileage from your decorating dollar if you spend the most on what has to last the longest and will get the hardest wear. For instance, if your budget is tight, invest in good hall carpet and cut back on the quality of the bedroom floor covering. Similarly, spend money on a good sofa, even if it means dining at a makeshift, skirted table until you can afford dining furniture.

In the long run you'll find that buying a few good pieces over a period of time is a wiser investment

than filling a space with less-costly and less-well-designed furnishings. One special piece of furniture, an elegant area rug, or a piece or two of original art can set the mood for an entire room and—more importantly—give you pleasure for years to come. Besides being a decorative bonus, one fine furniture piece or art object is an investment in the future—something that will reward you with many years of classic beauty and function.

This doesn't mean, however, that you must settle for a half-empty room while you work to complete your decorating plan. On the contrary. Today, you do not have to look very far to find exceptionally well-designed "interim" furnishings and accessories to suit every budget and style preference. Examples of interim furnishings include inexpensive wicker pieces from big import stores;

sofas, tables, chairs, and wall systems from life-style stores and mail order outlets; and unfinished pieces from specialty stores.

And, of course, there are always "finds" to be unearthed at garage sales, flea markets, secondhand shops, and auctions. By all means, fill in with these pieces now; later, when you can afford to replace them, you can move these good-looking standbys to less-public rooms, or sell them at your own garage sale.

But remember, furnishing a room with budget pieces requires an eye for good value. In addition to beauty and comfort, you'll want to look for pieces that are flexible, functional, and durable. Also, the more basic the lines, the more easily they'll mix with other furnishings.

# ACHIEVING AMBIENCE

**M**emorable rooms, like memorable people, have distinct personalities. In decorating parlance "personality" means the overall statement a room makes, the feelings it evokes when you enter, and what it says to you about the people who live there. This overriding mood, or ambience, is the heart of a successful room scheme. And, since ambience is a matter of personal expression, not specific styles, you can select from the entire spectrum of furnishings, choosing anything you like as long as it is consistent with the mood you want to create. To help you assess your surroundings, we'll show you a selection of rooms—some romantically nostalgic, some sleekly sophisticated, some casually country, all highly individual.

# AMBIENCE
## CASUAL

For all their easy-going appeal, casual room schemes do not just happen, they require the same selective preplanning as the most formal settings. Unlike a room that's merely decoratively disheveled, a well-conceived casual scheme is informal by design, not indifference. To arrive at a look that appears unpremeditated, always consider these criteria before choosing furnishings for casual living:
• Is it comfortable?
• Does it fit in naturally, or is it contrived and self-conscious?
• Will it be easy to live with, or will it demand special maintenance?

### CASUAL IS COMFORTABLE

The very essence of casual living is comfort. That means bodily comfort: Does it feel good to sit on, to walk over, to touch? There are secondary, more psychological dimensions to comfort, too. Furniture that seems to make demands upon us is inherently *un*comfortable. Sit-up-straight Victorian chairs demand decorum by their very attitude. Leather sling chairs, on the other hand, issue a visual invitation to sit back and relax.

Color also has its own comfort quotient—a very subjective one. Soft, restful colors may soothe the eye and psyche, whereas bolder colors are likely to excite, perhaps even agitate.

Over-elegant materials and contrived effects of any kind are contrary to casualness in decorating. Whimsy, however, adds a delightful dimension to casual

rooms. Personality pieces are welcome; so are elegant antiques, as long as they don't take themselves too seriously. For example, you could easily lead the casual life with a Louis XIV armchair if it were upholstered in, say, a bright cotton, but not in a formal velvet brocade or damask.

Maintenance is another important factor in casual decorating. If a piece of furniture is likely to need fussing over, you'll never be able to relax around it. Cull it from a casual room scheme, and opt instead for easy-care fabrics, surface soil protectors, and finishes that are as impervious as possible to household hazards. The same goes for accessories, including plants. Prima donna plants that make excessive maintenance demands are diametrically opposed to the easy life. Weed them out in advance.

*The seeming nonchalance that makes this lofty apartment living room so inviting is actually worked out carefully in terms of no-worry furnishings and calming neutral colors.*

# AMBIENCE
## CASUAL

1

2

**N**atural materials are inherently pleasing to the senses, and always at home in a casual setting. Most people are automatically at ease with exposed wood beams, walls, and floors, with growing green things, and with slate, tile, brick, and stone. Such basically honest materials rarely put on formal airs. If you're after a casual look, make the most of the architecture—mellow woods, natural light, and structural idiosyncrasies that will add charm to the scheme. In such a setting, the most casual furnishings are welcome: conformable modulars, handloomed rugs, nubby textured fabrics, and such artful accessories as old quilts, shell collections, and clusters of interesting weeds or dried flowers.

**1** The soaring architecture of this wood-warmed room lends itself to casual decorating. Natural wood surfaces finished with polyurethane varnish let the beauty of the grain show through. Furnishings are a blend of earth-toned hues.

**2** This casual "country" dining spot is actually high in a big-city apartment. The room's charm comes from the seemingly unrelated furniture mix—an industrial lamp over an old pine table, new Windsor chairs, and an old trolley-car seat. It's the straightforward, functional style of each piece that blends this maverick collection together.

**3** This once-dreary room has been cheered with paint and easy-living fabrics. White muslin, quilted for extra puff, covers the window seat cushion.

20

# AMBIENCE
## TRADITIONAL

There's a measure of comfort in the very word: "tradition." It implies time-tested furnishings, assimilated into a genteel blend of many styles from many periods. By nature, traditional decorating transcends passing trends and fleeting fads to become a melding of the best from the past.

It's a broad-brush category that embraces classic French furniture, as well as pieces by Thomas Chippendale, George Hepplewhite, and the Adam brothers of England. And, under its ample umbrella there's room for much more—selected Early American styles, French Provincial and elegant Oriental, even Art Nouveau and Deco, plus some of the finer pieces from the heyday of Victoriana.

This is not to say, however, that traditional furnishings are old hat. Decorating for present-day living calls for a lively interpretation of the past, since today's active homes simply have no room for museum-like collections of furniture.

Whether you are decorating with authentic antiques or with modern-day reproductions, enduring traditional schemes call for well-ordered arrangements, pleasing color blends with no strident contrasts, and, most of all, furniture pieces that will never go out of style. These pieces generally are straightforward and clean, with graceful curves and flowing shapes. And, a traditional room is the place for displaying accessories and mementos lovingly collected over the years.

Although a traditional room may have a degree of formality about it, the overall effect will be of welcoming hospitality. Let there be no harsh or jarring notes to disturb the room's calming continuity.

*This living room has fresh and very untraditional overtones, even though its individual parts are almost all in the best classic tradition. The marvelous mixture of pieces and periods assembled here includes an antique Victorian secretary, flanked by prints of four 19th-century American presidents. Both the French side chair, now resplendent in rich rose damask, and the handsome Italian import coffee table play up the curves of the imposing old secretary.*

*What really brings this room dramatically up to date is the bright yellow fabric that sweeps over all the upholstered pieces. Quilted to emphasize the contemporary floral design, the fabric gives a modern lift to the spirits and to the color level in this room dominated by dark woods.*

# AMBIENCE
## TRADITIONAL

**1** The presence of plaid adds decorative punch to this traditional living room. Note the detailing on the green wing chair—the same plaid has been used as piping.

**2** This inviting keeping room in a modern-day house is true to the traditions of earlier times. Rough-hewn beams and wide-plank floors are reproduced with care to serve as background for a collection of prized antiques.

**3** When a traditional room starts looking time-worn, call on color for a decorative lift. Here a bold scheme of yellow, peach, and pink gives the room new life.

**4** The bed in this English-style bedroom is a do-it-yourself project. Colorful mattress ticking wraps the mock four-poster made of 2x4s. The headboard consists of old door panels.

1

2  3

If you've set your decorating course in a traditional direction, you can liven up furnishings from the past with contemporary touches of fresh color, texture, and pattern.

4

# AMBIENCE
## ECLECTIC

**E**clectic is a fairly recent addition to our decorating vocabulary. Its dictionary definition comes right to the point: Made up of what seems best of varied sources.

The key word here is "best." Eclectic is not a catchall word for catchall decorating. Quite the opposite. An eclectic approach presupposes a sophisticated design sense, one that mixes elements with deliberateness and authority. Eclectic decorating is in gentle rebellion against past dictums that prescribed carefully matched and arranged furnishings. Once there were universally accepted rules for dressing a home. Today, it's one's own likes and dislikes that govern furnishings selections.

If you decide eclecticism is your kind of decorating, you'll have a lot of latitude to indulge your personal preferences. Eclectic interiors can embrace many periods and styles. They are, therefore, exciting to assemble and, because they are such highly personal reflections of taste, they are also fun places to live in or visit. Since every decorative element is unpredictable, there is always something new and interesting to look at and admire.

A collection of individual pieces often represent years of thoughtful accumulation. Many unusual items will result from forays to flea markets, auctions, and antique shops.

The most successful eclectic rooms, however, are masterpieces of selectivity. Although it's true that varied items can go into an eclectic scheme regardless of their design origin, it is not wise to abandon yourself completely to impetuous acquisition. You're apt to end up with a mishmash only masquerading as eclecticism.

## MOODS SHOULD MATCH

One sure way to avoid a hodgepodge is to apply this basic criterion to every piece you consider buying: Is it well designed and in good taste?

Although you're free to roam the design gamut, picking not only from different periods and places, but from different price strata as well, each element you choose must pass muster on its own merits. An old handmade quilt from the attic can have as much inherent beauty and integrity as an expensive hand-knotted rug from the Orient. Both qualify as tasteful and well-designed. Yet the *mood* of the two differs greatly. The quilt is basically informal and country in feeling. The Oriental rug, on the other hand, can go with the most formal furnishings, whatever their design or origin. This difference in mood becomes a useful yardstick against which you can measure the compatibility of disparate pieces. Is the piece appropriate to the overall formal or informal mood you want to maintain?

For example, you can mix classic French armchairs with an equally classic Chippendale camelback sofa, and dress the picture window in contemporary vertical blinds. Unrelated as the three elements are, they all have in common a formal quality that lets them live attractively and compatibly together under the same roof.

At the other extreme of the mood swing, you can create a charmingly informal eclectic room with a modern sweep of modular seating and a wall filled with gleanings from a country store. Raffia matting from the Orient might cover the floor, and the cocktail table could be a tree-trunk section topped with a round of smoked acrylic. Again, all the elements in this eclectic gathering hail from highly different backgrounds. The one thing they have in common that makes the room work is their basic informality.

## COLOR AS COORDINATOR

In a room filled with unlike elements, color is also a unifying force. It can smoothly blend assorted pieces into a pleasing whole. Repetition is your best ally in coloring an eclectic decorating scheme. Try to work within a simple, basic plan of only a few colors, and be sure to repeat each one often enough to give the room a well-balanced look.

As a part of your color plan, you might use the same pattern on several furniture pieces. A favorite eclectic technique is to choose a smart contemporary upholstery print to freshen up older, period furniture; or, conversely, use some old tapestry or rug pieces, for instance, to cover toss pillows for a contemporary sofa.

You also can unify a mixed bag of furniture from several time spans by keeping major accessory items all uniformly in the same style.

*Even though these furnishings are of mixed ancestry, the mood of the room is serene and integrated. Look carefully and you'll see just how different all the decorative elements are that contribute to this final effect.*

*The commanding presence in this room is the grandfather clock, with all the years of tradition it embodies in its scrolled and polished mahogany frame. Front and center, an ultramodern ribbon chair undulates like a sculpture across an old Persian rug.*

*In the serenely colored background is a pine schoolmaster's desk from early American days; angled over it is a collection of Japanese prints.*

*With its sky-lighted roof and minimally dressed windows, the architectural envelope of the room is inherently clean-lined and simple. It becomes a fitting backdrop for this carefully assembled collection of furnishings, each standing on its own design merits.*

# AMBIENCE
## ECLECTIC

**A**s the popularity of eclecticism has increased, many furniture manufacturers have stopped making only "suites" of carefully matched pieces, and have begun developing individual furnishings to meet our equally individual living needs.

Also, there are no longer restrictive room assignments for specific pieces of furniture. You can forget the labels *living room* table, *dining room* chair, *front hall* console, *boudoir* chest. The point is to use a piece where it pleases you most, not where a label or store grouping would have it. Classic pieces are particularly versatile. Keep this in mind when you move to a new house or decide to redo a room.

**1** Rebellion against the commonplace gives this room its unique appeal. For starters, there's the setting—hardly your average bedroom backdrop. Then there's the color scheme: A startling combination of peach walls and a deep saffron painted ceiling. The off-center contemporary bed is surrounded by a supporting cast of eclectic furnishings—a handsome Oriental screen, two antique English chairs, and a grouping of woven straw baskets. Adding even more dash to the decorating scheme are the large pillows covered with various batik print fabrics.

**2** An exciting tension between old and new exists in this eclectically decorated room. The basic environment is traditional, with the molding-framed walls, French doors, and classically simple fireplace. But tradition takes a sharp turn toward today with shiny, lacquered walls of dark brown and the modern artwork over the mantel. The sisal carpet and brass shell reading lamps are additional modern touches that play nicely against the antique atmosphere.

**3** Art—for drama's sake— sets this almost-stark dining room apart from its traditional beginnings. Carved wood and cane dining chairs contrast pleasantly with the sleek-and-shine of the black dining table. Everything in the room is uncluttered, from the floor-to-ceiling vertical blinds to the no-nonsense track lighting overhead. A plush underpaving of wall-to-wall carpet warms and softens the room, keeping it from becoming too austere. Additional drama is provided by the magnificent flower-filled glass vase.

In eclectic decorating, furniture is freed from its stereotyped roles for use in specific rooms, and can perform decorative and practical functions wherever needed in your house.

3

# AMBIENCE
## COUNTRY

**W**hy in this modern age of space technology and computer science should the simple furniture, tools, and handcrafts of an earlier time hold such appeal? Perhaps it's because "country style" furnishings have become synonymous with a way of life that's casual, comfortable, uncomplicated.

Whatever the reasons, country decorating is one of the freshest looks around. Never mind that the style is as old as the hills. Never mind either that these simple furnishings hail from many countries, rather than one.

All country furniture has some common characteristics. It is purely functional in design: sturdy, simple, and straightforward. The styles were adapted from the furniture of the aristocracy, and the pieces were handcrafted from materials common to the countryside.

Today, as in the past, these furnishings are totally unselfconscious and undemanding —with no hint of city-slick sophistication. Hallmarks include hand-rubbed and hand-carved woods, and hand-loomed fabrics; unpretentious furniture; and pleasantly uncomplicated color schemes. Country rooms are also identifiable by criss-crossed curtains, bright chintz and calico fabrics, braided rugs over bare wood floors, quilts and comforters, and homespun accessories.

Homey touches all, these elements are the backbone of country decorating. Working within this easy-going framework, you can create surroundings as delightfully down-home as a country cottage.

*Picture this room in a typical 1930s house with white walls, ceiling, and fireplace, and with a standard carpet on the floor. That's exactly the way it looked before two antique buffs turned it into the cozy room you see here. Now, the scheme expresses all the underlying appeal of country: uncomplicated, rich with color, and warm with the natural tones of wood, flowers, and simple accessories.*

*To begin, old carpet was ripped up and replaced with handsome pegged and grooved hardwood flooring. To bring the fireplace more into character with the new scheme, it was stripped and stained dark to blend with the mellow wood floor.*

*A cheerful floral glazed chintz on the upholstered pieces sets the color theme; an accent hue from the print was used as a dramatic change for the walls. To crisp up the scheme, the owners repainted the ceiling, moldings, and woodwork white. Homemade tieback curtains of cotton batiste hang at the windows. Furniture is a blend of English and American pieces, lovingly collected over the years.*

# AMBIENCE
## COUNTRY

**M**ore than just an assemblage of furniture, country decorating is a mood. It's a mood evoked most easily with decorative elements that are natural, handcrafted, and utilitarian (as well as decorative).

Natural ingredients include such materials as barnboard walls, sisal rugs, hand-adzed beams, and butcher-block table tops, all of which fit comfortably into country interiors.

Handcrafted items can include everything from San Blas Indian embroidery and old quilts to earthenware dishes and carved wooden decoys.

Utilitarian applies to many workaday objects that can be admired for their own sake, such as woven baskets, a weathervane, or a collection of farm tools. Above all, it's the basic integrity of these items

that makes them so appealing. That's why a handful of herbs, hung upside down to dry in the kitchen, makes an appropriate accessory in country-flavored schemes.

Refusing to take themselves seriously, country rooms easily accept the quaint and the curious, such as Victorian umbrella trees or old-fashioned penny banks and children's toys. There's also room for the outmoded and outcast: antimacassars, ancestral portraits (even though they may not be your own), antique bottles, and old medicine tins.

If country style is for you, then choose your color scheme from the quietly natural earthen tones or the unfettered, exuberant colors of, say, a patchwork quilt or a Grandma Moses painting.

**Color a country scheme as you like, in natural, warm earth tones, or in the uninhibited hues of a simple rag rug.**

**1** Much of the country furniture we now admire was, in its day, uncherished, simple furniture. As soon as the families who owned it came into means, they were quick to edge out the old pieces we now prize.

Happily, enough of the originals have survived to serve as models for the many pieces of country furniture that are being faithfully reproduced. This warm, wood-paneled dining room is a case in point, with its reproduction rush-seat chairs, plank-top trestle table, and slender pine cabinet.

**2** Country decorating reaches directly back to Early America for much of its inspiration. Here, a narrow rope bed, called a "hired-man's bed," becomes a sofa. It's covered with an old Pennsylvania quilt and a collection of family-made pillows. The pine coffee table is an authentic Early American treasure.

**3** Folk art and primitive American furnishings give this room its countrified personality. The setting combines a vintage camelback sofa and a pair of contemporary sling chairs. An antique blanket chest provides both storage space and a handy table surface.

**4** Rooms with a country decor need not rely solely on antiques and natural aging. This bed-sitting room incorporates both reproductions and a modern touch— the blue-and-white comforter on the bed. European in mood, this is country decorating handled the way our practical forebears would applaud; the armoire stores clothes, the table strips for serious work; even the lace tablecloth can go, harmfree, into the washing machine.

4

# AMBIENCE
## HIGH STYLE

**H**igh style denotes a very sophisticated look that's up to the minute but not avant garde. It appeals to people who are well-acquainted with the world of design, and who can afford to indulge their taste preferences.

High style excludes extraneous furnishings and accessories. It frowns on fads and is contemptuous of all things cute and contrived. Clutter is not a part of this look. A high-style setting is carefully pruned so each element is chosen for its distinctive lines and for its integrity of form and function.

Here even color is kept to a minimum, with hues drawn from the cool side of the spectrum to give a room a spacious and expansive feeling. Neutrals are effective, too.

Many high-style settings are expressions of the dictum that "less is more." But for all their elegant simplicity, the resulting rooms generally sidestep the ultra-spare look often associated with this minimalist decorating philosophy.

With a high-style approach, you have ample opportunity to express your tastes. You can build a room around an especially beautiful piece of furniture, no matter what its design heritage.

Elegant antiques are completely at home in such sophisticated interiors. Make them the centerpiece of the room, and build around them with quiet, non-competitive furniture and accessories. Or you may choose to highlight a dramatic painting or a handsome rug that expresses your personality in a single, refined stroke.

*The art of understatement is apparent in this large, high-ceiling living room. Furnishings are few, but their effect is powerful when played against the stark white walls and the gleaming expanse of the parquet floor. Simple elegance is evinced by contrasting textures, and a sophisticated mix of furniture styles. No matter that the pine-frame French chairs are from one era and that the bold geometric upholstery fabric is from another. The mixture of furnishings gives the kind of decorating panache that makes the high style look so special. The glittering mirrored bar to the left of the seating area adds dazzle to the setting and reflects the opposite end of the expansive room. All lighting—except for the simple brass floor lamp placed next to the sofa—is provided by recessed ceiling fixtures set on dimmer controls.*

**Succinctly defined, high-style decorating is restrained elegance; good taste expressed in its simplest terms.**

There's nothing "down home" about high-style decorating. What nostalgia is to the country look, reserve and restraint are to high style. It's urban and urbane, well suited to big-city apartments with their straight lines and precisely defined spaces, and to city people with their sophisticated and stepped-up lifestyles. Also amenable to the high-style look is contemporary architecture or any house that's stripped of an overdose of details.

Privacy needs and climate conditions permitting, bare windows and nearly bare walls are appropriate backgrounds for a high-style decor. If some type of window treatment *is* called for, consider something simple such as tailored vertical or mini-slat blinds, or unobtrusive shades. Fabric window treatments are rarely found in a high-style setting, but when they are, they're always uncomplicated and minimal.

Dramatic lighting is essential to the success of a high-style scheme. Frequently, ceiling-mounted spotlights, recessed, cove, and track lighting are used in lieu of conventional lamps. The more theatrical the lighting effect, the better.

Lustrous hardwood and parquet floors look well in a high-style decor, as do tightly woven carpets, nubby wool Berbers, colorful dhurrie rugs, and other striking area rugs. Also, slate and marble floors can be uptown elegant.

A high-style setting is not the place for an abundance of accessories or mementos. Stick with a few simple, but striking objects for best effect.

**1** A class act, from its quiet colors to the formal symmetry of the furniture arrangement, this high-rise living room really does make less into more. A scant half-dozen elements form an almost mirror image around a handsome dhurrie rug. The wall of vertical blinds at the windows accents the architectural look.

**2** An element of Oriental tranquility here transcends the obviously Eastern ancestry of the lacquer table and antique armchair from Burma. Calm colors and classic balance contribute an overall elegance that's as low-key as it is high style.

**3** Spare and unpretentious, this small living room has been stripped of frills. Furnishings are crisply functional, from the classic Hans Wegner "Peacock" chairs to the modular seating and the butcher-block bracket table.

# AMBIENCE
## ROMANTIC

It's the unpredictable combination of ingredients that makes romantic decorating such a delight for the eye. The idea is to indulge your imagination, to be fanciful and inventively free-thinking. Nothing heavy-handed belongs in a romantic setting. Choose what's fresh and unfettered.

Colors should be powder puff pretty, and patterns and prints lighthearted. Choose unponderous styles for furnishings, and try to avoid weighty, dark-colored pieces.

Art work can be just about anything you like as long as it's not too hard-edged graphic.

Windows, too, should be treated with a light hand. This is the place for plissé, Priscillas, and Austrian shades. It is also the place for balloon shades, generous helpings of lace, and swags and jabots made of ninon and taffeta.

The same approach applies to fabrics. Avoid too-practical tweeds, and too much heavy velvet. Polished cottons are much more in keeping with the romantic mood, in colors and prints that are frankly meant to be pretty.

And since you can be a bit fearless when you're romantically inclined, feel free to bring in a potpourri of different patterns and prints. As long as the patterns have a common color bond, they will add eye-catching interest to the room.

Soft, moody lighting is especially à propos for a romantic room setting, so avoid lamps and fixtures that are apt to cast a glare. Here's the place to indulge your fancy for whimsical lampshades of an earlier era.

*This delightful living room, with its Palladian doors and stained-glass windows, used to be the rectory of an old Southern church. Now it's home for two inveterate collectors of fanciful things, be they antique, traditional, or contemporary in design. The adventurous combination of furnishings includes two Italian armchairs, an antique French bench, and a white-glazed elephant-foot table. Other imaginative items in the room include a Tiffany floor lamp with tasseled fringe, and a charming old bird cage; two Queen's palm trees add stature to the setting. The miscellany of styles is anchored by an antique blue and white Chinese area rug. Walls are upholstered, not painted, with gray linen. Simple scallop-edged window shades offer privacy when needed, but do not detract from the beauty of the windows themselves.*

# AMBIENCE
## ROMANTIC

**1** The design inspiration for this scheme came from the countryside of 18th century France. It was a time when charmingly naive copies of elegant court furniture were created to meet the needs of country folk. A *bombé* chest in honey-toned pine typifies the graceful curving lines associated with fine French styling, as does the pine sofa table and the rush-seat armchair. The salmon-painted *boiserie* (carved wood paneling) is offset by the mellow hardwood plank floors. The same salmon color is picked up in polished cotton fabric that covers the matching loose-seat sofas, and is used for the tieback curtains. Because the fireplace is a natural focal point, all furnishings are comfortably arranged around it.

**2** Nostalgic and nice, this *un*stuffy front parlor also owes its allure to an earlier era. But its appeal is as fresh as today. Attics and antique shops yielded furnishings the collectors perked up with paint and colorful print fabrics. Plants, a brightly polished hardwood floor, and a frothy Austrian shade infuse the room with a youthful feeling despite its turn-of-the-century trappings.

**3** What gives this small bedroom its sentimental charm is the liberal use of a single small-scale print. Lavished on the walls and ceiling, the provincial pattern imbues the room with an open, airy feeling. Adding further to the old-fashioned atmosphere is a companion fabric used to upholster the headboard of the antique wooden bed, cover the pillows and box spring, and softly drape the circular bedside table.

# FURNITURE

**F**urniture is the essence of what makes a house a home. Strip a room of its furnishings and all that remains is an empty shell; a space devoid of all comfort, convenience, and decoration. But "comfort" and "convenience" are terms that mean different things to different people. It's important to select furniture that fits your way of living and your idea of what constitutes comfort in a home environment. This sounds simple enough, but all too often we end up with furniture, fabrics, and other items that just don't suit our homes—in either style or function. Impatience is often the culprit. We tend to "want what we want when we want it," then pay later (in more ways than one) for our haste. The secret is to take plenty of time to determine your own life-style, then to carefully select pieces that suit your personal preferences. This chapter is designed to help you shop for and buy furniture that you'll enjoy not only now, but for years to come.

# FURNITURE
## THE CLASSICS-ENGLISH/AMERICAN

I t took two centuries for American colonists to hew communities out of wilderness, fight for their independence, and develop a thriving nation. During those same two hundred years, some of the world's greatest furniture designs emerged, and not all those classics came from Europe. Infant America, with more vitality than sophistication, contributed its own adaptations of English furniture. The result was an English/American interchange that makes the two strains of furniture design nearly impossible to separate.

The purpose of good design is to serve the specific needs of the people and time when it is created. So, as people and life-styles change through the ages, furniture designs also change. The American colonists adapted the furniture styles of England that they had brought with them to suit their new needs, the native materials available—and the skills of colonial furniture-makers.

In England, furniture (as well as fashions, creative arts, even pastimes) was influenced by the current ruling monarch. We have the reign of William III to thank for turning the castle into a home. The Dutch William of Orange and his queen, Mary, were by royal standards a very domestic couple. For that reason, English furniture and rooms during the reign of William and Mary (1688–1702) took on intimate, livable proportions, giving us the prototype of our rooms today.

Most furniture of this period was of Dutch design extraction, modified and Anglicized. Walnut replaced oak as the primary wood, and furniture pieces seemed lighter, more slender, and more graceful than in previous periods. The rectangular silhouettes remained, but the introduction of curved lines softened the overall design. Much of this furniture was decorated with marquetry, displaying Dutch skill in veneering.

A typical William and Mary high chest displays this style's most identifying feature, the legs. They're straight, baluster-shaped, and are turned, tapering down to stretchers. The stretchers can also be tip-offs to a William and Mary design. Some are flat, serpentine-shaped pieces that crisscross diagonally from leg to leg, others arc or bow.

## AMERICAN TRANSLATIONS

While William and Mary furniture was developing in England, American colonists were concerned with survival—food and shelter. Not until these needs were met could furniture become important. And even when it did, limited space in cottages and lack of skill in furniture making resulted in pieces that were crude by English standards.

The simple lines of the trestle table, for instance, show how basic American furniture needs were. The ladderback chair is another example of 17th-century English furniture adapted to meet a new country's needs.

Native woods such as pine and maple replaced the fine furniture woods of Europe. And decoration, where it existed, reflected both the ethnic heritage of the colonists and the naiveté of their woodworking skills. Dutch colonists usually embellished their furniture pieces with painted folk art motifs. Other colonists used traces of carving in low relief, featuring simple designs. The later, undecorated furniture of the Shakers was so austere it looked almost modern in design.

## AMERICA'S DESIGN ROOTS

Most colonists patterned their furniture after English cottage furniture. The Windsor chair is an example, with its characteristic wheel-rim back and spoke-like spindles. Though named for the English castle, the Windsor chair is traditionally identified as American. Historic purists, however, tell us that perhaps the only truly American piece of Colonial furniture design is the Boston rocker, sometimes credited as another product of Ben Franklin's inventive mind.

Generally, the creation of American furniture was left to colonial carpenters who built basic pieces from what they remembered of English designs. Later, creative American cabinetmakers followed actual patterns of fine English furniture.

By the time America outgrew its infancy and entered the Federal Period (1780–1830), its skilled furniture makers produced pieces as beautiful as any in the world.

# FURNITURE
## THE CLASSICS-ENGLISH/AMERICAN

After William and Mary had helped to "humanize" the proportions of English furniture, Queen Anne ascended the throne and furniture design moved into a whole new realm of livability. For the first time, a woman had major influence on furniture style, and she placed the emphasis on grace and comfort.

The English during the early 18th century had more leisure time than ever before, and had more need for furniture to augment their newfound life-style. Designers created pieces specifically for serving tea, for playing games, and for sitting comfortably while enjoying either pastime. New members of the furniture family were tea tables, drop-leaf tables, and open-fronted china cabinets.

Queen Anne furniture was made almost exclusively of walnut, although that's where its similarity to earlier styles stopped. Lavish surface ornamentation disappeared; this new furniture achieved its own kind of beauty with veneers and delicate low-relief carvings. The shell motif was by far the most popular decoration, adorning chair backs, "knees" of chair legs, and aprons of chests. The gently curved cabriole leg that distinguishes the Queen Anne style became the dominant feature in furniture design for nearly half a century. Besides the characteristic curved leg, the pad foot of Queen Anne furniture is another clue to identification. Chairs, chests, and tables no longer had stretchers, and side-chair backs featured splats, often in fiddle shapes. The highboy, or high chest, is distinctly Queen Anne and embodies the best qualities of the period—graceful proportions, restrained lines, and exquisite detailing.

### DESIGNED FOR COMFORT

During the Queen Anne period, furniture became more than a mere household necessity. Now, comfort was a prime consideration. Seating pieces, for instance, were padded and upholstered. Chair designs featured seats with wide fronts to accommodate women's billowy skirts. And the popular wing-back chair, with its characteristic shape, originally was designed to protect the sitter's head from drafts.

### ENGLAND AFTER ANNE

Queen Anne was the last English monarch associated by name with a furniture style. In succeeding periods, the designers are the ones who have gone down in furniture history. The names of Chippendale, Sheraton, and Hepplewhite are synonymous with fine furniture.

Thomas Chippendale, who worked in the last half of the 18th century, transformed the graceful Queen Anne lines into heavier, more structural silhouettes. The cabriole leg gave way to a straight, square leg. The pad foot was replaced by the claw-and-ball foot, and the fiddle-back splat of side chairs became the carved and pierced back splat characteristic of Chippendale's work. After the import duty on mahogany was lifted in 1733, this fine wood replaced walnut as the favorite of English furniture makers, including Chippendale.

Though Chippendale introduced the furniture world to **chinoiserie** (a French term for anything Chinese style), these "Chinese Chippendale" pieces were created on consignment—strictly to please the cabinetmaker's clients. It's the camelback sofa, block-front chest, and side chairs that best typify the style of this great furniture maker.

### BACK TO THE LIGHT LOOK

The heavy lines of Chippendale furniture gave way to the lighter and airier work of Thomas Sheraton and George Hepplewhite. Both men were better known for their designs than their workmanship; it was from their pattern books that the furniture bearing their names was produced.

Sheraton, considered second only to Chippendale in English furniture design, created pieces characterized by a fragile, slender look. Delicate legs, either round or square, tapered down to a natural or spade foot. Chair arms are straight, and caning is prevalent, as are inlays of exotic woods.

Hepplewhite's style, like that of most other furniture designers, is best characterized by his chair designs. Legs tend to be plain, either fluted or reeded, and tapered to a spade foot; the chair back is usually shaped in the form of a shield.

TRESTLE TABLE

WINDSOR CHAIR

LADDERBACK CHAIR

BOSTON ROCKER

47

# FURNITURE
## ENGLISH/AMERICAN

QUEEN ANNE WING CHAIR

QUEEN ANNE HIGHBOY

QUEEN ANNE SIDE CHAIR

**BLOCK-FRONT CHEST**

**CHIPPENDALE SIDE CHAIR**

**CHIPPENDALE CAMELBACK SOFA**

# FURNITURE
## ENGLISH/AMERICAN

SHERATON SIDEBOARD

SHERATON SOFA

PENCIL POST BED

HEPPLEWHITE SIDE CHAIR

PEMBROKE TABLE

FEDERAL ARMCHAIR

# FURNITURE
## THE CLASSICS - FRENCH

During the 18th century, the tastes of the ruling monarchs still dictated French furniture design. And though the two most famous kings—Louis XV and Louis XVI—shared the same name, their tastes were vastly different.

### LOUIS XV

Louis XV had a flair for the romantic, and an inordinate love of luxury. The furniture designs that graced his court have an unmistakably feminine look about them. Pieces are smaller in scale and are intricately carved. All furniture lines are sinuously curved; symmetry and straight lines are absent. Pastel-painted wood finishes became popular during Louis XV's reign, as did the swollen fronts that characterize bombé chests.

The first upholstered armchair can be credited to Louis XV. The chair—called a bergère—is recognized for its inviting low slung lines, gently curved legs, and full-upholstered arms.

Rococo—an elaborate, frivolous form of furniture ornamentation—also ran rampant during the days of Louis XV. Supposedly an attempt to emulate nature through furniture motifs, rococo (a contraction of the French words for rock and shell) went a bit beyond the nature theme to include such things as cupids, hearts, doves, and muscial instruments.

### LOUIS XVI

The frills and adornments so loved by Louis XV lost favor when Louis XVI took the throne. In fact, furniture design did a complete about-face. Louis XVI was not the lusty, pleasure-seeking king his predecessor was. His pursuits were more scholarly.

During Louis XVI's first year of reign, serious exploration began at the ruins of Pompeii and Herculaneum, which encouraged a shift to classicism. Graceful lines and beautiful proportions were the order of the day.

Chairs, such as the **fauteuil**, featured straight legs and backs, with seats curved at the sides and front. Padded chair backs often hung on posts above the seats to accommodate **panniers**, the bustle-like pouffs worn by court women.

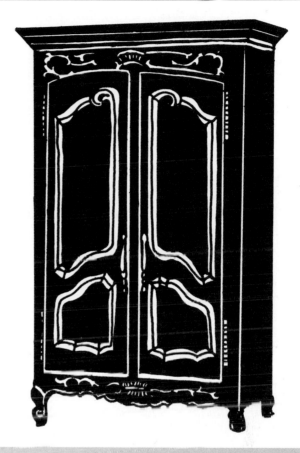

## ARMOIRE

Lines became rectilinear and, in France (as in late 18th-century England), straight, tapering legs all but replaced the longtime favorite cabriole leg.

### DESIGN IN TRANSITION

After the last Louis, France headed into a period of government by Directors, thus the term "Directoire" furniture. As a style, it's considered transitional, bridging the gap between Louis XVI and later Empire furniture. The lines show influences from both periods. Most pieces are straight lined, reminiscent of Louis XVI, though some pieces—chairs particularly—show Empire traits, such as rear legs curving outward and rolled back panels.

**FAUTEUIL CHAIR**

# FURNITURE
## THE CLASSICS-FRENCH

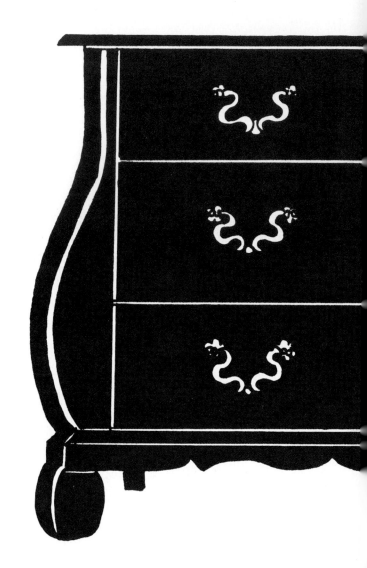

### RUSH SEAT CHAIR

#### COUNTRY FRENCH

Some of the most beautiful and charming French furniture came not from the court, but from the provinces. Rural craftsmen modified the elegant court designs to fit the needs of the people who lived, not in palaces, but in country cottages.

Most French provincial furniture is made from native woods such as pine, walnut, beech, and fruitwood. The lines are similar to those of Louis XV furniture, but are generally not as refined. Decoration is less elaborate than court furniture.

From country France came the versatile armoire—a 17th-century innovation originally designed to hold armor, then later (and now) used as a wardrobe or storage cabinet. Rush seat chairs, chests with low relief carvings, and delightful print fabrics also hail from the provinces.

BERGÈRE CHAIR

BOMBÉ CHEST

DIRECTOIRE CHAIR

# FURNITURE
## CONTEMPORARY

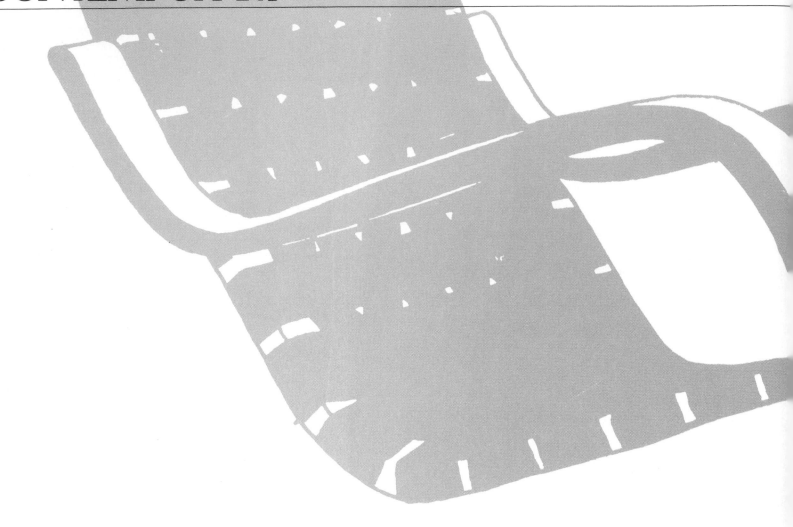

ALVAR AALTO PENSION CHAIR

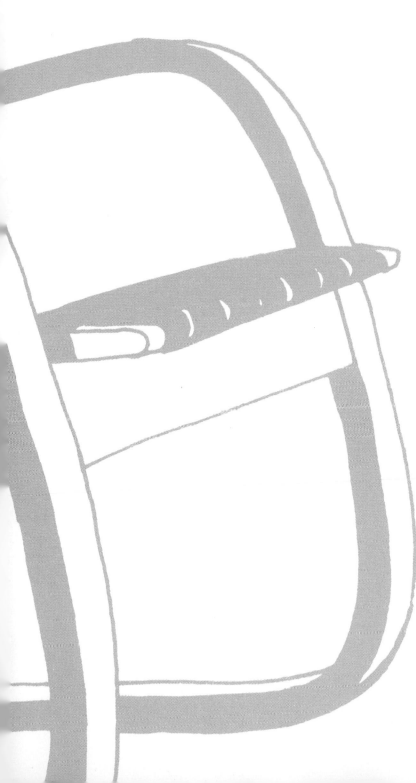

"Contemporary," like every popular furniture style before it, began with a few individuals working in their own personal ways. Innovative—radical sometimes—the 20th-century designer/architect/ furniture makers stripped away what was gaudy, frivolous, or fake to create furniture with simple, clean lines—furniture that conformed to human figures as well as their life-styles.

Contemporary furniture is practical and honest, emphasizing what's best about the materials, from natural wood to man-made plastics.

Technically, all furniture produced today is contemporary. But in the strictest design sense, "contemporary" refers to flawlessly proportioned pieces with simple planes and surfaces. In most cases, these contemporary designs are lower in silhouette than traditional furniture. Woods are left in their natural state, textures are emphasized, and decoration never interferes with function.

## THE BAUHAUS

If there is a definable starting time and place for contemporary furniture, it would be the 1920s at the German Bauhaus School of Art, Architecture, and Design. This school of experimental art had as its credo "form follows function," which gave students the freedom to experiment with materials, shapes, and designs—so long as the furniture first fulfilled its primary function without compromise.

The school attracted talents that became some of the world's best contemporary designers—Marcel Breuer, Mies van der Rohe, and Le Corbusier.

This invitation to be inventive also produced some exciting new furniture materials and construction methods. One of the earliest examples of avant-garde furniture design was Marcel Breuer's Cesca chair, designed in 1925. With this piece, Breuer introduced a new material, tubular steel, and, at the same time, pioneered a new design principle, that of a double-S-shaped support for a chair, rather than the conventional four legs.

In his Wassily lounge chair, Breuer, an architect and member of the Bauhaus faculty, gave the relaxing public the tubular steel chair, slung with leather to fit every curve of the body.

# FURNITURE
## CONTEMPORARY

**A**nother Bauhaus alumnus was Swiss-born architect Charles Edouard Jeanneret, popularly known as Le Corbusier. This designer firmly believed "the house is a machine for living," and to add to the convenience of home life his chaise longue, designed in 1927, features a seat that adjusts to any angle. The chaise of chrome-plated steel and painted oval steel tubes and sheets is considered one of **the** most relaxing chairs ever designed.

No wonder then that the Bauhaus School was a major design influence at the prestigious International Exposition of Modern Decorative and Industrial Arts in 1929. It was at this exposition, held in Barcelona, that Meis van der Rohe, second director of the Bauhaus School, introduced his now-famous Barcelona chair and table.

Though the Barcelona chair employs the same cantilever design principle as Breuer's chairs, it has its design roots in the ancient Greek flared-leg X chair. The difference between ancient Greece and 20th-century Europe is a graceful frame of steel supporting leather straps and tufted leather cushions. The chair, like its companion glass-topped table, displays the economy of line and beautiful proportions that characterize Mies van der Rohe's work.

### FUNCTION PLUS COMFORT

If "form follows function," it would seem that function included, among other things, comfort. All contemporary designers, not exclusively those of the Bauhaus, worked to make chairs and chaise longues to fit the body, ones that were molded to body configurations or, at least, adjustable to an individual's taste. Le Corbusier, of course, achieved this in his lounge chair. But Alvar Aalto, a Finnish architect, was equally concerned about comfort in his furniture designs. From experiments with laminated plywood during the 1920s Aalto created his famous Pension chair in 1946. He used his perfected laminated plywood technique in the same double-S cantilever principle that Marcel Breuer invented for his tubular steel chair. The result is a chair with the springiness of a plywood frame and the comfort of a form-fitting woven sling.

### MACHINE-AGE FURNITURE

"Machine-made" was not, at one time, the most complimentary description that could be applied to a piece of furniture. In fact, when furniture was first produced by machines, rather than by the skilled hands of individual craftsmen, the quality was poor to non-existent. In an attempt to duplicate handmade craftsmanship, cheap, machine-made furniture flooded the market and blighted the history of furniture design. To be successful, furniture would have to be designed specifically for machine production. And the best designers realized that.

By the end of World War II, contemporary furniture designers had wedded manufacturing technology with exciting new materials to produce furniture with a totally different look. New construction methods such as die-press stamping of plastic or plywood seats (the same process used to stamp out auto bodies) created new shapes in furniture. New names also appeared in the furniture field—some of them American.

### AMERICAN DESIGNERS EMERGE

During the '20s and '30s, most of the famous furniture designers were European or Scandinavian. It wasn't until the '40s that American designers began to make their mark.

Charles Eames, for instance, created his famous lounge chair and ottoman in 1945. Here was a shock-mounted chair with separate pads of molded plywood forming the base and seat. The contours of the wood provide unsurpassed body comfort, as well as a shape that's unmistakable.

Another example of machine-age furniture is the tulip-shaped pedestal chair, designed in 1957 by architect/designer Eero Saarinen. Shaped like a beautiful piece of sculpture, the back and seat are a one-piece molded plastic shell reinforced with fiber glass; the chair's stem and base are spun aluminum. The single base, replacing four conventional legs, was yet another departure in furniture design. This same pedestal concept was used by Warren Platner in his famous table.

MARCEL BREUER'S CESCA CHAIR

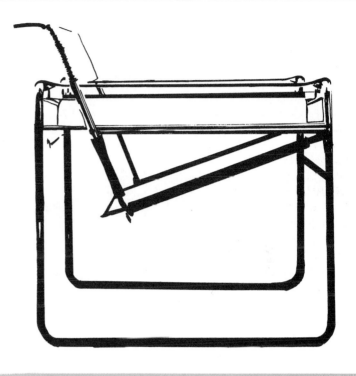

MARCEL BREUER'S WASSILY CHAIR

MIES VAN DER ROHE'S BARCELONA CHAIR

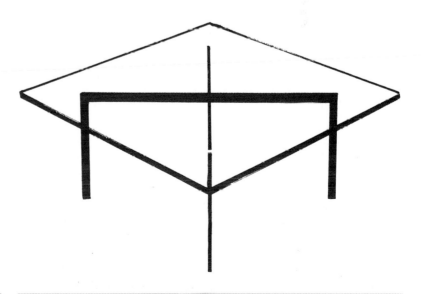

MIES VAN DER ROHE'S BARCELONA TABLE

# FURNITURE
## THE CLASSICS - CONTEMPORARY

LE CORBUSIER CHAISE LONGUE

WARREN PLATNER TABLE

EERO SAARINEN PEDESTAL CHAIR

PARSONS TABLE

CHARLES EAMES LOUNGE CHAIR AND FOOTREST

# FURNITURE /ANTIQUES

High technology and modern amenities have not diminished in the least America's love of antiques. A link with the past, respect for hand craftsmanship, the individuality of one-of-a-kind pieces, investment value—these are only some of the reasons for buying antiques.

No matter what motivates you in acquiring antiques for your home, you'd be wise to assimilate some background information before you go off, cash in hand, into the unpredictable world of antique shops and auctions.

## ANTIQUE—OR JUST OLD?

Is the piece you're interested in really an antique or just old?

To be precise, an antique (formerly thought of as anything made before 1830) is currently defined as anything 100 years old or older. But just because an item is antique by definition does not make it necessarily valuable.

When shopping the antique circuit, it doesn't take long before you realize that the prices of antique furnishings differ vastly. Some of the disparity comes from the dealers involved, but other differences are honest reflections of the furniture's features. For the antique-shopping novice, here is a list of things that can influence the price:

*Condition.* Naturally a piece of furniture in mint condition will command a higher price than one that is falling apart.

*Material.* Some antique furniture pieces—especially those of finer woods—soar to the top of the price scale. Accent materials, such as brass or silver hardware, leaded glass, or beveled glass also can raise the cost.

*Authenticity.* When a piece is signed, dated, or in some other way documented as to its age, manufacture, or ownership, expect to pay top dollar for the pedigree.

*Quality.* Any well-designed piece, beautifully crafted of fine materials is a choice, and costly, find.

*Availability.* The more scarce or rare a piece, the more sought after it is, and the more expensive it's likely to be.

*Source and origin.* If the piece was made by a famous craftsman, expect the price to be high.

## WHERE TO SHOP

Auctions, estate sales, and stores that specialize in antiques are the best places to look for antique furniture. Occasionally, you hear of someone finding a prize at a flea market or garage sale, but the chances are slim.

The secret to auction buying is to know what you want, know what you're willing to pay for it and then stick to that figure. Some guidelines for buying at an auction or estate sale:

• Obtain a catalog or description of the items to be sold—preferably in advance of the sale. In addition to information about the pieces to be auctioned, you'll find important facts such as the conditions of sale. These explain arrangements for payment, the deadline pieces have to be removed by, and the responsibilities of both the buyer and the auctioneer.

• Arrive at the auction early so you'll have enough time to inspect the items you're interested in. Plan to spend several hours to a whole day at an auction. Cutting yourself short of time may mean having to leave before the item you want is put up for bidding.

Make the rounds and check out each piece of furniture. If you find a piece in need of repair, figure in the cost of repair before deciding what your bid will be. Never bid on an item you haven't thoroughly inspected. You may not be able to see flaws or missing pieces from a distance.

• Be sure you understand the multiples you're bidding on. Is it a pair of chairs? Or just one?

• Make a note of the exact amount of your winning bid and always keep track of your bidding number.

• Get a receipt for all payments. Generally, the price you pay at auctions should be about two-thirds of what you'd pay for the piece in an antique shop.

One other suggestion seasoned auction shoppers offer: If you're particularly interested in acquiring a certain piece of furniture, try not to appear overly-anxious. Showing too much interest could tip off the auctioneer and bidding boosts could be engineered to take advantage of your eagerness.

*In this 1850s' town house, stately windows and oyster-white walls provide an imposing background for a collection of elegant antiques.*

# FURNITURE
## LIVING WITH ANTIQUES

**1** A single antique, placed out of context in a contemporary setting, can have an exciting effect on a decorating scheme. In this spacius entryway, a stately Victorian hatrack shares the scene with a thoroughly modern abstract painting. The effect is striking.

Also old, but not antique, is the colorful Oriental rug that tops the quarry tile floor. The juxtaposition of new and old brings out the best of both.

**2** A period room setting needn't have only authentic antiques. Here, a combination of real classics and reproductions meld beautifully in a modern-day home. The major pieces in this colonial-style living room are all reproductions; only the round tripod table and the handsome Federal slant-top desk are bona fide antiques. The Chippendale-style sofa (with its camelback and rolled arms), the Queen Anne side chair and wing chair, and the butler's table, with its cabriole legs, are all well-made reproductions readily available today.

**3** Many times antique buffs prefer to furnish a room as it might have looked hundreds of years ago. If you, too, are a purist, the important thing is to buy pieces that you can actually live with, not just look at. Fortunately, many Early American furniture pieces were so well constructed that they function as well today as they did when originally made. The furniture in this keeping room is 18th-century pine, a native wood that has mellowed with time. Shapes are simple and pieces utilitarian. The floor, consisting of old, uneven boards taken from the attic, provides additional character for the period decor. Authentic Early American accessories—tin candle sconces, pottery, and a collection of candlesticks—add finishing touches to this delightful setting. Simple handwoven tab curtains hang at the paned window.

# FURNITURE
## SECONDHAND AND UNFINISHED

Whether you're faced with a budget problem or simply have a sense of adventure, don't overlook the assets of secondhand or unfinished furniture. Smart shoppers have known for a long time that both "pre-owned" and new, but unfinished, furniture pieces can be not only bargains, but also beautiful items in their own right. As with anything, however, it's wise to bone up on buymanship pointers before you head for the sales or shops.

### SECOND TIME AROUND

Buying "secondhand" no longer has any stigma attached to it. Many people prefer these venerable pieces because of their good quality and construction, uniqueness, and do-it-yourself possibilities. Here are some places to shop for secondhand furniture:

*Auctions and estate sales* are always worth checking out.

*House and garage sales* give you a chance for real bargains since the venders aren't necessarily out to make a profit. Usually the objective is to clear out excess accumulations; many homeowners unwittingly price their merchandise far below market value. Now and then you hear of someone buying a really valuable item for a few dollars, but that's a rarity. Suburban areas are particularly good hunting grounds for good-quality furniture pieces because families there tend to move frequently and often don't want to transport old or large pieces to a new address.

*Consignment and thrift shops,* such as the Salvation Army, Goodwill stores, and St. Vincent de Paul outlets are good sources.

*Flea markets* may also produce some bargains.

*Newspaper ads.* Check them regularly for items you want. Then move fast before the competition does.

### QUALITY IS STILL QUALITY

If a piece of furniture was well made in the first place, it will probably be a good value when you buy it secondhand. Put every prospective purchase through these tests:
- Tables and chairs should be sturdy, not wobbly. Check how the legs are attached. Are there braces in corners and stretchers between chair legs?
- Check chests or pieces with drawers by pulling out the drawer and inspecting its construction. Are sides dovetailed? Are they varnished, but not painted? Unfinished wood will stick, painted wood may bind the drawer's movement. Are there dust boards or panels between drawers?
- Hardware should be attached with screws and bolts that go all the way through to the backside of the piece.

### FLAWS MAY NOT BE FINAL

Don't let the finish on a piece of secondhand furniture discourage you, unless, of course, a big chunk of veneer is missing. And even then, there's a solution. Check the underside of the piece to tell what the base wood is. You may want to remove all the veneer and simply finish the base wood.

Likewise, don't be put off by a piece that merely needs regluing. This is another flaw you easily can overcome. If, however, the piece you're eyeing has a spindle missing or a part that needs to be found or custom-made, be wary. Judge what repairs you can do yourself and determine how much you are willing to spend to restore the "bargain" in question.

### UNFINISHED FURNITURE

For years unfinished furniture had very little to offer in the way of selection. Most pieces were made of medium- to low-quality pine, usually decked out with brass-plated colonial hardware. In recent years, the picture has changed dramatically. Now, unfinished furniture is available in virtually every style, price range, and quality level. No longer limited to lumber and paint stores, unfinished furniture is available at many outlets, including stores that specialize in unfinished furniture only. Most of the major mail order catalogs offer unfinished pieces, as do many specialty mail order companies. Some of these even offer high-quality reproductions of museum pieces.

Selections range from practical, modular, and dual-purpose furniture to feature pieces such as roll-top desks and four-poster beds. Styles range from Early American to Colonial, Victorian, Shaker, French, and contemporary. You can customize simple-lined unfinished pieces in a variety of ways, depending on the hardware or finish you choose.

### WHICH WOOD?

Depending on the quality, unfinished furniture is manufactured of different woods, with lower priced pieces usually made of clear, soft white pine. This wood has little graining to add interest, so is best suited to a painted, lacquered, or antiqued finish.

Medium-quality furniture is often made of lodgepole or knotty pine, which is tougher and harder than white pine. This wood has the character of the knots to add a rustic touch to the finished piece.

Other good-quality unfinished furniture pieces are made of hardrock maple, birch, and aspen wood. Maple has a rich, grained look and takes a warm, mellow finish.

Luxury pieces are made of cherry and solid oak. When finished with care, these pieces look as elegant as a factory-finished piece—and you can choose the finish you want.

### CONSTRUCTION EQUALS COST

How a piece is constructed helps determine the price range it falls in. Low-end pieces will have bottoms and sides of fiberboard with frames nailed together. Drawers will generally be put together with staples.

Top-quality hardwood furniture most often features dovetailed construction with frames blocked and glued. Sides, doors, and drawers will be made of wood, and drawers will have center guides. Doors will hang true on their hinges.

Giving wood furniture a second chance at life usually means stripping and refinishing it. Depending on how much work you want to save and the money you have to spend, you may choose to have a professional strip your furniture, refinish it, or do both. On the other hand, if you have more ambition than you have money, or if you take pride in restoring your own furniture, you can do everything the pros do.

## THE PROFESSIONAL APPROACH

Having your furniture stripped by a professional is the easiest way to get the job done. However, it's the most expensive.

Before you have your furniture stripped professionally, you should know how the piece is going to be handled and what results are likely.

Since there are so many different methods for professionally removing old finishes, check with several companies. Ask what method each uses, and, if possible, look at examples of the shop's work.

One common procedure used by professionals is the "dip-and-strip" method. The piece of furniture is actually submerged in a vat of remover. After soaking, the furniture is hosed down with water to wash off the remover and old finish. Keep in mind that this method works only for items small enough to fit into a vat, and for those with parts not liable to damage by the solution and water. The dip-and-strip method has also been known to dissolve the glue on certain

pieces, so always inquire about the risks involved.

Never dip any veneered or softwood pieces, and be aware that furniture stripped by the dipping method will come back with the grain of the wood raised and in need of sanding.

A second process for professional stripping is to put the furniture in a machine that functions like a dishwasher. A chemical is recirculated over the furniture for several hours, then water is sprayed over it. Limitations are the same with this procedure as with the dip-and-strip method.

Some strip shops use muscle power to remove the finish. The pieces are washed in a vat of remover and scrubbed with a nylon brush or steel wool. Some shops follow this with sanding, others don't because sandpaper can damage the grain.

Check the Yellow Pages under "Furniture Repairing and Refinishing" for professional stripping firms in your area.

## DO-IT-YOURSELF STRIPPING

Before you start stripping wood furniture in your home, be sure you follow these precautions:
• Always work in a well-ventilated room. Fumes can be dangerous.
• Always wear rubber gloves to protect your hands.
• Keep all stripping products out of the reach of children.

## LIQUID NO-WASH STRIPPER

Basically two types of products are available for do-it-yourself

furniture stripping: a liquid no-wash stripping agent and a water-wash stripper.

To use a liquid no-wash stripper, you'll need a large metal container (a dishpan or roaster). Never use a plastic or rubber pan. You'll also need No. 3 and 0000 steel wool, nylon brushes, and a nylon scraper or spatula. A nylon toothbrush or bottle brush will come in handy for removing the finish in hard-to-reach areas.

Start your liquid no-wash stripping process by pouring plenty of remover into the pan. Then stand or lean the item you're stripping over the pan and wash the piece with steel wool and brushes. Work on one small area at a time and keep the surface of the furniture thoroughly wet with remover. If the furniture is too large to wash over a pan, dip the 0000 steel wool into the remover, squeeze out the excess, and rub a small area, keeping the finish damp with remover. When the finish is dissolved, wipe it off with a rag. Always use long strokes that follow the grain.

When your furniture is completely clean, buff the surface with No. 3 steel wool and allow to dry 20 to 30 minutes. Particles of steel wool may remain, so be sure you rub the surface thoroughly with a clean cloth. Or use a vacuum cleaner. Traces of steel wool left on the surface of the wood can ruin the final finish.

## WATER-WASH REMOVER

This stripping product goes on with a brush. Since a water-wash remover has a semi-paste

consistency, you'll have to spread and dab it on. Make sure the remover is applied generously to all surfaces.

Allow the remover to work from one to 30 minutes. Test its progress by scraping a small area. When the remover has completely penetrated the old finish, begin washing. The most effective way to remove the softened finish is to wash it with coarse steel wool or a towel soaked in detergent and water solution. Use a toothbrush on carved, intricate surfaces.

If you're trying to remove thick layers of paint or unusually tough coatings such as epoxy, you may have to repeat the stripping process. Use a scraper to remove all you can the first time, then apply a second (and possibly a third) coat without rinsing off the remover.

Water may damage wood veneers bonded with water-sensitive glue as well as other finishes. In these cases, or if you wish to raise the grain only slightly, rinse with mineral spirits or turpentine instead of water.

## ELECTRIC STRIPPING

A third way to strip wood is with a mechanical stripping attachment for your electric drill. It's a rotary disk fitted with flexible metal "fingers" that actually strip the finish from the surface. This disk comes in fine and coarse models.

## PREPARATION FOR PAINT

If you're going to paint a piece of wood furniture, you may not have to strip it first. Check to make sure the old finish isn't cracked or flaking. If the surface is reasonably smooth, you can prepare it for painting.

First wash off the piece of furniture, using turpentine, mineral spirits, or even a solution of dishwashing detergent and water to get rid of wax and dirt.

Wherever the old finish is chipped, "feather" the edges with sandpaper. Use 80 grit paper to sand away the rough edges, gently tapering the surrounding area of the finish until you can't feel where the chipped place was.

Use 200 grit sandpaper to sand every surface you want to paint. Sand until you've dulled the glossy surface.

## UNDER THE OLD FINISH

If a natural finish is the choice for your furniture piece, the next decision to make is whether you want the wood to remain the color it is or help its natural color along with bleach or stain.

Bleach makes the wood lighter colored and removes stains. Apply it to bare wood. Once the wood is lightened, you can stain it back to any color you want.

Stain colors and darkens bare wood. A variety of kinds and colors are available, but they work essentially the same.

## WHAT'S WHAT IN FINISHES

There are two approaches to finishing your stripped and prepared furniture. One is to apply a wipe-on oil finish, the other is to brush on a finish, using varnish, polyurethane, or lacquer. Each type has its advantages.

## OIL AND WAX FINISHES

Oil or oil and wax finishes are very easy to apply, and are a good choice if you want to give your furniture a natural, bare wood look. The oil soaks into the wood and offers protection from liquid spills (not as much protection, however, as is offered by varnish, polyurethane, and lacquer finishes).

Some manufacturers of oil finish products have a finishing wax topcoat for a slicker look. Any of these oil finishes are a good choice for furniture that won't get extra-hard wear.

To apply an oil finish, simply pour some oil on the furniture, wipe it around with a rag to get the surface wet, let it soak in for a bit, then wipe the surface dry.

## BRUSH-ON FINISHES

Both varnish and polyurethane form a hard, smooth surface on top of the wood. Polyurethane is impervious to water, alcohol, and almost anything else. Varnish is impervious, too, but not quite so tough as polyurethane. Use either finish on pieces that get extra-hard wear or where you want a gleaming "finished furniture" look. Both go on with a brush and are available in gloss, satin, and flat.

Lacquer or lacquer-like finishes are quick drying and don't build up as thick a coat as varnish or polyurethane. This finish can go on by brush or spray.

## TIPS FOR BRUSH FINISHING

Any finish you brush on takes a little time and technique. For best results, follow these rules:
- Before you start, put the furniture piece in a room where there won't be drafts to blow dust into the wet finish. Place a plastic drop cloth under the piece and cover the nearby area to help keep down dust. Then, wipe the piece thoroughly with a tack rag.
- Open the can of finish without shaking it. Stir gently if necessary, but avoid bubbles. Choose a good-quality natural bristle brush. Dip in the bristles only a third of the way. Wipe the brush off lightly on the side of the can and gently flow the finish onto the surface. When you have a whole panel finished, brush over it lightly with long, straight, overlapping strokes, using just the tips of the bristles.
- Leave the room and let the piece dry. Then sand lightly all over with 220-grit sandpaper and wipe the surface with a tack rag. Apply another coat, as carefully as the first.

## THE PERFECT PAINT JOB

To achieve the best possible painted finish on furniture, it's important to know the types of paints available and the characteristics of each.

Alkyd enamel, also called oil base paint, covers well and provides a hard, wear-resistant finish. It's easy to apply and any brush marks disappear as the finish dries.

Alkyd enamel is your best bet for most paint projects. It comes in satin, flat, and glossy finishes. Clean up with mineral spirits and allow four hours to dry completely.

Latex base enamel is not as glossy as alkyd base, but comes in flat, satin, and gloss. It dries quickly and cleans up with water while still wet. This paint is good for big pieces that don't get hard wear. However, latex base enamel doesn't cover as well as alkyd enamel, and even a hot coffee cup may soften the finish.

Lacquer gives an extremely smooth finish but requires careful surface preparation. It's fast drying and comes in flat, satin, and glossy.

## BRUSH UP ON PAINTING TECHNIQUES

Here are three good rules for brush technique:
- Get a 2-inch brush with a chiseled edge; natural bristles for an alkyd enamel, nylon bristles for latex.
- Dip the bristles only about a third of the way into the paint and strike off both sides of the brush against the can.
- Don't try to make the paint cover in one coat. When the first coat is dry, sand your furniture piece again, use a clean tack rag, and apply a second coat. Sand, wipe again, and apply a third coat of paint, if the piece needs it.

## SPRAY ADVICE

When spraying furniture, be sure to spray into all corners and crevices, then fill in the larger areas. Trigger off short bursts of paint and keep the can moving. Apply several very light coats. If the paint drips or runs, let it dry, then sand it away and start over.

# FURNITURE / RECYCLING PROJECTS

1 3

2 4

**1,2** Here, a has-been coffee table was given new elegance with a mottled *faux* tortoise finish. The technique is simple: First, strip the furniture piece, then apply a base coat of yellow ochre paint. Let dry for 12 hours, sand surface lightly, then repeat process. Next, apply 3 coats of clear shellac, allowing each coat to dry between applications. Now, squeeze tubes of raw sienna and black oil paint into separate containers. Thin each with turpentine to the consistency of thick ink. Using an artist's brush, apply the raw sienna and black oil paint to the tabletop in small strokes in an overlapping pattern resembling shingles on a roof. Now soak a natural sponge in turpentine and squeeze dry. Blot the slightly tacky surface with the sponge to mingle the colors.

Spatter black paint onto the tabletop by gently tapping the brush. This should create a mottled effect. After the top has completely dried, seal it with one coat of clear shellac.

**3,4** To update your old wooden furniture pieces with a new finish, try the technique used on this old oak desk and "lawyer's" chair. First strip and sand the piece. Mix one quart natural colorless stain with 3 ounces white colorant. (Add a few drops of rose madder to the mixture if you want to get a tinted effect.) Brush stain on furniture piece, covering only a small area at a time. Wipe off wet stain with a tack rag until you've achieved the desired color. Let the piece dry for at least 12 hours; clean the surface with a tack rag. Seal with several coats of polyurethane.

**5** Beds old enough to have some character are usually old enough to have miserable finishes. The solution? Simply paint the piece. After stripping and sanding, this bed was given a coat of alkyd-base primer to seal the grain thoroughly. Next satin finish alkyd paint went on. Choose any color you like. When the base color is thoroughly dry, carefully apply white paint to the edges of moldings or turnings for accent. Top your paint job with a coat or two of polyurethane.

Most furniture repairs are done to save money, to save the piece of furniture, or both. Knowing a few simple furniture repairs can put a less-than-perfect garage-sale bargain into the treasured collectible class. A little repair also can save a favorite piece of old furniture from exile in the attic. Here are some helpful tips to save damaged pieces.

## WOBBLY CHAIRS

A chair with the wobbles is one small step from disaster. Don't take chances. First, by all means, take the weak chair out of circulation until you can repair it.

When the symptoms are "shakiness," the condition is usually chair legs that need regluing. Stretchers also may have become unglued. Part of the problem is often that the holes legs and stretchers fit in are enlarged. Here's the cure:

Disassemble the chair. A towel-padded hammer will do the "demolition" job for you. Be sure to label each piece so reassembly will go smoothly.

Remove all glue from both portions of each joint. Scrape off what you can, then sand off the rest.

If, after sanding, the leg or stretcher fits too loosely into the holes, coat the joint with glue, then wrap with a layer of strong, fine thread.

Also, special metal fasteners are available for this purpose. To use them, file down one side of the joint and tape the fastener in place.

Apply glue and tap the leg or stretcher into the receiving hole.

Be careful no glue is left on the surface of the furniture. It will not accept stain and can ruin the final finish.

Draw joints tight by wrapping a rope or strong cord twice around the chair. Insert a small piece of wood between the two cords and turn it, tourniquet fashion, to tighten ties.

## LOOSE VENEER

When just a small area of veneer is loose, follow this simple procedure:

Lift the loose edge and squirt in a dollop of white glue. Spread the glue around, using a thin knife blade.

Put a piece of waxed paper over the glued area and a board on top; clamp it securely with a C-clamp or weight it down with a pile of heavy books or magazines.

When a large area of veneer is loose, or if you're replacing an entire section of veneer, use contact cement rather than white glue. Here's how to proceed:

Apply the cement to both the veneer and the undersurface, using a small brush. Allow cement to dry at least half an hour.

Carefully lay the veneer in place. Take care to be accurate; you won't get a second chance. Roll the veneered area with a rubber roller or a rolling pin.

## REMOVING DENTS

Here's where the auto repairman has an edge over a furniture fixer. Dents can simply be pounded out of metal; wood takes a different approach. There are several techniques for dent removal, depending on the severity of the damage. For a slight dent, stick shellac may be successful in filling it in. If not, try this:

Pierce tiny holes in the dented area, using a needle. Dampen the dent with a few drops of water. After the wood swells, rub lightly with rottenstone and oil.

If furniture isn't severely dented and wood fibers aren't broken, try this on a piece that you will be refinishing:

Lay several folds of damp cloth over the damaged surface. Apply a hot iron to the cloth for several minutes. In many cases, the steam swells the wood fibers and returns them to their original state.

Steam will raise the grain of the wood surrounding the dent as well, so you will have to do a little extra sanding to smooth the surface before finishing.

## FILLING CRACKS

The trick in filling cracks is to use a good wood putty and apply it carefully.

With a putty knife or small, thin-bladed knife, fill cracks with putty. Remove any excess putty with a rag or fine-grit sandpaper.

## REPAIRING DEEP SCRATCHES

To bandage a deep scratch on a piece of furniture you do not plan to refinish, try this:

Touch up the area with a stain that matches the rest of the piece.

With a tiny brush, fill the cavity with layers of shellac. Smooth the surface with extra-fine sandpaper and rub with rottenstone and oil.

## UNCRAZING A SURFACE

Too much exposure to the sun can cause a network of tiny cracks in wood finishes. If the condition is not severe, use this method for eliminating crazing:

Rub the crazed area with steel wool, then polish with paste wax. If the crazing is extreme, the only remedy to restore its surface beauty is to refinish it.

## SANDING—THE LAST STEP

After repair work is completed, there's still one important last step before your furniture is completely ready to have a new surface applied. That's sanding. This step is crucial and can make the difference between a professional-looking piece or a sloppy job.

If the surface is really damaged, start with a coarse- to medium-grit abrasive. If you're using a belt sander, be careful not to apply too much pressure. A belt sander cuts quickly and can gouge the surface of the wood. Don't use a belt sander on veneer. You can easily go right through the thin wood.

Remove dust and other residue after each sanding. Wipe the surface clean with a cheesecloth dampened with mineral spirits.

Sand with a medium- to fine-grit abrasive.

Dampen the surface to raise the grain (unless you plan to either bleach or water-stain the piece of wood). Using a very fine abrasive, finish sanding the piece by hand.

## CANING

Once you've mastered the skill of caning, you'll be able to restore more than an old chair's function. You also can restore a good share of the original charm, and save money.

You'll need about 300 feet of cane to reseat an average-sized chair. Cane width will vary, depending on the size of holes and their distance apart.

*Common-sized cane* should be used with 5/16-inch holes that are separated by 7/8 of an inch.

*Medium cane* is used for 1/2-inch holes that are about 3/4 inch apart.

*Fine cane* is for 3/16-inch holes placed 5/8 of an inch apart.

*Fine-fine cane* should be used for 3/16-inch holes separated by 1/2 inch.

*Superfine cane* is used for 3/16-inch holes that are spaced at 3/8-inch intervals.

*Carriage fine cane* is used for 1/8-inch holes that are drilled 3/8 inch apart.

To restore a seating piece, follow this procedure:

Repair and paint the chair first. Dampen the cane to make it pliable throughout all the following steps.

• Start caning at #1 (see sketch A). Fasten strand in the hole with a peg (golf tee or piece of 1/4-inch dowel sharpened at one end). Take the strand across to #2, underneath and up through #3, then across to #4, underneath and up through #5 and so on. Keep the strand taut and use pegs to hold it as you work.

• Fasten a second layer of strands at right angles over the first, using the same technique (sketch B).

• Remove pegs from the chair and fasten loose strands beneath the chair frame in knots around strands that run from hole to hole. Run the next layer of strands parallel to the first (sketch C), over the two previous layers.

• Start weaving (sketch D), using a caning needle. Each time you pull the strand through the hole, thread it into the needle and weave it across to the other side.

• Arrange dampened woven strands in pairs, forcing them close together in straight, parallel lines. To weave diagonally, follow sketch E, running two strands into each corner hole, with one hand above the chair and one beneath.

• Weave remaining diagonal strands from opposite direction (sketch F). As in previous step, be sure to run two diagonals into the four corner holes. When weaving edges, be sure the strand you're weaving with is run over or under the right already-placed strands. Completed caning will look like sketch G.

• Using binder cane, frame edges of woven caning (sketch H). Lay binder over holes and loop fine cane through each or alternate holes, securing the binder. Pull caning tightly so binder fits snugly. To finish, lap the binder over two or three holes, fastening down these ends together. After the last loop, fasten the end of the strand by plugging the hole from beneath or tying it.

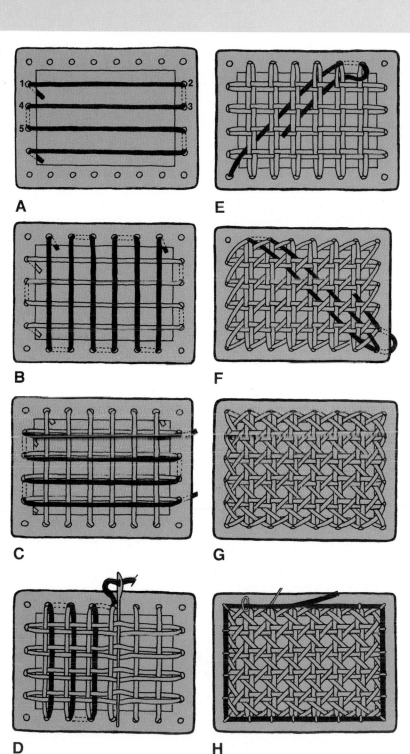

A

B

C

D

E

F

G

H

# PURCHASING PRIMER/BUYMANSHIP

Few situations in the world of buying and selling require the kind of thought and analysis that goes into making a furniture purchase. Furniture, as we all know, is a big-ticket item. But then, so is a car. The difference is, your sofa or dining table will very likely outlast your auto. And when you buy a car, you don't have to choose it on the basis of compatibility with the other items you house in your garage. Furniture is entirely different. Here an addition must coexist with present pieces.

But compatibility is just one consideration when buying furniture. There are many others worthy of your attention.

## WHAT'S YOUR FAMILY LIKE?

How you live determines (or at least *should* determine) what you buy. First, analyze your family structure. If there are young children in the house, there's no point in furnishing with formal, touch-me-not pieces.

How do you like to entertain guests? Do you prefer sitdown dinners or big buffets, small cocktail parties or big bashes?

How formal or casual is your life? Would you describe yourself as a "put-your-feet-up" kind of person or an individual who likes order and propriety at all times? All these factors should make a difference in the kind of furniture you buy.

## WILL IT FIT?

Before buying a new piece of furniture, envision it in your home. Where will you put it? Do you have the floor space?

To avoid problems before they begin, measure your room, then do a floor plan, putting in the existing furniture. Use ¼-inch graph paper and a scale of one square equals 1 foot.

When looking at your room plan, be conscious of traffic patterns. Will the new addition take up too much space or be in the way?

## BUDGET CONSIDERATIONS

Money is a major factor when shopping for furniture. Few of us can afford to make costly mistakes and all of us want to buy the best quality we can possibly afford. It's a good idea to decide in advance how much you can afford to spend. You will encounter a wide range of prices and quality in the furniture market. And there's a definite correlation between the two. The higher the price, generally, the higher the quality materials and construction. On succeeding pages we'll help you determine the quality of various types of furniture, but only you can define how much quality you can afford.

Getting the best possible quality for your money may take some special shopping skills. Look for sales or for close-outs of floor samples. And remember, classic pieces with simple lines are always a better buy than faddish items or furniture with a lot of *faux* detailing.

## THE WELL-ARMED SHOPPER

When you actually take off for the store, you will want to take some things along to make the shopping job easier. "Be prepared" is as good a motto for furniture buyers as for scouts.

Take your list of measurements and the floor plan of your room. Be sure you have a steel tape with you so you can measure the furniture piece in the store and compare the measurements with your at-home requirements. Don't trust your eye. A piece of furniture never looks as large in a store surrounded by other items as it does in your own home.

Also take along a notebook and pencil. You'll want to write down brand names, fabric content, sizes, special features or finishes and, of course, the price, in case you plan to do some comparative shopping.

The other items you'll need to have with you are samples of your present furnishings. For example, if the proposed addition is going in the living room, be sure you have a sample of the carpet, the wall paint or paper, and, if possible, fabric samples.

## SHOPPING TIPS

Successful shopping is a combination of imagination and know-how. It's the imagination factor that makes your home individual and exciting. It's also imagination that lets you see possibilities in furniture "buys" that other shoppers may overlook. But without some good common sense about buying practices, all the imagination in the world won't keep your budget in the black.

● Know what you need. Don't buy something just because it strikes your fancy on that particular day. The thing you thought you couldn't live without one day, might seem like a folly the next.

● Develop a master buying plan. Part of knowing what you need comes from having set some priorities and furnishings goals. If you have Chateaubriand taste and a hamburger budget, you may want to invest in just one good piece rather than fill the entire room with mediocre furniture. This doesn't mean you have to live in a bare room until you can afford the other pieces you want. There are plenty of inexpensive furnishings of good quality and design that fill the bill on an interim basis.

● Decide how much you can afford to spend. Study prices and take a good look at your budget. Determine how much strain your monthly expenses can take if you're contemplating credit buying.

● Find out as much as you can about the specific piece you're interested in. Read all labels, hang tags, and warranties. Learn what materials and construction methods have been used, what finishes have been applied, and what guaranties or warranties are offered.

● After you buy a piece of furniture, make sure you file all pertinent information with your household records. You'll need it if a problem develops.

*The combination living/dining room in this suburban tract house was given lots of character via casual, easy-care furniture and colorful artwork and plants.*

The furniture industry uses the term "case goods" to denote a large category of unupholstered items—cabinets, chests, desks, dressers, wall systems, and such. Some of these pieces are made of solid wood, but most are not. In fact, what *looks* like wood may not be wood at all—or at least not entirely. Most case goods manufactured today is constructed either of wood veneer, molded plastic combined with wood, or wood with a machine-printed grain. Some pieces are plastic, simulated by photo processing to look like wood.

So, how can you tell whether the desk you're buying is made of real wood or a photocopy simulation of wood? Your best bet is to read the labels.

## LABELING GUIDE

*Solid* indicates that all exposed surfaces (tops, side panels, and drawer fronts) are made of the solid wood named on the tag—without veneer. But wood on the inside of the piece may be different from the wood on the outside.

*Genuine* used with the name of a particular wood, walnut for instance, means all exposed parts of the piece are made of walnut veneer over hardwood plywood.

*Combination* is printed on the tag if more than one type of wood is used in exposed parts of the furniture. For example, genuine mahogany veneers might be used on all exposed panels (except for inlays and accents) and various other solid hardwoods might be used in all exposed solid parts.

*All-wood construction* means exposed parts are made of wood for the full thickness of the panels. Manufacturers may save costs on materials by gluing a thin panel of wood to a wood frame, giving the outward appearance of thick wood. To be sure you're getting the real thing, thump the panel. Genuine wood sounds dead; a panel on a frame produces an echo effect.

*Veneer* (A) refers to a material consisting of several (usually five in furniture construction) thin wood layers permanently bonded to each other with an adhesive. The core or center layer of the veneer is thicker than the others. For added strength, adjacent wood layers are bonded together with the grain at right angles. Wood with the most beautiful grain pattern is selected for the outermost layer or face veneer of a wood furniture piece.

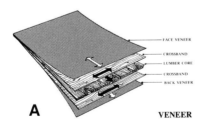

**A**        **VENEER**

FACE VENEER
CROSSBAND
LUMBER CORE
CROSSBAND
BACK VENEER

Veneer is durable, stronger than solid wood, and available at much less cost. It also provides more variety in wood and grain patterns than natural wood, since it can be matched to make unusual designs and effects. About 200 types of wood are available in veneers.

One more word about furniture labels. Some pieces have them; others don't. But un-labeled furniture isn't necessarily an indication of poor quality. If furniture isn't labeled with material information, it's up to you to ask the salesperson specific questions. You might also ask to see the catalog description of the merchandise.

## MATERIAL DIFFERENCES

Various manufacturers use different kinds and qualities of materials in case goods. But wood is the main ingredient.

Most good-quality furniture is built from natural hardwoods, but both hardwoods and softwoods are used in furniture construction. Contrary to what these terms imply, neither has much to do with the actual hardness of the wood.

*Hardwood* refers to wood from trees that lose their leaves each year. Oak, pecan, walnut, birch, maple, cherry, and mahogany are some of the most common hardwoods.

*Softwoods* are evergreens, such as pine, cedar, cyprus, spruce, fir, and redwood.

When you find a piece of furniture you like, find out whether it's made of wood. If so, what kind? Is it solid or veneer? But don't let the answer to the latter question alone determine whether or not you buy.

Today, fine wood furniture is made of both solids and veneers, but most is of veneer construction with solid wood parts. If constructed properly, both produce quality furniture.

There are also many new combination woods. These hybrid materials offer exceptional strength and durability.

*Particleboard,* a combination

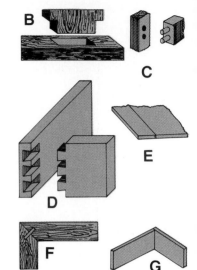

of wood flakes and resin binding agents pressed into sheets, is used for furniture in nearly all price ranges. In most cases, a hardwood veneer covers the particleboard.

*Hardboard,* composed of tiny threadlike wood fibers pressed together under heat, also looks like wood when it's woodgrain-printed and finished. But it's

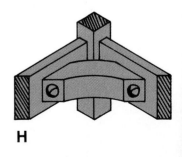

**H**

stronger and more moisture resistant than a number of woods.

The advantages of combination woods such as these is they allow manufacturers to hold down costs and still produce good-quality furniture.

## PLASTIC COMPONENTS

The addition of plastic parts to wood furniture is not as improbable as it might seem. Plastic can be molded and modeled to resemble wood carvings, moldings, and all sorts of decorative parts on furniture. Some of the places you're most likely to find molded polystyrene and polyurethane plastic components are on the fronts of cases, doors, and drawers.

Most plastic components look almost like the real thing. The basic difference is price.

## JOINING METHODS

Good-quality furniture construction depends primarily on how well the parts are joined.

There are four principal methods of putting furniture together: glue, screws, nails, and joints. All are used in varying combinations, depending on the kind of wood or woods, the purpose of the furniture, and its design.

In much of today's furniture construction, the most critical element is the adhesive. The number-one enemy of furniture is starved glue joints. However, the synthetic adhesives (technically, they're cement, not glues) have resolved that problem. Although fairly high priced, the synthetics are quick drying and permanent.

## WHAT KIND OF JOINTS?

More often than not, joints in wood furniture will be mortise and tenon, though they also may be dovetail, tongue and groove, or double dowel. (Butt joints aren't considered up to standards.) Regardless of the type, joints should be sturdy, smooth, and tight-fitting.

*Mortise and tenon* (B) is the strongest method of joining pieces of wood at right angles. This joint is usually used to secure the outer frames of most furniture pieces and to fasten top slats to back posts of chairs.

*Double-dowel joints* (C) are similar to mortise and tenon in theory, with dowels adding strength. You'll find these joints used in furniture frames and in joining legs to side rails of chairs.

*Dovetail joints* (D) are usually standard features for drawer construction.

*Tongue and groove* (E) is one of the oldest joining methods. Unfortunately, it is usually difficult to see whether this kind of joint is well constructed.

*Miter joints* (F) are found at corners of tabletops. Dowels, nails, screws, or a type of metal spine may reinforce this joint.

*Butt joints* (G) are the simplest and the weakest.

For added support at points of special strain and where rigidity is important, look for corner blocks (H). The blocks may be glued or notched and screwed in place.

## JUDGING GOOD CONSTRUCTION

Nearly every furniture manufacturer has special construction features and techniques, so hard and fast rules about what is good-quality construction are impossible to set. But here are some general guidelines on things to look for.

Back panels of case goods can tell a lot about the overall construction of the piece. In good furniture, the back panel is inset and screwed into the frame. In inexpensive pieces, the panel may be flush with the sides and simply tacked on.

Backs of top-quality pieces are sanded and stained to match the rest of the piece. In really high-quality merchandise, the backs may even be finished as nicely as the exposed panels.

Drawers are another good indicator of construction quality. Fine case goods will have center or side glides for easy drawer operation. They will also have stops to keep you from pulling the drawer out too far.

Drawers should be accurately cut with uniform space all around. When you move drawers from side to side, there should be no more than ¼ inch of play. A good piece of furniture will have dust panels between drawers.

On the best-quality pieces, all four drawer corners will have interlocking dovetail joints.

The drawer handles, knobs, or grooves should be evenly spaced. Insides of the drawers should be sanded smooth, stained or clear coated, and waxed.

When shopping, open and close doors on cabinets or armoires enough to make sure they don't hang open or swing shut. Push down firmly on the door when it's open. The hinges should be strong enough to keep it from sagging. Hinges and handles should be secure, and handles should fit your hands comfortably.

## FACTS ABOUT FINISHES

A furniture finish refers to the exterior wood surface. Generally this consists of protective materials applied to the finish. Sometimes it's actually the top layer.

Several clues to the quality of the finish are easy to see and assess. Check to make sure the surface material is hard, smooth, and evenly applied. Examine the surface for hairline cracks that run across the grain of the wood.

In addition to the popular furniture finishes (paint, lacquer, oil, or distressed) there are some special finishes, including catalyzed lacquers, polyurethane finishes, synthetic varnishes, and epoxies. There are also vinyl surfaces built right into the furniture, such as a wood veneer laminated with a sheet of vinyl, or a photographic print of wood grain which is reproduced on the underside of a clear piece of vinyl.

In most cases, the wood under the outside finishing layer will be stained, and this can be a key to good-quality construction. Look for dark or light spots indicating uneven application of the stain. On quality furniture the stain is sprayed on, then sealers, glazes, and clear lacquer are applied to enhance the wood grain. Lower grades of furniture are dipped in stain, then coated, with little or no attention paid to the beauty of the wood.

Feel under tables and chairs for roughness that might snag clothes. Also check to make sure the undersides of open shelves in hutches and other storage pieces are smooth.

More often than not, buying an upholstered chair or sofa is a considerable investment in both time and money. In return, you should expect—and receive—years of comfort and reliable service. Before you start shopping in earnest, stroll through the upholstered furniture departments of at least two or three stores. "Window shopping" in this manner will give you an idea of what's available, and what styles appeal to you.

Shop at stores you can depend on for good quality merchandise and knowledgeable salespeople. Sizing up upholstered furniture is tricky because most of the assets and liabilities are hidden. You can't rip off the covering to see what's underneath, but you can check information on the labels and hangtags and have important questions answered by the salesperson. If the salesperson is vague or unhelpful, ask to speak to the manager or buyer.

Judging the quality of upholstered furniture is a harder job than checking the quality of case goods. The difficulty here comes in not being able to see what's under the attractive cover fabric. So, up to a point, you have to rely on what a dealer tells you about the construction, springs, and cushioning of a piece, or on the illustrations in the manufacturer's catalog.

We intend to give you background information that will help you determine the quality of your prospective upholstered furniture purchase for yourself.

## THE FRAME

Unless a chair or sofa is made of molded plastic, it will have a wood frame. Good-quality frames are made of seasoned, kiln-dried hardwood that keeps them from warping. The manufacturer's information should tell you what kind of wood has been used.

Other features that indicate the quality of a frame are pieces joined by dowels and interlocking assembly of pieces (two pieces meshed jigsaw-fashion rather than simply butted together).

Corner blocks are another clue to the quality of construction. Good-quality furniture has corner blocks that are cut to fit, screwed and glued into position, and sometimes reinforced with a piece of plywood (A). Corner blocks stapled in place (B) won't give you furniture with long-range stability.

Look at the legs to see how they're attached. Although you can't see much of a chair's construction, this quality gauge *can* be seen and is a good tip-off to quality elsewhere in the unit's construction.

If legs are separate from the back rail of the chair, they should be made of interlocking pieces and joined to the frame with the same heavy-duty construction used for joining the other parts of the frame. If legs are simply screwed into the frame or screwed into metal plates attached to the frame, you may want to move up to a piece of better quality.

## SPRINGS ARE A CLUE

Springs do more than add resiliency to a chair or sofa. They also act as a barometer of quality. How many springs are used, how they're tied, and whether the spring area is reinforced are all indications of the quality of an upholstered piece.

Coil springs are familiar to most furniture buyers. Just remember, in quality furniture with coil springs, many coils cover the platform, while in inferior furniture coils are placed farther apart.

How coil springs are tied together is another clue to the kind of quality you're looking at. The best method is an eight-way tie, using substantial cord, with each cord anchored securely to the frame (C). A spring tied four ways (D) is definitely construction of lesser quality because a four-way tie is not adequate to hold the springs in the proper position.

The webbing under the springs is another checkpoint. In good furniture the webbing will be woven or laced so all bands are close together (E). Cheaper construction leaves enough space between webbing to put your fist through (F). Woven sheet webbing (rather than strips) also is frequently used, and should be reinforced with steel straps beneath each row of springs.

Another type of spring you may find is sinuous or non-sag springs, which look like wavy lines of heavy metal wire. These are generally used in the backs of very slim-lined furniture.

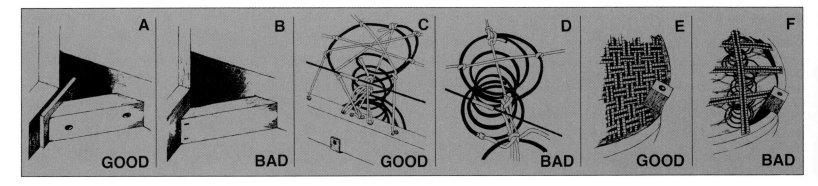

GOOD — BAD — GOOD — BAD — GOOD — BAD

## THE SOFT SIDE OF QUALITY

Cushioning or padding is important to the comfort and quality of a chair or sofa. Good-quality furniture has two or three layers of padding and most often a layer of fabric between the layers of cushioning.

*Spring-down* is one of the favorite cushioning methods in upper-end furniture. Here, individual coil springs are put into muslin covers. In some cases the coils may have their centers filled with polyurethane. Then these muslin-covered springs are inserted in a casing of fabric on a polyurethane block. Down is then blown into the channeled, down-proof muslin casing and the spring-filled core is wrapped with the casing.

*Polyurethane foam* and *natural latex foam rubber* are two other popular cushioning materials. For durability, comfort, and general appearance, polyurethane is your best value. It's strong, lightweight and flexible, yet provides soft, though resilient, seating. It's also completely nonallergenic. Most cushions start with a core of polyurethane and get a topping of polyester fiber to add softness to the surface and contour. Optional cushions such as spring down and down and feathers offer added luxury.

Don't be surprised to discover that instead of the traditional muslin undercover for filled cushions, there's a nonwoven fabric cover of synthetic materials. This cushion will perform the same as any other.

Most pillow backs are made with polyester fiber filling.

## JUDGING WHAT YOU SEE

The cover fabric of an upholstered piece is one of the first things you see. It's also one of the deciding factors in choosing a chair or sofa. But wise fabric selection means more than just choosing a cover that will look good in your home. Know how and why fabrics are graded (grading determines price) and learn about fibers and their characteristics. Then you'll be able to choose, knowing you've bought what's best for you and your budget.

## THE GRADE SYSTEM

The enormous range in price of upholstered furniture is often due to difference in fabrics used to cover them. And fabrics are graded according to their quality and design, and (for patterned fabrics) the amount of material needed to achieve a good pattern match in the furniture piece.

First decide how much use the chair or sofa will get and how long you expect it to serve you. If it's in for hard use, look for serviceable, tightly-woven fabric that will resist soil. You may want to think about vinyls or fabrics made from nylon or olefin. On the other hand a chair or sofa in a formal area can be covered in something less durable and more elegant.

There are two basic types of fabrics—flat weaves and pile fabrics. The flat weaves (damasks, satins, basket weaves, and tweeds) are made by weaving two sets of yarns. Pile fabrics (velvet, corduroy, and plush) are woven with an extra set of yarns to create the loop or pile effect. Fabrics with some surface texture will show less wear.

The manufacturers of upholstery fabric do not guarantee colorfastness or fading. All fabrics when placed in direct sunlight will tend to fade in varying degrees. However, synthetic fabrics will fade the least.

## FACTS ABOUT FIBERS

Two types of fibers are found in upholstery fabric: natural and synthetic. Naturals are those made from animal or vegetable fibers, including cotton, linen, silk, and wool. Leather is also in this group. Those natural fibers (other than leather, which is basically not a fiber) used in upholstery are usually combined with a man-made fiber in a blend to produce fabric with the best characteristics of both fibers. The exception is in printed fabrics, the majority of which are 100 percent cotton, which gives clarity and brilliance to the printed colors. In most cases, an upholstery fabric made of these fibers should be treated to resist stains and spills.

The man-made fibers include acetate, acrylic, nylon, olefin, polyester, rayon, and vinyl. Generally speaking, these fibers are extremely durable, take color well, and are much more resistant to fading than natural fibers. Nylon, olefin, and vinyl, are remarkably resistant to soiling.

## FABRIC FINISHES

The finishes applied to upholstery fabric provide an extra deterrent against fading, moisture, soiling, and staining.

Though finishes make fabric easier to clean, they do not make a fabric wear any better. Care of the fabric does that and is up to you. Remember, proper care will lengthen the life of your upholstery.

## TESTS FOR QUALITY

Don't just sit in a chair or on a sofa you're contemplating—bounce on it. This will give you an idea of how substantial the frame is. You shouldn't feel any wobbling or swaying.

Next, push your back into the back of the chair. You should neither hear squeaking or rubbing sounds nor be able to feel the frame. Also, the padding should be comfortable.

Check the padding on the top of the arms and on the front edge of the deck. If you feel the frame at all, this isn't top-quality merchandise.

Have your salesperson turn the chair or sofa up so you can see the bottom. If, when you pat the bottom, it sounds like a drum, you know coil and webbing construction is up to standard.

Check the outside panels of the piece. On high-quality furniture, these places will be soft and padded. You won't find that on less-expensive pieces.

Look at how the upholstery fabric has been applied. Is it straight? Do patterns match? Is the welting neat and even? If the upholstery and tailoring are sloppy, you can probably assume that the insides of the furniture are second-rate, too.

**P**lastic furniture no longer has to play the poor stepsister role to wood furniture. It has come into its own as an acceptable material with a remarkable record for good-quality design, good performance, and somewhat lower cost.

Plastics have gone beyond just being accepted; some are leading the way in modern design. Today plastic is being bent, molded, and blown into exciting shapes never before possible. Plastics also offer great opportunities for use of strong color, since color is an integral part of the material itself. Plastics have also made possible single-unit construction with no joints to weaken from time and use. The old wood frame found in upholstered furniture is now often made of molded shapes of rigid polyurethane, fiber-glass-reinforced polyester, or other structural rigid foams.

## A LOOK AT MATERIALS

Even though it seems a chemistry degree would be handy in deciphering what's what in plastics, it really isn't that complicated. Actually, only about a dozen of the thousands of compounds in the whole field of plastics are used in furniture. These 12 various kinds represent *families* of plastics, such as vinyls, urethanes, and acrylics. All of the 12 groups fall into two major classifications: thermoplastics and thermoset plastics.

*Thermoplastics,* in theory, can be melted down and re-formed. They can, therefore, be damaged by excessive heat.

*Thermoset plastics,* usually formed by the reaction of two or three ingredients, are less likely to be damaged by heat.

One of the most popular plastics in home furnishings is polyurethane, since it can be used in either its soft and flexible or hard and rigid state. From this plastic comes cushioning foam for upholstery and bedding, adhesives, and wood-finishing components. This same material, when rigid, can be formed into parts that look like wood or into free-form shapes for upholstered chairs.

## MANUFACTURING METHODS

Several procedures are used to manufacture all-plastic furniture. One of the most popular methods is molding plastic while it is in a hot liquid state, using a principle similar to that of making molded gelatin. Using thermoplastic materials, the resin pellets are heated until they become molten. Next they're injected into a mold under high pressure. When cool, the finished piece is removed from the mold.

A second manufacturing method involves heating large sheets of thermoplastic materials until they are soft enough to be bent or shaped.

## HOW TO JUDGE QUALITY

Plastic furniture, just like its wood counterpart, has features that indicate its quality, and a wise shopper will want to check for them before buying. However, these features are not at all the same quality points you would look for in wood pieces.

Though plastics have chemical differences, certain general characteristics are common to all plastic furniture pieces. Here's what to look for:
● Heavier gauge or thickness in plastic usually indicates better quality.
● Edges should be smooth.
● Surfaces should be flawless.
● Color and glossiness of a piece should be uniform.
● A piece that is finished on all visible sides indicates good-quality construction.
● Reinforcing elements should be hidden unless an integral part of the design.

## PRICES OF PLASTICS

Quality is quality no matter what the manufacturing material. And you get what you pay for. Even though some of the new plastic materials can be produced economically, the costs of initial molds can be extremely high. Therefore, when you shop for a good-quality plastic chair or storage unit you can expect to pay prices comparable to that of fine-quality wood furniture. However, as more quality plastic furniture is made, it will become lower in price.

## WICKER

The first fact to establish is that wicker is not a material, but a classification of furniture woven from any one of a variety of materials, including rattan, reed, willow, buri, raffia, latania, or any other pliant twig.

Each of these materials comes from a different source and each possesses different identifying characteristics.

*Reed* may be one of two things, a tall slender grass or the inner core of a rattan pole.

*Willow* is, of course, a common tree or shrub with tough malleable shoots. It's particularly long-lasting as a material for furniture because it retains its natural moisture well.

*Buri* is the spine or center stem of a small genus of palm.

*Raffia* is made from the leafstalks of the raffia palm.

*Latania* is a rope-like fiber procured from another member of the palm family. This material is hand-plaited when damp into taut strands for weaving directly onto furniture frames.

*Imitation wicker* is made from twisted paper or plastic and, with the application of several coats of lacquer, is hard to tell from the real thing.

## WICKER QUALITY CHECKS

Strength is one of the first things to check when shopping for wicker furniture.
● Lean heavily on a piece of wicker to make sure the furniture doesn't wobble or give under your body weight.
● Turn the piece over and check the underside. If the wicker furniture is good quality it will be sturdy and rigid with a frame that's at least 1 inch thick. Make sure all corners and joints are tightly wrapped with no loose ends.
● Check the finish. On good wicker the surface should be smooth to the touch, with no snags, rough edges, or hairy fibers visible.
● Notice how closely the wicker is woven. The best and most

expensive wicker is usually woven tightly of flexible reed strips made from the inner core of the rattan pole. Closely woven wicker is more durable than pieces woven in a loose, open design.

## RATTAN

Rattan is actually a woody vine that's a member of the palm family. This material, characterized by a tough outer shell over an inner bark and pithy core, is used for crafting some of the finest casual furniture.

The outer bark or peel is removed and cut into narrow strips that often are used to wrap the framework and joints of rattan pole furniture. The very narrowest strips of this bark are cane, used to weave chair seats and backs, furniture side panels, and accessories.

The poles themselves are sanded and seasoned for use as furniture legs and frames. The natural nodes, or growth marks, are carefully retained to add to the beauty of the finished furniture.

Rattan bends easily and holds its graceful curves well. It can be joined with nails, screws, or glue and accepts a finish well.

Mottled, fired, or scorched rattan is a golden variety of palm that has been burned between the joints for a tortoiseshell effect.

### HOW TO JUDGE RATTAN QUALITY

Here's a list of checkpoints to assure the quality of the rattan furniture you buy:

- Poles should be free of any dark blemishes that might indicate rotting.
- Growth nodes should be uniformly spaced (about 12 to 18 inches apart).
- Joints should be tightly and smoothly wrapped with genuine peel bindings.
- Rattan wraps or cane peel bindings should be glued and nailed to eliminate any possibility of loosening or unwinding.
- The finish should be smooth and fuzz-free.
- Test the furniture's strength the same as you would wicker.
- Check to make sure any cushions are comfortable, of good-quality fabric, and well constructed.

### BAMBOO

Though this material looks similar to rattan in that they both have growth nodes, the two have different characteristics.

Bamboo is hollow with a tough outer shell, which makes it less flexible than rattan. It is also more difficult to shape, splits easily, and doesn't take a finish well. Bamboo is best used for accessories and light accent pieces.

### EASY-TO-ASSEMBLE FURNITURE

This growing category of home furnishings (sometimes called "knockdown" or KD) comes in a carton with materials and instructions for easy assembly. In a matter of hours you have good-looking affordable furniture in your home.

Easy-to-assemble furniture is priced affordably because

manufacturers save money on the labor normally required to assemble furniture. Disassembled furniture also cuts shipping and delivery costs. What all this means is that you can buy furniture for at least 20 percent less than if it were assembled at the factory.

Quick-assembly furniture is usually clean lined and contemporary with a minimum of ornamentation, although traditional styles are available, too. The natural look predominates with an emphasis on wood grains and textured fabrics.

Materials include wood, fiberboard, plastic, and chrome-finished steel or wrought iron, with accents of rush, cane, or other woven reeds.

### HOW TO JUDGE QUALITY

To effectively judge the quality of quick-assembly pieces, you can't rely on the same standards you'd use for conventionally made furniture pieces. Materials and construction methods are entirely different.

Here are some tips to make judging the quality easier:
- Be aware that wood frames, even in high-quality lines, are most often of pine. Only a few groups have hardwood frames.
- Look for furniture that feels solidly built. Most stores will have samples set up. Check them thoroughly. And see how they are constructed.
- Sit on chairs and sofas. Do you hear any creaks from pressure? If the piece feels flimsy or unstable, it may collapse before too long.
- Chrome, iron, and metal frames should be electrostati-

cally finished on all exposed surfaces to avoid chipping and peeling.
- Check the tailoring of the upholstery, whether or not slings and cushions are reinforced with interlinings and what the filling is in cushions. Ask if replacement cushions are available.

In case goods, look for these things:
- Wood corners should be well-sanded and metal pieces free of jagged edges.
- Furniture edges should fit tightly with no cracks where the components are attached.
- Check drawers. You may not find dust panels or center guides, but all good-quality knockdown furniture should have side guides on drawers.
- Doors in cabinets should fit well and open smoothly.
- Shelves should have sturdy brackets that will support the weight of shelved items.
- Cabinets and chests designed to stack should fit firmly one on top of the other. If modular storage units are to be lined up, they should fit together snugly and evenly.
- Test units to see whether they will tip over when you pull out a drawer or open a door.

Each year, more and more stores are adding departments of quick-assembly furniture with a fair to good selection of affordable, portable pieces. Some cities have specialty stores dealing exclusively in this type of furniture.

The greatest share of this type of furniture is American-made, though some stores feature pieces imported from Europe.

# FURNITURE /CARE AND CLEANING

The better you care for your furniture, the longer it will last. Here are some practical care and cleaning tips for most types of furnishings.

## WOOD FURNITURE

Wood is extremely sensitive to too much heat and humidity. However, it can also be damaged by too little moisture. See to its climatic needs, then take good care of the finish.

Dust frequently, but be sure you're not harming the surface while removing abrasive particles. Always dust with the grain of the wood and lift objects to dust underneath. Never slide them around or you may scratch the surface.

Never use cheesecloth as a dustcloth unless you're sure all the sizing has been washed out. Don't expect a feather duster to really dust. It will push dust around, but not pick it up. A polish-treated cloth is good for a polished finish, but it may soften wax on a waxed finish.

Polish and wax only once every few months and use only polishes recommended for furniture. Always follow directions on labels and pretest any new wax or polish on a small, out-of-the-way area.

To help you maintain your favorite finish, here's a guide to the products to use.

*High-gloss* finish may be maintained with either a liquid polish or a paste wax. Let liquid dry, then buff. Paste wax requires rubbing to bring out the sheen.

*Satin-gloss* finish. Use a cleaning polish or cream wax without silicone.

*Low-gloss* finish. Use a liquid polish designed for low-luster wood or a cleaning wax that removes surface soil and protects the finish without producing a shine.

*Oil finish.* Wash periodically with a mild soap solution to which a few drops of mineral spirits or lemon juice have been added. Then apply boiled linseed oil. Dust the piece with a cloth dampened with clean water and glycerine or mineral thinner.

*Painted finish.* Wipe with a barely damp cloth or a sponge dampened in a mild soap and water solution. Avoid wax or liquid polish unless the label states it is recommended for painted surfaces.

*Antique furniture* should be cared for the same as high-gloss finish. Avoid a heavy buildup of wax.

## UPHOLSTERED FURNITURE

Vacuum upholstery once a week and turn cushions to distribute wear.

When a general cleaning is needed, check the fiber content of fabrics to see how they will react to shampooing. Always pretest each color in your upholstery to make sure there is no bleeding. Test in inconspicuous areas of the upholstered piece.

After making sure your furniture is safe to be shampooed, clean it with one of the spray foam cleaners on the market or whip up your own home formula. Never use soap on upholstered furniture, since it can't be rinsed off well enough and residue will attract soil.

Make a dry foam using a synthetic detergent and warm (never hot) water. Whip the solution until you can apply only the foam to a small area at a time. Use a soft-bristled brush or a sponge. Work quickly, scrubbing with a circular motion. Lift off dirty suds with a rubber spatula, dry sponge, or clean towel. Rinse with a clean cloth dipped in warm water and wrung almost dry.

Dry furniture as quickly as possible with windows open or an electric fan blowing.

Fabrics that can't be shampooed will have to be cleaned with a no-water cleaning solution. Read instructions carefully and apply sparingly.

## PLASTIC FURNITURE

To keep plastic looking its best, keep it clean by wiping pieces with a damp cloth or a cloth dampened in a gentle liquid detergent solution. Never use abrasive cleaners or furniture polish. Some manufacturers recommend automobile wax as a deterrent against the minor scratches plastic can acquire.

## WICKER FURNITURE

Protect your wicker furniture by using it only indoors, on a sheltered porch, or covered patio. Rain and direct sun can damage wicker.

Use a vacuum cleaner brush attachment to get out dust in woven areas. To clean, wipe with a damp cloth or wash with a soapy sponge. Rinse the furniture thoroughly, then wipe it dry. Rub on liquid furniture wax for sheen and extra protection.

## RATTAN FURNITURE

This furniture is made of a natural material that, like wood, needs moisture. If seating pieces snap and crackle with pressure, the furniture is calling for help.

Use a slightly dampened sponge, being careful not to wet the frame or penetrate the weave. Or spray a fine mist with a plant sprayer, then wipe it off with a cloth. Let rattan furniture dry before using.

## OUTDOOR METAL FURNITURE

Protect aluminum by spraying it with a clear lacquer two or three times a summer. Dull, unpainted aluminum can be restored by rubbing it with fine steel wool dipped in kerosene. Color-coated aluminum (and webbing) can be washed with a mild detergent solution. Rinse it well, then apply automobile paste wax to the aluminum.

Wrought-iron furniture stays looking good when you keep it painted with good exterior oil enamel in a gloss finish. This prevents rust and makes your furniture easy to clean.

## REDWOOD FURNITURE

To prevent darkening of the soft color, apply one or two coats of preservative to keep out some of the moisture.

Before application, scrub the surface with detergent, rinse well, and let dry.

If redwood has been stained, then waxed, all you need to do is wipe it down with a damp sponge.

# FURNITURE FIRST AID

| TYPE OF FINISH | PROCEDURE: SCRATCH REMOVAL |
| --- | --- |
| **Plastic** | Regular applications of automobile wax fill in minor scratches. |
| **Dark Wood** | Rub nutmeats (walnut, Brazil, or butternut) into scratch. Or touch up with furniture crayon, eyebrow pencil, or shoe polish in shade to match finish. |
| **Mahogany or Cherry** | Apply aged or darkened iodine. |
| **Maple** | Apply aged or darkened iodine diluted 50 percent with denatured alcohol. |
| **Oil** | Using a fine steel-wool pad, rub lightweight mineral oil, boiled linseed oil, or paraffin oil into scratch. Wipe dry. |

| TYPE OF STAIN | PROCEDURE: STAIN REMOVAL |
| --- | --- |
| **Water Marks or Rings** | Place clean, thick blotter over stain and press down with warm iron. Repeat. If that fails, try application of cleaning polish or wax. Or apply camphorated oil with lint-free cloth, rubbing with the wood grain. Wipe dry. Repeat. |
| **White Marks** | Rub with thin paste of wax and mineral spirits. When dry, apply thin coat of wax or cleaning polish. Or rub with cigar or cigarette ashes, using cloth dipped in wax, lubricating oil, vegetable shortening, lard, or salad oil. Wipe off immediately. Rewax. |
| **Milk or Alcohol** | Using fingers, rub liquid or paste wax into area. If that fails, rub in paste or boiled linseed oil and rottenstone (available at most hardware stores). Use powdered pumice for dull finishes. Wipe dry. Polish. Or apply ammonia with damp cloth. Polish immediately. |
| **Cigarette Burns** | Rub area with scratch-concealing polish. If that fails, apply rottenstone paste as for alcohol stain. If burn is deep, area may have to be refinished. |
| **Heat Marks** | Rub area gently with dry steel-wool soap pad a tiny area at a time, wiping up powdery substance. If that fails, rub with cloth dampened in camphorated oil or mineral spirits. Rub dry with clean cloth. Repeat. Or rub gently with fine steel wool. Wipe off. Repolish. |
| **Sticking Paper** | Saturate paper with lightweight oil. Wait. Rub area lightly with fine steel wool. Wipe dry. |
| **Nail Polish** | Rub area gently with fine steel wool dipped in liquid wax. Wipe away polish. Rewax. |
| **Paint Spots** | If paint is wet, treat like nail polish stain. If dry, soak area with linseed oil. Wait until paint softens. Wipe away paint with cloth dampened in linseed oil. If any paint remains, apply paste of boiled linseed oil and rottenstone. |
| **Candle Wax** | Harden wax with ice cube, catching moisture as ice melts. Using fingers, crumble off wax. Scrape remaining wax gently with old credit card. Rub with cloth dampened in mineral spirits. Or place clean, thick blotter over stain and press down with warm iron. Rub area with liquid polish. Wipe dry. |

# COLOR

Color comes first. Whether it's in first impressions, or in the final analysis of what makes a room work, color is the key to successful decorating. Without it, even the most expensive furnishings go flat. Conversely, color can turn everything, even the unsightly, into a visual pleasure. Color works magic, too, by visually stretching space, shrinking furniture, raising and lowering ceilings, and altering emotional levels. Add the fact that color is inexpensive, and you'll see why it is such a natural decorating asset. Today, there are all sorts of daring new color combinations that don't always fit the rule book. So in choosing your change of scene, don't limit yourself to the same drab old formulas. If all this sounds intimidating, relax. Everyone has an "eye for color," whether he knows it or not. All it takes is a little understanding of how color principles work. In the pages that follow we'll take you from color scheme to finished room.

# COLOR
## UNDERSTANDING ITS USES

There's no end of the rainbow when it comes to color. Sunshine is its source, and its beauty is truly in the eye of the beholder.

The human eye can perceive some 10 million different colors. That almost endless variety can be combined in an equally endless number of ways. Almost no color combination is wrong, *per se*. Consider the joyous abandon with which nature runs her spectrum of colors together, say in a field of wildflowers.

But when it comes to our interior landscapes, some colors and color combinations are definitely more successful than others. This chapter will help you sort through all the color options and settle on the best for your rooms.

### COMMON COLOR TERMS

*Primary colors*. These are the big three: red, blue, and yellow. Every other color starts out as one of these three. In traditional academic approaches to color studies, you'll find the primaries shown spaced equidistantly around a circle known as the *color wheel*. But since we're more interested here in practical decorating problems than in a textbook understanding of color, we'll forgo the standard color wheel and deal straightaway with how color can be used. If, for example, you use primary colors in decorating, you'll get an action room, one bright and full of visual bounce because the primaries offer color in its strongest form.

*Secondary, tertiary, and complementary colors*. These are color terms you should rec-

ognize even if you don't apply them directly in your own decorating plans.

*Secondary colors* are the three colors you'd come up with if you mixed equal parts of the three primaries: orange (from red and yellow), green (from yellow and blue), and violet (from blue and red).

*Tertiary colors* result when you mix a primary color with its nearest secondary color. The resulting hues are blue-green, yellow-green, yellow-orange, red-orange, red-purple, and blue-purple.

Secondary and tertiary colors, when used together, are known as *related or analogous color schemes*. (An example would be a room done in blue, blue-green, and green.) Because they get along so harmoniously, related colors generally have a calming and restful effect on a room.

*Complementary colors* are the colors most *unlike* each other—so totally opposite, in fact, they tend to neutralize each other and turn gray when mixed. Red and green are complements; so are blue and orange; yellow and violet. In a room setting, however, you *can* mix complements, and with lively results. Complementary color schemes are invigorating and require deft handling to succeed.

Here are some additional technical color terms that are helpful for you to know.

*Hue* is simply another word for color. Fire-engine red, fern green, burgundy, and aubergine are all hues.

*Saturation* means how *much* color is in a color, or how *satu-*

*rated* it is with the basic hue. For example, both pink and fire-engine red are officially "red"; the difference is in the saturation, or *intensity,* as you'll sometimes hear it called.

*Value* refers to the lightness or darkness of a color. White has the brightest value of any color; black the darkest. You'll soon learn how the value of a color has major effect on the way it behaves in a room setting.

*Tints* are colors closest to white in value. Most pastels fall into the category of tints. *Shades* are colors closest to black in value. Deep purple, midnight blue, forest green are all called shades.

*Neutrals* are the "un-colors": black, white, gray, brown, and beige. Because they are so easy on the eyes, neutrals are a welcome addition to any color scheme.

### THIRD DIMENSIONS

*Finish, size, and space* are more words you're apt to come across when dealing with color.

*Finish* refers to the physical surface of the color, that is, whether it's slick or dull, smooth or textured. Finish can affect color, too. The exact same color on a lacquer-finished Parsons table, for example, will appear much brighter and lighter than it will on a swatch of linen upholstery fabric.

*Size* and *space* also affect the appearance of color. You may love that tiny touch of persimmon in your Oriental rug, but go easy in transferring it to an entire wall. The larger the area of color and the closer you are

to it, the brighter it will appear. This is why you should always work with large samples of paint colors and fabrics when you're considering living with a color in a big way.

Conversely, the eye tends to blend colors seen at a distance. Impressionist painters understood this optical phenomenon, streaking their canvases with separate colors and letting the eye of the beholder do the mixing.

In decorating, such color magic can cause mischief. For example, a crisp black-and-white tweed slipcover can turn into dull gray at a distance. Be forewarned that the same optical illusions apply to small-patterned fabrics and wall coverings and to tweedy carpets. Again, your surest safeguard against such unintentional color accidents is to bring home a large swatch of whatever you intend to use in your room plan.

*One color plus white equals an almost foolproof color scheme. Here, a scintillating shock of pure turquoise is cooled by generous areas of white. Yards and yards of eyelet drape the windows and canopy bed in this nostalgic bedroom. The shirred, ruffled fabric adds softness when played against the sleek shine of the painted floor.*

# COLOR
# ITS MANY MOODS

So far, we've concentrated on the physical nature of color, the side the eye sees and understands. More important, perhaps, is the emotional effect color can have on how we feel.

Its effect is very real. Although all of us have somewhat different reactions to different colors, there are categories of color that can be counted on to affect all people pretty much the same way. No mere whim inspires experts to paint hospitals and institutions in cheerful or calming hues, or professional designers to put warm reds on restaurant walls. Bright colors fight depression; neutrals are soothing to the spirit, and red encourages a sense of warmth, and even stimulates the appetite.

## WARM OR COOL

Color can indeed raise or lower the visual temperature in a room. No mystery here: Nature sets the thermostat. The warm colors are the colors of sunshine—reds, yellows, and oranges. The cool colors include blues, greens, and violets. Before you attempt to translate these properties into a color scheme, study the room itself. What kind of natural light does it get? Warm sunshine from a southern exposure or cool bluish light from the north? Southern exposures generally fill a room with rich, bright light. Thus, if you overemphasize the warm side of the color spectrum, you might end up with too much of a good thing. Better to balance the room's natural attributes with a generous helping of cool or neutral colors.

Save the warms for a north-facing room where they can help compensate for the room's paler personality.

Natural light is not the only consideration, of course, especially for apartment dwellers and families whose at-home hours are mainly in the evening. Artificial lighting has such dramatic effects on colors that it's essential to evaluate color samples in the kind of light they'll be seen in. Don't bother taking a fabric swatch to the door of the store to see it "in the light" if it will be viewed under artificial light at home. Take the swatch home, instead. As a rule, incandescent lights add a warm, yellow cast to colors. Fluorescents, however, tend to cool down colors and bring out their greenish-blue bias.

It's not the bulb alone that can affect the quality of light in a room. So do the texture and color of lamp shades, and the other colors you already may have in the room. The light that reflects from, say, a green carpet or a red brick wall can influence the color of everything else in the room—another good reason to do your color selecting in the room itself. If you understand such optical caprices in advance, you can make them work for, not against, your decorating plans.

## COLOR:
## THE MOOD-MAKER

As important as the site and light in the room you're decorating is the way the room will function. Will it be a place for jovial gatherings or quiet relaxation? Warm colors are so naturally convivial and conducive to activity, they are obvious choices for kitchens and family rooms, children's rooms, and nurseries. Studies tell us that infants react instantly and happily to strong, bright colors. Commonly used pastels are actually too sophisticated for them to appreciate.

The cooler side of the color spectrum leads to introspection and calm, the mood you might seek for a living room or master bedroom. The more subtle, grayed tones also assume a kind of sophistication and formality that makes them right for both traditional rooms and elegant contemporary scenes. On the other hand, bright, warm colors come on strong enough to carry rooms that are young and fun in feeling, whether they are Early American informal, ultramodern and slick, or uninhibitedly eclectic.

Which brings us to another psychological dimension of color: its passive or aggressive tendencies. Simply put, the "passive" colors are light in value, and usually content to remain in the background. The cool colors mainly fall into this passive category. Because the eye often looks right past them, light, cool colors tend to open space up visually, a neat trick to remember when you're dealing with smaller rooms. It follows that the "aggressive" colors, the warm hues and shades that are dark in value, will move in on the eye, filling space and making their presence felt in a room. There will be times when you'll be happy to harness the power of dark, warm colors to make a large room seem smaller, to add an element of coziness to overwhelming space, or simply to camouflage such problems as overhead pipes.

*Inspiration for this subtle, sophisticated color scheme came from the large delicate watercolor hanging above the sofa. Pillows in soft shades of yellow and blue punctuate the white of the sectional sofa and repeat the colors found in the patterned wall-to-wall carpet. The pastel blue striped fabric is repeated on the upholstery of the French arm chairs and on several large floor pillows. Greenery in both the living room and the glass-walled garden room add yet another element to the Monet-like color scheme. A change in flooring—from carpet to wood—defines the garden room and provides just the right touch of visual contrast for the setting. Two French reproduction chairs and a small round table provide a perfect spot for lunch or afternoon tea.*

Color has an amazing ability to affect not only the overall look of a room—its furnishings, fabrics, and accessories—but the moods of the people within it.

# COLOR
## ITS MANY MOODS

Another factor that should be considered in planning a color scheme is your family's tastes. What colors do they respond to? What colors do they feel most comfortable with? *You* might love an all-pastel living room, for instance, but how well would it wear (literally) with children? Feelings about colors vary as dramatically as tastes in anything else. That so many colors are named after foods (think of lemon yellow, coffee, tomato red) attests to our sensual attitude toward colors. It would be a mistake to make unilateral decisions when you choose a color scheme for the public areas of the house. Private bedrooms and baths excepted, all other rooms should reflect, as far as possible, the family's collective personality. This doesn't mean decorating by committee, however. Take a tip from professional designers, who interview everyone in the household and make careful note of color likes and dislikes. The designers use this information to assemble several color schemes that they hope will please the entire family. Often, since fabrics, wall coverings, and carpets come in such variety, it's possible to assemble the same basic room plan in a number of different colors (or "colorways," as they are called), and let the family vote for their favorite.

Whether you're redecorating one room or several, keep the house's overall balance in mind. Especially where you can see one room from another (as the hall from the living room), color coordination is extremely important.

1

1 Color rules can be bent, and beautifully, if you understand the effect you are after. Here, the pat approach would have been to paint the walls of this tiny dining room a space-making light color. Instead, a more exciting tack was taken by covering the walls in a deep, strong blue. Salmon adds a surprise spark of color on the chair cushions and in the art work. The aggressive blue serves to bring the walls forward, and makes the room conducive to candlelit dinners and lingering over coffee.

2 Gray-blue, toned down to a restful tint, points up the sophisticated simplicity of this town-house living room. In deference to the handsome presence of the tall windows, everything else is neutralized with white. The statement is so strong and direct that other colors simply aren't needed. A unique and personal idea: children's christening clothes framed simply in clear acrylic boxes and hung as "art" over one of the love seats.

It's a good idea to get a reading of your family's favorite colors before embarking on a decorating project. This is especially important when choosing colors for "public" rooms.

# COLOR
## PICK A PATTERN

**N**ow for the nitty-gritty: how to get a color scheme out of your head and into your room. You probably already have a starting point, since few of us ever approach a decorating project with a totally naked room. Assess the furnishings you want to keep, looking for a color combination you can build your new scheme around. A rug, a painting, a quilt— all can provide inspiration.

One of the easiest and surest sources for a successful color scheme is a print fabric. Professional artists have already worked out the color harmonies for you, so success is assured if you follow this simple formula and expand the fabric's colors to embrace your entire room.

• Use the dominant color in the fabric for the largest areas in the room—the walls or ceiling— with at least an echo of it in the floor treatment.

• The next brightest color can go on large, upholstered furniture pieces and the window treatment without overwhelming the eye. It's a good idea to repeat a bit of this color at floor level, too.

• The sharpest color in the fabric becomes the accent color in the room. Use it sparingly in art and accessories.

Two other important pointers to remember about color scheming are: Never give two or more colors equal importance in a room. Let one dominate, the other play counterpoint. And, never use a color just once. If you bring in a zesty yellow throw pillow, for example, add corresponding yellow touches elsewhere—on curtain trim, for instance.

*In this bedroom, the floral chintz fabric sets the color scheme. But hues from the print are used in a variation on the usual formula. Here, some of the design's bolder (rather than quieter) hues take over the major decorating tasks. Bright pink from the pattern covers three walls and lines the underside of the canopy. The fabric itself, rich in soft, soothing brown tones, is shirred on the fourth wall, used topside on the canopy, and for the comforter, and draperies. Antique gold, another strong color from the print, appears on the dust ruffle and as trim on the canopy. Cooling pale blue carpets the floor and also stripes the canopy liner. Accents from the fabric's flower-strewn print are used for a pile of dusty-pastel bed pillows.*

Another, almost no-fail way to set a color scheme is simply to play favorites. Start with one color you particularly like and build around it, drawing on colors that are close enough not to jar the eye with contrast. This is called a related color scheme and it's easy to see why. You're working with colors that are close kin to each other, colors that are all in the same family. Blue and green and violet are the cool cousins; blue-green, green, and yellow-green make a spring fresh combination; yellow, orange, and red tones are hot and lively. The color spectrum then slides back to the quieter deep red, violet, and blue range. Take any slice from this rainbow of related colors and build it into a room scheme that will automatically be compatible. The major caveat here is not to combine too many colors. Remember, one color must always dominate a scheme to make the room successful. As part of the basic scheme, three colors are generally as many as the eye wants to handle in a room. However, you can vary your palette almost endlessly by playing those three colors up and down the intensity scale from light to dark. Into this harmony of basic colors, you can, and should, introduce an accent color, a small, strong counter note that will bring the room to life. Complementary colors (those most unlike your basic colors) make effective accents. In a room cool with blues, for example, introduce a dollop of strong orange, blue's opposite number, and watch it set things vibrating.

1 Who says "country" decorating must be cozy and quiet? Instead of the time-softened shades you might expect in a room filled with mellow pine furniture, the colors in this braided rug and patchwork quilt are sharp, spicy, and downright contemporary. Related tones in the rug range from pink to red, to blue and green, and back again. With bold accents like these, other colors are restfully subdued.

2 Soft bonbon colors enrich this living room well beyond its monetary budget. The squashy sofa is homemade; a box spring and mattress are agreeably disguised in a wrapping of fabric and polyester batting. The color magic, accomplished with bathtub dye baths, flows through a whole spectrum of restful, related harmonies taken from a favorite poster. Both poster and sofa now create a warm, glowing color unit that contrasts softly with the crisp checked floor.

2

95

# COLOR
# FAIL-SAFE SCHEMES: NEUTRALS

No longer are neutrals synonymous with colorless or uncommitted. Today's positive outlook toward neutrals is far different from the old idea that they are "safe" colors for unsure decorators to fall back upon. That attitude put the world in wall-to-wall beige a decade or so ago. Now, artfully blended into a "no-color" or "bleached-look" scheme, the neutrals can be sophisticated, urbane, and, best of all, surprisingly easy to work with. (The same can be said for the pastels. Once regarded merely as pale shadows of more vivid hues, now pastel tints offer exciting color schemes.)

## THE NATURE OF NEUTRALS

If you've ever walked a beach at low tide, or studied a snowy meadow in winter, you have seen neutrals at their natural best. Think of the bleached pebbles against the wet sand, of the polished gray driftwood, and flaxen marsh grasses. Visualize the white snow over dark rocks, the setting studded with dried weeds and bare trees in variegated shades of gray and brown.

If you also have noted the myriad textures in these landscapes, then you have an understanding of what it takes to turn a palette of neutrals into a relaxing room scheme rich with visual interest.

## TWO WAYS THAT WORK

There are two sound approaches to creating a neutral color palette in a room. You may opt for the entire range of "un-colors"—browns, beiges, grays, taupes, and whites—working a number of them into a soothing scheme. Since all such neutrals get on harmoniously together, the risk of visual cacophony is virtually nil.

Or, you can select just one basic neutral and use it everywhere, varying its intensity and texture so you can eventually orchestrate that one-color note into a full-bodied symphony. This is called a monochromatic or one-color scheme.

A handsome example would be a living room planned around desert hues. Walls might be covered in warm, rich camel tones; the seating, a sweeping modular unit upholstered in sand-toned linen-like fabric; and the rug, nubby-textured in shades of dark-weathered wood. Visualize the play of textures as the colors shift from light to dark. Add a dramatic accent color, such as terra cotta, in the accessories, and you have all the visual interest any room needs.

## NEUTRALS KNOW FEW BOUNDS

The quiet of neutral schemes makes them a natural for small rooms where their "non-aggressive" attributes can be used to coax limited space into looking larger. Expanses of unbroken, subtle neutrals seem especially appropriate in sophisticated, contemporary rooms, where even the furniture is refined to a basic simplicity. No extraneous detail is needed. No intrusive color allowed.

Neutral and monochromatic schemes are not reserved, however, for modern habitats alone. Period furnishings seem to gain new presence when placed against a background of calm colors because the pieces aren't forced to compete for attention.

The silhouettes of antique or unusual furniture pieces show to even better advantage. And remember that the furniture wood itself contributes yet another neutral ingredient to be blended into the color scheme.

Architectural details in a room also can be counted as neutrals: wood floors, beamed ceilings, marble or tile fireplaces, slate floors, or metallic touches in the fixtures.

For the most part, metallic or mirrored surfaces simply reflect what's there and, like chameleons, assume the colors surrounding them. Keep this in mind when you select glass tables or seating pieces with chrome bases. Copper and brass count as neutrals, too, but they will add a distinct, warm color note of their own while mirroring the color mood of the room. Be sure to pre-program the effect of such shiny surfaces into the overall color scheme.

## ADD PATTERN AND TEXTURE

Long after loud, blatant color schemes have passed from popularity, the comfortable neutrals will still be hanging around. The only pitfall in using these quiet colors lies in getting things a bit *too* bland. That's easily avoided by such things as balancing light, medium, and dark color values around the room.

Pattern and texture, two important ingredients in any color scheme, also become absolutely essential when you are dealing with neutral or one-color rooms. It is the contrast in textures and the variety of shapes that make the beach and bleached winter scenes so visually pleasing.

In a room scheme you also can use what comes naturally—straw, wicker, wood, dried flowers and weeds, nubby wool, and soft suede—all in wonderfully no-color colors.

The dimensions of texture and pattern are so important, in fact, that we devote a separate discussion to them toward the end of this chapter.

*An eloquent understatement on behalf of neutral colors, this monochromatic living room proves that basics can be beautiful, and far from boring. Cooling, eye-restful white on walls and flooring increases the illusion of spaciousness and emphasizes the beauty of fine modern furnishings like these. The flat-weave Indian rug and sleek furniture provide needed pattern and texture. Modular seating pieces and the clear-glass coffee table are purposely kept understated to emphasize the striking rug design. In the nearby dining area the stripped-down no-color look is restated with a glass-topped table and stylish chrome-and-cane Breuer chairs. Personal possessions add warmth to this contemporary scheme.*

# COLOR
## FAIL-SAFE SCHEMES: ONE COLOR PLUS WHITE

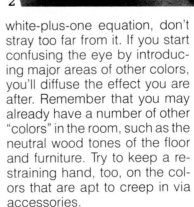

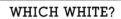

The easiest decorating arithmetic can add up to some of the prettiest rooms around: Simply take white and add one other color to it.

White is the most amenable of neutrals. Cool and calm, it can smooth over architectural oddities and make small spaces seem to expand. Conversely, white can come on bright and crisp in eye-popping contrast to strong colors. Absolutely *nothing* can clash with white, so it will work with any color companion you choose.

You really have to keep in mind only one thing as you plan a white-plus-color scheme, and that is proportion. As in any color scheme, one color must dominate and make the major statement in the room. White will assume this role willingly, if you choose it for the walls and

woodwork, and confine the other color to furniture and accessories. Or, white can play second-in-command, offering visual relief from a really strong, intensely dominant color on the walls or other major areas.

### WHITE PLUS A BRIGHT

Since you are virtually assured of success with a white-plus-one-color scheme, you can let the other hue be a dynamite one. Bright blue and white are a classic combination. Strong green, deep maroon, chrome yellow, vibrant brown: White lets them be exciting without overtaxing the nervous system. Even a real shock of red can be controlled with strokes of white, deftly applied.

Once you've chosen the color you want to add to your

white-plus-one equation, don't stray too far from it. If you start confusing the eye by introducing major areas of other colors, you'll diffuse the effect you are after. Remember that you may already have a number of other "colors" in the room, such as the neutral wood tones of the floor and furniture. Try to keep a restraining hand, too, on the colors that are apt to creep in via accessories.

### POWERFUL THREESOME

There is one exception to this two's-company advice: You can bring black into the picture. Black and white plus one color forms another fail-safe formula. Here, too, the "plus" can be any other color you like, so long as it's strong enough to stand up against two such boldly con-

trasting color personalities. Red is a classic addition to the trio. It is *the* zinger for rooms where you want a lot of action, as in family rooms and kitchens.

### WHICH WHITE?

Once you've picked the partner to use with white, give some thought to just which white it shall be. Especially in paint colors, you'll find an amazingly wide selection. There's warm white with a bit of yellow or umber in it, good for schemes where you want to add a touch of warmth and coziness. Then there's the cool, crisp white that has a bit of blue about it; use it to cool too-sunny rooms or add crispness to clear, clean colors. Bright or stark white, with no hint of other color, is a good mixer with most hues.

**1** Rich red, spread over the walls of this country-flavored living room, calms down considerably under the influence of the white-painted moldings and white-covered furniture. Notice how the other neutrals in the room, the pine and rattan furniture and the sisal rug, also exert a quieting influence on what could have been a strident effect.

**2** Likewise, bottle green, uncorked for the walls, might have been overbearing in such great sweeps. Instead, it becomes serene and visually refreshing confined as it is within a framework of white. Thanks to the sharp color contrast, the white-painted moldings provide all the ornament the windows need. Their strong vertical force is beautifully counterbalanced by the long, horizontal line of the sofa, covered in bright white.

**3** White assumes the major role in this elegantly eclectic room. Rolled over the walls and molding details, white becomes the quiet foil against which prized period furniture pieces are shown off to best advantage. For all the room's formal antiques, however, it is hardly an intimidating room. Credit the playful use of exuberant colors in the pillows that replay hues from the bold abstract painting. Upholstered in white, the rolled-arm sofa becomes the perfect centerpiece for the pair of Louis XVI armchairs that complete the point-counterpoint use of white and strong color in the room.

3

# COLOR
# VISUAL TRICKS TO PLAY

**C**olor is a consummate magician. The French call its kind of magic *trompe l'oeil,* which means, "fool the eye." Count on it to magnify a room's best assets while discreetly masking the less-than-perfect proportions.

We have already discussed the passive or aggressive qualities that make some colors loom large visually, and others fade quietly out of sight. Here are some of the ways you can put these qualities to work in solving decorating dilemmas.

## SPACE-MAKING

Because light colors do not assert themselves, they open up space and make it look larger than it really is. For this reason, ceilings traditionally have been painted white; the lightness overhead seems to raise the roof and give the room a more expansive feeling.

The same color trick works with walls, especially where the space is broken into disconcerting nooks and crannies. White or a light color helps blend these disparate walls together so you perceive them as one free-flow of space.

Underfoot the same principle can produce a different visual response. Instead of overlooking light colors at floor level, we are very much aware of them. The eye has long been conditioned to expect dark foundations for most rooms, so a white or light-colored carpet virtually pops into our visual field. The same applies to floors that have been bleached or painted a light color. You'll want to take this into account as you propor-

tion the dominant and secondary areas of color in your room plan. Overall, unbroken expanses of light color tend to create the illusion of gracious space.

Pale colors also are lifesavers in rooms where natural light is meager. Pale tones enhance all kinds of light, whether it comes through a window or from man-made sources. This is another reason why most ceilings should be painted a light color—and most lampshades should be translucent white, or at least lined in white, to reflect the most possible illumination.

## SPACE-SHRINKING

Occasionally, overly generous space can simply be too much of a good thing. In this situation, put the opposing power of dark colors to work. These deep shades can help make large space seem small and cozy. For example, a ceiling that's painted brown seems to come down into your line of vision. It automatically makes the room look and feel warmer, more intimate. This trick is especially effective in older homes with unusually high ceilings. You can even exaggerate the effect by bringing the dark color down from the ceiling onto the walls as far as a picture molding or some other natural line of demarcation.

Another way to harness color's power to push space around is to use dark/light, quiet/bright colors in carefully plotted contrast, For example, you can visually square up a too-long, too-narrow room by painting the short end walls

dark and the long side walls light. The short walls will seem to step forward, and the long walls shrink in importance. This is an especially useful technique for a long, dark hallway. Whatever contrasting colors you choose, keep them light to compensate for the hall's lack of illumination.

The same legerdemain will make the most of important structural elements in a room. Overhead beams, chair rails, wainscoting, or architectural moldings become outstanding decorative elements when you paint or stain them in deliberate contrast with the ceilings and walls.

## CAMOUFLAGE AND DISGUISE

Furnishings respond to color magic, too. An oversized sofa or chair will dwindle to manageable size when you slipcover it to match the color of the wall behind it.

You can literally paint away such unwanted features as awkwardly placed doors and windows by applying this same kind of color camouflage. Treat the openings as part of the wall and paint over them, frames and all. Try this in a small hallway cut up with lots of doors and watch the overcrowded condition disappear. As for that awkward window or that outdated fireplace, dress it to match the wall, and it will do a vanishing act, too.

Color also can help tie together a melting pot of mixed-heritage furnishings. And the color source needn't be expensive; all you need is a can of

paint or a few yards of fabric. Just be sure that one dominant color theme runs throughout your room redo.

And watch how easily a splash of fresh new paint or stain can knock years off a time-worn chair or chest. (See some suggestions for recycling old pieces in the "Furniture" chapter.)

Earlier we mentioned color's talent for "fool-the-eye" decorating. Why not test it for yourself by painting a fake scene on a wall or window. You'll add dimension, and often whimsy, to a room. For starters, paint an outdoor scene and a half-raised window on a blank powder-room wall, add a collection of colorful circus animals to the wall in a child's room, or paint a window-box full of posies on the *inside* of the kitchen window.

*A lot of color magic is quietly at work in this elegant all-gray bedroom. The monochromatic color scheme blends the varied architectural and furnishings elements into a setting that's serene for sleeping. The light, quiet gray tones make the space look and function expansively, a carefully calculated interplay of textures keeps the room from looking dull. Rich velvet textures in the carpet, and on the love seat and channel-quilted bedspread, contrast with the slick laminate built-ins along the headboard wall. And the staccato pattern of the vertical blinds is repeated in the angular lines of the ceiling beams.*

*Lacquered white for sharp contrast with the black-painted ceiling, the beams visually lower the ceiling to create a more intimate bedroom setting.*

# COLOR
## CREATE YOUR OWN

**Y**ou can make your own modern art with nothing more complicated than canvas and colorful dyes. Even with only a modicum of talent, good results are assured if you follow these easy instructions.

### CANVAS WALL MURAL

Mix dye (half water, half dye) in a container. On a drop cloth, lay out the canvas (the mural shown is 4½ feet by 5½ feet), then mark a rectangle, leaving a three-inch border to wrap around a canvas stretcher. Sponge down the canvas until it's evenly wet, then dye. (The more wetness, the more the dye will bleed at the edges of the stripes.) Move the canvas only when it's dry, then spray on stain repellent for extra protection. Mount the canvas on stretchers and it's ready to hang.

### PAINTED PILLOWS

Cut out 18- or 20-inch squares of artists' canvas. Using the same dying solution as the

painting, apply the dye to a hot-water wet canvas, using small brushes. When it's dry, have it cleaned to set the dye. To sew the pillows, cut un-painted plain canvas to back of painted canvas and sew, right sides together, leaving a 6-inch opening for the stuffing. Clip corners, turn right side out, then stuff with polyester fiberfill. Slip-stitch the opening closed.

# COLOR
# THE IMPORTANCE OF PATTERN

**P**lain color is exactly that: plain. Only when you add the zest of pattern or texture do you bring out all the potential in a decorative color scheme. Mixed in with plain-color surfaces, these elements provide the contrast that makes a room interesting.

As we said earlier in this chapter, one sure way to a successful color scheme is to follow the lead of a single pattern. Take the colors from it and use them as the color palette for your entire room.

## TWO OR MORE PATTERNS

If, on the other hand, you choose to use more than one pattern, the success of the mix will depend largely on two criteria: contrast and compatibility. Several patterns can go together, provided they are different enough in design, yet have a compatible color in common. Classic examples are geometrics and florals. A stripe and an all-over flowered pattern work nicely, as long as they share a common color denominator. If you keep that color constant, you can even add a third pattern, perhaps a small plaid. Stripes, flowers, plaid: The patterns have enough contrast in design to stand up to each other, and, providing they share the same color, they'll work well together.

To make it easier for the home decorator to put together a foolproof pattern mix, more and more manufacturers are offering collections of coordinated fabrics and wallpapers, even bed linens. You can choose from as many as five or six patterns, all specially planned by design experts so that any one or several motifs will blend compatibly. And you'll be able to select from several different color ranges.

You also can mix up a mélange of patterns all alike in design, but decidedly different in *scale* (or size). A room rampant with gingham checks, for instance, will look interesting, not merely busy, if the designs contrast sharply in scale while keeping colors similar.

You'll also want to consider the size of the room itself in relation to how much and what scale of pattern you use. For example, a small-scale design used sparsely in a large area will be insignificant and spotty. Put the same pattern into more limited space, and it will work beautifully. Conversely, a large-scale print usually looks best in a large space. (There's always an exception, however: a single burst of pattern used in a small room very often can be quite effective.)

## PATTERN HAS WEIGHT

Avoid clustering all your patterned pieces together. Because patterns tend to take our attention, they carry more visual weight than solid colors and must be evenly distributed to keep the room balanced.

Remember, too, that pattern can come from a number of sources, such as a collection of art objects, a picture grouping, books on open shelves, the backs of chairs lined up around the dining table. Be sure to consider all these elements in your pattern plan.

**1** A good pattern is worth repeating, so blue-and-white gingham appears in shirred panels on the walls, in tieback curtains, and the banquettes used for seating at the table. Other color-related prints can be added, so long as they don't overstep their second-place role.

**2** If you saw them individually, you'd never guess how graciously the five, yes, *five,* different patterns in this living room can get along. The clue to their coexistence is color compatibility, and a decided difference in the design and scale of each. Large areas of quieting neutrals provide needed relief for the eye.

Most rooms need the punch of pattern to bring a color scheme to life. Success in choosing, using, and mixing patterns depends on two criteria: contrast and compatibility.

2

# COLOR
# THE IMPORTANCE OF TEXTURE

Texture is the last dimension of color in decorating, but certainly is not the least in effect. Subtle though it may be, the interplay of surface finishes is the final touch without which the most colorful room would be lacking.

Textures fall into two basic categories: *smooth* and *rough.* As you might expect, smooth textures imply refinement and sophistication. Therefore, they tend to be fairly formal in feeling. Think of satin and glass, of polished mahogany, crystal chandeliers and brightly gleaming brass.

On the other hand, rough textures evoke a casual atmosphere, where life can be lived in comfortably informal fashion. Homespun fabrics with open weaves and nubby finishes fall into the casual category, along with handwoven rugs and strongly textured brick, plaster, or stucco walls. Rough-hewn beams bring a kind of primitive vigor to a room, as do wide-plank, pegged wood floors. The effect is quite different from the well-mannered look of parquet, even though both floors present a polished, smooth surface.

### COMPATIBILITY IS IMPORTANT

As a general guideline, you will want to keep textures compatible with the overall atmosphere of the room; that is, formal or informal, smooth or rough. However, there are times when the classifications get a bit fuzzy, and you must rely on your own eye and judgment.

More important than a strict application of the formal-informal rule is the interesting interplay of various textures. Too much slick and shine can be cold and intimidating; on the other hand, a room scheme can bog down in all thick, rough textures. The secret is a varied balance. Play slick and shiny against rough, tactile textures. A glass cocktail table looks exciting when placed on a nubby-pile rug. Suede cushions play off nicely against a sleek, leather-covered sofa. Lush fringe adds a margin of textural interest to draperies made of a silken fabric.

Contrast in textures affects more than just the overall mood of the room. Smooth, shiny textures seem lighter and less bulky than deep, rough surfaces. A chrome and glass table "floats;" a dark oak one takes up more visual space.

To make a room seem smaller, use rough, thick, or rich textures. They tend to advance visually and dominate. Lower a ceiling that is too high by adding rough-hewn ceiling beams, and give weight to the floor with a shaggy area rug.

To make a small room expand visually, use light, airy, smooth textures. See-through materials, such as glass, and reflective surfaces, such as chrome and mirrors, negate bulk and add spaciousness.

Finally, textural finishes also affect color itself. Broken-surfaced, heavy textures make a color seem less intense. They disburse the light and diffuse color. Remember as you plan your room that a satin pillow, for instance, will look lighter and brighter than the velvet sofa it was dyed to match exactly.

1 Texture assumes the leading role in the play of neutral colors across this room. Although the major pieces of furniture, the 1872 piano and the Victorian secretary, are ornate and heavily carved, the room's overall mood is light and airy. Credit the sleek floor and chrome chair, the lacy metal radiator cover, and the spiky stalks of dried weeds around the room.

2 A simple description of the colors in this room just wouldn't do it justice. It might sound bland and boring; beige, off-white, tortoise shell, green. But a mix of textures adds vigor and variety to the scheme. The key is the calculated juxtaposition of smooth, hard, and shiny surfaces with those that are rough and rich, both visually and tactilely.

# ROOM ARRANGING

When it comes to arranging or rearranging a room, it's not the amount of space you have that counts; it's the imaginative way you use it. And since space is a precious commodity for most of us, it only makes sense to seek the best possible arrangement solutions for any given size or shape of room. Although there's no single "right" way to plan a room scheme, some room arrangement principles invariably apply: Proper scale, balance, and proportion are the three most essential ingredients in a successful room arrangement. But you also can call on a number of other decorating "tricks" to make a room look and function the way you want it to. Here are some imaginative ideas to help you shape the space at your place.

# ROOM ARRANGING
## THE BASICS

The right arrangement may well be the most essential ingredient in successful decorating. No matter what furniture you have to deal with—antique or new, elegant or informal, abundant or spare—the life of your room depends on the way you relate the pieces, to each other and within the overall room space.

Room arrangement needn't be a puzzlement. Just as formulas exist for creating successful color schemes, guidelines exist to eliminate the frustrations of arranging a room so it works as well as it looks. First of all, consider how the room will function, the furniture pieces you will need, and the physical space and shape of the room itself.

### FIRST THINGS FIRST

When setting out to arrange a room, keep in mind three important considerations:
• Convenience
• Comfort
• Composition

Convenience and comfort *must* come first and, fortunately, they are the easiest to cope with. Although *composition* (meaning balance, scale, color, and so on) is important, it is a matter of aesthetic judgment best made after the prerequisites are met. So for now, let's look at the criteria involved in achieving the basics of convenience and comfort.

Ask yourself some basic questions at the onset. What do you want the room to do? In the living room, for instance, how do you want the room to function both for your family and for guests? How much seating is required? How much open floor space? Do you want to serve dinner in the room? Entertain large crowds? Include a spot for music or hobbies? For a family room the questions (and perhaps the answers) will be much the same.

For a bedroom, answers should come from whoever will live within. For example, if your bedroom is large enough, it can be as useful for daytime activities as it is for sleeping. What furniture will you need? A bed, of course, and a lot of storage. What about a desk for quiet pursuits? A love seat or chairs for lounging?

### SIZE UP YOUR SPACE

Once you know what furniture you will be working into the arrangement, consider other important factors: the room's actual architecture, the size (including ceiling height), the location of windows and doors, and the presence (or absence) of immovables such as fireplace, picture window, or built-in cabinets or shelves.

To qualify as "convenient," a room arrangement should promote an easy flow of traffic throughout the room. In other words, avoid blocking a passageway with furniture and don't put a chair where it occludes a window or closet you'll need to reach. As a rule of thumb, you'll need to allow double its width of clearance for a door that opens into a room. And keep traffic lanes at least 3 feet wide for people to move freely and comfortably through the room.

### PLAN FIRST ON PAPER

You can go about arranging a room in two ways: One is the push and shove method, where your aching back does all the work. The other—the one we recommend—involves plotting on paper first. Measure your room's dimensions and chart them, letting each foot of space equal ¼ inch on graph paper. Measure and mark all architectural features: doors and windows, nooks and crannies, closets, fireplaces, built-ins. Also note the locations of other fixed features such as electrical outlets, light switches, wall sconces and chandeliers, radiators and heating ducts. Using the same scale (¼ inch equals 1 foot), draw and cut simple templates for every piece of furniture in the arrangement. If you don't plan many changes in fabric or colors, you may want to crayon in the basic color of each piece before you cut it out. This way you'll have a clearer mini-picture as the room shapes up.

### FIND A FOCAL POINT

The first step toward an actual arrangement is to find a focal point for the room, an element around which the furniture will revolve. In a living or family room, this focal point may be a fireplace, a picture window framing a beautiful view, or even the television set. In a bedroom, it's usually the bed. In any room where such an obvious center of attraction is lacking (and certainly, not all rooms have a natural focal point), you must create your own. For example, you can hang a dramatic painting or lay a handsome area rug, then orient your seating pieces around it. Or center an impressive piece of furniture—a large breakfront or armoire—on one wall, and position the sofa and chairs opposite it.

Once you've achieved your focal point, everything else will fall into place according to function and size. In a living or family room settle the seating pieces first because they're usually the largest and most important. A few more basic rules make this easy:

• To encourage conversation, chairs should be no more than 8 feet apart. Also, they should face each other, more or less, because straight-line arrangements make comfortable eye-contact almost impossible.

• Every seating piece requires a table comfortably within reach for glasses, ashtrays, and, usually, lamps. (Lighting also can come from floor lamps and overhead fixtures as long as each seating piece gets enough illumination for comfort.)

• A coffee table used in front of a sofa should be set about 14 to 18 inches out to allow ample leg room.

• End or chair-side tables should be approximately as tall as the arm of the chair or sofa they're serving.

*To take full advantage of its gracious floor space, this country French-inspired living room is formally arranged around its natural focal point, the fireplace.*

# ROOM ARRANGING
## SUCCESSFUL SOLUTIONS

The third major consideration that must go into any successful room arrangement is its composition, the visual image that results when the furniture has been placed to meet the first two standards, comfort and convenience. Good composition can be defined in terms of balance and scale, color and pattern.

To be well-balanced, a room must have a pleasing distribution of large- and small-scaled pieces of furniture and accessories throughout. Achieving balance is often more a matter of visual weight than actual size. A sofa, for example, "weighs" as much as a pair of lounge chairs with a table between them. A breakfront is as big, visually speaking, as a pit seating group. You can use an area rug to add weight to a small game table and give it visual clout enough to balance a large sofa on the opposite wall.

The *scale* of the pieces in question is an important part of this balancing act. For instance, you can't expect a delicate Chippendale tea table to carry as much visual weight as a low-to-the-rug slate-topped cocktail table. Nor will you get the same heft from an open-arm French-style chair as from a high-back English leather wing chair. The same is true for accessories. A small lamp on a massive table will look lost at sea, and a large lamp on a dainty table will look like an elephant out of place.

Here are tips on playing up and down the scales to make furniture look light or heavy, large or small, without sacrificing comfort and convenience.

● To increase visual space in a small room, use glass or see-through acrylic tables instead of chunky ones of wood. Furniture with chrome or mirrored surfaces performs similarly.

● Choose chairs with open arms (or no arms) and leave legs unskirted to keep the scale light.

● When space is small, look for well-scaled furniture that does two jobs in one—such as a high-low table that serves as a coffee table, then rises to the occasion, literally, as a dining-height table at mealtime.

● Conversely, add visual heft to a lightweight seating group by placing it on an area rug.

● Use one large-scale furniture piece or a wall of built-ins to visually anchor a room arrangement.

● If the room is large and furniture sparse, don't line it up soldier-fashion around the room; instead, group pieces together in an island arrangement away from the walls to make the furniture seem more important.

*Color* is another element that can be used to visually balance a room's composition. Bring it on strong and dark when you need to anchor part of a room and give it visual weight enough to balance off another area. Dark fabrics used for upholstery will give importance to unprepossessing chairs. Or, you can reverse the process and use color to make heavy furniture practically disappear. Try upholstering an oversized sofa to match the wall covering it rests against. Presto! The sofa seems to flow into the wall—and out of the cumbersome, heavyweight class.

Where there's a wall, there's many a way to arrange furniture in a room. But when that wall space is interrupted time after time, the only solution may be an arrangement that free-floats in the middle of the room. In this relaxed living room, the four walls are all given over to architectural features: a floor-length window worthy of flaunting, French doors, a fireplace, and entryway (as you see from the floor plan). Centering the checked sofa in open space opposite the fireplace is a splendid solution for the broken-up space.

With a handsome Chinese area rug anchoring the seating area, the rest of the floor is unencumbered for easy access to the doors, window, and secondary furniture arrangement—the round table and chairs in the far corner. In proper balance with the overall open-air ambience of the room, lightly scaled cane-backed occasional chairs, and a cherished antique rocker flank the sofa—and complete the convivial conversational grouping.

# ROOM ARRANGING
## SUCCESSFUL SOLUTIONS

**1** Color comes quietly to the rescue in this problem-sized living room. High and handsome, but hardly wide, the space measures a mere 14x14 feet wall-to-wall. A generous helping of low-key color coaxes the stingy space into feeling expansive—lightening the floor and blending the standard-size sofa neatly into the wall. Because the space is so limited, the owners wisely opted for floor lamps instead of the usual (and heavier-looking) end-table-plus-lamp combination. They selected nicely scaled open-arm chairs instead of fully upholstered lounge chairs to complete the seating group.

**2** In this pocket-size living room the small-scale furnishings are purposely all in space-expanding neutrals. A pair of sofas facing each other at right angles to the window wall forms the nucleus for comfortable conversation and also helps divert traffic on the left. The acrylic table provides plenty of room for snacks, yet the clear material makes the table almost invisible.

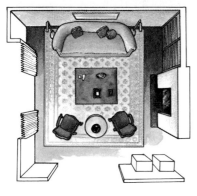

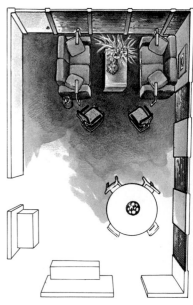

You've just seen how color can visually change the scale of a room or its furnishings to create a cohesive room composition. Color can perform other arrangement artistry, also. Carefully chosen and deliberately dispersed, it can pull disparate elements into a compatible grouping, tie together completely separated areas, and, conversely, visually divide the space within a room.

When you face a problem in arranging a room, remember that light, cool colors seem to stretch out space, and extroverted ones move in to fill it up. Using this guideline, you can "shrink" a large seating arrangement by coloring it to match the wall. By covering stingy floor space in neutral carpet, you can open it up visually for more generous furniture arrangements.

On the other hand, you can use color to carve too-ample rooms into manageable areas. To set off one section of a room for dining, for example, paint the wall a warm color in contrast to the living area's cooler hue. Applying the same principle underfoot, use small area rugs (even over carpet) to help demarcate different furniture groupings and activity areas.

2

# ROOM ARRANGING
## SUCCESSFUL SOLUTIONS

One of the old ground rules for successful room arrangements insists that you keep furniture close to the walls at all times. That rule must have been enshrined before the time of tempered glass and wide-open rooms. With today's architecture, walls aren't always around when you need them to arrange furniture against, which necessitates an entirely new approach to the subject.

One answer is to set furniture on the diagonal. Unorthodox as it may seem at first, furniture placed at an angle to the walls focuses attention directly into the room, rather than around its perimeter. A free-form arrangement works especially well in rooms cut up by lots of window and door openings. And since seating isn't rooted in one place, it's easy to rearrange it as needed.

Another variation on the theme is the island arrangement. Again, the furniture grouping doesn't rely on the walls for support, although pieces may be squared up with the walls. Seating arrangements, especially, can benefit from being pulled closer together. You'll make conversation easier and give ordinary space a special new look at the same time.

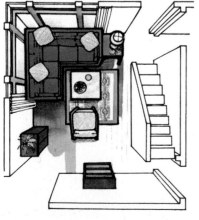

**1** In this wide-open, glass-wrapped living room with little solid wall space, the bright red sofa right-angles against the glassed-in corner. Because the contemporary sofa is long and low, its back aligns neatly with the windowsills. The hefty sofa is offset by a lounge chair, and everyone can share the smashing view. Two tables—a small one at sofa side and a large, but light-looking, glass-topped cocktail table—are the only other furniture pieces the grouping needs.

**2** Things aren't always squared up today, and happily so in the case of this wonderfully country-warm room. A half dozen upholstered modular pieces have been gathered into a great U that faces the fireplace. Because the diagonal arrangement meets all the room's seating needs so nicely, the rest of the floor space is free, in this case making room for a dining area that also can share the fireside glow. The inherent flexibility of modules makes them marvelous space-savers.

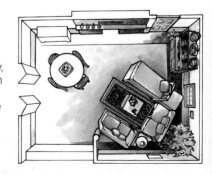

# ROOM ARRANGING
## SMALL-SPACE SOLUTIONS

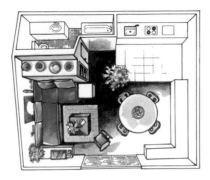

**W**ith the right room arrangement, you can live big in small spaces, coaxing many activities from tiny areas. The idea is to *not* overcrowd the space you have with excessive furniture and chaotic colors. Be compact without being claustrophobic. Keep backgrounds simple and light in color; lean toward lightly scaled furniture that does double duty in a single space.

Then employ a few special tactics to make your limited space seem larger than it is: mirrored walls, hidden lighting, built-ins that solve storage problems vertically—not at the expense of precious floor space. (Try to keep the floor as uncluttered as you can so the room looks more spacious than it has a right to.)

Opt for wall- or ceiling-mounted lights rather than floor lamps or space-taking lamp-table combinations. Hang dramatic picture groupings to counterbalance heavy, floor-bound furniture arrangements. Choose upholstered pieces that can hug the wall, and let occasional chairs serve both the living and dining areas.

When you're coping with an all-in-one-room living and dining area, measurements become especially critical. To guide your planning, remember:
- A dining space for four requires at least 8 square feet.
- You should allow 20 to 24 inches of table space for each setting.
- Leave almost 3 feet of pull-out room behind each chair. Squeeze inches elsewhere if you must, but don't let limited space cramp your dining style.

Little spaces can mean a lot more livability than you might imagine from a glance at a floor plan. This one-room habitat functions spaciously and graciously beyond its square footage, thanks to a well-planned furniture arrangement and a few stretches of imagination.

For openers, the entire room has been painted with warm white—over walls, ceiling, and all built-ins. Unbroken expanses of single neutral or pastel color like this help any small room take on added size visually. Another space-stretcher is the old mirror-on-the-wall ploy. Here, mirror panels seem to double the room's dining space. Furniture that does more than one job is a must in tight places. These sofas, really beds barely disguised in bright fitted sheets, tuck snugly into a corner. Wall-mounted lighting and minimal clutter combine to maximize both the good looks and the livability of this everything room. Even if you're blessed with more ample space in your own home, the expansive (and inexpensive) ideas applied here could live happily in your busy family-room environment.

When you must cope with cramped quarters, less is indeed more. Pare furniture to a minimum to free up maximum floor space, and keep things light, in both color and scale.

# ROOM ARRANGING
## SPACE-MAKING SOLUTIONS

**S**pace that looms too large can be more than a bit intimidating. Instead of attempting to deal with a really big room on its own overscaled terms, bring it within manageable size by decoratively dividing it into different areas. This is an approach that works equally well whether you're taking on an old house with generous propor- tions, or planning a multifunc- tional family room. It also solves a number of living needs in a largish, one-room apartment. The idea is to separate the space into different areas that serve different functions, and still maintain a feeling of visual unity throughout the room. That may sound more at cross- purposes than it really is.

One successful means of separating activities is to use furniture pieces as dividers. Your blockade can be a series of almost anything: open and freestanding shelves, a screen, bookcase, built-ins, a piano, sofa, or any other large piece of furniture. Place the furniture at a right angle to the wall to form an effective division of living space.

Another way to achieve over- all unity in a multifunctional room is to opt for one-color backgrounds or variations on a single color. Spread the same hue lavishly over the floor and walls. Or, repeat the same fab- ric on the wall and on major up- holstered furniture pieces. It's also a good idea to keep win- dow treatments similar if they can be seen simultaneously from all areas.

Try to replay patterns or colors across your various ac- tivity groupings. Such repetition helps the eye perceive the dif- ferent areas in the room as one harmonious plan.

**1,2** To divide and unify at the same time isn't quite as difficult as it may sound, as you can see from the one-room apartment shown here. Although now redefined physically by a beautiful bookcase divider unit, the space still works as one generous whole, thanks in large part to the rich green used over all the walls and to the sisal carpet that flows through both areas.

The divisionary bookcase becomes a much needed wall in the living room, while facing away from the newly defined "bedroom." Freestanding and glassfronted, the divider contributes privacy without blocking the open feeling within the room.

3

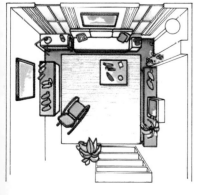

It may sound as if it's a new math equation, but it's actually an old and time-honored formula for arranging furniture in a small room: Subtract to add extra space. That is, subtract all nonessential furnishings, streamline the room to serve its purpose, and keep furniture you need light in scale and airy so the total effect is uncluttered, unencumbered, and unerringly suited to the room's function.

Again, the more floor space you can leave free, the more open and easy the room will feel. So, again, opt for wall-hugging arrangements and wall-hung lighting fixtures.

You also can gain an illusion of space by raising the roof, figuratively. Use tall shutters or screen panels, a stately piece of furniture, or an oversized picture to extend the vertical dimension of a room.

**3** Low, lean, and light, this apartment's little living room manages to lead a highly productive life without an ounce of excess fat in its furnishings. Sofa, tables, and butcher-block shelving units cling close to the walls around the room's perimeter, freeing most of the floor space for easy inflow and egress. From the Haitian cotton covering on the oak-framed sofa to the graceful rocker and glass table, the furniture feeds the illusion of space.

# ROOM ARRANGING
## FURNITURE THAT'S FLEXIBLE

1

2

**R**earranging a room is a sure way to accomplish an almost-immediate change of scene. If you program some flexibility into a room from the very beginning, you'll eliminate later backaches when the furniture is recast in new roles.

One way is to buy built-in flexibility—furnishings that can lead several different lives. Today's multi-use furniture easily adapts to our less structured lives and more malleable spaces.

A bedroom (and bedroom furniture), for instance, can do double duty (and more), serving as a study, hobby workshop, sitting room, or an entertainment center. Only after-hours does this versatile room turn sleeping spot.

If you entertain frequently in limited space, you'll find flexible

furnishings a boon for company occasions. Planning ahead can ease the upheaval. Buy a drop-leaf table you can keep in hiding behind the sofa. Trade the desk lamp for candles and set out the buffet. Gather in the extra dining chairs that have wandered off to the living room or hallway.

For a party, shift furniture in the living room to make conversation and traffic flow easily. Break seating groups into small, intimate arrangements, augmented with pullout benches or floor pillows. (And retrieve those extra chairs from the dining room.)

Or, for really large-scale bashes, try a different tack. Clear out excess furniture (especially if it's the stackable and storable kind) to make standing room for a crowd. Free up floor

space and you'll keep your guests convivially mingling and mixing.

And as easily as pulling a rabbit from a hat, you can transform almost any space into instant sleeping quarters for guests. You'll find sleepers (from single to queen size), discreetly hidden away in sofas, chairs, chests—and even wall systems. To make the transition from day to night an easy one, use lightly scaled, easily movable coffee tables and chairs nearby.

Because you best know the ways you intend to live in your rooms, approach each furniture arrangement with secondary plans in mind. An alternative arrangement can shift the focus of your room and gain you more living functions from the same space.

**1** This bedroom makes a marvelous double agent, a room for much more than sleeping. Generous freestanding bookcases create a division between the sleeping and study areas, providing ample storage on one side and a privacy wall on the other. The sleeping side is backed with panels of colorful fabric, stapled top and bottom to strips of wood lathe.

**2** Stowaways would love this bedroom, literally built from modular plastic drawer units. They're tucked under and all around the bed, ready for rearrangement at a moment's notice. Here, the drawers have been used to create a storage-laden mattress platform, a bedside table, and two towering chests. The tranquillity of this almost-all-white room is magnified by a mirror that wraps around the window from floor to ceiling.

3

## AMAZING MODULARS

One of the most versatile problem-solvers around is changeable, rearrangeable modular furniture. Sized and shaped to fit together in countless configurations, modulars let you buy only the pieces you need to fit your style, your budget—and your space.

Modular components not only include chests and wall systems for storage, but comfortable upholstered seating as well. When first introduced, modular seating was strictly contemporary, square in shape, and large in scale. Now you also can find traditional styling with soft curving frames and wood or metal trim. And, in response to today's small room sizes, new modulars are often compact and small-scaled.

At the other end of the seating spectrum are systems that can be stacked building-block fashion to suit a variety of conversational needs.

Modular pieces (both seating and storage units) not only help you cope with difficult floor plans, but also assure that you're never stuck with a static arrangement. Simply regroup them for a change of scene or to handle new living and entertaining needs. And modulars are always ready to move—to another room or a new home.

**3** Six flexible pieces create an island of comfort on an area rug in this living room. Several basic units make it all happen: the square, the square with a back, and the square with back and arm (corner piece). There are even upholstered tables for added flexibility. These modules provide almost all the furnishing this room needs—now, or later, when a different configuration is called for.

# WINDOWS

**B**efore you redecorate, explore the window-treatment options available today. The possibilities are practically limitless, and good results are guaranteed if you give your windows careful thought instead of treating them as an after-thought, as often happens. Consider first the window itself. If it's a beautiful architectural asset—or, if the view it affords is spectacular—then perhaps the best "treatment" is no treatment at all (privacy and climate permitting, of course). Even if privacy or energy factors are essential, you can still select any number of coverings that won't detract from a window's appeal. And if the window is nothing to rave about? You can camouflage an eyesore or make a so-so window something special in countless ways. No matter what their size or shape, all windows offer exciting opportunities to express individuality. On the following pages, we'll show you many practical and decorative options for your windows.

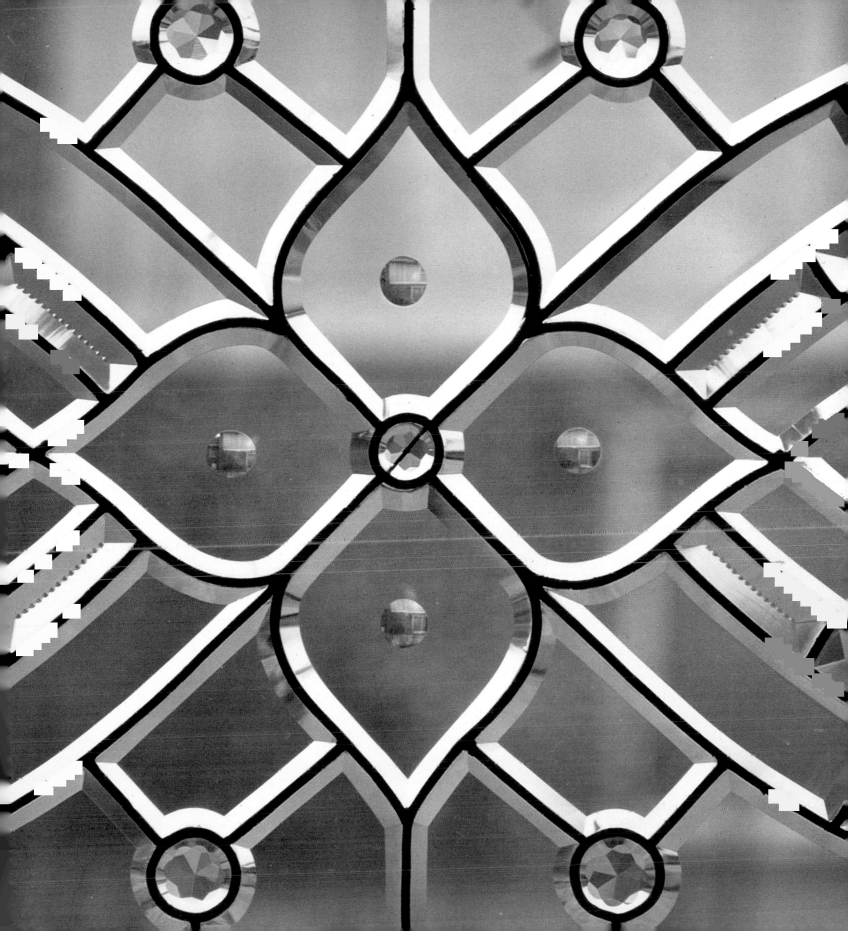

# WINDOWS
## FABRIC TREATMENTS

**A**lthough the possibilities for window treatments are many and varied, the odds-on favorite material is still fabric. And the perennial winners of style popularity contests continue to be classic draperies and curtains.

Every fabric has unique characteristics. Color and pattern are only two considerations. Weight, texture, and fiber content must be taken into account as well.

Why then, don't all homes and all window designs look alike? For the same reason a woman wearing a crepe de Chine cocktail dress doesn't look the same as a woman wearing a sport dress of denim. Some fabrics just naturally lend themselves to formal, elegant treatments, while others are more suited to casual or tailored window treatments.

### MULTI-FUNCTIONAL FACETS

Seemingly, a window treatment's job is simply to hang there and look attractive. But that's certainly not all it's capable of. A successful window treatment also may have one or more of a dozen other decorating jobs.

For instance, fabric window coverings are the surest, and easiest, way to soften the angularity of a room's architecture. Softly pleated draperies or billowy curtains of a gossamer sheer fabric bring a softness and sense of grace to a room by taming the severe planes of walls, floor, and ceiling.

A window treatment also can change the visual dimensions of the window it's dressing. In a room with skimpy windows, oversize draperies create the illusion of larger, more spacious window areas. The style and placement of draperies can make windows look wider, taller, or more dramatic in proportion than they really are.

On the other hand, window treatments also can make a window look tailored and compact, without appearing severe. For example, a shirred curtain, mounted inside the window casing, will slim a window and its treatment to the bare minimum, while still providing the softening appeal of fabric to a room.

### THE GREAT FABRIC COVER-UP

Windows, particularly in older homes, are not always where you would like them to be. However, badly placed windows, like badly sized or shaped ones, can be helped out of their awkward state and into new beauty by planning a treatment that masks their flaws. To treat a series of badly placed windows, convert them into one cohesive design element with a single unifying covering. Treating mismatched windows with draperies identical in size and style will blend the various window sizes and placements in the viewer's eye, creating the impression of uniformity.

### ADD PATTERN AND COLOR

Every room needs its share of pattern to be lively and exciting. And pattern can range from subtle tone-on-tone designs to large-scale, bold prints for a design statement that's anything but quiet. The choice is yours. So is the choice of where in your room to use pattern. For many people, pattern on the walls or in the floor covering involves too large an area for visual comfort. It also may represent too large an expense to change, if tastes are inclined to tire easily. It's for these cautious-about-pattern people that window treatments present a natural outlet.

Window fabrics also offer a chance to add color to a room in measured proportions.

### STYLE-MAKERS

Nothing underscores the decorating style of a room the way window treatments do. For instance, a formal 18th-century English room is made even more elegant with tall, slender window treatments of tieback draperies that are topped with sculptured cornices or with swags and jabots. A country atmosphere becomes more relaxed and comfortable when windows are treated to casual curtains in gingham or chintz. A fabric window treatment also can be up-to-the-minute contemporary fashioned from open-weave casement cloth or textured fabrics in comfortable neutral colors.

*Wispy lace tablecloths float from wooden cafe rings and rod to give this room its romantic charm. Fabric-store lace, available by the yard, will create the same effect.*

# WINDOWS
## FABRIC TREATMENTS

**F**abric window treatments also can create a focal point for a room. If your room lacks a natural attraction such as a fireplace, a dramatic built-in, or other architectural assets, create your own with an impressive window treatment.

Bay windows or bow windows are the easiest avenue for creating a focal-point window treatment. But any window can be imbued with the kind of unique beauty needed to turn it into a center of interest.

Try unifying a series of windows with a single window treatment, or adding a lambrequin around a skimpy window to make it look more impressive. Or give a squat window stature by bringing the window treatment to the ceiling line with a valance or cornice. Also, try layering a treatment with tieback draperies over contrasting underdraperies—perhaps all under a window-spanning valance or swag.

Sometimes the choice of fabric is enough to turn a window into the room's focal point, particularly if the fabric also shows up in other areas of the room. By using the same fabric for furniture covering and window treatment you've established an important design element in the room. For even more drama, create a furniture arrangement that leads your eye from the coordinating furniture to the window treatment, and you've formed a definite visual center of interest.

A fabric window treatment also can be a blending device in a room infused with many colors. A sure way to bring a sense of order to an area is by

selecting a window fabric that ties together the colors floating loosely around a room.

When choosing a fabric window treatment, don't underrate its ability to save precious energy. Granted, not all window coverings are energy efficient. But by choosing a heavy fabric, lining the draperies, and combining them with a secondary window covering such as underdraperies or shades, heat loss through the window area can be greatly reduced. Avoid sheer or loosely woven fabrics, unlined draperies, or single-layer window treatments if you're out to save energy. (See pages 148–149 for more about energy-saving ideas.)

A fabric window treatment can help solve many decorating problems; for example, count on it to create a stylish focal point in an otherwise ordinary room.

**1** The elegance of this dining room window treatment comes from lavish drapery panels, fashioned extra long to balloon over the tightly braided tiebacks, then cascade to the floor in a puddle effect. The crown molding at the ceiling level demurely hides the drapery pleats and forms a slim architectural heading. Underdraperies of delicate sheer fabric complete this sophisticated treatment.

**2** Each of the windows in this handsome bedroom has been treated to soft sheer under-draperies, then topped with heavier eggshell-toned draperies to assure privacy and complete light control. Overdraperies have a bordering band of deep blue-green fabric, color-keyed to the wall and pillow covers.

**3** Fabric window treatments don't need yards and yards of material to be effective. In this dining room, curtain panels hung from spring tension rods decorate the lower two-thirds of the window. The rod casing is sewn 3 inches down from the top of the curtain panel to create the pert ruffle that edges the simple, but striking, window style.

**4** Pairs of curtain rods are the secret ingredient for this innovative window treatment. One rod is installed at the top of the window, the other at the ceiling line. Curtain panels are sewn together in the area between the two rods, forming a self valance. The lower portions of the curtains fall free and are caught by tie-backs of the same fabric. Here, a salmon-colored chinoiserie print plays the solo part in patterning the room.

# WINDOWS
## FABRIC TREATMENTS

1  2

Traditionally, when we think of fabric treatments we envision windows swathed in heavy draperies. In today's decorating, this picture isn't necessarily true. Fabric coverings range from minimal to maximal and can suit any decorating style.

On the spare side are classic swags, valances, and jabots. Often teamed with draperies, these simple treatments also can go solo in traditional rooms where furnishings are refined and restrained. Or, a single panel of lace, shirred on a rod mounted inside the window casing, also makes an elegant and understated accent.

In contemporary rooms, simple fabric window trims can help soften the hard-edge look of metal and glass furniture. Airy casement cloths work well when hung in straight panels, stretched taut over the window surface or draped softly in panels hung on traverse rods.

For another slick, contemporary look, use sliding fabric panels, mounted either on a track or in wood frames. You can use panels in a color or pattern to accent or quietly background other furnishings.

Vertical blinds, with fabric-covered slats, offer a decorative opportunity to add trim, textural interest; or, repeat a pattern you have used elsewhere in the room. (You will read more about verticals later in this chapter.)

At the other extreme are window coverings that layer more than one treatment on top of the other. As in clothing fashions, the layered look offers both good looks and practicality.

Overdraperies paired with sheer curtains aren't new. But replace the sheers with a semi-transparent roll-up shade, top it with tieback draperies in a perky floral or geometric print, and you have a fresh new window covering. For a finishing touch, add a matching fabric valance. You'll find drapery rods to handle both drapery and valance in one unit.

Another variation on the layered theme is a combination of plain and print. Choose a pretty print fabric and laminate it on a roll-up window shade (buy lamination kits at window hardware shops). Add side draperies or tiebacks in a solid color from the print; border the draperies in a strip of the print.

Here's a double-decker idea that combines fashion, privacy, and energy conservation. Hang two tiers of solid-color cafe curtains on the window; push the top ones open to let in light. Then frame the window in a coordinating print fabric used to cover screen panels. The screens can be open during the day and closed at night for complete privacy and to save energy. Band the cafes in gimp, ball fringe, or other decorative trim in an accent color taken from the pattern.

3

4

**1** Fabrics in a room can be impressive in their coordination and repetition. Or they can be impressive in their singularity. This low-key bedroom in soft colors follows the latter course and combines two distinctly different fabrics and window treatments for an outstanding decorative effect. Both of the room's window areas are sheathed in a semiopaque shade covering. But that's where the similarity ends. The windows backing the bed feature classic draperies in a fabric that matches the bed's headboard. The side windows sport a toast-and-cream patterned fabric fashioned into curtain panels, shirred onto a wood cafe rod, and tied back with bands of matching fabric.

**2** Coordination is the key in this sunny living room. The same fabric is used as window dressing, furniture upholstery, wall covering, and even for the cabinet lining. Forming a focal point for this area is the bay window which displays four favorite window treatment techniques, plus matching fabric on the wall above and below the window panels.

The center panel of the bay is skirted with a lower-half cafe curtain dropped from wooden rings and a rod. A small valance flounces over the top of the center section. Side windows are shuttered, then topped with panels of pleated, tieback draperies.

Use of only one pattern and one color is what makes this scheme so successful.

**3** Simplicity in a window treatment is every bit as attention-getting as flamboyance. In this understated traditional living room, a single swag and one jabot decorate each fireplace-flanking window. Viewed singly, the windows present an unexpected asymmetric image. View them within the space of the room's end wall and they bracket the focal-point fireplace, forming an effective (and imaginative) treatment for this country style room.

**4** This charming country scheme demonstrates how to add color and style at your windows with only a minimum of fabric. The soft balloon effect is created by sewing three rod pockets in a fabric panel. The trick is in mounting the rods. Install the top rod at the top of the window casing; then position the other two slightly higher than the rod pockets so that the fabric will drape over each rod in a balloon effect. If sunlight is a problem during part of the day, you can mount sun-filtering roll-up shades behind the short valance; to keep the view unencumbered, the shades can roll out of sight when unneeded.

# WINDOWS
## SHADES AND BLINDS

Certain rooms and certain decorating schemes call for window treatments that are trim and tailored with no fuss or frills. And that's where shades and blinds step front and center. Whether your interior environment is sleek and contemporary or rugged and comfortably casual, there's a nondrapery window dressing that's right for how you live.

Some natural attributes of shades and blinds are the ability to provide privacy and light control. And, shades and blinds are available in materials that range from semi-opaque to completely room darkening. Though window shades and blinds come in a wide variety of materials and styles, all have this in common: they're practical, easy to install, and just as easy to maintain.

### SOLO OR ENSEMBLE

On their own or teamed with other types of window treatments, shades and blinds are equally effective. They can be quietly *au naturel* in matchstick or bamboo blinds, subtly colored in woven-wood blinds, sleek and austere in the various hybrids of venetian blinds, or alive with color and pattern in the fabric varieties, such as Roman or Austrian shades.

**1** Woven-wood blinds are both window treatment and mood-maker in this casual, tinged-with-the-tropics living room. This member of the shades and blinds family lets light filter through, gently bathing the room in a warm glow. Woven-woods are a breeze to install. Hooks screw into the wall or woodwork to support the blind hung from them.

**2** Vertical blinds, hung floor-to-ceiling are the perfect window treatment in an area where the focus is on line and form. In this subtly colored dining room, the whole design emphasis is on beautifully simple shapes and strong graphic lines; the room calls for a clean, architectural treatment like this. Vertical blinds are particularly practical for city apartments. Louvers close for complete block-out privacy, yet offer infinite control of view.

**3** Mini-slat venetian blinds create a trim window treatment as they hang neatly inside the bright blue surround of this trio of windows. Completely adjustable, these blinds allow absolute control of light and privacy. They make an ideal window covering for a plant-filled breakfast room. An inside-the-casing-mounted blind, such as this, is a space-saving window covering that lets you show off woodwork or an eye-catching wall.

# WINDOWS
## SHADES AND BLINDS

**A** ny window with woodwork or details too pretty to hide is a good candidate for shades or blinds. Both can be installed inside the window casing, allowing molding to frame them the way a picture frame augments the painting it surrounds.

If, however, your window has only ordinary garden-variety trim, then mount your shades or blinds on the window casing, edge-to-edge, to mask the molding while dressing the window.

### THE OPTIONS

Once, a shade at the window meant a standard white or off-white roller shade. As a functional privacy-producing, light-blocking window covering it was fine. But it offered little in the way of design. Now all of that has changed. Even today's roller shades come in a wide range of colors and in textures that run the gamut from sophisticated moirés to heavily textured homespuns. Both plain fringe and ball fringe are available as trims, as well as sculptured bottom edges that give the old roll shade a distinctive new silhouette.

You'll find shades made of fiber glass, fabric, open-weave mesh, and of course, the old standby shade cloth that comes in a full complement of densities from translucent to completely opaque.

Over the years, venetian blinds have greatly improved their decorative status. Now, in addition to the standard variety, venetians are available in several slat widths, in horizontal or vertical styles, and in a palette of decorator colors. The tailored, one-inch mini-slat blinds also are available in metallic finishes, linen weaves, wood, perforated styles, even gingham checks.

Mini-slat blinds can be custom ordered in a combination of several different colors, with the slats arranged in whatever fashion suits your design scheme. These blinds are all available in precision measurements that allow you to fit even oddball windows in older homes.

Factory delivery time for custom orders is about 30 days.

### WOODS AND WEAVES

Another category of window shades and blinds is the whole richly textured family of woven woods. Choose a style that is predominantly wood with only subtle traces of warp, or choose a heavily woven blind that looks like an impressive tapestry with only a hint of wood showing. Colors in the slats themselves

3

4

range from light to dark wood tones; some slats are painted white or popular decorator colors. (Less-expensive plastic slats come in sharp accent colors.)

Yarns used for weaving present a range of colors from neutrals and earth tones through brighter accessory colors. And woven designs, though usually vertical or horizontal stripes, do come in geometric patterns as well.

## FABRIC SHADES

Fabric is also very much a part of the shade scene. Roman, Austrian, and balloon shades offer home decorators the chance to add the softness, pattern and color of fabric to a window and still retain the trim, slimmed-down look of a shade.

All three types of fabric shades have vertical tapes through which pull cords are drawn to raise and lower the shade. Roman shades feature flat, tailored panels that raise in a series of soft horizontal pleats. Austrian shades have wider, fuller panels that create a billowy, festooned effect even while lowered. Balloon shades offer the smooth line of the Romans, but with a puffed bottom edge that is similar to the Austrian style.

**1** French doors are always a decorating challenge. Here, a wall-spanning Roman shade was the solution. Attached to a wood cornice board above the door frames, the shade can be raised to allow easy egress, lowered to protect privacy and sun-fragile furnishings. Heavy white duck was chosen for its stability.

**2** When rugged texture is in order, a woven-wood blind is the answer. In this handsome room full of natural textures, the blind's sun-warmed yarn colors contrast nicely with its natural wood slats. The window becomes a fully functional accessory. Some varieties of wood shades feature their own valance that masks the installation hooks.

**3** Interesting molding and a deep recessed window called for a window treatment that would show them off. This bottoms-up Roman shade in a fresh floral print dresses the window with pattern, yet still shows off the classic molding.

**4** Balloon shades combine the best features of both Roman and Austrian shades. Here, a balloon style is framed in deep rich wood trim. Semi-sheer yellow fabric is gently pleated for a smooth look when the shade is closed. When it's raised, the fullness of the pleats fluff out into this whimsical bunting effect at the bottom edge.

135

# WINDOWS
## SHUTTERS AND SCREENS

A successful window treatment must be functional and attractive. But in the category of shutters and screens, you can add still another attribute. These window coverings are also distinctly architectural. They're a compact, space-saving solution to treating window areas that demand a structural look.

And this family of window coverings has great versatility. Shutter panels, for instance, are available in louvered styles (adjustable or stationary), solid panels, vertical vaned panels, or open framework panels into which you can insert shirred fabric, decorative glass, grillwork, or acrylic. Shutters in a variety of styles are available (usually unfinished) through local lumber dealers, or they can be custom-made, if your windows or taste dictates.

You can finish shutters with wood stains, in sharp accent paint colors, or use blend-into-the-wall tones. Try covering solid-panel shutters with fabric, wall covering, or laminated plastic.

Shutters and screens are good window mates for traditional draperies and curtains. Combine shutters with cafe curtains or pleated draperies.

**1** Solid shutter panels are a sophisticated way to unify a ribbon of small windows that cut up a wall. Here, carefully matching the wallpaper from wall to shutter, these flush-with the-casing panels seem to slip out of sight when closed. The street side of the shutters is painted a solid color to blend with the exterior of the home.

**2** Three tiers of wide-vaned plantation shutters accent the vertical lines of this window treatment, making it appear tall and stately. Lacquered navy blue and played against light furniture and floors, these shutters turn a run-of-the-mill window into an impressive bit of decorating.

**3** The Japanese solved the problem of letting in light, yet providing privacy when they came up with the shoji screen. In this smartly styled kitchen eating area, translucent panels in the sliding screen bathe the area in light while creating an interesting geometric-patterned wall. The shoji panels are installed behind a black lacquer frame that is built around the existing door frame. Panels slide aside to allow passage through the glass doors.

# WINDOWS
## PLANT WINDOWS

There's no better way to reinforce the "natural" look in decorating than with window treatments that help bring the outdoors in.

As window coverings, plants are about as natural as they come. Their lush foliage can filter light softly and gently, and create a fresh, garden-like atmosphere in a room. All of which makes a plant-laden window a comfortable decorating touch for a sun-room, porch, or casual family-living center. Plants also offer a window treatment you can change at will. More privacy? Simply add more plants. Less light? Then use denser plants.

Plants are a subtle window covering that bridges the gap between what's growing outside your window and the interior environment in which you live. In seasonal climates, plants create a welcome breath of fresh air year round.

### GREEN THUMB DECORATING

Don't forget that this is a living window treatment. Choose plants that will do best in the amount of light a particular window provides.

Be aware, too, that seasonal differences in the amount of natural light can affect the health of your greenery. In the summer, when the days are longest, plants in south, east, and west windows may burn easily unless something, such as a deciduous tree outside, provides shade for them. In winter, days are shorter, but the sun can be intense.

Remember, plants in small pots will require more frequent watering than ones in large containers. And, during heating months when humidity may be lower in your home, your green window covering will require more watering.

1 2

**Plants and windows go together like wine and cheese. Each is made better by the presence of the other.**

**1** A greenhouse window not only adds dimension but doubles the amount of light in this planning area, which previously had only a skimpy window and no decorative character. The mélange of geraniums and begonias in natural clay pots gives the area life and color, yet masks the view of a neighbor's house. Make sure shelves on which plants rest are moisture resistant and easy to clean.

**2** Shelf standards and brackets, spanned by cut-to-size glass shelves, create a simple yet effective staging area for plants. For visual interest, vary the sizes and shapes of plants, as well as the types of containers. Here, cuttings sprout in clear and colored glass containers, and potted plants thrive in glass, ceramic, and terra-cotta planters.

**3** In this open-to-the-outdoors area, verdant plant growth cascades from ceiling-hung pots. Rugged redwood beams anchor the hefty metal-link plant hangers that support a variety of green leafy plants.

**4** This garden room is a delight year round, thanks to its plant life. Windows here are naturally decorated with gigantic floor-standing plants and sprawling plants hung from the bulkhead above the banks of French doors.

Even the ceiling-reaching ficus in the corner of the room stretches its branches over a section of the doors to filter sunlight and add to the atmosphere of this porch turned solarium.

# WINDOWS
## FOCAL-POINT EFFECTS

**1** The wall-to-wall effect of shoji screens creates a striking focal point in this subtly Oriental-flavored apartment. Not only does this effective window treatment act as a center of interest, it also sets the mood for the rest of the decor. And the beauty of this kind of commanding window treatment is that you don't have to have windows of monumental size. Let this wall-covering arrangement of sliding screen panels cover windows, surrounding wall space, even window-flanking storage areas if you choose.

**2** Here casement windows are framed in white molding and covered with a chevron design created with strips of masking tape. The clean, geometric window treatment is set off by striking charcoal flannel-covered walls (fabric is stapled to the walls at top and bottom).

**3** Like a beautiful jewel, this beveled-glass, leaded window is the outstanding feature in this comfortable dining area. Because the antique glass panel was smaller than the three-sectioned window it fronts, the glass was encased in a ½-inch plywood frame, cut to fit the window opening. Then, to add dimension to the window, a plywood casing was attached to the frame. The entire unit is hinged to swing up for window cleaning.

Windows, as the source of light in a room, have a natural talent for commanding attention. So turning a window into the room's focal point isn't all that difficult. Just remember, to be a visual center of interest a window and window treatment must be impressive either by size, placement, material used, or the treatment's execution and detail.

### THE RIGHT SETTING

For extra emphasis, recruit the area surrounding a window. When a wall is painted a high-contrast color, your eye is automatically drawn to the area. The same visual magnet is at work when a window is surrounded by frame or molding.

# WINDOWS
## BUDGET IDEAS

1
2

There's a window treatment to suit every personality and life-style. There's also a window treatment for every budget, so don't think you have to take a big chunk out of your decorating fund to achieve an effective window treatment.

### CUT MATERIAL COSTS

One way to trim costs while decorating your windows is to go for low-cost materials. Instead of expensive yard goods, try window coverings crafted of twine, paper, or recycled fabrics and handwork. A trip to local secondhand stores may produce old lace tablecloths or crochet pieces to either stitch together or starch stiff and hang from monofilament threads. Curtains of patchwork pieces are not only easy on the budget but colorful and smart in a casual setting. Secondhand stores and rummage sales also can turn up enough raw material for machine patchwork.

### CUT THE COVERING TO SIZE

Another way to cut the fat out of window costs is to plan treatments that aren't expected to cover the entire window. Decorate rather than cover the glass area, provided, of course, that privacy isn't a factor.

Crown the top of the window with a valance or cornice. Or use freestanding screens at either side of the window. Try slim, stationary drapery panels tied-back at either side. These decorative design ideas require only a fraction of the yards of material needed for a fully functional treatment such as pleated traverse draperies.

**Imagination can be more important than money when it comes to creating your own one-of-a-kind window design.**

**1** An inexpensive bamboo shade takes on a custom look with the addition of bands of colorful yarn. Simply weave yarn over and under the existing warp threads of the shade to introduce exciting color and texture to your window. It's a one-of-a-kind treatment all for the price of a discount-store bamboo shade and a few strands of yarn.

**2** Beaded and beautiful. This lighthearted window treatment is a throwback to Casablanca and the Casbah.

Here, wooden beads are strung on picture wire, then attached to wooden strips fastened to the top of the window frame. To anchor the bead strands more securely, use a second wooden strip attached to the bottom of the window frame.

If bead stringing isn't your favorite pastime, prestrung wooden or glass bead curtains are available at import shops.

**3** Macrame makes a window treatment that's low in cost and high in decorating effect. In this dining area, natural hemp twine has been knotted around three dowel rods, cut to pressure fit inside the window casing. The macrame can be as complex or as easy as your skills dictate. Either way, the result is a window covering that's in harmony with a casual, naturally decorated room.

143

# WINDOWS
## BUDGET IDEAS

Using what you already have is still another way to create budget window treatments. By installing shelves in front of your window, you can display collectibles, glassware and dishes, plants, art pieces, shells, bits of driftwood, or anything else that interests you. The window becomes an attractive background for your collection, and your hobby becomes an interesting, constantly changing, window treatment.

By suspending inexpensive objects in front of your window you also can save substantially over the cost of conventional window coverings. You can string anything from beads or empty thread spools to can lids pierced with designs.

**1** Colorful tumblers, stored on glass shelves are a budget decorator's substitute for a stained-glass window. Screw the 2x2 wood frame together and put it up, either by using furniture levelers as is done here or by screwing the frame into the window molding. Drill holes for dowels, then add glass shelves, cut to size at your local paint and glass store.

**2** A cornice, window shelves, and lace-covered macrame hoops join forces for this highly individual (and low-priced) window treatment.

To create a cornice, screw 5-inch-long boards to the ends of a board cut the same length as the width of the window. Wrap with fabric and staple in place.

Lace is wrapped and stapled to the back of the hoops.

Even the most unlikely materials can be turned into fashionable window trims when you apply your ingenuity.

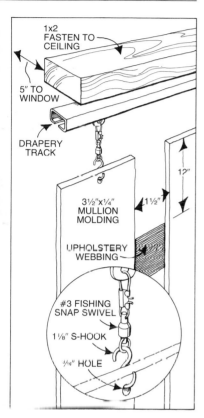

1x2
FASTEN TO CEILING

5" TO WINDOW

DRAPERY TRACK

12"

3½"x¼" MULLION MOLDING

1½"

UPHOLSTERY WEBBING

#3 FISHING SNAP SWIVEL

1⅛" S-HOOK

³⁄₁₆" HOLE

**3** Use this wooden curtain as a window treatment or room divider.

To duplicate the natural pine curtain, drill ³⁄₁₆-inch holes in the top of 3½ x ¼-inch mullion molding. Lay slats on the floor, carefully spaced, then staple upholstery tape to them as indicated in the drawing above.

Position a 1x2 board 5 inches from the window and attach to the ceiling using hollow wall anchors. Then screw drapery ceiling track to the 1x2. Using 1⅛-inch S hooks and #3 fishing snap swivels, attach slats to track as shown.

You'll find fishing swivels available in black, brass, or chrome at sporting goods stores.

3

# WINDOWS
## BUDGET IDEAS

**1** Custom draperies can cost a bundle, but there are ways to skirt some of the expense. In this dining room, for instance, a wall of French doors has been beautifully (but inexpensively) treated with Indian cotton print bedspreads. The spreads were trimmed slightly longer than the doors to allow for top rod pockets and bottom hems. Tiebacks allow easy access to the French doors.

**2** Here a quilted bedspread—salvaged from a bedroom redo—plays a new role as a customized curtain. The cut-down panels came from the corner sections of the spread, so the border trim now serves as decorative edging on the curtains. The raw edges simply were turned under and machine-stitched. A simple rod with clip-on cafe rings holds the clever treatment.

**3** The recycled roll-up shades in this eclectic living room are of snappy red-and-white print. Fabric panels cut slightly larger than the shade rollers allow for machine-stitched side hems and bottom slat pockets. Then, panels were stapled to the original rollers and the shades hung inside the window casing. Fabricating roller shades works best if you choose tightly woven cotton, linen, rayon or blends in a medium-weight fabric. These fabrics will withstand the tension without losing their shape and aren't too bulky to wrap neatly around the roller. If the shade will get heavy use, the face material should be lined with fabric or a paper backing designed for fabric lamination.

Windows let you view the world—and they let in the cold during the winter. As much as 30 percent of your home's total heat loss passes through your windows. And with ever-increasing utility costs, that's reason enough to plan energy-saving treatments for your windows. Here are some suggestions to help cut heating bills in winter and air-conditioning in summer, to say nothing of doing your part to help save our diminishing resources.

## INSULATE WITH AIR

Dead air between the outdoors and the room is your biggest ally in keeping conditioned air inside. For instance, storm windows or "sandwiches" of glass, with all cracks tightly weatherstripped, are your first line of defense.

You also can create dead air space between the glass and the room with fabric, which might in turn cut winter heat loss through the glass up to 80–90 percent.

In the summer, dead air will keep heat from moving in, but you also will need to turn back the sun's rays with reflective material. Several products are available to help you.

## SAVE WITH SHADES

Ordinary window shades can cut costs of heating and cooling. A window with a light-colored opaque roller shade, mounted within the frame, admits 47 to 54 percent less heat in summer than an unshaded window. Even a translucent shade reduces heat loss.

Some regular roller shades have special sun-filtering or aluminized backings that add even more to their energy-saving abilities.

In winter, the reduction of energy loss can be helped with a window shade, too. On a north or west window, for instance, you may save as much as 31 percent.

Specially designed energy-saving shades offer even more spectacular protection from cold and heat.

To reduce utility bills, look for reflective solar shades. Though made in different ways and of a variety of materials, these shades all work on the same principle: They trap dead air and bounce heat away from the room in summer or back into the room in winter.

Some solar shades look like big sheets of transparent film. When they are drawn, you can see out, but outsiders can't see in. This filmlike material is made of a reflective aluminum layer that's sandwiched between two sheets of polyester film.

These shades are not inexpensive, however. Price for a high-quality shade to fit an average size (6x4-foot) window is $60 or more. But the investment may be worth it when you can keep out as much as 80 percent of the heat from the glass. Solar shades also control glare and filter ultraviolet rays that fade upholstery and other fabrics.

Check the thickness of the film when shopping for this type of shade. Some are made of film that is only one millimeter thick; three or four millimeters of thickness are a must for a top-quality, durable shade.

If shades made of solar film are used on extra-large windows (more than 120 inches wide), you will need a cord and reel for raising and lowering the shade.

There are also other reflective shades to choose from. Some resemble aluminum foil, with a plain or textured surface. Some are of quilted aluminum, with a reflective plastic film vapor barrier and a translucent fiberfill insulation. One shade has metallized material laminated to white vinyl, with a layer of fiber glass scrim sandwiched between for durability. You turn the silvery side toward the glass in the summer and it reflects the heat back outside. Switch the shiny surface to room side in winter and it will reradiate furnace heat into the room.

Another good form of window protection is a thermos-style shade. It actually works on the principle of a vacuum bottle. The material is made of hundreds of tiny segments, with air space sealed into each segment. The shade has a highly reflective white pigment embedded into the material.

Still another aluminized foil shade is made of five tissue-thin layers that inflate when the shade is pulled down, creating two and a half inches of dead air space in front of the window.

Solar shade material may be attached to special roller shades, with a heavy bar at the bottom to keep them from curling when drawn. Some foil materials can be laminated to the back of a regular window shade or to other fabrics.

Most of the special solar control shades must be custom manufactured and you may not find all the various types in your area. Look in the Yellow Pages of the telephone directory under "Windows—Insulating Fabrics" or "Solar Equipment and Materials."

## CONSIDER DRAPERIES AND LININGS

Draperies are another way to conserve energy, providing you make a wise choice of materials and styles. For instance, draperies made of tightly woven, bulky fabrics will provide fairly good insulation. Add a thermal or reflective lining and you have a substantial weather barrier.

Custom-made draperies give you the most choice in energy-saving options. Most department and home furnishings stores will custom-make draperies with weather-resistant linings, as will stores specializing in solar materials. They usually have the lining material for sale by the yard, so you can attach an energy-saving lining to existing draperies.

Some of the same aluminized fabrics used for window shades can be attached easily to draperies at top and bottom with staples or tape. Or they may be used separately as free-hanging curtains behind draperies and hung on the same hooks.

For seasonal efficiency, you may prefer a highly reflective aluminized material laminated to vinyl and left free-hanging. It can be switched to face the window in summer and the room in winter to take advantage of its reflective properties.

One of the best insulating fabrics for drapery linings is Milium, a metallic-backed cotton cloth that has been used for years as lining for winter coats. Milium is a fairly expensive material for drapery lining and often is used with high-priced, luxurious face fabrics. Milium prices vary from store to store.

Foylon, a foil-backed polyester, developed from the same technology that produced silvery space blankets, is another good insulating and reflective fabric.

In addition to aluminized materials, there are linings of thin or heavy cotton and of Dacron backed with foam and vinyl. These linings rely on white or silvery colors for reflection.

Vinyl backings, formerly stiff and undrapable, have lost their rubbery surface and now feature soft embossed textures that let curtains hang gracefully. Some vinyl backings feel like suede or soft cotton. (If the vinyl you choose is very lightweight or inexpensive, it may have a tendency to curl at the bottom.)

An added benefit of many foam and vinyl linings is their room-darkening and sound-deadening qualities.

Prices for weather-resistant linings range from around $3 to $10 per yard plus a labor charge for putting in the insulating lining.

When you buy window coverings with energy-efficient linings, be sure to check washability of the finished draperies. Some insulating linings are washable, but others must be dry cleaned.

Ready-mades also offer you curtains and draperies with insulating linings; they are available everywhere from discount stores to the most expensive home furnishings departments.

Ready-mades, of course, are considerably less expensive than custom-made draperies. As a rule, the linings will not be of the same high-quality fabrics, but many of them will be effective weather barriers.

Most linings of ready-mades are of cotton or Dacron, laminated to foam and vinyl, and often laminated to the drapery fabric as well.

Good-quality ready-mades, lined with insulating fabric, will cost from $25 up, depending on style, size, and face fabric. The lower-priced ready-mades may have a too-thin cotton lining or thin foam backing that may deteriorate or crumble in a short time.

## TRAP WARMTH WITH WOODS

Woven-wood blinds and draperies are ideal for keeping out cold. Wood is a good natural insulator, and when combined with thick, tightly woven yarn, it provides very good protection against heat loss.

When shopping, make sure the slats and reeds are of wood. Some lower-priced woven shades have slats of plastic, which do not provide as much insulation.

Woven woods are not cheap. A high-quality shade for a window 36x42 inches will be at least $90.

The more yarn used, the higher the cost, and the better the quality. Look at the back of the woven wood shade to check its energy-saving features. Hold the shade up to the light. If there is much light leakage, that means energy leakage as well.

While woven woods are excellent for saving energy in winter, dark woods and yarns absorb sunrays in summer, adding unwanted heat to your house. Either choose shades of light-colored woods and yarns or add a reflective roller shade to save on air conditioning costs.

Wooden blinds will help keep heat in during winter, and white metal or aluminum slatted blinds will reflect summer heat.

However, when used alone, slatted blinds, whether hung vertically or horizontally, do not rate as high in year-round energy savings as do most other window treatments. They do not provide a close enough seal to hold the dead air between window and room.

Wooden louvered shutters also help to some extent in retaining heat in a room, but here again, there are air leaks.

## PERMANENT WEATHER SHIELDS

In addition to shades and draperies are films that coat the glass, deflecting the sun's rays and reflecting as much as 81 percent of the sun's heat. Some films have flow-on coatings of tinted liquid plastics that harden on windowpanes. Another type is a thin sheet of plastic that bonds to the window with an adhesive or with static pressure. In some cases, aluminum particles or coatings are applied to the plastic sheets.

Other outside devices designed for windows include solar fiber glass screening, thermal shutters, and reflective or solar glass panels. For information about these products, check your local lumber yard, building supply dealer, and firms specializing in solar equipment.

## CONSERVATION TIPS

What you do with the window treatments you use can help the energy picture, too.

Mount blinds and draperies outside the window frames if possible. Air may leak along edges of an inside-the-frame mounting.

Mount draperies from floor-to-ceiling and be sure draperies overlap in the center. Hold fabric firmly to the wall at each side with strips of Velcro fastener glued to the walls and sewn to edges of draperies. Use cornices and lambrequins to help seal tops of windows. (The one exception to striving for a tight seal would be use of a dark-colored drapery in the summer that would trap air, build up too much heat, and damage the glass.)

In winter, always be sure to draw shades and draperies at night or on dark, overcast days. Open them on sunny days.

Keep your windows clean—especially during the winter—since clean glass lets in more sun and warmth.

Remove screens in winter. The mesh will reduce sun's rays by 20 percent.

Don't just close windows. Latch them to make as tight a seal as possible.

149

# WINDOWS /HOW-TO HANDBOOK

Window shapes have a distinct bearing on window treatments. So start your window decorating by analyzing the size, shape, placement, function, and character of your windows. These sketches of the most popular window types should help you identify yours.

• **Picture windows** have one large, stationary pane of glass, sometimes flanked by smaller windows (either sash or casement) that can be opened for ventilation.

• **Double-hung sash windows** are the most common type. Some double-hung sash windows have only two large panes of glass; others have several smaller panes within each half of the window. This type of window opens from either the top or the bottom.

• **Sliding doors** are large panes of glass set into tracks enabling them to slide in front of each other for access through the door. One pane usually is stationary, the other movable.

• **Ranch windows,** or strip windows, are distinctly horizontal in shape. Most often found in contemporary homes, these windows are frequently used in bedrooms and are usually set high in the wall.

• **Corner windows** are usually two double-hung sash windows placed side by side in the corner of a room. This window placement gives you the same window treatment opportunity as two side-by-side windows

anywhere else. Treat them as two separate windows or as one large one.

• **In-swinging casements** open by means of a crank the same as any standard casement. The difference is in the direction the window swings. These casement windows open inward, creating a decorating challenge that requires a carefully planned window treatment.

• **French doors** open either inward or outward and the direction of the swing determines design opportunities. Inward opening French doors present the same problems as inward opening casement windows, though both types of French doors dictate a treatment that will not obstruct traffic.

• **Louvered windows** are those with horizontal panes of glass that open outward to any desired angle, much the way shutters function. These windows usually open and close with a hand crank. Treat louvers the same as you would any other window, since the movement of the glass does not interfere with a window treatment.

• **Bay window areas** consist of three or more windows set at angles to one another. They can be any type or combination of windows, including sash windows, picture windows, casements, or louvered windows. There are special rods and fixtures available to fit all shapes of bay windows.

• **Slanting windows,** most often

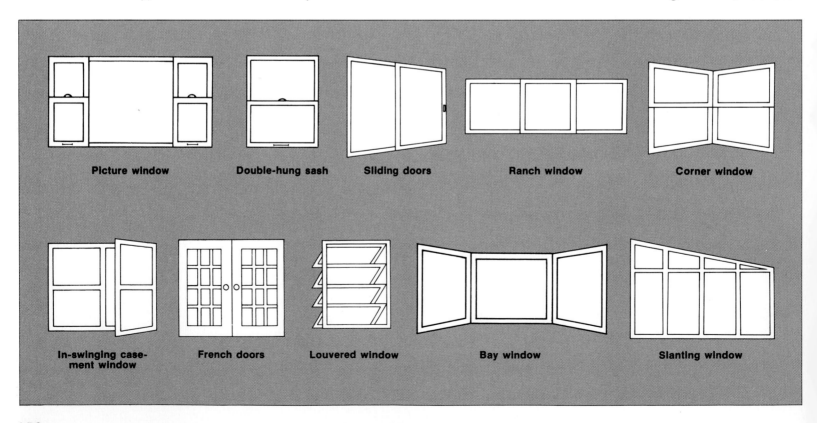

Picture window     Double-hung sash     Sliding doors     Ranch window     Corner window

In-swinging case-ment window     French doors     Louvered window     Bay window     Slanting window

found in contemporary houses, are a combination of large panes of glass at the bottom, topped by irregularly sized and shaped windows above. Decorating these windows often requires ingenuity.

Window treatments can be as plain or as fancy as you want. But most of them are some variation of the treatments below. Learning about these basic window designs gives you a head start in creating your own treatments.

• Two-way traverse rods create classic drapery treatments that pull from both sides toward the center. This is probably the most popular window treatment, although with imaginative finishing touches it can be as distinctly individual as any other window treatment.

• One-way draw traverse rods allow you to stack all the drapery fabric on one side of the window. When closed, draperies look the same as with a two-way traverse. Rods are available to pull right or left.

• Shirred curtains are straight panels of fabric, gathered right on the curtain rod. These curtains do not pull back, but can be tied back if desired.

• Cafe curtains are panels hung from traverse cafe rods or from rings that slide along a rod manually. These curtains usually feature scalloped edges at top, or pinch-pleat headings.

• Double-hung traverse draperies give you two separate pairs of draperies per window, and each drapery opens and closes independently of the other. This layered look usually features an underdrapery of a sheer fabric with an opaque overdrapery. Hardware is available to give you a stationary curtain panel under a conventional traverse overdrapery if you prefer.

• Decorative traverse with cafes features a cafe curtain treatment over the lower portion of the window, with full draperies hung over them and held back by decorative hardware.

• Ruffled tiebacks, or Priscilla curtains, are usually gathered right on the curtain rods and crossed over on the upper half of the window.

• French door traverse rods are one-way draw rods attached to the top of the doors, not to the molding. This allows the doors to open inward without disturbing the draperies, whether open or closed. Specify one right-hand and one left-hand draw when buying these rods.

• Draw draperies with a valance gives an extra touch to classic treatments. A ruffled or pleated valance is hung at the top of the draperies—or well above them if you want to add visual height to your windows.

• Sliding fabric panels create a tailored window treatment and are a good solution to sliding doors or a group of mismatched windows. Panels are hung from ceiling track systems.

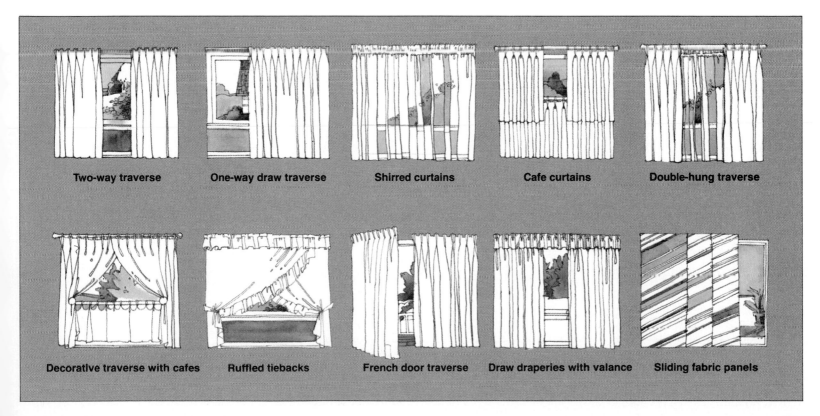

Two-way traverse  One-way draw traverse  Shirred curtains  Cafe curtains  Double-hung traverse

Decorative traverse with cafes  Ruffled tiebacks  French door traverse  Draw draperies with valance  Sliding fabric panels

Replacing your draperies isn't something you do every day, so it's best to be armed with as much information as possible before you begin your shopping foray. Here's information that should make the hunt easier.

## MAKE YOUR DECISION AT HOME

Taking swatches of your carpet, upholstery, and wall paint to the store with you can help with preliminary selections, but when it comes to making a final decision, do it in the room the draperies will be used in. The type of light (both natural and artificial) and the areas of surrounding color and pattern have a visual effect on your window treatment. So take draperies home on approval or buy ¼ to ½ yard of drapery fabric. Study it at the window, then make your choice.

## FABRIC FUNDAMENTALS

Some of the most important qualities in a window treatment, such as durability and easy care, are direct results of the fabric you choose. The fiber, the dyes, the weave, as well as the finish applied to the fabric, all work toward creating a window treatment that will live up to your expectations.

Fibers, for instance, are of two kinds, natural and synthetic. Cotton, wool, silk, and linen are natural fibers. Cotton, linen, and wool are the most durable of the natural fibers. Silk, though exquisite, is more fragile and thus less popular for use in draperies.

Synthetics used for drapery fabrics include acetate, acrylic, nylon, polyester, rayon, and glass fibers. You can choose from several brand names by different manufacturers in each fabric category.

*Acetate* is noted for its soft touch, good draping qualities, quick-drying properties, excellent crease retention, and sun, moth, and mildew resistance.

*Acrylic* is best known for its soft, wool-like hand, and its resistance to wrinkles, mildew, moths, and fire. Some acrylic fabrics are washable; others must be dry-cleaned.

*Nylon* fabrics are strong and pleat well. They can be washed or dry-cleaned and are wrinkle resistant and will not sag or stretch. Bright yarns are more sun resistant than the duller yarns.

*Polyester* fabrics or blends of polyester and other fibers are popular because of their easy-care properties. These fabrics are durable, drip-dry, and wrinkle resistant, as well as high in sun resistance and crease retention.

*Rayon* often is blended with other fibers. Basically, it is soft, drapes well, is inexpensive, and is wrinkle and abrasion resistant. Because of the diversity of rayon blends, be sure to read the hangtags carefully.

*Glass fiber* is remarkably easy to care for. Fabrics of these fibers drape well, need no ironing, and dry rapidly. They are excellent resisters of sun, mildew, moths, and fire.

Some fabrics are blends of natural and synthetic fibers to bring out the best qualities of each fiber.

When you're shopping, always look for fiber content labels that explain the fabric's care and characteristics. File these care labels for reference to help you maintain the fabrics correctly for longer life.

Fabric weaves can be plain, twill, satin, knit, or a variation of these. Just remember, the more closely woven a fabric is, the greater its durability and stretch resistance.

Fabric finishes are the extra touches that give your draperies special characteristics. Finishes are available to provide easier care; to add body, luster, and crispness to the fabric; to make fabrics moth-, water-, and shrink-proof; to make them mildew, bacteria, and flame resistant; to provide wrinkle and crease resistance; and to make them stain and soil repellent.

Read labels on your draperies or drapery fabric to find out what finishes have been applied, what they do, and how long they will last. If finishes aren't permanent, find out whether the fabric can be refinished and what the cost might be.

## WHAT'S AVAILABLE IN DRAPERIES

If you've decided to buy your draperies or have them made, as opposed to sewing them yourself, here are the choices you have:

There are ready-mades, special order ready-mades, made-to-measure draperies (or factory-made customs); workroom customs; and draperies selected through a department store's in-home shopping service. The in-home service gives you factory-made customs, but with some design options usually found only in workroom custom-made draperies.

To simplify your shopping, let's take a look at each of these drapery categories.

## QUICK AND LEAST EXPENSIVE

Ready-mades can offer many advantages to the drapery shopper with limited time or decorating dollars. An appealingly large selection of fabrics, colors, and patterns are available in ready-mades and, of course, you can walk into the store, walk out with your drapery purchase and within an hour have them hanging in place at your windows. Of all types of draperies available, ready-mades are the least expensive. You'll find the prices of these ready-to-buy-and-hang draperies are about half the price of workroom customs and 40 to 60 percent less than the price of factory-made customs. However, ready-mades have a drawback.

They come only in standard sizes, so if your window is irregularly shaped, sized, or positioned, you may be forced to buy something more custom than these stock ready-mades.

Standard sizes in ready-mades are 63 inches long by 48, 72, or 96 inches in width per pair, and 84 inches long by 48, 72, 96, 122, or 144 inches in width per pair. Width is usually not a problem, but it's impossible to buy a floor-to-ceiling drapery in ready-mades.

Ready-made draperies are available unlined, fabric-lined, and thermal-lined.

## FROM THE FACTORY

Factory-made customs also are referred to as special-order ready-mades or as made-to-measure draperies. Translated, each label means the same. You choose your fabric from store samples, provide the window measurements, and the draperies will be made to your size specifications (up to 108 inches in length).

Prices in this category of window covering vary greatly—differences are often due to the fullness of the drapery and the quality of workmanship.

You can expect made-to-measure draperies to arrive in four to eight weeks, depending on the volume of the store you ordered from.

## UNLIMITED SELECTION

Draperies made in the workroom of either a retail store or a decorator shop are referred to as workroom customs. They're the high end of the drapery buying spectrum and offer you unlimited selection of fabrics, styles, and sizes. They also are delivered to your home and, for an extra fee, someone will install drapery rods and hang your draperies for you. This type of drapery usually calls for a professional measurement at the start to prevent any mistake in width and length. The measuring service generally is considered part of the job and comes at no extra charge to you. Charges for workroom cus-

toms depend on the price of the fabric, whether the draperies are lined or unlined (there's an additional charge for lining fabric, of course, though the labor charge differences between lined and unlined draperies are not much), the labor charge, and the price of the hooks. This type of drapery will cost you about twice what ready-mades of a similar fabric would cost, providing they were available in the size you needed.

Installation charges vary, depending on whether you live in your store's town or outside its normal delivery area. Installation charges depend on the number and type of drapery rods involved.

Workroom customs will take from four to eight weeks for delivery, depending on the availability and arrival of fabrics ordered.

## SHOP AT HOME

Several national department stores offer you the convenience of shopping for draperies in your home. And at the same time, you can get some design advice from knowledgeable personnel (though they usually are not professional interior designers). Your draperies also will be installed for you, all without leaving your home. Here's how the in-home service works.

After you've selected your fabric and any new drapery hardware needed, a measurement is taken and you're given an estimate based on the price of the fabric and the style you've decided on. Styles vary widely, and many different treatments

and customizing ideas are available. Costs of these draperies are nearly as high as workroom custom draperies, with only a slight saving in the labor charge. This saving results from the difference in the workrooms of a very large drapery construction operation and those of small custom drapery shops.

The waiting time for these draperies is usually from six to eight weeks.

## TO LINE OR NOT TO LINE

If you're hanging anything other than sheers or casements, a lining fabric can be an advantage. Though, in many cases, drapery linings aren't essential, they are worth considering for a number of reasons.

For instance, a lining will help your draperies hang more smoothly with deeper, richer-looking folds. They protect your carpet and furniture fabrics, as well as the fabric of the draperies themselves, from sunrays. And, in these days of concern for energy conservation, drapery lining is one of the easiest, most effective ways to reduce heat loss through the glass during winter months and stop infiltration of heat in the summer. For extra energy saving, go a step beyond regular fabric linings and choose thermal lining.

There's one more advantage to drapery lining—one easy to overlook if you're viewing your draperies only from inside your home. Your draperies are also seen from outside and linings will give a uniform appearance to your house's exterior.

## WHAT'S QUALITY?

Quality affects cost. That's true in draperies as well as in anything else you buy. But the old saying, "you get what you pay for" is also true. In draperies, good-quality fabrics and workmanship are definitely worth the increase in price. Good construction is essential to appearance as well as to the wearability of your draperies. Here are some of the points to check when shopping for your draperies.

Straight hems and square corners indicate good-quality construction. If hems and corners are anything but straight, your drapery will never hang well. Stitching should be neat and straight.

If the fabric you've chosen has a design, pattern matching is another key to the quality of workmanship. Patterns should match perfectly, not only in the seams within each panel, but also from one panel to the other when hung at the window.

You may have an opportunity to choose how full you want your draperies, consequently determining how deep the pleats will be. Full draperies with deep pleats will cost more but will hang better and look better. And only a high-quality workshop will offer you that choice.

Deal only with reputable outlets, whether it's a local retail store, a national department store, or a private decorator shop. Ask to see draperies made by the firm you're dealing with and judge the quality of their workmanship before you decide to order from them.

**Y**our draperies and the rods you hang them from are inseparable. You need to know the length of the rod to accurately determine the drapery width. And to establish how long a drapery rod you will install, you must have some idea how large an area you want your draperies to cover. The best way to solve this which-comes-first riddle is by following these two rules of thumb.

For ready-made draperies, buy the width that best covers the area you want treated, then buy and install an appropriate length rod, taking into consideration your drapery panels will have to overlap 2 inches at the center and must cover the "returns" on each end. (Returns are the areas between the front edge of the rod and the wall or casing it's mounted on.)

For custom-made draperies or draperies you sew yourself, determine the exact area you want covered, buy and install the rod, then use the rod to establish the measurements of your finished draperies.

## MEASURING TIPS

When measuring for draperies and drapery hardware, always use a steel tape. A cloth measuring tape may stretch somewhat, giving you inaccurate measurements.

To avoid costly errors, always write down all the measurements as you make them. Don't rely on your memory.

Measure every window you intend to treat, even though several windows in a room may appear to be the same size. Size is deceptive, and certain windows, particularly those in older homes, can vary slightly in their measurements.

## INSTALL THE ROD

Drapery hardware may be mounted in four ways: on the wall, on the casing, inside the casing, and on the ceiling. Rods to be mounted on or inside the casing can be only a certain length: the distance from outside edge to outside edge of the casing or the distance inside the window casing. Rods mounted on the wall or on the ceiling can be any length you want. The window size doesn't have to determine the size of the rod or the finished drapery.

Rods that are longer than the width of the window visually expand its size and give the window more importance than it might have on its own. Rods mounted on the wall influence the length, as well as the width, of the draperies. If desired, you can place a wall-mounted rod at the ceiling line, giving you a floor-to-ceiling drapery effect. If not installed at ceiling height, wall-mounted rods are usually placed 4 inches above the window glass to mask the heading and hardware when the window is viewed from the outside.

The length of the rod establishes how much of the window will be exposed. If you're not using an extra-wide drapery for a special decorating effect, you will want to compute just how wide your draperies have to be to pull open and yet reveal the entire glass area of the window. This means allowing extra space at either side of the window for the draperies to "stack" when opened. This "stackback" can add up to nearly one-half the width of the glass.

To help figure the stackback for each window, simply divide the window's glass width by three, then add 12 inches. This will give you the total stacking area required for a pair of draperies. To determine the position of your rod, divide the stackback figure in half, measure that distance from either outside edge of the glass, and make a mark. The distance between these marks represents the length rod you will need.

When planning for decorative traverse or cafe curtain rods, take into consideration that the measurement of the rod does not include the finials or end pieces. If space is tight or you're working on a corner installation, be sure to figure the size of the finial into your window treatment.

## MEASURE FOR DRAPERIES

With the rods installed, you're ready to measure for your custom-made draperies.

Start by measuring the length of the rod from bracket to bracket. Then add 4 inches for overlap at the center of the window plus the measurement of the returns. The sum of these measurements will give you the finished width of your drapery *(see sketch).*

To establish the finished length of your draperies learn these "rod-and-rule" tips:

To find the length of draperies or curtains hung by hooks from conventional traverse rods or curtain rods, simply measure

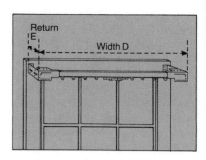

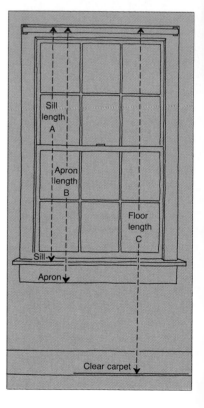

from the top of the installed rod. If you are planning to use decorative traverse rods or cafe rods with rings, measure from the bottom of the rings.

Personal taste and the type of installation dictates where the hem of your draperies will be. The usual lengths are from the top of the rod (or the bottom of the rings) to the sill, apron, or floor *(see sketch).*

Draperies and curtains hung from wall-mounted rods usually fall to the bottom of the window's apron or to the floor. Full-length curtains and draperies should barely clear the floor or carpet. For rooms with baseboard heating, be sure to choose a style and length that will not interfere with the air flow of the heating unit.

Draperies and curtains hanging from rods installed on the casing most frequently go to the windowsill or to the bottom of the apron. And curtains hung from inside-the-casing mounted rods should drop only to the sill.

## DOUBLE-CHECK MEASUREMENTS

Because we advocate double-checking all drapery measurements, we'll do the same and once again run through the basics of measuring width of standard draperies, plus several other popular window treatments.

*Draw draperies:* Measure the length of the rod, plus the returns and overlap at the center. Remember that one-way draw traverse rods have no overlap.

*Cafe curtains:* Measure the width of the rods between the finials. To determine the length of each tier, measure from the lower part of the clip or ring on the upper rod to 3 inches below the clip or ring on the lower rod. This is the finished length (including overlap).

If you're using decorative cafe rods, you may want the bottom rods and rings exposed rather than hidden. In that case, measure from the bottom of the ring on the top rod to the top of the lower rod.

For the lower tier, measure from the bottom of the ring on the lower rod to the desired finished length (to the sill, the apron, or the floor).

*Recessed window curtains* (mounted inside the casing): Measure the length from the top of the rod to the sill.

*Shirred curtains:* Finished length is from 1 inch above the top of the rod (this allows a 1-inch heading above the rod pocket) to the desired length—the sill, apron or floor.

## INSTALLATION IS IMPORTANT

Measuring accurately, installing the right rod in the right place, and selecting quality draperies all contribute to a professional, finished look at your windows. But all those quality-conscious preliminaries are a waste of time if you do a haphazard job of installing your curtains or draperies.

The hooks you select play a big part in how a drapery panel hangs. Several types are available; one that's right for each drapery and rod combination. If in doubt, the rod package will recommend a type of hook for you to use.

Hook placement determines the placement of the drapery or curtain heading in relationship to the rod. Learn where the heading should be for each type of rod, then place the hooks appropriately.

For a conventional traverse rod installation (or for curtain rods), the heading top should be level with the rod top. This

conceals the rod when the window treatment is closed.

With decorative traverse rods or cafe curtain rods, you'll want the rod and rings to show, so the top of the heading should come to the bottom of the rings.

A properly installed drapery or curtain covers the entire casing of the window. Pleats should be straight and the space between the pleats should be smooth and even when the draperies are closed. The same smooth, sleek look should be evident in the return area from the outside front edge of the rod to the wall surface. Overlaps should be smooth and the two drapery panels should line up evenly at the center when the draperies are closed.

## GETTING THE HANG OF IT

How you hang your draperies can make a big difference in the way they operate on a traverse rod.

Start by hanging the panels at the master slide in the center of the rod. Then attach a drapery hook in each slide, working toward the end of the rod. Don't skip rings or slides if there are more than you need. To leave extra slides on the rod may cause them to twist and interfere with the operation of the traverse rod. Instead, push them to the end of the rod and slip them out of the unit.

If draperies are to have a professional look when they're opened, the headings have to be trained to fold up neatly.

To train draperies hung from a conventional traverse rod, place your finger behind the drapery heading in the center of

the space between two pleats. Bring your finger forward and hand press the drapery heading, creasing in the center of the space. Continue this procedure across the entire heading of the drapery. By creasing drapery headings in this fashion, you determine where they will fold when opened and you control the symmetry and neatness of the window treatment.

To train the headings of draperies hung from decorative traverse rods, use the same procedure, but rather than crease the heading forward away from the window, crease it backward, toward the window. In this case, the drapery hangs below the rod so there is space for excess folds of fabric to recede, creating a trim silhouette.

The next step in "breaking in" your draperies is to train the folds in each panel. To form attractive, professional-looking folds, open up the draperies and finger press each fold. Using tape, heavy twine or a strip of fabric, tie the folds loosely in position. The panels should stay tied for two or three days to train the fabric into the even folds you want. Untie the draperies and let any wrinkles hang out.

## DRAPERY CARE

To add to the life expectancy of your draperies, have them cleaned regularly. Embedded soil can eventually deteriorate fibers. Regular cleaning is important, but always send draperies to a reliable cleaner or laundry. Be sure to tell your cleaner the fiber content of the draperies.

Choosing the right drapery hardware is essential to the success of your window treatment. If you're contemplating a new window design, it's a good idea to become familiar with what's available in rods and hooks. You'll want to find the best rod for your particular situation. On these two pages we show you the most popular standard rods, but be aware that custom variations of these types are also available through your local drapery dealer.

## FUNCTIONAL RODS

This popular category of drapery hardware includes *single curtain rods (1), sash rods (2),* and *swivel end sash rods (3).*

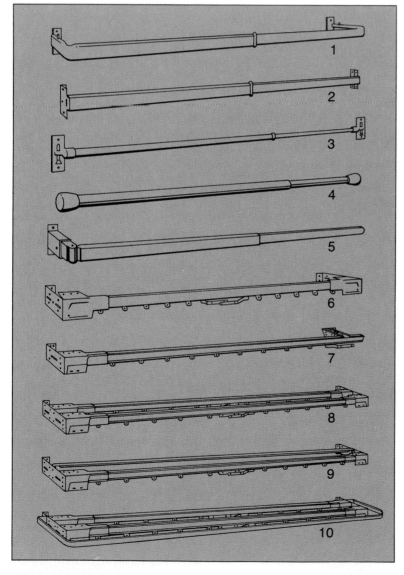

These rods most often are used for shirred curtains or simple cafes. They're usually made of metal in white or off-white, and their lengths can be adjusted.

Sash and swivel end rods allow you to hang lightweight curtains over windows where the rods (and the window covering) must be close to the glass.

*Spring tension rods (4)* fit snugly between the two sides of a window casing, which makes them ideal for shirred curtains hung inside the window frame and in difficult-to-treat locations. These rods can be inserted into rod pockets at the top of a flat curtain panel. Curtains are then gathered right on the rod. For a snugger curtain installation, use a spring tension rod at both the top and bottom of the window with two rod pockets sewn into the curtain panel.

*Drapery cranes (5)* are the appropriate hardware where installations have to be flexible. On French doors or in-swinging casement windows, this drapery rod, with its hinged bracket, allows the free end to swing out away from the door or window.

Traverse rods come in a wide variety of combinations. The *conventional traverse rod (6)* is used with classic pleated draperies that pull from the center to either side. A *one-way-draw traverse (7),* lets you pull your drapery back to one side of the window or the other. This rod is ideal for corner window installations or in areas where there is no room on one side of the window for the draperies to stack. One-way traverse rods are available in either a right- or left-hand draw.

*Double traverse rods (8)* let you hang two pairs of draw draperies and open and close each drapery independently of the other. This is the rod to choose in situations where you want a layered look with an underdrapery you can open to expose the window.

Combinations of traverse rods and curtain rods are also available. The *traverse-and-plain-rod (9)* is your choice for a layered window treatment featuring draw draperies over a shirred curtain. And if you prefer two pairs of draw draperies, topped with a valance, this *triple rod (10)* is the one to choose. The curtain rod outside the pair of traverse rods allows you to gather a valance or use a stationary pleated valance to top off a layered window treatment of two pairs of draperies.

## DECORATIVE RODS

Decorative traverse and cafe rods let the functioning hardware of your window treatment step front and center and become a gleaming decorative accent as well. These rods are used for cafe curtains or standard pleated draperies in situations where the drapery rod need not be hidden.

*Decorative traverse rods (11 and 12)* look just like cafe curtain rods, but they let you attach your pleated draperies with hooks inserted into the slides of the rod just as you would into the slides of a conventional traverse rod. These decorative traverse rods are available in a variety of styles and finishes, including brass, antique brass, wood finishes, white, antique white, black, bronze, antique gold, chrome and pewter.

*Cafe curtain rods (13)* are available in metal made to look like wood and in natural wood. These rods are used with cafe rings, and curtains are opened and closed manually, rather than with the pull cord of decorative traverse rods.

In addition to these standard rods are specialty rods that can handle any window need. See your local drapery hardware dealer.

Corner rods, for instance, are available to treat two windows on adjacent walls. There are special rods for bay and bow windows, as well as bendable track that can be recruited to fit nearly any problem window. Ceiling track systems let you hang your window treatment from the ceiling.

## MOUNTING HARDWARE

Drapery rods can be mounted four ways: on the wall, on the casing, inside the casing, or on the ceiling.

For visual expansion of the window size and to allow room for the draperies to stack, mount rods on the wall. For wall installations, try to locate wood studs. If successful, use 1¼-inch wood screws to install the rod. If mounting rods on hollow walls, use special fasteners such as toggle bolts.

Rods mounted on the wall should be placed at least 4 inches above the window glass so hardware and heading will not be seen from the outside.

Mounting curtain rods on the casing does not allow for space to stack the draperies on either side of the glass. However, this installation is very effective for stationary draperies or curtains of semi-sheer fabric.

## HOOKS AND WHERE TO HOOK THEM

Although drapery hooks all perform the same function, a variety of them are available, and each one is used in a different situation.

The *round pin-on hook (14)* is used with closed-bottom headings where draperies or curtains are hung from curtain or sash rods.

The pointed top *pin-on-hook (15)* is used with closed-bottom headings where curtains or draperies are hung from conventional or decorative traverse rods or hooked to cafe rings.

*Pleater hooks (16)* are used exclusively with pleater tape, where each prong of the hook is inserted into a pocket of the tape, creating the pleat.

*Slip-on hooks (17)* are used for draperies with open-bottom headings, where they slip up under the heading and clamp around the pleat.

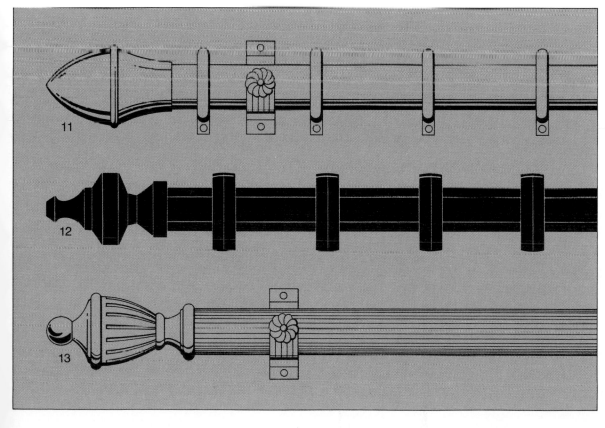

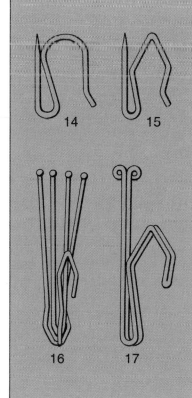

Although shades and blinds have been popular window treatments for a great many years, some confusion still exists as to which is which. Blinds refer, most accurately, to window coverings made of vertical or horizontal slats, such as woven woods, Venetian blinds, or vertical blinds. Shades are basically of two kinds: the simple roller shade and the more complex Roman shade and its variations. To control light, shades move up and down to cover or expose the window glass. Woven-wood blinds function much the same way. Venetian blinds admit light according to the angle of their adjustable slats; these blinds can be raised or lowered. Vertical blinds are drawn back like draperies to expose the window area.

## SHADE SHOPPING

Roller shades are the simplest, most basic shade treatment, but don't let that fool you. Within the category of roller shades, you'll find everything from vinyl-coated cloth to vinyl embossed with shantung, moiré, floral, or linen-like patterns. You can choose from many colors and a variety of personalizing touches such as trims, appliqués, pulls, tassels, scallops, and valance designs. With this kind of selection, your shades can blend quietly into the background or play a major role in your decorating scheme.

You can select a shade to function exactly the way you want. Translucent roller shades, for instance, filter the sunlight, and opaque shades act as room darkeners. Special backings assure complete privacy, still others help save energy.

Most standard roller shades are mounted to be pulled down from the top. However, special installations allow for the bottom-up variation. These are used mostly in skylights and with odd-shaped windows.

If you'd rather not see the roller, a reverse roller shade is your answer. This variety, when hung, rolls toward the window, concealing the roller. A reverse roller shade is particularly effective at a window where you need extra space between the glass and the shade, such as when a crank would interfere with the placement of a conventional roll shade.

Roller shades mount easily with brackets and can go inside the window frame, outside the frame on the casing, or on the ceiling. Each mounting method has its advantages. Inside-the-casing installation, for instance, results in a slim, space-saving roller shade treatment that lends itself to a layered window fashion, with draperies or curtains used over the shades. By mounting a roller shade on the casing of the window, you completely cover the window and cut out any light that might leak in. An on-the-ceiling installation creates the impression that your windows are taller and more impressive than they really are. Just make sure your mounting method will not interfere with the operation of doors or windows.

The other half the shade market, Roman shades and their variations, raise and lower with cords in the same way venetian blinds do. Created of fabric, these shades are seen in three styles: the basic Roman shade in which the fabric forms soft horizontal folds as the shade is raised, Austrian shades that fall into graceful scallops, and balloon Romans that gather into soft puffs when raised.

Roman shades can be mounted within the window frame using a spring-tension curtain rod or attached with hook-and-loop fastening tape to a board mounted on the window frame.

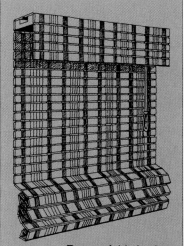

**Roman-fold shades**
Raised and lowered by a cord strung through rings on back of the shade, these blinds gather into soft folds when pulled up. Pull cords may be anchored to lock shade in any position. A valance covers the hardware.

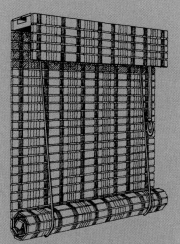

**Cord-and-pulley shades**
Cords roll this woven-wood shade up from the bottom, showing the reverse side of shade material. An automatic cord lock holds the shade in any position. A valance covers the headrail for a finished look.

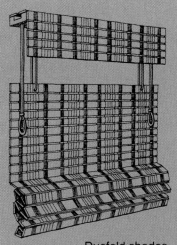

**Duofold shades**
This Roman shade can function as a top-down or bottom-up window covering. The same headrail and cord locks serve both operations. Lowering this shade from the top allows light but safeguards privacy.

## SIZING UP SHADES

Measuring for shades is critical. For an inside-the-casing installation, measure the width of the window opening (both top and bottom) and deduct ½ inch from the narrowest measurement to allow for clearance. Select a shade closest in length to the height of the window opening.

For an on-the-casing installation, measure the casing from outside edge to outside edge. Choose a shade or blind in the nearest size. A roller shade can be cut to size. If you have to trim a wood, bamboo, matchstick, or vinyl-slatted blind, cut equal amounts off each side. Vinyl slats may be cut with scissors,

wood slats and support bars with a fine-tooth saw.

If you prefer to mount the shade outside the window frame, plan for your window covering to overlap the window frame a minimum of 3 inches in width and length.

## BLIND BASICS

Blinds are basically of three varieties: woven woods, venetian blinds, and vertical blinds. Let's start with venetians.

Decorating with venetian blinds is easier than ever before, since mini-slat blinds offer a rainbow of colors, plus metallic finishes, linen-looking surfaces, check patterns, even perforated slats. Order a single

color or any striped or decorative color combination you want. The wide-slat blinds are more limited in their colors than the narrow ones are.

Venetian blinds can be mounted inside or outside the window casing, on the ceiling, and with hold-down bottom rails, if desired. Use them alone or in combination with draperies or cafes.

To measure for custom-made blinds, use a steel tape or wood ruler and write down exact dimensions (within the window opening for inside-casing installation, from edge to edge of the casing for an outside installation). Your dealer will calculate the exact size of the blind so slats will clear the window

frame. For installation, either inside or outside the casing, you will need at least 1 inch of flat surface on which to attach the brackets.

Vertical blinds feature movable louvers the same as venetian blinds. Louvers rotate a full 180 degrees to adjust for any light or privacy situation. These blinds are available pulling open from left to right, from right to left, or from the center to the sides. Louvers may be of either translucent or opaque shade cloth, vinyl, or aluminum. And, as an added touch, valances are available.

Mount vertical blinds inside or outside the casing, free-hanging, or with a bottom track.

Once seen only in commercial buildings, vertical blinds now are used extensively in homes. The most spectacular effects occur when verticals are used to cover large window walls in contemporary homes.

Woven-wood blinds are increasing in popularity with the trend toward natural decorating. These blinds are fashioned of long strips of wood held together by decorative vertical yarns (woven aluminum blinds are also available in some areas).

Woven woods often are made in several colors to create an interesting pattern at the window, and your choices here range from subtle natural-colored yarn and wood to bright accent-colored yarn and painted wood slats. You also may add customizing details to your woven woods.

On these pages you see the six most commonly used installations of woven-wood blinds.

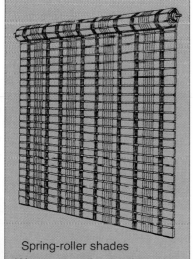

**Spring-roller shades**

Woven-wood shades are mounted on heavy-duty rollers to create a window covering that operates like a conventional shade. Narrow slats are most effective and windows should be less than 6x6 feet in size.

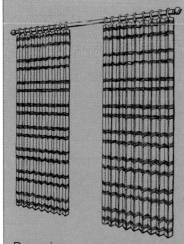

**Draperies**

Vertical slats create the drapery effect in these woven woods. Prepleated draperies can go on any heavy-duty traverse rod. Mounted on slim tracks, unpleated material falls into rolls or accordion pleats.

**Cafe curtains**

As in the draperies, slats run vertically and the yarns horizontally in these cafes. Choose narrow or wide slats and tops with straight or scalloped valances. Prepleated curtains can be mounted on any cafe rod.

Sewing is saving when it comes to draperies. And sewing your own lined or unlined draperies is not as difficult as you may think. If you can handle a sewing machine, follow instructions, and work carefully, you can do a professional-looking job.

## MEASURE METICULOUSLY

Always use a steel tape or wood ruler for accurate measurements. Start by measuring the area the draperies will cover. To this finished length measurement, add 11 inches for hems on unlined draperies (6 inches for the bottom hem, 5 inches for the heading covering the stiffening material). Add 7 inches to the finished length for lined draperies (6 inches for the bottom hem and 1 inch at the top).

If the fabric has a design repeat, determine how many inches apart the repeat is and divide that figure into the length measurement of your panel. If the result is a fraction, buy enough yardage for one more full pattern repeat per width. Plan for a full pattern motif at the heading of floor-length draperies and, if necessary, a portion of the design at the hem. For shorter draperies, place the full design at the hem and a portion, if necessary, at the heading.

To establish the width of your drapery panel, measure the rod from bracket to bracket. Double the measurement (or triple it for extra fullness), add the space of the returns, plus 4 inches for overlap at the center of the two panels and 8 inches for side hems. This sum, divided by the width of the fabric chosen, will tell you how many widths of fabric each panel will require. Add 1 extra inch in width for every seam where two cuts of fabric are joined. Divide this final figure in half to determine the unfinished width of each panel.

If you're using pleater tape, you can determine the width of your drapery panels by pleating tape until you reach the desired finished width. Remove pins, measure the tape and add appropriate inches for the seams and hems.

## CUT WITH CARE

Lay the fabric on a flat surface. Always be sure to cut with the true crosswise grain, established by pulling a thread in the fabric, then cutting along the thread line.

Cut away the selvages or clip them to prevent puckering seams. Cut a master fabric panel, then lay it on the remaining fabric and cut all other panels.

If lining draperies, cut the lining fabric 6 inches shorter and 3 inches narrower than the face fabric.

## ONE STEP AT A TIME

Carefully complete each step of the sewing process, finishing the same step on all panels before moving to the next step.

First, sew fabric cuts together, using an interlocking fell seam (sketch 1).

Next, finish hem, whether you're sewing lined or unlined draperies. Turn up 3 inches of the drapery fabric and press in place. Turn this pressed hem a

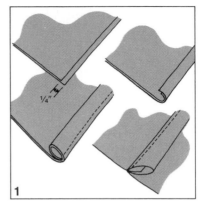

second time and press (sketch 2). Position weights according to sketch and tack in place. Hand hem or machine-stitch bottom hem.

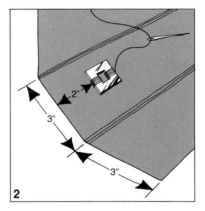

To hem lining, turn under 1 inch and press. Turn hem a second time. Press and stitch.

## LINED OR UNLINED

If you're sewing unlined draperies, your next steps are the placement of the stiffening to create the heading, then the side hems. If sewing lined draperies, reverse the procedure and sew the side hems, then the heading.

For unlined draperies, cut a piece of stiffening material 4 inches shorter than the width of the drapery panel. Place the material on the wrong side of the fabric, 1 inch down from the top edge and 2 inches in from each side edge. Fold the 1 inch of fabric down onto the stiffening and stitch along the top, folded edge. Then turn the entire stiffening material over toward the wrong side of the fabric and stitch down.

Next sew side seams, turning 1 inch under and pressing down. Repeat, turning the hem a second time. Press and stitch. Miter corners where side hems and bottom hem meet.

For lined draperies, lay the lining fabric on top of the drapery fabric, right sides together, with the tops of both the lining and the drapery fabrics even. Pin the edges of one side of the two fabrics together and stitch ½ inch in from the cut edge (sketch 3). Place the two other side edges together and sew with ½-inch seam allowance. (Remember, drapery fabric is wider than lining fabric so the two will not lie flat.)

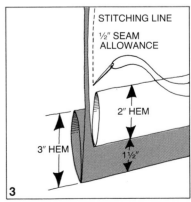

STITCHING LINE
½" SEAM ALLOWANCE
2" HEM
3" HEM
1½"

After sewing side seams, turn the panel right side out and press down, positioning lining

1½ inches in from folded edge of drapery panel. Press. Miter corners where side seams meet the hem.

To create a heading of buckram or crinoline, cut stiffening material the width of the finished, pressed panel. Turn the panel wrong side out again and place the buckram at the top edge of the panel with the bottom edge of the stiffening material ½ inch below the top edge of the drapery panel. Stitch down, then turn the panel right side out. The stiffening is hidden between the drapery fabric and lining. Press down and pleat.

If using pleater tape, place drapery fabric right side up and lay pleater tape on the top edge with pocket openings facing up. The tape should overlap the drapery fabric ½ inch and extend ½ inch at each side. Make sure end pockets are equidistant from the ends of panel.

Sew the tape ¼ inch from the edge. Turn the drapery over and fold back tape so it lies against the lining fabric. Allow ½-inch margin between the top of the pleater tape and the top fold of the drapery panel. Press.

To give pleater tape a finished appearance, fold under the overhanging ½ inch of tape on each side and sew it to the drapery lining edge. Stitch along bottom edge of pleater tape, below the pockets.

## PERFECT PLEATING

Since windows and draperies vary in size, there's no set rule for the spacing or the depth of pleats. The most common spacing of pleats is 4 inches apart

but you may prefer to place your pleats closer. There is, however, a guide for pleating draperies that can be used no matter what spacing you decide on. To help you with this formula we'll give you an example as we go through this procedure step by step.

First, determine your finished, pleated panel width, including returns and center overlap. (Let's assume that measurement is 36 inches.) Then subtract the space for the return (a conventional traverse rod is usually 3½ or 4 inches from the wall, so we'll subtract 4 inches from 36, leaving 32 inches).

If you have determined your pleats will be spaced 4 inches apart, divide this figure (32 inches) by 4 to find out the number of spaces between pleats on your drapery panel (32 divided by 4 equals 8, or 8 spaces).

Next subtract the space of the returns from the *unpleated* width of your panel. (Let's say, in this case the result is 60 inches.) Divide this figure (60) by the number of spaces (8). (The result is 7½.) Subtract your 4-inch-between-pleats space from this figure (7½) to establish the amount of fabric in each pleat (3½ inches).

Start pleating by measuring 4 inches (or the space required for the return) from the outer edge of the panel. Mark with a pin. Continue marking pleated areas and spaces according to the formula given above, until you have the entire width of the unpleated panel marked for pleating. Be sure you finish with a 4-inch space at the center edge. This will accommodate

the overlap at the center of the drapery.

To form a pleat, fold through the center of the space marked for the pleat and pin it down. On the right side of the fabric, stitch from the top to the bottom of the stiffening material *(sketch 4)*. Backstitch or tack to reinforce the pleat. With the basic pleat formed, use any of the following variations of decorative pleats.

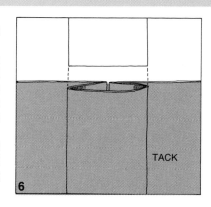

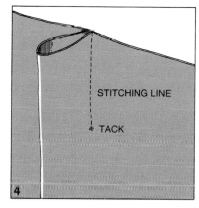

Pinch pleats *(sketch 5)* are formed by dividing the large pleat into three smaller ones and stitching at the lower edge.

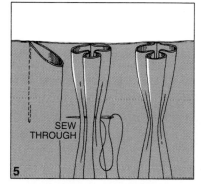

French pleats *(sketch 6)* are like pinch pleats, but are not creased. Divide basic pleat into 3 smaller pleats; sew through bottom of pleat.

Box pleats *(sketch 7)* are easily formed by pressing down the basic pleat and tacking at both the top and the bottom edges.

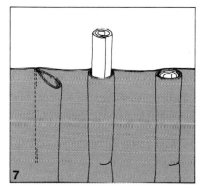

Cartridge pleats *(sketch 8)* are box pleats, but are untacked and have cotton or rolls of buckram inserted to give them their shape.

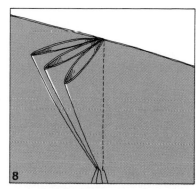

# WINDOWS/FABRIC SHADES AND SWAGS

If you can sew a straight seam and lace a skate, you can create your own Austrian and Roman shades. Here's how to make these popular, practical fabric shades.

## THE ELEGANT AUSTRIAN

These glamorous shades most often are made of sheer or semi-sheer fabric and trimmed at the bottom with fringe.

To measure and cut fabric, first determine the length and width of the finished shade. The length of the shade should be two or three times the length of the area to be covered, plus 1 inch for the bottom hem. The more fabric, the fuller the draping of the shade.

To the finished width measurement, add 2 inches for each side hem, plus 2 to 4 inches for each shirred section. The more fabric allowed for shirring, the deeper each scallop will be.

Scallops in Austrian shades are most often 12 inches apart, though you may place them from 10 to 15 inches apart.

Start sewing Austrian shades by hemming the sides. Turn under 1 inch of fabric and press it down. Turn the hem over a second time, press and stitch.

Ready-made shirring tape makes Austrian shades a breeze to create. This tape has cords woven into it that create the shirring of the fabric. The tape also has rings to draw pull cords through for raising and lowering the shade (sketch 1).

Start by sewing a strip of tape at each side, placing the tape 1 inch in from the finished outside edge. Begin 1½ inches below

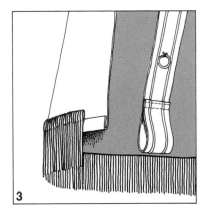

the top edge of the fabric and continue sewing tape until you're ⅜ inch from the bottom edge. Allow about 2 or 3 inches of excess tape to hang below the bottom edge of the Austrian shade.

Decide how many scallops you want in the shade and divide the width of the shade by this number to determine placement of the rest of the tape strips. Position and stitch to wrong side.

After all tapes are stitched, knot the cords loosely at the top and bottom so they don't pull through while you're working on the shade. Turn up excess tape at the bottom and stitch to make loops (sketch 2).

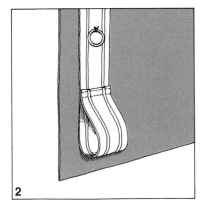

Finish the bottom of the shade by turning ⅜-inch fabric toward the front side of the shade and sewing fringe over it (sketch 3).

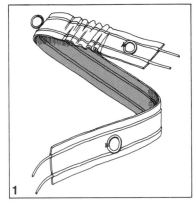

Next, finish the shade's top edge. Since the shade is, at this point, wider than the window, place small pleats at either side of the shirring tape strips to achieve the exact width of the window. Then turn down ½-inch hem at the top. Turn the hem to the wrong side and make sure pleats are secured in the hem.

To hang an Austrian shade, sew hook-and-loop fastening tape over top hem of shade. The tape's other side will be attached above the window.

Before shirring an Austrian shade, cover a metal rod with fabric casing and insert the rod through the loops of shirring tape at the bottom of shade.

The shirred look of an Austrian shade is created by pulling up the two cords in each strip of tape until the shade is the desired length. Make sure each tape is shirred to the same length and that the rings on the tape are horizontally level. When the shirring is done, knot the cords together at the top of

the shade, but don't cut them. You'll need to release them for cleaning.

To install an Austrian shade, cut a length of traverse cord for each strip of shirring tape on the shade. The cord should be long enough to go up the shade, across the top, and back down the side of the curtain. Tie each cord to the covered rod at the bottom, then thread it up through the rings.

Window hardware should include a board the shade is fastened to and screw eyes on the underside of the board through which is strung the traverse cords. When the cords are threaded through screw eyes, gather them at one side of shade. Then lower shade to its full length and knot traverse cords under the last screw eye. Cut all cords except one for raising the shade.

## TRIM AND TAILORED ROMANS

Roman shades are very similar to Austrian in construction, though they are less formal and require less than half the fabric. To create this horizontally folded window shade, cut fabric the size of the window plus extra inches in width for side hems. Cut the fabric at least 3 inches longer than window measurement to allow for the bottom hem.

Two types of Roman shade tape are available. One has rings sewed to it, the other features punched holes through which you thread pull tape. With either type, cut strips 1½ inches longer than the finished length of the shade.

Turn and stitch the bottom hem. Then turn the 1-inch side hems. Now, turn the hems to the wrong side of the fabric and sew tape over the top of the hem.

Sew additional strips of tape at evenly spaced intervals. Tape strips may be placed from 10 to 14 inches apart. Be sure all rings are parallel so the shade will pull up evenly. Let excess tape hang below the shade's bottom hem. This tape will be turned up and stitched down to form loops through which to slip a fabric-covered rod.

At the top of the shade, turn down a ½-inch hem and finish it with the fastening material used to attach the shade to the window.

To install a Roman shade, attach traverse cords or pull tape to the bottom rod. String the cord up through the rings or pull tape up through the pleater tape loops. Then thread it through screw eyes, gathering all the cords at one side. Tie them together and cut as with Austrian shades.

## THE SENSUOUS SWAG

These drapery toppers can be finished and attached to a board above the window, or they can be draped over a cafe curtain rod. The swag itself can be rounded, triangular, or any other decorative shape. Jabots are the hangings on either side of the swag.

To use a cafe curtain rod for a simple swag, drape the curtain over the rod with jabots in back and the swag in front (sketch 4). To create a double swag for a large window, drape the swag as shown here (sketch 5). A

double swag is made in four pieces, two swags and two jabots attached to each other.

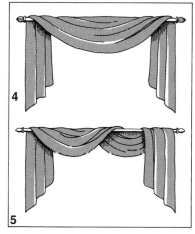

To make a swag, measure the width of the area to be covered. That represents the top measurement. However, to drape nicely, a swag must be larger at the bottom than at the top. Here's how to figure this bottom measurement according to the depth of the swag.

First make a diagonal line pattern (sketch 6). Start with a piece of muslin ½ to 1 yard wider than the swag's top.

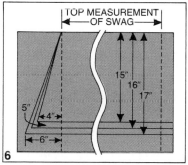

In the center of this material, mark the width of the swag top. From each outside mark, drop a straight line down to the bottom edge of the muslin. Measure 15

inches down this line (the popular depth of a swag) and make a mark. From this mark, measure 4 inches out toward the outside edges of the muslin. Then draw a diagonal line from the mark to the top edge mark. For a swag 16 inches deep, make a mark 5 inches out from the vertical line, for a 17-inch swag, the mark should be 6 inches out (increase an inch in width on both sides of the swag for each additional inch of depth).

Next decide how many folds the swag will have. For four folds, divide the diagonal line into five parts. Mark muslin pattern, use to cut swag fabric.

To drape swag, pin it to the edge of a bed or the back of a sofa so it hangs straight down. Then pin the markings for the first fold by taking the fabric at the point of the first mark and bringing it to the top of the swag. Do this on both sides and smooth the first fold from center of swag outward toward the sides. Next bring up and pin second fold, then third. Continue until all folds are pinned.

Cut off any excess fabric (along the diagonal line) and trim bottom of swag to leave 3 inches below the last fold.

Make a ¼-inch hem at the top and tack sides well to keep folds in place. Add trim.

Jabots are usually 25 inches wide and can be any length, though 27 inches is typical for a short jabot. The inside edge is usually the depth of the swag, and the bottom horizontal edge is 4 inches (sketch 7). Finish the jabot by turning a ¼-inch hem and adding trim, or by lining.

If you line the jabot, cut the lining fabric the same size and

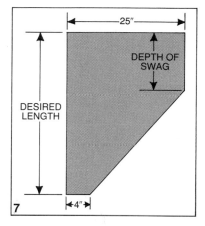

shape as the jabot. Stitch the two pieces right sides together, leaving the top edge open. Turn right side out and overcast open edge.

Pleat the jabot with three pleats. Fold the first pleat 4 inches from the outside long edge. Fold over the remaining two pleats, one on top of the other or spaced as desired. Stitch pleats in place. Reverse the pleating for the jabot on the other side of the swag.

To hang the swag on a cafe curtain rod, attach snaps, buttons or hook-and-loop fastening tape to the top edge of the jabots, and snaps, buttonholes, or fastening tape to each end of the swag (sketch 8).

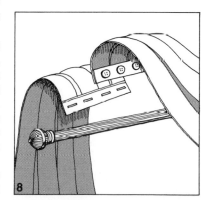

# WALLS AND CEILINGS

**W**alls and ceilings are more than the packaging your furniture and accessories are wrapped in. They are decorating elements in their own right and account for the largest portion of color, pattern, or texture your room will have. So a room's background is not something to toss off lightly in your decorating plans. Walls can set the mood of your room, can warm it or cool it, visually expand it or contract it. They can showcase your design imagination or reflect your skill as a do-it-yourselfer. And with the wide variety of materials available on the market today, your walls don't have to look like anyone else's. Careful selection of material and color will turn ceilings into decorative assets, too.

# WALLS AND CEILINGS
## BEAUTIFUL BACKGROUNDS

**W**alls wrap a room in a cocoon of color, texture, pattern—and style. They're an accompaniment to the rest of your decorating scheme. But, like a perfectly orchestrated symphony, the elements in your room must work together; so plan walls that harmonize with floor, ceiling, furniture, window treatments—even with any adjoining rooms. Walls are a valuable decorating synergist that you should put to work.

Quiet or upbeat—you can create almost any mood with the appropriate wall treatment. Choose patterned wall coverings in bright colors and you bring your walls front and center to establish their visual importance.

On the other hand, when you opt for wall coverings in soft colors and subtle textures, you make walls seem to disappear, creating an easy-going mood.

Dress walls in traditional wall coverings and you set a formal tone. Perky provincial patterns are perfect for a cheerful Early American environment; bold splashes of color create a modern milieu.

faces, including brick and wood. Toned-down hues (or tints) of one of your scheme's major colors will help make walls compatible with the overall room design.

A sparsely furnished room may demand strong color on the walls to keep it from looking sterile. A bright, cheerful accent of color—either an entire wall or even part of a wall—will fill in the spaces no matter how limited the furniture.

### CHECK THE EFFECTS OF LIGHTING

Consider light in choosing wall colors. The effect of a color changes in varying light, from day to night, from lights full up to lights dimmed. Decide first when you will use the room most, then check your chosen paint or wall covering in the same light as in your room.

For super-sunny rooms, a muted variation of your color will help control glare. For a lightless room or one used mostly at night, add punch with lighter, more vibrant tones.

### SHOW YOUR COLORS

Wall color figures strongly in any decorating scheme, simply because it represents such a large portion of the room. But that doesn't mean walls have to be the room's dominant feature, unless, of course, you want them to be.

To put the focus on furniture and away from walls, choose neutral wall tones. White is the obvious choice, but don't overlook natural colors and sur-

*This contemporary setting in a turn-of-the-century house gets a good measure of its charm from walls covered in lush forest green. Shiny dark lacquer (really deck enamel) applied to the walls of this long narrow room causes them to advance, creating the illusion of a smaller, more intimate space. To add visual height and prevent the dusky color from overpowering the room, the ceiling is shimmery, silver radiator paint. As counterpoint for the dark walls, the oak floor is sanded and bleached to a tawny biscuit tone, then sealed.*

# WALLS AND CEILINGS
## BEAUTIFUL BACKGROUNDS

B eautiful as they may be, walls can do much more than add color or pattern to a room. Many also serve as sound absorbers; others visually divide or unify space.

### SOUNDING OFF

Unsettling sounds, reverberating around the room or coming from a room nearby, often rob an area of its pleasant mood. Correct choice of materials for both walls and ceilings can muffle and mellow sounds.

Wood paneling helps deaden sound from room to room; cork or other insulating materials also offer protection.

Other alternatives include fabric, felt, or carpet. Ceilings of special acoustical materials also will help. Although these coverings don't deaden sound completely, they can cut down the echo effect and help maintain a comfortable sound level in the room.

Furniture and a sound-absorbing floor covering provide all the control you need in many rooms. But certain situations, such as reading or music areas, require still more sound barriers. In this case, special materials used on walls and ceilings are your best allies.

### DEFINING SPACE

Open planning, used in many homes today, calls for definition of areas to keep the space from seeming cavernous. Use wall treatments to define and visually separate different areas, or allow the space to flow gently from area to area with only subtle color shifts.

Coordinated but different wall coverings are perfect for defining wall spaces. Companion patterns are designed for just such go-together diversity. An equally attractive technique is to use different tones of paint, such as a sweep from lightest beige to espresso brown, to set off space in a unified way.

Any area suffering from the blahs can benefit from an accent wall. When the effect of a fantastic view or architectural focal point is absent, create your own. Eye-catching wall-paper, bright paint, *faux* brick (easily applied from do-it-yourself kits), stucco, and photo murals are only a few ideas. Just make sure your accent wall is strong enough to contribute to the room's character.

### ALL THROUGH THE HOUSE

Each room has its own personality and needs its own particular wall treatment. But give some thought to the modulation from one room to the next.

For rooms opening directly onto one another, closer harmony is necessary. Walls of the same color draw the eye into adjacent areas and visually combine two rooms, giving the impression of spaciousness.

**Controlling sound or setting the stage, whatever its purpose, a wall deserves to be both practical and beautiful.**

**1** Formality need not be stuffy. Here old, dark wood paneling was pretentious and gloomy; a new paint treatment turned the room into a pleasant place for elegant entertaining

Persimmon and blue cover the major flat surfaces in this easy, but elegant, paint face-lift. White paint accents the molding and beams to define the color panels and original woodwork, and the dark floor gives a touch of drama to this basically soft scheme. Tie-on seat cushions in a persimmon and white print echo the wall coloration.

**2** Brick walls, especially old brick walls, can provide a beautiful background for all types of furnishings—modern, eclectic, or traditional. The walls of this room came out into the open after hiding for years behind plaster.

Exposing the brick may, however, give you more than you bargained for, including crumbling mortar or a window or door previously covered. If you're concerned about a total exposé, just a section of old brick wall (such as around a fireplace) gives great effects—without uncovering too many defects.

To hang artwork on a brick wall, you'll need a drill plus nylon or metal screw anchors or expansion shields. Make the holes the same size as the anchor since a tight fit is essential for strength.

**3** Hang fabric just for the fun of it or use it to cover walls in bad repair. Here, shirred fabric is held taut on rods anchored at ceiling and floor. Artwork is suspended from an L-shaped hook protruding between two lengths of fabric.

3

# WALLS AND CEILINGS
## THE POWER OF PAINT

**N**ever underestimate the power of paint and what it can do to wake up a dull, drab, or out-of-date room. Paint not only is the least-expensive material to use on your walls (and other furnishings as well), but also takes no particular talent to apply and goes on speedily.

### PAINT TYPES

The most popular paints are latex and enamel.

• *Latex paint* is water based for easy cleanups. It dries fast and goes over many interior surfaces, including plaster and masonry, as soon as they have dried and hardened. Latex is not the best choice on wood or materials made from wood products, such as particleboard. If you paint over existing latex, wash the walls and let dry before applying new paint.

• *Alkyd enamel* has almost replaced oil paint because it dries faster and has little odor. It is tougher than latex, so it's ideal for soil-collecting, often-cleaned areas such as the bath, kitchen, children's rooms, and all woodwork. Also use alkyd enamel over wood or wood-based materials to minimize stains leaking from the back. Before painting over old enamel or oil paint, sand the surface so new paint will adhere.

• *Specialty paints* are available for specific jobs. Texture paint lets you apply surface interest with your brush. This water-soluble, latex-base paint has a silica sand additive that usually is heavy enough to create a stucco-like texture.

• *Epoxy paints* are special formulas designed for use on bathroom fixtures and tile. Some types of epoxy paint are premixed, others require adding the hardener at time of use.

Other specialty paints include fillers for painting cinder

It is easy to create colorful decorating effects right out of the paint
can. Just check the wealth of paint
samples, and conjure up something
special for your walls.

blocks, cement paint for water sealing, and other primers and sealers that prevent old stains from bleeding through a new covering of paint.

## PAINT FINISHES

Flat, high gloss, and semigloss finishes are available in the two main paint types. Each has its own advantages.

• *Flat paint,* with its suedelike softness, is good on most walls except those subject to frequent soiling. Although some flat paints are scrubbable, the cleaning results are less satisfactory than with other finishes. Dark, flat paint shows stains more than lighter varieties.

• *Semigloss paint* combines the softness of a satiny surface with the durability and washability needed in heavy-use areas, such as kitchen, bath, and children's rooms.

• *High gloss* is the most washable finish. Stains penetrate it least, and soil comes off most easily. Glossy paint also has a decorative effect, giving a lacquer or enamel look.

## PAINTING TIPS

Here are a couple pointers to remember when painting:

Paint chips are too small to use as a guide for determining what a color will actually look like on the walls. You'll be safest in the long run if you buy a can of paint and cover at least 6 square feet of wall to be sure the color is what you want.

Paints generally dry lighter than they look in the can, but the cumulative reflection of four walls tends to intensify color.

**1** Shiny, cola-colored walls give this traditional decor an up-beat look. The lighting was planned to enhance and highlight the lacquer-like quality of the paint. (High-gloss paint accentuates any imperfections, so take extra care in preparing the wall before painting.)

White paint on the ceiling, doors, and moulding keeps the dark color from becoming overpowering.

**2** Rather than turn your back on an architectural oddity, play it up with paint. Here a coat of bright orange latex paint turns a tiny alcove into a focal point and decoratively sets the space apart from the rest of the white-walled room.

**3** This fool-the-eye mirror "frame" is nothing more than paint. To create a similar, just-for-fun framing effect, attach a plain mirror to the wall using clear mirror clips, then draw lines 5 inches out from the four corners. Round the corners, pencil in the rest of the "frame," and fill in the sides with paint colors of your choice.

Painting will go rapidly and smoothly if you select equipment and supplies wisely.

Let your paint dealer advise you about primers, brushes, pads, rollers, and other needs. He also can help you decide on the amount of paint to buy.

Generally, a gallon of paint will cover about 400 square feet. Provide the dealer with the size of your room (the total length of all walls multiplied by the room's height) and the number of openings. If you plan to use a different type of paint on woodwork and doors, be sure to say so.

Buy the brushes, pads, or rollers designed for the type of paint you will use.

• *Brushes.* A natural bristle brush is best for use with alkyds, but not for water-based paints. A latex paint will make natural bristles stick together and become mop-like.

The newer, inexpensive disposable "brushes" that have foam instead of bristles attached to the handles are adequate for many projects. The small ones are especially good for trim and tiny grooves.

An expensive high-quality brush will last for years if cleaned well after use. However, an inexpensive brush or a throw-away one may be a better investment if you paint only occasionally.

• *Paint rollers* make quick work of coating large, flat surfaces. Make sure you have the right roller cover for your type of paint. Mohair, with its short tightly woven nap, is best for glossy finishes; a lamb's wool cover should be used with solvent-based paints. Synthetic foam covers are all-purpose.

The 3-inch-wide trim rollers can get into areas too tight for a full-size roller. Or you may find

using a small brush to paint trim gives you more control than a roller does.

• *Pad painters,* made of a carpet-like material or foam attached to handles, spread paint easily and evenly on almost all surfaces. They're ideal for painting shakes, screening, and wide expanses of walls.

• *Paint trays.* A flat pan won't do as a paint container for a roller. You need a regular slanted, metal or plastic paint tray with grooves to help work plenty of paint into the roller cover or pad. Throw-away plastic insert trays will save on cleanup time.

## STEP-BY-STEP PAINTING GUIDE

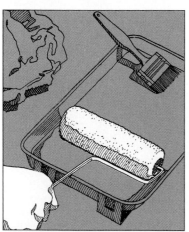

**1** First, prepare the walls: Fill cracks, patch plaster, scrape and sand damaged areas, clean off dirt, and coat surfaces with the necessary primer. Then assemble your painting supplies. In addition to brushes, rollers, paint pads, and pan, invest in plastic drop cloths and an extra roller "sleeve" for each different color or type of paint you use.

**2** Fill roller with paint by rolling it into the lower end of the tray, then smoothing the load on the slanted surface until paint is distributed evenly around roller. Fill roller with as much paint as it will take without dripping.

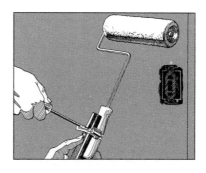

**3** Paint ceiling first, using a brush or roller attached to an extension rod. Or erect a simple scaffold if you prefer. Paint in 2- or 3-foot strips across the shorter dimension of the ceiling. Use a small brush or trim roller to get into corners.

**4** Start painting walls by cutting in edges (painting a narrow strip at ceiling line, around doors and windows, and along baseboards) using a brush, edging roller, or paint pad. Lap marks won't show on flat paint. If that is the type paint you are using, do all the edging around an entire room before painting the rest of the walls. With glossy paint, however, it's best to do one edge at a time and fill in with the roller immediately.

**5** Switch to a roller or paint pad for the rest of the walls. If you used a brush for edging, run the roller close to the trim, over the brushwork, because a roller leaves a different texture than does a brush. Some rollers have guards that will prevent smearing trim. Paint the open area of the wall first, so the roller is dryer when you get near the trim.

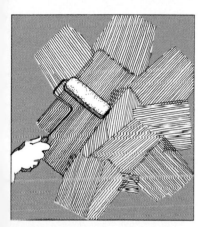

**6** To paint large wall surfaces, roll a big M on the wall and then fill in. Strokes should *not* be only parallel, straight up and down, or across; for best coverage, roll on paint every which way.
   If you're using glossy paint, finish up with vertical strokes to give the surface a smooth appearance. Use slow, smooth strokes so you won't spray tiny drops of paint. Always wipe up any spills or drops of paint immediately after they occur.

**7** Painting woodwork and features such as raised door panels is time consuming, but don't rush this part of the job. If you are using the same paint for walls and woodwork, paint woodwork as you come to it. If it will be another color or a higher gloss, do it after painting the walls. A small trim roller or an edging brush with tapered ends will make covering grooves and molding easier.

**8** Paint a door in this sequence: door frame first, then the top, back, and front edges of the door itself. If the door is paneled, paint panels and molding, then the rest of the door, starting at the top. If you can't remove hardware, paint around it with a trim brush, then fill in flat surfaces with a regular roller or larger brush.

**9** Windows also take time and patience. Adjust the window so you can paint the lower part of the upper sash first. Then raise upper sash almost to the top to finish painting it. Do lower sash next. Continue by painting the recessed part of the window frame, then do the frame and windowsill.

**10** Paint the baseboard last, using a brush or roller. Do the top molding and base shoe, then fill in space between. Protect flooring or carpet with masking tape or with a cardboard or plastic guard held flush against the bottom edge of the baseboard:

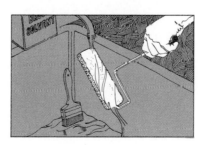

**11** Cleanup chores include the room and the equipment. Remove masking tape; wipe or chip off with a razor blade scraper any drops of paint you may have missed. Clean brushes, pads, and rollers according to directions on the paint can label.

# WALLS AND CEILINGS
## WALL COVERING CHOICES

**W**hen a room needs pattern, texture, or a little extra spark, nothing does the job better than a beautiful wall covering. And selection has never been greater. Here is information to help you determine the wall covering right for you.

### KNOW YOUR NEEDS

The type of wall covering you choose will have a bearing on wearability, washability, removability, and, naturally, the cost. First, know what you expect of a wall covering. Then zero in on the type best suited for your needs.

• *Machine-printed papers* are moderately priced. The selection is wide, and most are well-designed and durable. One reason these papers are moderately priced is because they're printed on high-speed presses, which reduces the cost of manufacture.

As a rule, machine-printed papers are pretrimmed, which means the selvages are cut off. Pretrimming is a big help for do-it-yourselfers.

• *Hand-printed wallpapers* are more costly than most other kinds, with prices varying a great deal depending on the background material used. Though this type of covering is called "paper," the selection also includes designs printed on linen, foil, vinyl—even silk.

Ordering hand-printed wallpapers may mean a wait of several weeks. These papers are usually not pretrimmed, and fragile coverings should be hung by a professional. Some may even need lining papers.

• *Washable wall coverings* include several types of materials that range from "wipe-offable" to downright scrubbable.

Plastic-coated wallpaper allows you to wipe off spots with a damp cloth. Vinyl-impregnated, fabric-backed papers, and polyvinyl chloride wall coverings are labeled "scrubbable," meaning they can withstand frequent brisk scrubbings over a long time. Grease and smoke stains will come off with no damage to the surface.

• *Prepasted papers* already have an adhesive coating when you purchase them, so they save a do-it-yourselfer time and effort. Just dip them into water or wet the back with a sponge. Prepasted papers also have another work-saving advantage. They can go over old wallpaper (except vinyl), as long as the paper is smooth and tight to the wall.

Prepasted paper also comes in 12-inch squares for even easier installation than rolls.

• *Strippable wall coverings* can be pulled off the wall in full strips without steaming or scraping. The main advantage of this type of wall covering is the ease of removal when it comes time to repaper or paint. It's a particularly good advantage with vinyl, as you should never try to hang new wall covering on top of old vinyl. Most fabric-backed vinyls are strippable, but some other vinyls are not.

Any wall covering can be made strippable if a quick-release adhesive is used. However, only fabric-backed, fairly heavy grades of wall coverings are actually durable enough to be used again.

When applying strippable papers, you must follow instructions to the letter and use the adhesive recommended. Check with your dealer.

• *Grass cloth and fabrics* are laminated to paper and sold in rolls in wallpaper stores. Some of these specialty coverings are cork, felt, burlap, and synthetic or natural fiber grass cloth. Cork is glued to a paper in feather-thin slices. Felt, which has insulating and sound-deadening qualities, is now moth- and flame-proofed. Burlap is available in a gamut of colors and is often vinyl-coated for soil resistance. Grass cloth comes in a wide range of colors and textures from smooth to nubby. All these coverings are hung in the same way as regular wallpaper, but should be used with lining papers for best results.

• *Cushion-backed wallpaper* is a washable vinyl covering designed to mask cracked plaster or imperfect wall surfaces. It also can be used on rough concrete- or cinder-block walls. The embossed cushion and woven glass fiber backing prevent this wall covering from conforming to the irregular surface of the wall.

### DECORATING DECISIONS

Once you've established the type of wall covering best suited for your room, your lifestyle, and your budget, you can move on to other decorating decisions. Wall coverings can perform several functions, and the function may guide you to a specific choice of covering. For instance, to hide bumps, uneven ceiling lines and other wall flaws, use a concealing overall pattern. With good walls you want to play up, choose a more subtle effect with small prints, textures, or even the sophisticated shimmer of Mylar. As is true of paint, wall coverings with light-colored backgrounds will make your area look larger and more open; small prints on dark backgrounds tend to close the walls in, creating a cozy, intimate look.

For a totally coordinated effect, many wall coverings are available with matching or companion print fabrics to be used for window treatments or on furniture.

*The serenity of white, used lavishly in the furnishings, sets the tone in this high-style bedroom. However, it's the introduction of the subtle taupe and white wall covering in a contemporary plaid that gives the room its extra touch of sophistication. Angles in the ceiling are minimized by the placement of the wall covering; the pattern draws the eye down and into the room. Wall coverings are great disguisers for architectural defects, since they can distract as well as attract the eye.*

# WALLS AND CEILINGS
## HOW TO HANDLE WALLS WITH WALLPAPER

**1**

**2**

**W**allpaper provides almost an endless number of solutions to myriad decorating problems. It can be used to camouflage badly marred or uneven walls, blend cabinets or appliances into the background, soften irregular architectural features, create a color scheme, or set a particular decorative mood. In addition, wallpaper can be teamed with matching fabric lavished on walls, ceilings, pillows, upholstered furniture, and window coverings for an easy, unified look.

There's such variety of wallpaper patterns and styles to choose from today that the problem isn't so much finding a paper you really like as it is narrowing your selection and making a final choice.

**1** You won't find any cabinets in this kitchen—not unless you look closely. All are artfully camouflaged with a beautiful bandanna-print vinyl wall covering, as is the dishwasher and refrigerator.

Even the door hinges are painted to blend with the brown tones in the print; the doorknobs are covered with paper to match. A ventilation fan hides behind one of the cabinet doors—pull the doors open and on goes the fan.

**2** Here is an example of how wallpaper can set the style of a room. The large-scale pineapple print, reminiscent of designs used in Colonial times, looks hand-stenciled even though it was bought by the roll. To emphasize the architecture, the woodwork was painted dark red, a color taken from the paper. Because this design makes such a strong decorative statement, furnishings in the room are kept as simple as possible so as not to compete.

The patterned paper also helps to unify wall spaces cut up by windows, doors, and the projecting fireplace.

**3** Even though a room may be traditional, you can liven things up by adding some not-so-traditional touches of your own. Many of today's wall coverings come with matching or coordinated fabrics. If you find a pattern or print you like, go all the way and swath your room (or a small nook like this one) with a dramatic duo of paper and fabric. It's the repetition of the single floral print pattern that helps give this cozy retreat its country charm.

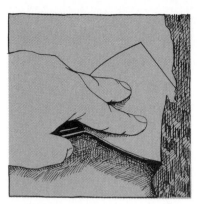

A wide wall scraper and a steamer do a fast job of removing old, loose wall covering.

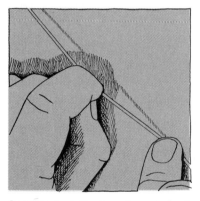

Snap a chalk line for a true vertical where you plan to line up your first strip.

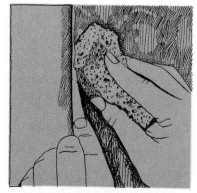

Smooth wall covering onto wall by wiping with a clean sponge or a paperhanger's brush.

Attention to detail is the key to having the finished job look as if it were done by a professional. Take time with each of these important stages.

## MEASURING AND ESTIMATING

Wall coverings come most frequently in double- or triple-roll packages. The estimated amount of usable paper in a single roll will cover 30 square feet. (Most rolls actually contain 36 square feet of paper, but an allowance is needed for trimming and matching.) Widths range from 18 to 28 inches; some heavy vinyls are 54 inches wide.

Always check to see that the rolls are color matched; this should be no problem, if all rolls are from the same dye lot.

To determine how many rolls you will need, measure the distance around the room. Multiply this figure by the wall height from baseboard to ceiling line. Add up the square footage of all windows, doors, and other openings that will be left uncovered, and subtract this from your total. To be doubly sure of your measurements, you may want to draw your walls with windows and other openings on graph paper and recheck your figures. Allow extra footage for necessary waste—how much depends upon the amount you will lose in matching the paper's pattern. (Many dealers will help translate your figures into the number of double or triple rolls you'll need, if you provide exact room measurements.)

To be on the safe side, order an extra roll for future patches, and as a margin of error. It's better to order too much than to run short and have to wait for a second order to arrive. Most dealers will take back unopened rolls, except in cases of costly special-order papers.

Unless your wall covering is prepasted, now is the time to choose the proper adhesive. Follow the wall-covering manufacturer's suggestion for the adhesive to use for this particular product.

If your walls need a primer, check with your dealer as to the type that will work best with the adhesive you will be using.

## PREPARING WALLS

All walls must be free of grease if the adhesive is to work. So begin by washing walls, using a solution of water mixed with detergent or household ammonia. Kitchen and bath walls definitely should be washed thoroughly.

*Handling old wall coverings.* The old covering may or may not need to be removed. Vinyl should always come off. If your new covering is paper, old wallpaper can stay, providing it is still tight at seams and edges with no overlapping. If, however, your new covering is vinyl, remove the old paper.

Fabric- and paper-backed vinyls and strippable papers are removed by lifting a corner of a strip and pulling. If the paper backing adheres to the wall, leave it as a liner for the new wall covering.

Unstrippable papers are a bit harder to remove. If the covering is impervious to water, sand the surface so water can penetrate to the adhesive. Apply water to the paper. For large areas, rent a sprayer. For small areas, apply a mixture of warm water and vinegar with a brush. Proportions are ½ cup vinegar to a pail of water. Use a scraper to remove the paper, then remove the old paste by washing the walls with a solution of mild soap and hot water.

*Prepare painted walls.* Wait a month before papering over any newly painted wall. For old gloss or semi-gloss oil-based paint, roughen with coarse sandpaper to make a good surface for the glue. Seal water-based paint with a priming coat of fast-drying glue sizing.

Unpainted walls need special treatment. Plaster should be at least a month old, and a priming coat of glue sizing should be applied.

Wallboard and other paper-faced surfaces need sealing with an oil-based primer (which can be very thin). Let the primer dry for at least 24 hours.

*Make necessary repairs* as you would for painting, including sealing and priming cracks and holes and countersinking any nails.

*Paint the woodwork and molding* and allow ample time for it to dry before hanging the wall covering.

## TOOLS FOR THE JOB

Tools specifically for wall covering are available separately or in kit form. In addition to a pasting table, ladder, drop cloth, and kraft paper, you will need:
● A razor knife and plenty of sharp new blades
● A wide (6″) putty knife

- A pasting brush or roller (For prepasted wall covering, you need a water tray and sponge instead of a pasting brush.)
- A smooth brush
- A seam roller
- Yardstick
- Scissors
- Two plastic pails (one for paste and one for water)
- Large clean sponge
- Broad wall scraper
- Plumb bob
- Screwdriver

## THE GREAT COVER-UP

Start with plenty of work space. Before tackling the rolls, make your first plumb-line mark, usually in a left corner. Determine the placement of the plumb line by measuring the width of the wall covering out from the corner. Subtract ½ inch and mark your plumb line. (The first strip of wall covering goes to the left of this line and is pressed into and around the corner.)

Cut the first two strips after lining them up so their patterns match. Trim selvage if necessary.

Starting with the first strip, paste and "book" it by placing it on the table wrong side up and spreading paste on it from the center to the top edge of the strip. Fold the top half of the strip back to the center, pasted surfaces together. Be careful not to crease the wall covering. Repeat with the bottom half.

While this strip is resting, paste the second strip. If you cut all the strips for a wall at one time, mark one end "up" and number strips consecutively.

Hang the first booked strip by opening the top half and lining up the motif at the top. Smooth and position on the wall to the left of the plumb line, working from the center to sides without stretching the covering.

For prepasted paper, reroll strips, patterned side in, starting from the bottom. Then place the roll in the water box so the top of the strip comes out of the box. When ready to hang the strip, place the box on the floor below where the strip will be hung. Then just draw the roll up onto the wall and smooth into position along the plumb line.

Careful brushing with the wall brush will help to eliminate air pockets; a pinhole will take care of the rest. After checking positioning, trim the strip at top and bottom, and go on to the next strip. Line the second strip up with the first, butting it up to the edge of the first strip carefully. After 15 minutes, smooth the butted edges with the seam roller. Remove squeezed-out paste with a sponge and clean water (except on flocked or raised patterned coverings).

Check your work periodically to see that the strips are properly lined up. Start a new plumb line on each wall and after doorways just to make sure your strips are all straight. Do doorways and windows as you come to them.

## UPHOLSTERED WALLS

Upholstering a wall is a bit more complicated than simply stapling fabric to the wall, but it is very effective. The upholstering covers up badly scarred walls, helps muffle sound within the room, and provides some sound deadening from room to room. It also gives a feeling of softness to an area.

The materials you need are a fabric with a pattern that conceals seams (such as stripes or prints), quilt batting to cover the wall in a single thickness, a sewing machine, and a staple gun and staples.

To begin your wall upholstering, staple the quilt batting over the entire surface of the wall. Staple batting 2 inches in from the edges at the top, bottom, sides, and around windows and doors. Place staples about a foot apart. After attaching the edges, staple randomly over the entire wall surface to anchor the batting and keep it from sagging.

Prepare the fabric by cutting strips the height of the wall from floor to ceiling, plus an extra 1½ inches at both the top and the bottom. As you cut the strips, be sure the fabric pattern matches.

Sew strips together along side edges with a minimum ½-inch seam. Make one large fabric piece as wide as the wall, allowing an added 1½ inches at each side. Press seams open on the reverse side of the fabric.

Attach fabric to the wall by folding the top 1½ inches under the quilt batting, then stapling through both backing and fabric. Place staples at 3-inch intervals. Then stretch fabric to the base and staple, pulling taut so no ripples occur. *Make sure the design of the fabric is vertical and straight.* Cut out inside doors and windows, leaving a hem to turn. Staple around openings. Finally, staple fabric down the sides at each end of the wall. Cover staples with trim if needed.

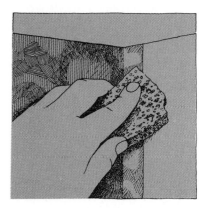

Extend covering ½ inch around the corner. Plumb next strip; it should overlap corner strip.

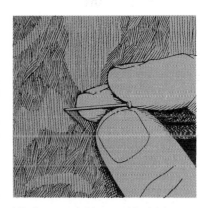

Work out wrinkles and bubbles, using a pin to release trapped air if necessary.

For protruding fixtures you can't disconnect, cut an X in the covering and slip it over fixture.

# WALLS AND CEILINGS
## OTHER COVERINGS

**M**ention wall coverings and almost everyone thinks of paper, vinyl, or similar materials you buy by the roll. But there are plenty of other materials that can be used in ingenious ways to cover walls. For a step beyond traditional "roll goods," consider these alternatives.

### BY THE SHEET

Some materials can go on in large (usually 4x8 feet), rigid sheets. These panels are fast to apply and can camouflage less-than-great walls.

*Plywood paneling* is available in a wide variety of wood surfaces ranging from rustic to elegant. For a special effect, check your local dealer for unusual wood veneers.

*Hardboard panels* are more economically priced than plywood paneling and offer surfaces simulating brick, wood, or a variety of other photo-reproduced patterns.

*Plastic laminated paneling* has, for years, sheathed walls in baths and kitchens. However, this durable, water-resistant material now has moved into other areas of the home. Laminates can go on any wall where the decorating scheme calls for easy-care surfaces that need to withstand hard knocks. Wood, colors, or patterns are laminated to the surface, which is then laminated with a finish impervious to almost anything.

*Pegboard* (perforated hardboard) is the proverbial workhorse for hanging storage. Its patterned surface makes it good for any informal area—with or without a hang-it-all purpose for the wall.

### BY THE PLANK

*Solid wood planks* are a good, but rather expensive, choice if you want a beautifully grained natural surface for your walls. And there's no end to the wall treatments that can be created with planks. Apply them vertically, horizontally, diagonally, in a board-and-batten configuration, or in parquet patchwork. Finish planks with any stain you want. Or, if you prefer, leave them unfinished.

*Wood strips* that can be cut with a knife are also available. This easy-to-handle material lets you create your own wall designs right on existing wall surfaces.

*Laminated wood veneers* are trickier to use than roll wall coverings, but are applied in a similar way. They're handsome answers for walls with unusual contours.

### BY THE SQUARE YARD

*Carpet* creates interesting wall treatments that give a room softness and texture on vertical surfaces, at the same time deadening sound.

Apply carpet to walls using waterproof latex adhesive. While the mastic is drying, use tacks to hold the carpet in place. Let the adhesive dry for several days before removing the tacks.

### BY THE SQUARE

*Tiles* are as varied as pebbles on a beach. They come in a wide selection of materials including ceramic, natural slate, resilient flooring and carpet.

Use the specific adhesive recommended for each material.

*Cork* makes a hardworking cover-up for bad walls. It also adds a warm, natural color and earthy texture to a room.

### MORE OPTIONS

Several other materials can add interest to your walls, if what you're looking for is something out-of-the-ordinary.

*Bamboo* generally is purchased as roll-up shades. Simply hang a shade from hooks at the ceiling line, then anchor it by stapling or nailing through the thickest canes at 1-foot vertical and horizontal intervals.

*Clay bricks or stones* are available in both the nail-on or glue-on variety. Some offer a fire-resistant wall surface.

*Recycled objects* can create some of the most exciting walls around, and at some surprisingly low costs. Try old wine labels, sheet music, record covers, maps, or packing boxes.

**There's no excuse for a drab-looking wall. With a little creativity, your walls can be as varied as your imagination.**

**1** Your local liquor store is the source for an imaginative wine-crate wall treatment like this one. Used in a party room or wine cellar, the crates are particularly apropos. These crate ends simply are nailed to the wall. For best results, first measure the wall space to be covered, then arrange the crate ends on the floor for the design effect you want before you fasten them to the wall.

**2** Straw mats (generally used for sunbathing) make interesting natural-texture wall coverings. Start by stapling the 4x8 foot mats along the ceiling edge. If you're covering a plaster wall, staple the mat to the back of ceiling molding, then use screws to attach the molding to the wall. In either case, pull the mat taut and staple the lower edge into place. Variations are Japanese *tatami* mats or grass carpet squares, which can be stapled into place.

2

To create a wall treatment more distinctive than most, consider something other than the old standards of paint and paper. Here are four dare-to-be-different examples.

**1** Floor-to-ceiling mirrors set in niches on either side of a double doorway create this arcade effect. Originally, only one door connected the living and dining areas, making both spaces seem cramped. By adding another door and extending both to the ceiling, the room became the high-style showcase you see here.

**2** Ordinary squares of sand-paper, glued to the walls (and door) in a grid design, give this dining spot an anything-but-ordinary appearance. A galvanized trash can serves as an unusual (and inexpensive) table base.

**3** Natural pine boards take on new appeal when placed diagonally on a wall. To duplicate this contemporary treatment, start in one corner; nail up a 1x4-inch mitered pine board from ceiling to floor at a 45-degree angle. Nail remaining boards parallel to the first; space ½ inch apart.

**4** Corrugated cardboard may be a mundane material most of the time, but when used as a wall covering, it takes on a sophisticated status. Available at stationers and packing goods companies, the cardboard comes in a number of widths. To apply, coat the *walls* with vinyl paste, then position the cardboard on the walls.

3

2

4

With everything paneling has going for it, no wonder it's such a popular wall-covering material. It is long-lasting, easy to maintain, and —in either the solid wood plank variety or the factory-finished sheets—is one of the most handsome wall treatments.

## PICK YOUR PANELING

In these days of high-cost lumber, solid wood planks are luxury items, but you can enjoy the same good-looking walls with synthetic reproductions of wood panels. They're moderately priced, and some simulate the woodgrain so authentically it's hard to tell the man-made from the nature-made.

Prefinished wood paneling, commonly available in 4x8-foot sheets or in planks, are of these basic types: plywood, which is a sandwich of wood; particleboard and flakeboard, both made of compressed wood chips; or hardboard, made of compressed wood fibers. Any of these may have a veneer of real wood, or they may have a simulated woodgrain or a decorative pattern printed on the surface. Many of the factory-finished surfaces have the texture, as well as the appearance, of real wood.

There is also a low-budget paneling available—a somewhat new type of particleboard called "waferboard." It's less than ½ inch thick and is about half the price of regular plywood or hardboard paneling.

Although the wood look is the most popular of all panelings, the decorative patterns of prefinished panelings are almost unlimited. You'll find designs that simulate patterned wallpaper, damask, burlap, bricks, fieldstone, stucco, terra cotta tiles, marble, wicker, or leather.

Some panels resist moisture, but others can't withstand the dampness of basements or bathrooms. Discuss your project with your dealer for advice about the best type of paneling for your installation.

For special projects, you can buy prefinished paneling in sizes other than the standard 4x8 sheets. There are shorter or narrower planks for diagonal installations or for use as wainscoting. For high-ceilinged rooms 10-foot-long panels are available.

When buying paneling, tell your dealer the floor-to-ceiling height and the corner-to-corner width of each wall to be paneled. For sheet paneling, you will need one panel for each 4 linear feet of wall. Unless the wall is mostly windows, doors, or other openings, don't deduct openings from your calculations.

If you're paneling with boards instead of sheets, have your lumber dealer help estimate the amount you will need, especially if the boards are going on diagonally. Ask about returning uncut boards for a refund.

## PREPARE THE WALLS

Before paneling, check to see whether walls are perfectly plumb and flat. To do this, hold a board against the wall and look for gaps. Also check walls for evidence of decay or moisture. Remove old molding carefully if you plan to reuse it.

When paneling a below-ground level room, attach sheets of plastic as a vapor barrier between panels and walls.

If a wall is straight and in good condition, clean it with a household cleaner and apply the paneling directly to the wall surface. Otherwise, install furring strips to give you a level nailing base for the panels. Furring strips, nailed to wall studs, are also necessary if you are installing paneling over a masonry wall, wallpaper, or peeling paint.

For sheet paneling, begin by applying two furring strips that span the width of the wall. Nail a strip ½ inch above the floor, using a level to make certain it is absolutely horizontal. Nail and level the second strip ½ inch below the ceiling. If the wall is very irregular, you may have to nail shims (thin scraps of wood) behind the strips to ensure a flat base for your paneling.

Next attach a vertical furring strip over each stud, making sure each strip is straight. Shim out where necessary. Sheet paneling must be supported at the edges and every 16 inches vertically. Vertical board paneling requires extra furring strips, attached horizontally at intervals of 24 inches to give the boards a grid-like support. For boards applied horizontally, diagonally, or in a herringbone pattern, use the furring pattern recommended for sheet paneling.

## APPLYING THE PANELS

Before you install panels, condition them for at least 48 hours by stacking them, with furring strips between, in the room where they will be used. This lets them adjust gradually to the temperature and humidity of the area. Without conditioning, the panels may expand or contract after installation.

Plan the arrangement of panels carefully. Place them next to one another along the walls you'll be paneling, and shuffle the order until you find a pleasing sequence of tones and grains. When you have determined the panel positions, number on the back and stack them in the order you will be using them.

The first panel must be cut so its outer edge is perfectly vertical. Trim top and bottom panel edges to leave ½-inch gap at both the floor and ceiling. This sliver of space makes it easier to fit panels into place and compensates for any settlement. If you use a hand or table saw to cut panels, they should be placed face side up. Place panels face side down when using a saber or portable circular saw.

Loosely attach the first panel (with a couple of nails driven part way in) a few inches from the starting corner. Check against a plumb line to be sure the outer edge is perfectly vertical.

Then use a pencil compass to follow the line of the corner from ceiling to floor. The pencil side of the compass will scribe the exact configuration of the corner on the face of the panel. After marking the panel, pull out the nails and take the panel down from the wall. With a coping saw, cut along the scribed line.

Test-fit the panel into the corner and check that the outside edge is straight with the plumb line. This way, even if the corner is not plumb, the first panel's outside edge will be.

Paneling may be applied to walls using only nails or a combination of nails and special paneling adhesive. If not using an adhesive, attach the first panel after butting it gently into the corner. Leave a ½-inch space at both top and bottom. Nail the panel solidly to the furring or studs at 16 inch intervals.

If you are using grooved sheets of paneling, the grooves should be positioned over the furring strips or studs. Nail into grooves wherever possible, and use a nail set to countersink nails. Fill in the holes with wood filler colored to match the panels. If nails are already color-matched to your paneling, drive them in flush with the panel's face.

To use both an adhesive and nails, apply beads of adhesive to the furring strips or walls, using a caulking gun. Butt the panel into the corner and press it firmly against the adhesive. With a couple of nails, attach the panel to the furring or wall, about an inch from the ceiling.

Next, pull the bottom of the panel away from the wall a little and insert a small block of wood behind it. This gives air space so the glue will set.

As soon as the adhesive is ready (approximately 10 minutes), remove the wood block, and press the panel firmly into place.

Now drive in nails at the top and bottom of the panel. Then,

using a rubber mallet, tap the panel tightly against the adhesive. Wipe off any excess adhesive that oozes out from the panel's edge.

The height of a wall may differ in various areas of the room, so measure and cut each succeeding panel just before you are ready to apply it. Don't cut all the panels the same size or at the same time.

Butt each succeeding panel gently against the previous one and attach the same way you did the first panel.

Plan ahead. If you find fitting the last panel on a wall will be a tight squeeze, remove a few inches from several preceding panels to make the last one fit.

The last panel on a wall should butt gently into the corner. Start the next wall with a panel butted up against the face of the previous panel.

## FINISHING TOUCHES

When all the panels are installed, add molding and trim to give the wall a finished look. The trim also masks any imperfections along the floor, ceiling, or around the frames of doors and windows. Use nails or special construction adhesive to hold ceiling molding in place.

Baseboard molding should be nailed to wall studs, never to the floor. This lets the floor expand and contract with humidity changes.

If the floor is crooked, there will be cracks between the molding and the floor. You can cover these cracks by using a base shoe (a quarter-round molding) nailed to the baseboard or to the floor.

## INSTALLING TILES ON THE WALL

Whether you plan to install tiles of ceramic, cork, mirrors, plastic or resilient flooring, you should follow the same rules for measuring, marking, and laying out the squares. However, you will need a different type of adhesive for the various kinds of tiles. Your dealer can recommend the right type.

Here's the equipment you'll need for tiling (some of the specialized items may be available to rent from your tile dealer):
● Tile cutter to cut accurate straight lines
● Nippers to nibble out curved cuts on tiles
● Notched trowel (with serrated edges) to spread adhesive to just the right thickness
● Notched spreader to get into tight spots

If you are installing ceramic tiles, buy, for the main areas of the wall, regular field tiles in 4½- or 6-inch squares. Use smaller trim tiles to round off edges and go around corners.

## PREPARE WALLS

For successful tile installation, the wall must be smooth and firm. Clean off any loose wallpaper or paint. Joints in a new drywall should be sealed.

Plan your layout carefully, starting at the center of the wall. Drop a plumb line at the wall's midpoint, then mark off the width of the tiles on the wall, working toward the edges. You should come out with equally sized cut tiles at each corner.

Remember that floors, as well as walls, may be uneven. Measure from the ceiling to the floor

to find the wall's lowest point. Mark a level line one tile width above the low point. Begin the installation by setting a row of full tiles above this line.

To install your ceramic tiles (squares of other materials are applied in much the same way, except that most of them will not need the grouting ceramic tiles require), spread the adhesive by using the trowel's notched edge, combing out the mastic in beaded lines. Set the first full tiles into place, with space in between each tile for grout. After you have checked that a tile is square with its neighbor, press it firmly into the adhesive.

The field tiles of ceramic will go up fast, so set all of them before turning to the more tedious task of trimming and fitting tiles around pipes, fixtures, and the edges of the room.

To apply ceramic tiles around edges, measure the space, and score the tiles. Then, using a tile cutter, cut them to fit. Smooth edges using a wood file, and press tiles into place.

For fitting tiles around pipes, tub, or light fixtures, nibble out semicircular notches with the nippers until the tile is the right shape and size.

Pack all joints with grout, then smooth the grout with a rounded object such as the handle of a toothbrush. This will compact the grout further.

Use a wet sponge to wash off excess grout, being careful not to damage joints. Let a ceramic tile installation cure for about two weeks, then coat the grout with a special sealer designed to ward off dirt and mildew.

# WALLS AND CEILINGS
## CREATE NEW WALLS WITH SCREENS

1

2

The familiar folding screen or the straight-hanging fabric panel are no longer just bit players on the decorating scene. Today these functional favorites can play just about any part you want, whether it's bringing beauty to a nondescript corner, hiding storage space, or dividing one room into two.

You can find or design a screen to suit any furniture style from contemporary to country. To stage your own screen play, buy a screen that's ready to use, embellish an unfinished one, or construct your own.

**1** When walls aren't where you want or need them, the answer is to improvise. Here, for instance, an attractive foyer effect was created with a folding four-panel screen. The screen came unfinished from a catalog store. To give it decorative dash, two widths and three colors of adhesive-backed tape were applied to the canvas panels in a zingy design. Add a large plant at one side and your new "hallway" is complete.

**2** Taming the expanse of this wide-open room is a bold contemporary fabric panel suspended on a rod from the ceiling. Weighted at the bottom to keep the fabric taut, the panel slides along the rod to diffuse sunlight at one end of the room and to form a corridor effect at the other.

**3** Shirred fabric in a colorful floral print adds country airs to this antique-looking spindle-top screen. But it does more than serve as a smart backdrop for a mix of country and contemporary furnishings. The store-bought screen (with its original panels of sheer fabric replaced) neatly camouflages a mixed bag of stereo equipment and other storage on shelves behind it.

# WALLS AND CEILINGS
## EMPHASIZE THE ARCHITECTURE

1

2

If you're fortunate enough to have a house with interesting architecture, don't hide it, flaunt it. A home with built-in character gives you a decorative head start; the trick is to use architectural assets to greatest advantage. One way is to eliminate distractions that would diffuse the interesting effect. For instance, to show off a classic element, keep the surrounding wall covering simple.

**1** To accentuate the architecture in this turn-of-the century dining room, all molding and trim were painted to contrast with the walls. The gunmetal gray paint emphasizes the early-era feeling of the room, and provides a sharp counterpoint for the mellow yellow of the papered walls.

**2** A full 18 feet tall at its peak, this angular wall demanded strong treatment. The problem was an unusually sunny area that also called for some restraint. The solution was to pick up one of the colors from a favorite Oriental rug—in this case, a brilliant blue—and splash it on the angular wall. Wood paneling gives the textural interest the wall needs and keeps the solid color from becoming overwhelming.

**3** Raising the roof can have interesting results. Here, the addition of a triple dormer window, with ceiling raised to the roof lines, created this spacious aerie. The bed, placed directly into the luminous space, becomes part of the overall design, as does the chandelier.

# WALLS AND CEILINGS
## ARCHITECTURAL ASSETS—FIREPLACES

One of the most impressive architectural assets in any home is a fireplace. Automatically an attention-getter, it draws your eye in an exciting, magnetic way, and is the crown jewel of any wall. A fireplace definitely deserves special consideration in your wall decorating scheme.

However, now that dwindling energy supplies are skyrocketing the costs of other heat sources for our homes, fireplaces are taking on another very important function, that of providing auxiliary heat. For all its beauty, an energy-efficient fireplace is fast becoming more than a mere luxury, it's an addition you should consider if your home doesn't already have one.

A fireplace is a natural focal point both your family life and decorating plans can revolve around. Even in warm months when it's off duty, a fireplace can be filled with flowers or fresh greenery for decorative effect.

Take a look at your fireplace itself. Think of it as a major piece of "furniture" that has evolved through the ages along with all the other architectural elements in our homes. If it's to be the focal point for your room, the character of your fireplace (and such accouterments as andirons, screen, fenders, and tools) should be in keeping with the other room furnishings. An Early American room warms to natural mantels and wrought-iron accessories. More traditional rooms take to carved wood paneling and tile- or marble-faced fireplaces. Contemporary fireplaces can be faced in stone, set in mirrors or simple brick surrounds, and need not have a mantel at all.

Remodeling an existing fireplace or adding one from scratch usually is a major (and costly) undertaking, but it can be as easy as a trip to a fireplace or home center shop.

---

### A FIRESIDE CHAT

Every conventional (that is, built-in) fireplace has basic parts that make it work:
- *The firebox* is the chamber that contains the fire itself.
- *The hearth* is the very bottom of the firebox. The part that comes into the room is called the *extended hearth*.
- *The throat, smoke chamber,* and *smoke shelf* are all above the firebox and are designed to channel smoke and ashes upward into the flue.
- *The flue* is the vent or hollow stack that carries away the unwanted products of the fire's combustion. Often, it takes away the wanted heat, as well; more about that later.
- *The damper* is the control device built into the top of the firebox so you can regulate the flow of air, both up and back down the flue. Always keep a damper closed when there's no fire; otherwise, your hard-bought heat will go right up the chimney.
- *The surround* is the area that does just that, surrounds the firebox opening. The surround can be decorative, but it always should be noncombustible material, such as brick, stone, marble, or tile, unless you are dealing with a *zero-clearance* firebox (right).

---

### WHAT SHOULD YOU BUY?

Now that you have a handle on a fireplace's anatomy, look at the options available. A conventional, masonry fireplace generally requires installation by a skilled craftsperson so it functions efficiently and safely. On the other hand, any reasonably handy person can install, new factory-built fireplaces, and save as much as one-third of the cost of a conventional masonry fireplace. If you're interested in adding a built-in fireplace to your home, explore the many improved prefabricated firebox units that have been mandated by the energy shortage. Some important features to look for are:
- *Heat circulation.* Instead of channeling the fire-warmed air up the chimney, new units draw air from the room, heat it in chambers around the hearth, then send it to the room directly through a series of ducts. Some new firebox units even have ducts that reach outside for air instead of drawing on what's inside the house. With proper ductwork, some units can heat as many as three rooms. To speed the process, fans are an available option. Other units offer heat-amplifier blowers to return warm air quickly.
- *Glass doors.* Because a fire must feed on air, it sucks in what's most readily available, usually the already-warmed air you want to keep in the room. Glass doors prevent this loss, especially at night when a fire dies down.
- *Zero-clearance fireboxes.* This kind of firebox has two or three insulating walls, and can be safely positioned next to a combustible surface, such as a wood wall.

---

### FREESTANDING FIREPLACES

The "good old days" are here again. Paralleling the rise in energy costs is the resurgence of interest in freestanding fireplaces patterned after the old wood-burning stoves of yesteryear. Actually, the freestanding fireplace is a kind of hybrid, bridging the gap between conventional built-in fireplaces and true stoves. (They are back, too, and highly touted for their energy efficiency. The main difference is that stoves are practically airtight so you can't actually see the fire, not as aesthetically pleasing as freestanding fireplaces.)

Freestanding fireplaces are available in many decorative styles, ranging from colonial-traditional to handsome contemporary, and can be placed almost anywhere you want a warm spot: in a corner, along a wall, or even in the middle of a room (local fire codes permitting). Some units are designed in the round—a nice feature for open-plan rooms. To achieve maximum efficiency from a freestanding fireplace, look for the same features as those for a built-in fireplace: glass doors, a heat-circulating chamber, fan or blower, and outside air intakes.

However you arrive at a choice of fireplace for your home, you will be adding a warm new dimension to family living, as well as easing energy demands.

You can trace the "come hither" warmth of this focal-point fireplace directly to the marvelous texture of the old, worn bricks. They literally embrace the fire itself, then run wall to wall and floor to ceiling, giving rich earthen overtones to the entire room. Blessed with a fireplace wall this unusual, the room's furnishings are quietly neutral so they don't compete for attention.

This built-in fireplace warms both the room and its atmosphere, literally. The wood wall paneling and simple lines of the wood mantel give this fireplace an inviting, traditional look. And through a system of carefully engineered air intakes and return ducts, the fireplace puts the warmed air back where you want it—in the living room—not up the chimney. It's a good investment that's good looking, too.

Flowers, both real and stencil-painted, refresh this farmhouse fireplace during the months a fire is out of season. Literally picked from the flowered wall covering below the bedroom's chair rail, the stenciled flowers capture the simple charm of this 100-year-old house. The design offers a touch of color that's *never* out of season. A roughhewn brick surround neatly "frames" the fresh flower arrangement.

Versatile freestanding fireplaces such as this one offer the quickest, most economical means to a cheerful open hearth. They come in many colors and styles and can complement any decor. Although some models are more energy-efficient than others, all have an exposed flue pipe to radiate extra warmth. Most freestanding units can be installed almost anywhere—along a wall such as here, in a corner, or in the center of the room. (But be sure to check local building codes first.)

Decoratively speaking, a fireplace can be a focal point all year long. Heaped with greens, this high, wide, and handsome hearth during the off-season is still the center of attention in the dining area of this remodeled house in historic Old Savannah. Potted plants, an armload of dried flowers, or even a cluster of grasses and weed pods can serve the same attractive purpose; the natural arrangement will add interest to an off-duty fireplace all through the summer months.

An antique updated, this elegant marble fireplace takes warmly to its new role as focus for a room full of contemporary furnishings. Neutral grasscloth-covered walls and a gathering of good art objects are perfect complements to the refined lines. Centuries old to be sure, period fireplaces such as this are still very much of-the-moment in their smart simplicity. It's best to accent this austerity by keeping mantel arrangements uncomplicated with but a few well-chosen accessories.

# WALLS AND CEILINGS
## COPING WITH DEFECTS

**D** isguising a home's defects can be a challenge. To do this kind of sleight-of-eye decorating is just a matter of recognizing your home's architectural impediments, then employing easy-to-master design solutions.

### ROOM THE WRONG SIZE?

When a room is smaller than you'd like, you can visually push the walls out by using a light color. Conversely, if your room has all the intimacy of a vacant ballroom, bring in the walls and create a snug visual effect by using a dark color. If you want pattern on your walls, keep the room from looking small by choosing a design with an open and airy background. To reduce the visual space of a room, use small patterns, bold geometrics, or strong plaids.

### AWKWARD PROPORTIONS?

The technique for altering proportions within a room is much the same as for visually changing the overall size of the area. If a room is too long and narrow, pull in the end walls by painting them a dark color or by adding deep-tone paneling or wall covering. If you're dealing with a pint-sized space, visually expand it with white or light hues. If your room is monotonously square, change the boxed-in effect by making one wall a special feature. Use a dramatic wall covering, a strong color, or an eye-catching corner-to-corner wall arrangement.

### MISPLACED CEILING?

A ceiling can be raised or lowered visually through the use of color and pattern. To make a lofty ceiling look lower, paint it dark. For a still lower effect, bring the ceiling color down the walls a few inches.

A low ceiling can be "lifted" by painting it a light color. A vertically accented covering on the walls will move your eye upward, creating the impression the ceiling is farther from the floor than it really is.

**1** Stripes provide an orderly answer for amalgamating the odd angles of this dormer-niche powder room. Your attention goes to the handsome wall treatment, not to the crazy-quilt angles of the architecture. To crown this wall decor, a strip of paper creates a border at the ceiling line.

In small places such as this, avoid designs with large motifs that will split up when going around corners, destroying the unity of the pattern.

**2** Sheets, gathered and stapled to walls, create a softness few other wall treatments can match. Best of all, who would know (or care) if the wall underneath was cracked, chipped, or otherwise marred. Here, the same sheeting covers a makeup table and mirror.

**3** Sometimes the best way of coping with defects is just to go along with them, pointing them up in a way that's fresh and fun. The tent-like quality of the ceiling in this small, dormered room stands out because of the punchy geometric pattern used to cover it. Squat doors to the room's storage areas are accented with matching striped paint.

**4** An unusual cove ceiling with a correspondingly unusual dormer called for a wall treatment that would conceal the collection of odd angles. Most often, this kind of angled area is simplified and unified by a print that has no obvious repeats. Which is exactly what was used in this bedroom. The small floral pattern covers the walls, ceiling, and, in a fabric version, the window. Note how the window treatment doubles as a canopy effect, turning this architectural tough spot into a success story. To add a final touch, the quilt and pillows echo the wall-covering motif.

193

# WALLS AND CEILINGS
## FAKE ARCHITECTURE

**A**rchitectural purists insist on the real thing—real molding, real wood, real plaster relief on walls or ceilings. But there are ways you can cheat a little and still create a wonderful architectural flavor.

### WHY ARCHITECTURAL DETAILING?

More than just appearance is at stake when you're adding architecture to a room. Certainly, giving an area some character and personality is an important improvement; but, besides glamorization, architectural details accomplish several other decorating coups.

• Architectural detailing can define space within a room or tie unrelated spaces together.

• You can re-create a design style or create the feeling of a particular time and place through the architectural accents added to your home.

• Proportions of walls can be altered with well-planned architectural accents.

### ARCHITECTURAL ADD-ONS

Before you start supplementing your walls, decide what atmosphere you want to create through architectural additions. Then keep in mind that you don't have to limit yourself to typical "architectural materials" such as wood trim or reproduction molding. Other, non-architectural materials (such as paint, ribbon, and fabric) can accomplish the same effects.

Some wall details most often used to denote a mood or highlight a design style are:

*Rustic*. Roughhewn paneling, beams, stucco, or other strong textures on walls and ceilings give a room a rugged, casual feeling.

*Outdoors indoors*. Treillage can create a garden feeling. Use lattice for an entire wall, as a divider, to decorate corners, or to disguise columns.

Walls surfaced with brick, exterior siding, or shingles also can create an outdoor flavor indoors.

Realistic photo murals or stylized mural wall coverings can create almost any outdoor scene, including the vast panorama of a seascape or moonscape.

*Early American*. Plate rails a foot below the ceiling and a chair rail about 30 inches from the floor are practical as well as decorative when creating an Early American room. Other traditional treatments include paneling and half-paneled wainscot effects. Create these with real molding or wood, or use paint and a wall covering to do the trick.

*Victorian nostalgic*. Floral printed wall coverings that have cake-icing-pretty ornamental moldings speak of the Victorian era. Use composition reproduction moldings and medallions, wood moldings, or paint and wall-covering borders for the look of molding. All of these create an old-fashioned effect.

*Modern utilitarian*. Cork, peg, and chalkboards, heavy duty industrial paints and wall coverings, even industrial-style resilient flooring brought up the walls add to the modern utilitarian style. Use bright paint to accent functional units, including exposed pipes, radiators, fuse boxes, or air heating vents. These former "eye-sore" elements can be transformed into attractive, architectural accents in this colorful style.

*Modern sophisticated*. In this sleek, slimmed-down look, traditional architectural add-ons are unthinkable. But a striking architectural effect can result from the addition of mirrored panels, swaths of high-gloss lacquer paint, even bands of carpet on the walls. These materials, when used in an accent capacity, create the impression of architectural detailing.

### EYE-FOOLING IDEAS

Moldings should be scaled to the walls they accent. Trim should be neither too heavy nor too skimpy. Always use a level when positioning molding, and lay out your molding design on the wall using removable tape. When the arrangement is right, mark the position, remove the tape, and apply the molding.

Mirrors double the size of a room, but make sure the views reflected are worth seeing twice. Never let a mirror wall be so eye-fooling that someone could walk into it.

**You can simulate structural changes by using a whole range of exciting and easy-to-do decorating techniques.**

**1** Two-inch-wide grosgrain ribbons coordinate the entire scheme of this enchanting dining room. A lush terra cotta paint used on the lower half of the wall is matched in floor-length draperies. Black and sharp green ribbons are the drapery tiebacks. The same ribbons glued along the wall create the effect of a chair rail. Overlap the ribbons slightly to conceal the seams. Note how the white baseboard separates the dark color of the wall from the floor and adds a high contrast spark to the area.

**2** Each linear element in this room is outlined with blue and white stripes cut with precision from a single roll of wall covering. By carrying the stripes up to the ceiling and around the top of the wall, the effect created is definitely Art Deco. Matching navy paint updates and melds otherwise undistinguished woodwork into the new design. The gold on the walls echoes the age when Deco was the decoration rage.

**3** Paneling and molding, too? Certainly, when the effect is as smashing as this. This great look is simple for even the less-than-handy. Instead of being mitered, each corner of the molding is completed with a small square block, so all molding is square-cut and easily applied. Plan your pattern of molding first, then use a level to line up both horizontal and vertical pieces. Paint molding before you apply it, cover up any nail holes with plastic wood, and retouch these right on the wall.

2

3

# WALLS AND CEILINGS
## EYE-APPEALING CEILINGS

No wall scheme is complete until the right ceiling crowns it. What's overhead is just as important as what's underfoot and what surrounds.

Decide first whether you want to subdue the ceiling or make it dramatic. In most instances, keep ceilings simple so the eye is drawn to other more interesting parts of the room.

*Paint.* White paint will pick up the wall color through reflection, and usually is the best choice for a low ceiling. Higher ceilings can take tints of lighter hues or even dark, intense colors.

More dramatic ceiling treatments may involve applying something other than paint. And since gravity is working against you as a ceiling decorator, start by making sure the ceiling surface is as secure as possible. Scrape, patch, and repair as you would for walls.

*Wall coverings.* Almost any wall covering can go on a ceiling when it is securely attached. Usually, strips of wallpaper are hung across the shortest distance for ease of handling, and patterns can be repeated and matched up along the walls.

*Ceiling tiles* are handy for covering ugly or damaged surfaces. They can be glued with a mastic to good surfaces, or stapled to furring strips nailed in rows at right angles to the ceiling joists. Make a layout before applying tile. This guarantees that the border tiles where the ceiling and wall meet will be even size.

*Dropped ceilings* are good for altering room proportions and for finishing off areas such as attics or basements. Ceiling materials include wood-plank looks, decorative tiles, and acoustical tiles. Metal grid systems used to support the ceiling sections are suspended from the joists above and anchored along the side walls.

**It's easy to go to new creative heights when you use a bit of ingenuity to decorate oft-overlooked ceilings.**

**1** In this bright-banded play-room, each wall closet sports color-coded doors to help children confine clutter. Panels of industrial enamel climb up over the angled ceiling for a lively, unified wall and ceiling treatment. The enamel is topped with high-gloss marine varnish for extra shine.

**2** The openwork lattice-look of the ceiling in this turn-of-the-century sun-room results from fabric that hides a sagging ceiling. Two sheet patterns are combined—one as the ceiling's center, the other as a border for both the ceiling and the upper portion of the walls. A simple white molding caps the solid walls. Wall-covering adhesive attaches the fabric to ceilings. In small rooms, staples along the wall edges may be enough to secure the fabric in place.

**3** Here's a different way to define a dining area and add architectural interest at the same time. A network of slats hangs from the ceiling on nylon fishing line, creating an illusionary, floating effect. Determine how far from the ceiling you want the slats to hang, then cut the fishing line in equal lengths. Loop a piece of line around the end of each slat, then wind the free end around cup hooks screwed into the ceiling. Keep winding the line around the hook until the slats are level.

3

# FLOORS

In more ways than the obvious one, the floor is the foundation of every room. It is the "fifth wall," so to speak; a surface that demands both practical and decorative consideration. What you select as a floor covering will have a strong influence on the way a room looks and functions, so be sure to explore the many options—carpet and rugs of all kinds, resilient vinyls, tiles, wood, and numerous other materials—before making a final choice. You'll find flooring materials to fit every budget and style preference, with an enormous selection of colors and patterns. Quality of the various coverings can vary greatly, so always buy the best you can afford. And if you choose to go beyond the range of ready-made floor coverings, there's a whole realm of custom-coverings you can create yourself or have specially designed for you by a professional in the field. This chapter gives you plenty of ideas to put your floors in focus.

# FLOORS
## PRACTICAL CONSIDERATIONS

Eye appeal and function are the two most important considerations when selecting floor coverings for your home. No matter how much wear a room is in for, there's a floor covering that can handle it—and look good in the process. There's never been a larger selection of colors, patterns, and materials to choose from; so finding the right product won't pose a problem. In fact, if you encounter a problem at all, it will be in narrowing down your choices and making a final selection from the many options available.

### FLOOR CHOICES

Some of your choices are obvious, some more imaginative; so, don't be tied to tradition.

*Carpet,* installed wall-to-wall, gives you softness, color, texture, and possibly pattern. Remember also to figure cost of cushion and installation.

*Rugs,* either room-size or areas rugs, offer many of the same characteristics as carpet. In addition, they are portable and can be shifted around to distribute wear. Rugs may require a finished resilient or hard-surface floor surrounding them, depending on their size.

*Resilient floor coverings,* either sheet goods or tile, offer easy maintenance, and a wide range of colors, patterns, and textures. Location and use may influence your choice. It may be possible to save money with a do-it-yourself installation.

*Wood floors* add elegance and beauty to a room scheme. You can strip, sand, bleach, or stain and finish wood floors to your liking. You can also paint them with deck enamel or good-quality interior enamel and then seal them with polyurethane. Or add stencils or painted designs.

*Ceramic tile, quarry tile, brick,* and other hard-surface materials lend natural beauty, plus rugged textures. You can install these yourself, if you're handy, but most people opt for professional assistance.

### THE FUNCTION FACTOR

How a floor covering will be used may have a strong influence on what you choose. It will definitely determine your choice of color, pattern, and texture.

In a hard-use area, plan for a top-quality resilient covering, hard-surface material, or heavy-duty carpet that's closely woven with low pile. A medium color with a sprinkling of texture is your best bet for keeping your floor looking good.

Only in low-use areas should you consider delicate colors, or ultra-plush surfaces.

Remember, the less upkeep time you have to spend, the more practical your choice should be.

### STYLE CONSIDERATIONS

Floor coverings, like any other design element in your home, can work for you in your overall decorating scheme. Decide what part you want your floor to play, then choose a covering that will accomplish this end. Here are some examples of what various floor coverings can do.

*Make a small room look bigger.* To do this, avoid pattern and use one solid color, preferably a lighter tone. A solid or slightly textured resilient covering will do the job, as will a flat pile carpet. Or try a wood floor, either bleached and varnished, or painted a light color.

*Add pattern to a room.* With all the patterned floor coverings available, you'll have a wide selection. Choose a resilient covering or carpet with an overall design. Or select a patterned area rug to accent an otherwise neutral setting.

*Unify space within a room.* You'll need one great expanse of floor covering—carpet or tile—to do this. Avoid area rugs or room-size rugs, as they tend to chop up space.

*Define areas.* If your challenge is to create the effect of separate areas within a room, rely on several area rugs, used to delineate spaces.

*Form a focal point.* When you want your floor to be the decorative focus in a room, choose an unusual treatment or material, such as an exquisite Oriental rug or an area rug with a spectacular design.

### SHOPPING TIPS

Once you've narrowed down your choice of floor covering, shopping will be easier if you follow these guidelines:
- Determine roughly how much you have to spend on your floor.
- Measure the room or area you want to cover. This will help you establish a general cost figure. (Your dealer will measure the space accurately before he writes the order.)

If you're choosing an install-it-yourself floor covering, be sure your measurements are precise.
- Gather all the information you can about the type of floor covering you are considering. This will save you from disappointment later about a covering's performance.
- Pull together samples of upholstery, drapery, or other furnishings in the room, and take them with you on shopping trips.
- Choose a reliable dealer, one who is well-informed about the advantages and disadvantages of various flooring materials, and who offers a wide choice of products.
- Find out about a dealer's services and charges for such things as installation and future repairs, if needed.
- Buy the best quality you can afford. In the long run, cheap products are likely to cost you more because they're apt to wear out sooner than good-quality materials.

*This bedroom came with an old oak floor that was structurally sound, but not worthy of showing off with a natural finish. For a something different effect, sparkling white porch and deck paint was applied, giving the room an airy, country cottage look. Porch and deck paint requires little maintenance to keep up its appearance. The same effect, both visually and functionally, can also be created by painting the floor with a good-quality oil base enamel, then applying several coats of polyurethane to protect the surface from scuffs and scratches.*

# FLOORS
## CARPET

For years carpet—especially wall-to-wall carpet—was considered the quintessence of fine floor covering. With today's eclectic tastes, however, carpet is by no means the *only* choice for a high-fashion floor; yet it remains universally popular. Its beauty, softness, and sound-control qualities are hard to surpass. And the choices of soft flooring materials, in general, are now broader than ever, ranging from wall-to-wall carpet to room-size and area rugs; from tough, hardworking tweeds to luxurious, pastel plushes.

### CARPET AND COLOR

Carpet adds incomparable qualities of quiet and comfort to a room. Luxurious to both body and soul, carpet is also a wise room choice for some sound bottom-line reasons. Square yard for square yard, you buy a more "furnished" feeling with carpet than with any other floor covering. Even when a room has next to no other furnishings, it looks less empty with the underfoot color and comfort of carpet.

This leads us to the space-expanding capabilities of wall-to-wall carpet. An unbroken sweep of color, especially when it's light in hue, fools the eye into seeing more floor area than actually exists. If you're really tight for space in a small room, make the carpet and walls the same light color.

Conversely, a darker tone of carpet will give a room an intimate, cozy feeling.

The right choice of color on the floor can work some other visual magic, too. Carpet in a sunny, bright color can "warm" a room that lacks natural light; cool colors, such as green, blue, and purple, tend to tone down an overly bright room.

On the practical side, don't forget that light colors will show soil, dark colors lint. You'll have to weigh your decorating preferences against the amount of upkeep required.

Whatever color family you select, you'll find a myriad range of tints and tones to choose from. When you narrow your choices to a few favorites, ask the store salesperson to let you take samples home.

Only by studying a color in your own home environment can you really be sure it's right for you. The colors of other furnishings in a room, as well as the amount of natural light, will affect flooring colors. Artificial light tends to "gray" colors, so check your samples in both daylight and under nighttime lighting. Remember, too, that a whole floor of carpet will intensify the color and make it look far more vibrant than your small sample.

### INSTALLATION OPTIONS

You can choose wall-to-wall carpet, permanently installed over a cushion. Or, select your carpet from a roll (widths range up to 15 feet wide); then have it cut into a room-size "rug." Loose-laid carpet should fit within a foot or less of the room's perimeter. In a rectangular room, a room-size rug creates a look similar to permanently installed carpet, but still allows you to roll it up and take it with you when you move. And, loose-laid carpet can be turned periodically to distribute wear and tear evenly.

### PRACTICAL ADVANTAGES

Because of materials and construction, carpet has some inherent characteristics you may find advantageous over other types of floor coverings:

*Sound absorption* is one of carpet's most appealing features, particularly in condominiums, town houses, or older homes with high ceilings.

*Softness.* If you're trying to combat the angularity of a room's architecture, carpet can help. With its yarn construction and gentle surface texture, carpet is a natural softening agent.

*Versatility.* Carpet needn't stop at the floors. It's equally effective as a wall covering or to sheath platform furniture.

*Easy maintenance* is another consideration in selecting a floor covering. Many homeowners prefer vacuuming carpet and giving it an occasional shampoo to cleaning a resilient or hard-surface flooring. The choice, of course, is dictated by your personal housekeeping preferences.

Some low-maintenance varieties of carpet will challenge any floor covering for easy upkeep. Look for types made to take hard wear, and choose colors and textures that mask soil and lint. But remember, a carpet's color and texture do only that, *mask* soil and lint. You'll have to rely on fibers and construction for durability and cleanability.

*Warmth*—both psychological and real—is a carpet characteristic appreciated more each year. In an energy-conscious home, carpet can help eliminate the cold that radiates from a chilled hard-surface floor.

*Camouflage.* Unlike resilient or hard-surface floor coverings, carpet can go over an existing floor, no matter what its condition; there's no need for a new subfloor. Carpet also tends to mask any irregularities in the surface levels of a floor.

*Carpet is a flexible floor covering. It's so flexible, in fact, that it moves easily from the floor to cover walls or furniture.*

*That's the case in this renovated town house. Where three rooms had been previously defined by ordinary walls, now is one large expanse of living area with carpet, neutral in color and rich in texture, spanning the entire space.*

*The carpet runs from the floor up and over the seating platforms that fill the newfound space, supplementing the store-bought seating near the fireplace.*

*To create this architectural look, wood frames were covered with plywood, wrapped in layers of foam rubber, then sheathed with the same carpet used on the floor. Although they may look built-in, the individual pieces are actually separate and freestanding, so they can be moved about the room as needed.*

It's not hard to see why carpet is the soft touch in flooring. It's posh, plush, quiet, and versatile. It imparts a feeling of luxury and, at the same time, is easy on upkeep.

New carpet represents a sizable expense. To ensure the best return on your investment, you need a basic understanding of carpet fibers and construction. Here's a summary to help you shop wisely.

## START WITH CONSTRUCTION

Most carpet is made by one of four different methods—tufted, woven, needle-punched, or hand-knotted.

*Tufted carpet* is made on fast, efficient tufting machines that function the way a sewing machine does. The yarn is punched through a pre-formed backing material. A coating of latex adhesive locks the yarns in place, which then are given a second backing or, in some instances, a cushion of high-density foam rubber, sponge, or vinyl cushion.

*Woven carpets* are made on power-driven, high-speed looms. Each type of loom (velvet, Wilton, or Axminster, which accounts for these famous carpet names) produces a different carpet finish, but the weaving principle is the same. Pile, weft, and warp yarns are interlocked into a solid fabric.

*Needle-punched* construction uses hundreds of barbed needles to interlock a mat of fibers on a prewoven fabric core, producing carpet resistant to water, insects, mold, and sun. Needle-punch carpet is for indoor/outdoor use and for installation in baths and kitchens. Carpet cushion is also made this way.

*Hand-knotted* and hand-tufted carpets and rugs usually are made in the Middle East according to centuries-old traditions and patterns. These handmade floor coverings are often one-of-a-kind works of art, and are inherently expensive.

## FIBERS

Although the fiber you choose has an important bearing on both price and wearability of carpet, fiber isn't the whole story. You can buy a good fiber, used in a poorly constructed carpet, at bargain prices. But make no mistake, it's not really a bargain. On the other hand, any fiber that's put into a well-made carpet is going to cost more. But you can expect both better appearance and longer wear—and consequently, better value for your money.

Although the list of carpet fibers by brand name is overwhelming, only four major man-made fibers are actually on the market—nylon, acrylic, polyester, and polypropylene. (Wool, of course, is a natural fiber and it continues to be a favorite fiber of those who can afford to pay for the best.)

## CHECK THE DENSITY

One of your best guides to quality is the density of the finished carpet. The deeper and denser the pile, the better. Closely packed pile that is firmly secured to the backing is the mark of a good, long-wearing carpet. One way to check pile density is to bend back a corner of the carpet to see how much of the backing shows. The more backing you see, the less fiber you have to walk on—and the

less durable the carpet will be. Denier and ply affect carpet density. *Denier* refers to the fiber size and weight. *Ply* is the number of strands twisted together to form a single yarn. For instance, a carpet made with three yarns twisted together in each tuft is considered a three-ply yarn carpet. In general, the higher the figures for denier and ply, the better the carpet quality.

## CONSIDER TEXTURE

The next thing to consider when you're shopping for carpet is the finish of the surface. Among the surfaces you will find are:

*Plush* has a luxurious, velvety look, with even cut pile. This carpet shows footprints easily and though some people find this shading appealing, others do not.

*Saxony* is a combination of plush and a short shag, giving a rich, surface finish.

*One-level looped* carpet is just what the name implies. The carpet is made with tufted loops all the same level and left uncut. This is a durable surface with an interesting pebbly look. It can take hard wear, particularly in its super-short variety, which is used in kitchens and other areas where it's important to keep soil and spills on the top surface.

*Two-level looped* carpet is formed of a high- and low-looped pile left uncut.

*Cut-and-looped* carpet is similar to the two-level looped style except the lower level of loops is left uncut and the top level is sheared, which creates a sculptured effect.

*Embossed carpet* is another variety of multi-level loops. This style creates a lush sculptured appearance.

*Random-shear* refers to a carpet created of one-level loops and sheared yarns.

*Frieze or twisted-pile* carpet looks similar to plush, but the yarns aren't cut. They're given a tight twist that is locked in by a heat-setting process.

*Shags* are formed of long pile yarns, either looped or cut.

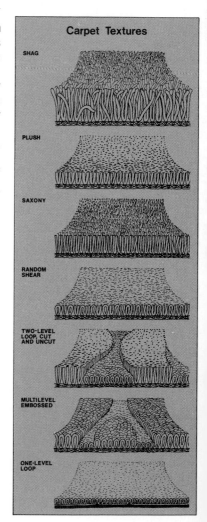

**Carpet Textures**

SHAG

PLUSH

SAXONY

RANDOM SHEAR

TWO-LEVEL LOOP, CUT AND UNCUT

MULTILEVEL EMBOSSED

ONE-LEVEL LOOP

# CARPET AND RUG FIBER FACTS

| | Characteristics | Advantages | Disadvantages | Cleanability |
|---|---|---|---|---|
| **Wool** | Deep, warm, rich look. Excellent resiliency and abrasion resistance. Good, warm, natural feel. | Excellent durability. Flame resistant. Springy and crush resistant. | Does not reproduce light or bright shades well. Can be damaged by aklaline detergents. Needs mothproofing. | Greatly resists soil, but cannot be cleaned as easily as man-made fibers. |
| **Acrylic** | Closest to wool of man-made fibers. Nonallergenic, resistant to mildew, moths, and insects, wide choice of colors available. | Is crush resistant and springy. Resists sun. Low static generation. | May pill (form beadlike balls of fiber on the face of the carpet). | Cleans very well. Greatly resists soil since dirt has less tendency to cling to smooth fibers. |
| **Modacrylic** | Is literally a modified acrylic. Often used alone in bath and scatter rugs; almost always blended with acrylics in carpet. | Abrasion, mildew, and moth resistant. Nonallergenic. Is easily dyed. Is added to acrylic to aid flammability resistance. | May tend to pill. | When used in blends, it's easy to clean and maintain. In some rugs, it can be machine-washed. |
| **Nylon** | Wide choice of colors and excellent color retention. New nylon has excellent bulk, is soft to touch. Special additives make it static protected. Good resiliency. | Exceptional durability, strongest man-made fiber. Resists abrasion, mildew, and moths. Nonallergenic. Continuous filament fibers minimize pilling, fuzzing, and shedding. | Without special additives, nylon can present static electricity problem. Pills in cut filament (staple) loop pile constructions. | Can be very resistant to soil stains, most acids, and solvents. Excellent cleanability, even spot cleaning of stains. Hides dirt, so requires less-frequent cleaning. |
| **Polyester** | Resembles wool in look and touch, and comes in a variety of textures. Good color selection and retention. Resists moths, mildew, and is non-allergenic. | Great durability. Almost no pilling or shedding, good abrasion resistance and resiliency. Sheds moisture. Can be used almost anywhere indoors. | Cool to the touch; lacks the "warmth" of other fibers. Is susceptible to oil-based stains. | Good cleanability. Resists most soiling. Has less static electricity build-up than untreated nylon, so soil clings less. |
| **Polypropyl-ene olefin** | Primarily styled in loop and random-sheared textures. Is very strong and wearable, moisture resistant, nonabsorbent. Resists abrasion, pilling, and shedding. | Extremely durable. Good for heavy traffic areas both indoors and out, with proper backing. Fibers can withstand weather and moisture. | In lower grades, may crush and flatten. | Excellent in ease of cleaning. Less static than other fibers, so dirt does not cling. Is the most stain resistant of all present fibers. Resists almost all acids and chemicals. |

A good cushion is essential to a carpet's longevity. It's also important to underfoot comfort, since it's the cushion that creates a softer walking surface, insulates cold floors, helps absorb noise, and prevents the carpet from slipping and shifting. What's more, cushioning adds to the luxurious look and feel of carpet. Unless the carpet you choose comes with its own high-density foam backing, or is the flat-weave variety, you'll want to invest in a cushion when you buy carpet or a room-size rug.

## CUSHION TYPES

Your choice of a pad or cushion should be influenced by how thick you want your carpet to feel, the quality of carpet itself, where it will be used in the house, and how much wear it will get.

For most areas of the home a 40-ounce padding is usually adequate, but for stairs or heavy traffic areas, a 48-ounce cushion may be a wiser investment. Most cushions are priced according to weight per square yard.

Several different materials are used to create carpet cushions. Each has its own characteristics, advantages, and price variations.

*Felt padding* may be all animal hair, or a combination of felt and fibers. The former provides excellent insulation and long service, but it is quite scarce, and thus, expensive. A blend is less expensive and somewhat less effective than all-hair felt padding. Combination hair-fiber paddings are often rub-berized to eliminate shedding and skidding underfoot.

One caution: If a family member is allergic to animal hair, you'll want to avoid this type of carpet cushion. Nor should you place all-hair padding on radiant-heated floors. The cushion's outstanding insulation attributes will defeat the purpose of this type heating.

*Fiber felt padding* eliminates the allergy problem, but, as the least expensive of the felt products, it also is the least durable and may wear out before the carpet.

*Foam rubber* is a fairly costly cushion but it gives good wear in return for your money. This non-allergenic, mildew-resistant cushion is available in both flat finishes (recommended for hard-use areas) and in waffled finishes. The waffle cushion feels softer underfoot but is not as long wearing as the flat finish variety.

*Sponge-rubber* carpet cushion comes in both flat and waffled finishes,too, and is very soft underfoot. This cushion is less buoyant than foam rubber and is not recommended for outdoor use.

*Urethane foam* padding offers many of the same attributes as foam and sponge rubber. If you're concerned with floor-level heat or dampness, urethane will be your best cushion choice.

*Gas-filled polyester fibers* bonded into a cushion are one of technology's latest contributions to floor comfort. This pneumatic cellular pad is made of small, gas-filled polyester fibers. It's an excellent insulator and, for that reason, should never be used over radiant-heated floors.

*Self-cushioned* carpet is made with a layer of latex cushion bonded to the underside. Since this lining is usually thinner and less dense than a separate cushion, it may be slightly less resilient. However it has its advantage: Self-cushioned carpet can go directly over concrete or other subfloors.

## A LOOK AT LABELS

When shopping for carpet, some of your "required" reading should include the back of the carpet itself. Here's where you'll find a label (required by law) and, in some cases, a guarantee.

The label should include the country of origin or the name of the place where the carpet was made. It should also state the exact type of fibers used to make the carpet.

Where two or more fibers have been combined, the proportions of the blend must be defined on the label, with the majority fiber given first. (For example, 80 percent wool, 20 percent acrylic.) The majority rules in fiber blends, so this carpet will look, feel, and perform more like wool than acrylic. The manufacturer has blended in the small amount of the second fiber, acrylic, to take advantage of its special features, such as easy cleanability.

The label will also include the name of the manufacturer, which is one of your best guides to buying quality in a carpet. With fibers constantly being refined and changed, a reputable manufacturer and retail store offer the greatest assurance that you're buying a floor covering you'll be satisfied with.

Check the carpet label for the name and number of the pattern, as well as the color. Note any special finishing treatment, such as moth-proofing or a stain retardant.

## WHAT'S GUARANTEED

Carpet guarantees seem complicated, but not if you know what to expect.

You should know that any specific carpet you're looking at may have as many as three guarantees.

The fiber is usually guaranteed by the manufacturer. Some fiber makers put the guarantee in writing, which amounts to guaranteeing the fiber against 10 percent wear in five years. Other fiber manufacturers may not come right out and state it, but that's the generally accepted terms for fibers. Remember, this guarantee is for the fiber only and has nothing to do with the construction of the carpet.

Carpet is generally guaranteed for one full year by most manufacturers. And, in most cases, a reliable dealer will stand behind the manufacturer's guarantee, or make the same guarantee if the manufacturer doesn't.

Make sure you find out from your salesperson just what is guaranteed and for how long. And have the exact terms of the guarantee written on your sales slip. Then file this information so you can keep an accurate record of your date of purchase and conditions of sale.

# YARDAGE, COST, MAINTENANCE

## THE COST OF FLOOR COVERING

Since a floor-covering purchase represents a major investment, you should make your decision with long-range plans in mind.

As we've already said, be cautious about floor covering "bargains." Don't even consider a carpet that isn't distinctly labeled, showing fiber content and manufacturer.

When budgeting for your carpet, remember the price will not include cushioning and installation, so the price-per-yard of the carpet alone is only a part of your total purchase price.

Estimate yardage and price, using the charts at right. But don't rely on your own measurements in making a purchase. Have a salesperson come to your home and take the final measurements. Your dealer will figure any extra yardage needed for matching patterns or covering odd-shaped areas of the floor.

## CARPET CARE

Getting the best performance from your carpet requires giving the right kind of care. Vacuum frequently to remove surface dirt before it works its way into the pile. Shampooing a carpet is recommended every one to three years and may be accomplished in several ways.

The *dry method* calls for sprinkling powder-type cleaner onto your vacuumed carpet, brushing it into the pile, then vacuuming it up. This method is easier than the wet method but is less thorough in cleaning.

The *wet method* can work on all types of carpet, provided you take precautions. Do not use soap, ammonia, washing soda, or any strong household cleaning agent. Use only the mild detergent sold specifically for carpet cleaning.

*Foam spray* coats your carpet with a thin layer of cleaner. After it's sponged in with a sponge mop, let it dry, then vacuum.

*Professional cleaning* is a thorough process to remove embedded soil. Contact a reliable carpet and rug cleaner for information about on-location cleaning, plant cleaning, dry-cleaning, spot removal, re-dying, reweaving, and repairs.

## FIRST AID FOR CARPET

Here are some quick-care tips to help you solve common carpet problems.

*Fuzz* is created by loose fibers left in the carpet when it was sheared. Vacuum frequently.

*Pulled loops* should never be pulled out. Instead, cut them back with scissors so they are even with the pile.

*Static electricity* is often a problem in cold, dry weather and is more predominant with some types of carpet than with others. A room humidifier or antistatic spray will help reduce static electricity.

*Pile matting* is a condition that occurs under the weight of furniture or with constant traffic. Remove matted spots by steaming them with a hot iron over a damp cloth or by using a steam iron. Avoid pressing the iron down on the carpet. Brush the pile up after steaming.

### ROLL GOODS CHART*

| Feet | 12 | 15 |
|------|------|------|
| 9 | 12 | 15 |
| 10 | 13⅓ | 16⅔ |
| 10.6 | 14 | 17½ |
| 11 | 14⅔ | 18⅓ |
| 11.6 | 15⅓ | 19⅙ |
| 12 | 16 | 20 |
| 12.6 | 16⅔ | 20⅚ |
| 13 | 17⅓ | 21⅔ |
| 13.6 | 18 | 22½ |
| 14 | 18⅔ | 23⅓ |
| 14.6 | 19⅓ | 24⅙ |
| 15 | 20 | 25 |
| 15.6 | 20⅔ | 25⅚ |
| 16 | 21⅓ | 26⅔ |
| 17 | 22⅔ | 28⅓ |
| 17.6 | 23½ | 29⅙ |
| 18 | 24 | 30 |
| 18.6 | 24⅔ | 30⅚ |
| 19 | 25⅓ | 31⅔ |
| 19.6 | 26 | 32½ |
| 20 | 26⅔ | 33⅓ |
| 20.6 | 27⅓ | 34⅙ |
| 21 | 28 | 35 |
| 21.6 | 28⅔ | 35⅚ |
| 22 | 29⅓ | 36⅔ |
| 22.6 | 30 | 37½ |
| 23 | 30⅔ | 38⅓ |
| 23.6 | 31½ | 39⅙ |
| 24 | 32 | 40 |
| 24.6 | 32⅔ | 40⅚ |
| 25 | 33⅓ | 41⅔ |
| 25.6 | 34 | 42½ |
| 26 | 34⅔ | 43⅓ |
| 26.6 | 35⅓ | 44⅙ |
| 27 | 36 | 45 |
| 27.6 | 36⅔ | 45⅚ |
| 28 | 37⅓ | 46⅔ |
| 28.6 | 38 | 47½ |
| 29 | 38⅔ | 48⅓ |
| 29.6 | 39⅓ | 49⅙ |
| 30 | 40 | 50 |
| 30.6 | 40⅔ | 50⅚ |

*Find room dimensions in dark type and read square yardage in body of the chart.

### TILE CHART

| Square feet of room | 9x9-inch tile | 12x12-inch tile |
|------|------|------|
| 1 | 2 | 1 |
| 5 | 9 | 5 |
| 10 | 18 | 10 |
| 20 | 36 | 20 |
| 30 | 54 | 30 |
| 40 | 72 | 40 |
| 50 | 89 | 50 |
| 60 | 107 | 60 |
| 70 | 125 | 70 |
| 80 | 143 | 80 |
| 90 | 160 | 90 |
| 100 | 178 | 100 |
| 200 | 356 | 200 |
| 300 | 534 | 300 |
| 400 | 712 | 400 |
| 500 | 890 | 500 |
| 600 | 1068 | 600 |
| 700 | 1246 | 700 |
| 800 | 1424 | 800 |

Waste allowance: 1 to 50 sq. ft.: 14%; 50 to 100 sq. ft.: 10%; 100 to 200 sq. ft.: 8%; 200 to 300 sq. ft.: 7%; 300 to 1,000 sq. ft.: 5%.

# FLOORS
## AREA RUGS

**V**ersatile area rugs are playing a bigger-than-ever role in floor fashions. Whether used alone or in conjunction with carpet, area rugs offer an excellent way to personalize a room with color and pattern, to define space, and to add softness and warmth to hard-surface floors. Open-plan houses are especially amenable to the use of area rugs because the on-flowing spaces call for definition of various activity areas.

On the practical side, area rugs offer the advantage of being portable—a big plus if you move a lot. They also make great cover-ups for wall-to-wall carpet that's damaged in spots or badly soiled.

Area rugs are available to suit every taste, budget, and decorating scheme.

For traditional, formal rooms, look over the impressive array of Oriental rugs in rich, tapestry colors. Equally elegant for formal settings are rugs made after the French styles of Aubusson and Savonnerie.

Contemporary and eclectic schemes are prime candidates for the sophisticated beauty of dhurrie rugs. These flat-woven rugs feature designs ranging from primitive to highly complex, stylized versions. Unfortunately, they are hard to find except in large cities. Other rugs well suited for contemporary settings are ryas from Scandinavia, flokatis from Greece, Indian rugs, and rugs with bold graphic designs.

Early American decors are at home with braided or hooked rugs and colorful rag rugs.

**1** Two bold geometric area rugs in this room define separate seating areas and—at the same time—decoratively unify the large space. Compatibility of color and scale keep the pattern of the upholstered wing chairs from competing with the rugs.

**2** An area rug can spark the color scheme of an entire room. Here a striking dhurrie rug does just that—in rich shades of blue, gray, pink, yellow, and white. Two love seats covered in raspberry amplify the pink hue found in the rug.

# FLOORS
# ORIENTAL RUGS

**A**uthentic hand-knotted Oriental rugs are more than mere floor coverings; they are a treasured art form that dates back to about 3000 B.C. Through the centuries, people have always appreciated the beauty and richness that fine Oriental rugs provide.

Fine antique Orientals are the rugs preferred by collectors and connoisseurs, but these rugs are becoming more and more difficult to find and are generally quite expensive. Fortunately, today's machine-made reproductions of the famous hand-knotted Orientals offer affordable (but by no means inexpensive) facsimiles of the real thing.

These handsome, well-made reproductions come close to duplicating the rich, soft colors and the intricate patterns of authentic Orientals, but are made on power looms and are sheared by power instead of being hand knotted and hand clipped.

Also available are Oriental-design rugs that have the design printed on the surface of the pile. These rugs are not as high quality or as striking in appearance, but they offer many people the opportunity to achieve an Oriental look at an affordable cost. The thing to remember is that machine-made floor coverings, even though they're in authentic Oriental patterns, are not true Oriental rugs—even if they're made in the Orient. Law requires these facsimiles—such as rugs made in the U.S. on power looms—carry the label "Oriental-design" or "Oriental-style" on the backing.

*A spectacular Persian area rug sets the pace for this eclectic living room, and proves how beautifully a traditional design can underscore a contemporary room. The oranges and earth tones in the rug are translated onto the updated French-style armchairs, loose-cushion sofa, and even the dramatic contemporary painting that dominates the wall. Although this is an authentic Kilim, you could obtain a similar effect with a less-expensive reproduction rug.*

*When shopping for an Oriental rug, take along a sample of your curtain and upholstery fabrics to see how they look with the rug. However, remember that an Oriental rug, like a fine painting, is a long-term investment and will be used through many decorative changes. It's wise to decorate to complement the rug, rather than pick an Oriental rug to fit your present scheme.*

**B**uying an authentic Oriental rug is vastly different from selecting just any run-of-the-mill floor covering. You are actually acquiring a one-of-a-kind handmade work of art, an heirloom to be appreciated and passed on to your children's children.

Because it has a life expectancy of two centuries or more, the older a rug is the rarer and, as a rule, the more valuable it is. The New York Antiques Society defines an "antique rug" as 100 years old or more. Many such antiques have been counted in estates and handed on as inheritances. Fortunately, the art of rug-weaving has been passed from generation to generation in the Orient, resulting in a constant flow of new beauties from East to West, at least until recent years. Now dramatic upheavals in the social structure of the rug-producing countries, most notably Iran (formerly Persia), threaten to diminish, if not end al-together, the supply of authentic hand-knotted Orientals.

## ORIENTAL ORIGINS

Rug-making as an art arose in small villages that once flourished in the so-called "rug belt" from northwestern Africa clear across into China. It was a totally vertical industry from sheep-raising to shipping. At one time, even the dyes for the wool were distilled by hand from all-natural ingredients. Today's collectors are inclined to prize (and pay more for) rugs from the pre-chemical dye era before 1850 or so.

Most of the exotic names of Oriental rugs merely tell us the cities or regions where their characteristic styles originated. Kirman (or Kerman), Sarouk, Bokhara, Isfahan, Afghan, Heriz, Tabriz, Samarkand, Bergama, and many more small areas achieved world renown through their rug-weaving arts. You'd have to study an ancient map to pinpoint these exotic, faraway places today.

An Oriental rug may have been made by an individual or a single family, especially if the rug comes from a primitive rural region. Usually these rugs are somewhat coarse, with a simple design, and a fairly deep pile.

Rugs of more complex designs are rarely produced by a person or family. Specialists (such as artists, dyers, weavers, and finishers) are employed by a small rug manufacturer.

It often takes an expert to identify a rug by its pattern, because artists in one region may have borrowed designs and colors from other Oriental regions. And many rugs—especially those commissioned by American companies, may be adaptations of Oriental designs.

### BOKHARA

### KIRMAN

### SAROUK

## IDENTIFYING ORIENTAL RUGS

As a general guide, Oriental rugs belong to one of six major groups, each named after the tribe or region that first created them.

*Persian.* Persia, now Iran, is the most famous of all the rug-making countries, with rugs known for their soft colors and elegant all-over designs. Some of the famous pattern names of Persian-made rugs are Heriz, Isfahan, or Kirman, Kudistan, Sarabend, Sarouk, and Tabriz. But many other less famous names are in the catalogs of rug collectors.

*Turkoman.* Also known as Turkmen (the variations in spelling can pose problems for the amateur Oriental rug collector), these are the famous "red rugs" from central Asia. Woven by nomadic tribes who used the madder plant to achieve their characteristic red and red-brown dyes, the Turkoman rugs include the Afghan, Bokhara, and Samarkand designs. Bold and basically geometric, these rugs are known for their repeated *guls,* a medallion-like design derived from a flower.

*Caucasian.* Made in central Asia but seldom with the brilliant red favored by the Turkoman weavers, these rugs have crowded designs and strong geometrics, not unlike American Indian motifs.

*Chinese.* In most Chinese-made rugs, the colors are the soft shades we associate with silks, and the designs include recognizable symbols, such as trees, animals, dragons, and clouds. The Chinese also sculptured their rugs, cutting back the pile to give dimension to certain motifs.

*Indian.* Carpet-weaving was introduced to India with the ruling Mogul dynasty in the 17th and 18th centuries. Persian designs still dominate in India, but the skillful village weavers have, for years, crafted first-quality rugs inspired by French Aubusson and Savonneries.

*Turkish.* With designs akin to both Caucasian and Turkoman rugs, the Turkish weavers are known for their prayer rugs made in brilliant, contrasting colors.

## EARMARKS OF AUTHENTICITY

Shopping for an Oriental rug should, first and foremost, be a matter of choosing a color and design that delights you. If you prefer an authentic Oriental rug, you should familiarize yourself with some of these checkpoints that will help you successfully evaluate various rugs.

• Material should be noted. High-quality rugs are made of long staple sheep or lamb's wool. A cotton warp may be used. (Some Oriental-design rugs are made partly with synthetic fibers. The life expectancy of these rugs will be considerably less than the 200 or so years expected of top-quality Orientals.)

• Construction is an excellent indicator of authenticity. All true Oriental rugs are made by hand with the yarns knotted through a backing made of linen or cotton. The back of an imported rug is apt to be rough, while the backing of a domestic rug will show smooth and even yarns. The more knots per square inch, the better the rug's quality. A really fine Persian carpet may have upwards of 500 to 1,000 knots per square inch, accounting for the rug's long life and lustrous beauty. With hand-knotting's desirable irregularities, there's little chance you will confuse an antique rug with a modern, machine-loomed Oriental (which, as we mentioned before, may be a high-quality rug in its own right).

• Surface is another good indicator of Oriental rug quality. After the yarns are knotted, they are clipped to form a dense, plush surface. The pile of a good-quality Oriental should be soft and silky, not coarse or brittle.

• Fringe is yet another distinguishing characteristic. On an authentic Oriental rug, the fringe is an integral part of the floor covering, created by the loose warp ends of the foundation. American-made rugs, on the other hand, have fringes added on after weaving.

## WHERE TO FIND TRUE ORIENTALS

Fine Oriental rugs occasionally turn up at estate sales or auctions, but your best bet is with a reputable, established large-city dealer. You'll also find a good selection of machine-loomed (and now and then, hand-loomed) rugs at fine department stores. In small cities, a local interior designer may be able to help you by showing you brochures, or by directing you to a reliable dealer in a nearby larger city.

## SHOPPING TIPS

Take time to learn as much as you can about Oriental rugs. Read books on the subject, and study color photographs of different rugs so you become familiar with the various types and their characteristics.

When you're ready to buy, make sure you see the rug on a floor, not just hanging on a wall. Some carpets have creases or bubbles, curl at the edges, or pucker at the corners. Look at the rug in position on the floor to make sure it's right.

Inspect every inch of the rug, both front and back, to make certain its appearance hasn't been tampered with. Sometimes, a rug's balding spots are covered with colored inks. Patches, however, are acceptable if executed skillfully.

On old or antique Orientals, the back of the rug usually looks somewhat brighter than the front, the result of dirt or natural fading. Fading should be negligible if vegetable dyes or properly applied synthetic dyes were used.

An antique look can be achieved by bleaching and forcing wear of an Oriental rug, but neither process should shorten the rug's life.

Be sure to check a used Oriental for overall signs of wear in the pile, the fringe, and the backing. Be especially alert for signs of dryrot, a condition you can detect by folding the rug with the pile inward and pulling. Dry rugs will crackle. Check the backing for loops that are worn down to the foundation. They'll soon pull out, creating bald spots on the front.

# FLOORS
## WOOD

For countless centuries, richly polished, gleaming wood floors have been a hallmark of elegant living. And rightly so. Unlike most synthetic materials, wood is inherently warm, pleasing to look at and nice to touch. And it's one of the best insulating materials there is. Woods are as different in grain, color, and texture as the trees from which they are cut. And for durability, few materials can match its toughness. Like fine silver, wood—properly cared for—simply becomes more beautiful with time.

Although our love of wood has never diminished, at one time, wood floors all but disappeared under countless square yards of wall-to-wall carpet. Recently, however, wood floors have resurfaced in all their natural beauty, and are prized more than ever in both contemporary and traditional decors.

### WHAT WOOD IS RIGHT?

All wood is beautiful. It's your personal preference that's the determining factor.

Many of the finest floors are constructed of hardwood, the product of leafbearing trees such as red or white oak and walnut. Floors made of the soft woods produced by cone-bearing trees are equally acceptable, both aesthetically and functionally. As proof, many of the random-planked pine floors laid by our ancestors have not only stood up to the passage of two centuries, but are still as attractive as ever.

Wood flooring has come a long way since the days when colonists hewed trees by hand and fitted them with pegs. Today you can select from an incredible variety of woods—with many styles, finishes, and colors—as easily as you choose carpet or resilient floor coverings.

In some cases, the most dramatic floor choice might be mellow, dark-stained oak chosen to show off a treasured Oriental rug. A pine floor is a good choice for a casual or country-style environment, sparked, perhaps, by a colorful braided or rag rug. Even parquet floors are now available pre-packaged and ready to install—a boon for the budget-minded.

### FLOOR SHOW CAST

To help you with your wood flooring decisions, here's a quick guide to some of the most popular types you're likely to find.

*Strip flooring.* This is the most widely used type of wood flooring. The strips are long, narrow boards that come tongue and grooved and end matched, in a variety of widths and thicknesses. Most floors are of 2½-inch wide strips, a standard $^{25}/_{32}$-inch thick.

*Plank flooring.* Wider than ordinary strip flooring, planks are available up to 12 inches wide and are especially effective laid in random widths. Some planked floors are plugged with wood or brass for a creative, custom-looking finish.

*Block flooring.* The name says it. This flooring is produced as a block or as a laminated block, cross-banded with plywood. When designed to look like parquet, it is called "parquetry." Use this floor for visual interest.

*Parquet floors* are made of small pieces of wood laid to produce geometric patterns such as checkerboard, herringbone, and basketweave designs. Skilled do-it-yourselfers can lay their own parquet floors made of 12x12-inch squares. Some parquet squares are available with a special foam backing for sound insulation and comfort underfoot.

### THE DIFFERENCE IN WOODS

Since most wood flooring is about equal in strength, the difference in price rests primarily on aesthetic appeal. This means, the nicer the grain and the fewer imperfections, the more costly the wood.

The best grade wood is *clear,* free of knots as the name implies. Next, come *select, No. 1 common, No. 2 common,* and, finally, *1½-foot shorts,* which are remnants from the other grades.

Before you decide on a particular grade of wood, think about the atmosphere you want. You might be willing to pay for a luxury wood floor in certain rooms, yet in others you may want the rustic feeling you get from a lesser grade wood with its character-giving imperfections.

As we've said, most wood floors are made of oak. But with improved manufacturing techniques and the refinement of veneers on hardwood plywood, other woods such as birch, beech, and pecan are beginning to be used. Some of today's newer wood floors are impregnated with special plastics to give them extra durabilty.

## YOUR PRESENT FLOOR

Don't get the idea that a wood floor is a luxury choice available only to homeowners who are building or remodeling their homes. If you have your heart set on wood, investigate your present floor. If you live in a home that was built in the 1930s or before, there's probably a hardwood floor under the carpet. Pull up a corner to see. It may not be in perfect condition, but professional refinishing may be all that's needed to recapture its beauty and character. Newer homes, in contrast, often have a softwood floor that may lend itself to a painted finish.

**1** From the planked and beamed ceiling to the honey-colored parquet floor, this cozy family room is framed in the warmth and beauty of natural wood. Here, the checkerboard parquet floor is left austerely beautiful. No area rug or soft floor covering separates the wood of the floor from the wood of the furnishings. The effect is an open, spacious area that capitalizes on the richness of natural wood grains.

Though this room is casually Colonial in its furnishings and accessories, the same floor could underscore a formal and very elegant setting as well. Parquet in this time-honored pattern would also suit a contemporary room.

**2** Wide-planked and gleaming from wall-to-wall, a wood floor enhances this wide-open and uncluttered family room. The natural wood floor, deep in tone, provides the perfect foil for a pair of unmatched Oriental rugs, and gives the sparsely furnished room a mellow feeling of warmth. Even though this floor is exposed to constant use, a polyurethane finish keeps it looking beautiful.

# FLOORS
# WOOD: HOW-TO TIPS

**W**ood is inherently tough and takes everyday use in its stride. But your wood floor is like anything else you value. If you want to keep it looking its best, it needs to be cared for properly.

## AN OUNCE OF PREVENTION

By keeping the floor as clean as possible, you eliminate the major source of surface destruction, common dirt and grit. Even the smallest particles of soil, when ground in under daily use, attack the floor by first wearing away at the wood's protective coating of wax or varnish, then at the grain itself.

Vacuuming and damp mopping are the simplest and most effective forms of wood floor maintenance. If a floor is really dirty you can scrub it, but be careful not to let water remain on the wood long enough to swell and bleach it.

## FIRST AID FOR SCRATCHES

Children, pets, and furniture sometimes are unkind to wood floor finishes. But remedies are available to help you restore your floor's beauty.

Repair any small surface scratches with steel wool and a solvent, such as cleaning fluid. Dampen the steel wool with the solvent and rub with the grain until the scratches disappear. Then rinse and refinish the spot to blend with the rest of the floor.

Major assaults on the floor may call for more thorough efforts. If the gouge is deep, sand it out, then use a brush to work wood filler into the spot. Let the filler set overnight, then sand it smooth, working with the grain. After sanding, refinish.

## REFINISHING FINESSE

Nothing makes a house feel quite as revitalized as fresh, newly finished wood floors. If you have the option, do the floors *before* you move in. It's a dusty, noisy job that requires wide open spaces to work in.

If you choose, hire a professional floor refinisher who will, with machines and crew, finish the job in a day or two. However, floor refinishing is a do-it-yourself project that's well within the capabilities of anyone who is fairly handy and relatively patient.

You'll need an upright drum sander for the open floor areas and a disc-type edger for working close to the baseboards. You can rent both these tools at hardware stores or rental firms.

Only three major steps are required to refinish a wood floor: sanding off the old finish, filling in any cracks and gouges with paste wood filler, and, finally, applying the protective finish.

If you want to change the color of the floor, apply a stain before finishing it. And, if you choose any finish other than polyurethane, you will want to apply a paste wax after the finish is completely dry.

Polyurethanes are relatively new and relatively expensive compared with more traditional varnishes and penetrating sealers. They're easy to apply and remarkably good at protecting the floor under a hard, gleaming surface.

Before you begin refinishing your floor, arm yourself with a good set of instructions on how to operate the sanders, and be sure to follow the specific directions for the stain and finish you choose.

## BLEACHING FLOORS

For sheer decorating drama, nothing can beat the sophisticated beauty of a white-bleached floor.

And although it's not impossible to bleach and finish a floor yourself, the process is tedious and the bleaching compounds are caustic. The best choice is to call in a professional who has the proper protective equipment and experience with this technique.

The bleaching procedure requires successive applications of bleaching compound, followed by sanding and neutralizing before the finishing coat is applied. Although not a simple process, its beautiful effect makes the effort worthwhile.

## PAINTED FLOORS

Paint can make the best of an ugly or badly worn wood floor. In addition, it can add a special charm all its own. New, tough deck enamels come in colors that beg to be brought indoors. Or you may use any good-quality enamel paint under a tough protective coating of polyurethane.

You needn't stop with plain paint, either. Spatter-painted floors are classics from the Early American era and are easily created with a stiff-bristled whisk broom.

If you're even slightly artistic, you can achieve such special underfoot effects as *faux* marble, original freehand designs, or patterns stenciled from traditional sources.

*Contrast is the key to decorating with effect. In this exciting living room contrasts result from playing lights against darks, starting with the floor.*

*No other floor covering choice could do what this sleek bleached wood floor does to bring out the beauty of the deep-green enameled walls.*

*In addition to providing contrast, a floor this light in color performs another special decorating job. It tends to make the room look larger and more spacious. But to capitalize on this effect, keep the floor as exposed as possible. Hiding it under area rugs or massive furniture will destroy its visually expansive characteristics.*

*Don't worry about a bleached floor's being impractical. Bleached wood, no matter how light, is easy to maintain, if protected with polyurethane.*

# FLOORS RESILIENTS

**R**esilient flooring has come out of test tubes and into our homes to create surfaces that wear like iron and look like almost any material you want. Now brick, slate, wood grains, even marble, show up in this tough and easy-on-the-budget flooring.

More than mere substitutes for natural materials, resilient sheet goods and tiles are a flexible, practical decorating material in their own right.

With modern printing, embossing, and finishing technology, resilient tiles and sheet goods now go far beyond the kitchen (where now-extinct linoleum was once prerequisite) to compliment any floor in the house. In a living room, for example, you can bring floor space up-to-date with a broad sweep of white vinyl that looks like brick or marble. Upstairs, where flagstone from a quarry would be too heavy, use its synthetic counterpart.

## EASY UPKEEP

Also thanks to modern technology, the beauty of man-made floors is more than surface deep, often outdoing the real thing in both wearability and ease of maintenance. Most resilient floors demand little more than a damp-mopping or buffing to keep their no-wax finishes looking great. And should the sheen dull with constant wear, your dealer has an acrylic-based dressing you simply apply to the dulled areas.

New developments in floor covering products and mastics make installation easy.

**1** In this country-style bedroom, what looks like a slab slate floor is actually vinyl. It simulates the color and texture of natural slate without the weight, the installation problems, or the rigid coldness of the real thing.

For a different slant on country decorating, try brick, quarry tile, wood grain, or fieldstone—all in practical vinyl.

**2** Using colorful, solid vinyl tiles, it's possible to create a custom floor such as this one. Looking for all the world like a modern painting, the floor was designed by the homeowner, but installed by a professional tile layer. The 12-inch-square tiles were cut to their specific shapes then fitted together to form the exciting floor "painting."

Using the same material and texture in various decorator colors, then keeping the walls and furnishings a non-conflicting white guaranteed success.

2

As the name implies, resilient flooring is a hard-surface covering with a bit of give and bounce. Although a high-quality resilient floor usually is a sizable investment, remember that the flooring will withstand constant use for many years and still retain its good looks.

Today's market offers a wide variety of resilient flooring, in an equally wide variety of prices. Your shopping challenge will be in narrowing the selections down to just one.

## SHEET FLOORING

Resilient flooring is available in two types: sheet goods that are sold from rolls, and individual square tiles.

Each is right for certain areas and certain applications. Both are made of vinyl, either solid or blended with other materials. (Linoleum, by the way, no longer is manufactured. You may hear dealers use the term, but what they're talking about is vinyl.)

Sheet flooring comes in a roll-like carpet, and is sold in 6-, 9-, and 12-foot widths, which lets you buy the length you need to fit your room. Although sheet flooring is almost twice as expensive as comparable grades of vinyl tiles, it is available in richer colors and in more patterns than tiles. Sheet goods also have the advantage of being nearly seamless.

With few exceptions, you can install sheet vinyl on any floor, including below-ground-level basements. You'll hear this referred to as "below-grade." Because some backings can't cope with certain conditions, be sure to consult your dealer before you buy.

Sheet flooring comes in two types: inlaid and rotovinyl.

*Inlaid vinyls* are the top of the line in sheet flooring because they are solid vinyl. The wear surface is built up, layer by layer, of tiny vinyl granules fused under heat and pressure. Inherently thick and soft, some inlaid vinyls have extra layers of foam to provide added comfort underfoot and to muffle footsteps and other noise.

Although inlaid vinyls cost considerably more than other types, they provide enough extra wear life to justify the initial investment. Like a fine Oriental rug where the surface goes all the way to the backing, in inlaid vinyl the color and pattern last until the flooring wears out completely.

Because inlaids are heavier than other resilient floorings, they are difficult to install. If you feel at all uneasy about your skills, call in a professional for any permanent installation of sheet flooring. Matching patterns and fitting around a room's irregularities is an art that often requires a professional's skill.

*Rotovinyl* floor coverings are made by a process that combines photography and printing. The use of photography makes possible realistic images of stone, brick, slate, and wood, for instance.

Once the photographic image is printed, a "wear layer" of clear vinyl or polyurethane goes on top. The thickness of the layer determines how long your rotovinyl floor will hold up. You'll want at least 10 mils of pro-

tection for reasonable quality; the most expensive rotovinyls have wear layers 25 mils thick.

Another guide to buying durable rotovinyl flooring is the amount of cushioning built in. Test by squeezing or stepping on the prospective flooring to see whether it's soft, yet firm. Next, dig in a thumbnail and check to make sure the indentation recovers.

Do-it-yourselfers will have a much easier time with rotovinyls than with heavy inlaid flooring. In fact, apartment dwellers or homeowners who expect to be on the move in the near future can merely loose-lay the flooring in place, that is, cut it to fit like a rug but not cement it down permanently.

## RESILIENT TILES

Easiest of all for the do-it-yourselfer to tackle are floor tiles. Here, you're getting color- and pattern-excitement that goes down a square at a time, rather like fitting together an easy puzzle.

To eliminate any confusion over which tiles to buy, here's a brief look at the types available.

*Solid vinyl tiles* are top-of-the-line for the same reasons inlaid vinyl is. The wear layer goes all the way through, more patterns and colors are available, and the tiles are easy to install and easy on the feet.

*Vinyl asbestos* tiles, known as "v-a" in the flooring industry, are a vast improvement over the old asphalt tiles you may remember; yet they still manage to remain moderately priced. Easy to install and long wear-

ing, v-a tiles are resistant to burns that could spoil solid vinyl. They also shrug off such other household hazards as dents, scuffing, and grease.

Other tile types include new vinyl composition floor tiles that eliminate asbestos filler and are even more resistant to wear and soil than v-a. Some asphalt, rubber, and cork tiles still remain on the market, but they offer few, if any, advantages over the newer vinyls.

Two more benefits of modern technology are the self-sticking tiles that simplify installation and new finishes that need no waxing, available on both sheet goods and tiles.

## INSTALLATION GUIDELINES

Most tiles and sheet goods can be installed over old resilient floors (except over cushioned ones). But the old floor must be in basically sound shape—that is, smooth surfaced and firmly bonded to the subfloor. Otherwise it might be necessary to cover the old flooring with underlayment (¼-inch sheets of plywood or hardboard). That extra step can cost about $5 a square yard for materials and labor over and above the price of the new floor and its installation.

The alternative is to install cushioned vinyl flooring that can go over floors in relatively poor condition. And, unless your old floor is really woebegone, you can skip laying new underlayment, too. Large holes or gouges will still have to be patched, however, for your floor to be smooth.

## RESILIENT AND HARD-SURFACE FLOORING

| Types | Characteristics | Advantages | Disadvantages | Cleanability |
|---|---|---|---|---|
| **Asphalt tile** | Porous, resists alkalis, low cost | OK on cement, below grade | Noisy, dents, needs waxing | Hurt by grease, harsh cleansers |
| **Vinyl cork tile** | Handsome, sealed surface | Quiet underfoot | Not for heavy traffic | Similar to vinyl tile |
| **Rubber tile** | Handsome, clear colors | Excellent resilience, quiet, durable | Expensive, slippery when wet, must be above grade | Resists dents and stains, hurt by strong detergents, grease |
| **Vinyl-asbestos tile** | Resists alkalis, easily installed, low cost | Durable, colorful | Not quiet or very resilient | Resists grease, easily cleaned |
| **Vinyl-cushioned sheet** | Wide range of colors, patterns, surface finishes | Superior resilience, quiet, comfortable, stain resistant | Expensive | Easily maintained, some with no-wax feature |
| **Vinyl sheet** | Wide range of colors, patterns, surface finishes | Good resilience | Moderate price | Easily maintained, some with no-wax feature |
| **Vinyl solid tile** | Often simulates natural materials | Easy to install, durable | Fair resilience | Stain resistant, easily maintained |
| **Wood** | Natural or painted | Good resilience, durable | Fair stain resistance | Easily maintained |
| **Brick, slate, quarry tiles** | Natural look, exciting shapes | Durability, beauty | No resilience | Needs waxing, good stain resistance |
| **Ceramic tile** | Colorful, many shapes | Beauty, no staining | No resilience | Clean with soap and water only |
| **Marble** | Costly, formal | Beauty | Hard underfoot, stains easily | Needs waxing, stains hard to remove |
| **Terrazzo** | Permanent, multicolored | Durable, hides soil | Limited design, permanent installation | Easily cleaned |

# FLOORS
## OTHER OPTIONS

Y ou have plenty of flooring options besides conventional coverings of carpet, vinyl, and wood. Some of the most exciting, high-fashion floors are of *non-resilient* materials—clay tile, slate, brick, marble, and terrazzo. These hard-surface floorings generally call for professional installation, and require more upkeep than other materials. However, the beauty of non-resilient floors is well worth the extra effort required.

*Clay tile* comes in two forms —quarry tile and ceramic.

*Quarry tile* is a baked clay product usually found in an unglazed form that can be installed with mastic on almost any base. It's durable, but may require a stain-resistant sealer because some tiles are very porous. Quarry tile is highly impact-resistant, but will chip if dealt a severe blow. Colors include natural shades of terra cotta, buckskin, and earth browns.

*Ceramic tile* is non-fading and very resistant to wear and heat. It is easy to clean, but as with any tile product, selection of grout is important. Porosity and physical makeup of the grout can cause maintenance problems.

*Slate* is highly stain-resistant, and is relatively easy to install. It does, however, scuff in heavy traffic areas, and needs waxing.

*Marble* floors are rare in many new homes today because installation is quite expensive. Well suited for elegant, formal settings, marble is hard underfoot, stains easily, and needs regular waxing.

*Terrazzo* is a man-made product consisting of marble or stone chips set in a binder of cement, then polished to a smooth, shiny finish in a multicolored effect. It requires a solid concrete base for installation. The finished floor is highly resistant to moisture and stain.

*Brick,* new or old, is a wonderful flooring choice for rooms with a country or rustic flavor. But as you might expect, brick floors are hard underfoot, and need waxing occasionally to look their best.

**For a something-special flooring, consider one of the many non-resilient, hard-surface materials available today.**

**1** Glazed quarry tiles are an asset in this garden room; they add to the natural outdoor mood and complement the rattan furniture. Damp mopping is all that's needed to keep waxed quarry tile looking its best.

**2** A close look at this floor reveals a cost-saving surface trick that offers dramatic results. The floor is ordinary concrete scored into squares. After the concrete was fully cured, a stain was applied and the surface sealed. The floor has all the appeal of a quarry tile surface at a fraction of the cost.

**3** Scored mosaic tiles, in pristine white, add floor-level interest to the kitchen area of this open-plan house. The subtle geometry of the tile's pattern is a nice counterpoint to the slick surfaces that cover the rest of the room.

**4** A single sweep of travertine marble gives this long hallway really elegant appeal. Once only seen in stately, formal homes, marble has found more and more contemporary applications.

3

4

# FLOORS
## MAKE YOUR OWN

**D**own through the ages, handcrafted rugs have been an important folk art in virtually every country. To join in the time-honored tradition, crochet a rag rug of your own.

Rag rugs can be a potpourri of colors or a subtle monochromatic blend of one hue. They can be round or oval, tiny hearth rugs or styles large enough to cover most of the floor. But no matter what color, shape, or size, crocheted rag rugs all offer limitless decorating possibilities.

All you need is a rag bag full of old clothes, fabric scraps or remnants. Or if your rag bag is bare, shop garage sales and thrift shops for inexpensive, usable materials. Altogether you'll need the equivalent of nine yards of 45-inch cotton or cotton-blend fabric to make a rug 3 to 4 feet in diameter. Use a size J crochet hook and the simple stitch diagrammed here.

### CROCHET A RAG RUG

Begin by cutting or tearing the fabric into strips not less than ¾ inch wide or more than 1½ inches, depending on the fabric's weight. A heavy, dense fabric, such as denim, should be torn into narrower strips; a medium weight fabric like sheets can be 1 inch wide; and lightweight cotton should be widest, 1½ inches. Just be sure to make all strips of the same fabric the same width.

Machine-stitch the strips together as shown in diagram 1 to make lengths you feel comfortable handling.

Using a size J crochet hook and your fabric "yarn," chain 6 stitches (diagram 2), and join them into a ring with a slip stitch (diagram 3). Now, in the first stitch of the ring, make a single crochet stitch (diagram 4). When completed, make another single crochet in the same stitch to increase (diagram 5). Repeat in all six stitches of the ring.

Continue single crocheting (diagram 4) increasing in every other stitch for the second row and thereafter as necessary to maintain the rag rug's circular shape and flatness. To change colors or add new strips, join a new strip to the preceding one, stitching it by hand.

Continue working in single crochet, increasing occasionally and changing colors as you choose, until the rug is the desired size.

To finish the rug, cut the last 3 or 4 yards of fabric strips narrower and narrower (down to about ⅜-inch wide at the end) so the last round of the rug naturally grows smaller and smaller.

*Worked in a palette of blues and white, this circular crocheted rug is a whorl of subtle color accenting the warm wood floor of a comfortable country dining room.*

*For nostalgic good looks as well as practicality, probably no other floor covering does what an unpretentious rag rug does. And remember, your rug is as washable as the fabric you've crocheted into it. You can launder at home any rug made of cotton or cotton blends that will fit into your washing machine.*

**1. Join strips of fabric together on the diagonal. Trim seam.**

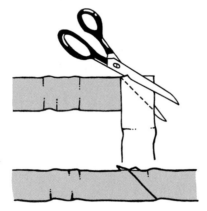

**2. Crochet a chain of six stitches.**

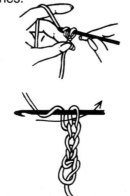

**3. Join chain into a ring with a slip stitch.**

**4. Work entire rug using a single crochet stitch, steps A–E.**

**A. Insert hook into second chain from hook, under the upper two strands.**

**B. and C. Draw up fabric.**

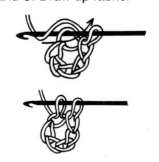

**D. Loop fabric over hook.**

**E. Draw fabric through the two loops. Insert hook into the next stitch, and repeat from Step A.**

**5. To increase, do two stitches (Diagram 4, A–E) in one loop.**

# FLOORS
## MAKE YOUR OWN

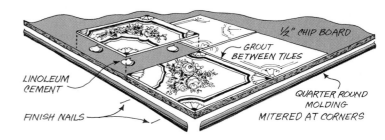

**1** You can create a *faux* flagstone floor with heavy brown wrapping paper, ordinary white glue, and polyurethane varnish. It's a mellow, natural look that's easy to achieve, simple to care for, and gentle on your budget.

**2** Not all area rugs have to be soft. Here's one that's rigid—a portable patio of ceramic tile cemented to a base of chipboard.

It gives the effect of a permanently installed tile area, but it's completely portable.

**3** Patchwork takes to the floor in this vinyl-tiled room with its inlaid "area rug." Colored tiles are cut to form an eight-point star, then set into the solid background. A crisp band of green borders this contemporary interpretation of an Early American craft.

½" CHIP BOARD

GROUT BETWEEN TILES

LINOLEUM CEMENT

FINISH NAILS

QUARTER ROUND MOLDING MITERED AT CORNERS

## FAUX FLAGSTONE

You can flatter even the most unsightly floor—and save money while you're at it—by creating a *faux* flagstone covering with inexpensive brown wrapping paper. Here's how:

**1.** First clean the floor thoroughly. Scrape off any loose paint or adhesives. Patch all cracks. Countersink any nails that may have popped up. Then sand the floor smooth.

**2.** Next tear the brown wrapping paper into irregular shapes, making them look as much like flagstone shapes as you can. Be sure to vary the sizes to give the finished floor an interesting mixture of shapes and sizes. Remember, tearing the paper is important to the overall effect. If you resort to scissors, you won't have the soft, ragged edges your paper shapes need to carry off their charade as flagstones.

**3.** Combine white household glue and water in equal parts. Brush or roll the mixture onto one side of the paper. Position your "stones" on the floor, making sure the shapes are overlapped and the entire floor surface is covered.

**4.** Smooth out any wrinkles, using a rolling pin or a wallpaper seam roller.

**5.** To protect the pretend flagstones, finish the floor with four or five coats of polyurethane varnish. Let each coat dry overnight before applying the next. Although this building-up of the top coat takes time, it's worth the effort. When finished properly, your fake flagstones will wear almost as well as the real thing, even in a kitchen.

## PRACTICAL AND PORTABLE

You *can* take it with you, when it's a movable area "rug" made of ceramic tiles cemented to a chipboard base.

Use this idea to brighten one end of an apartment living room, or to set off a dining area in a dramatic way. You'll find this floor is as practical as it is portable, since ceramic tiles are impervious to nearly everything and clean with a damp mop. And this "rug" is a snap to make. Study the diagram on the opposite page, then read through the instructions below.

**1.** To make this ceramic unit, cut ½-inch chipboard to fit the size of the finished tile surface. Figure the measurements of the tiles, allowing space between the tiles for grout. The chipboard should be flush with the outside edges of the tiles.

**2.** Lay the tiles on top of the chipboard, leaving space between them to add the grout. (Grout seals the crack between the tiles and gives your tile topper the look of a permanently installed floor.)

**3.** When all tiles are positioned, remove them one at a time and use vinyl adhesive to glue them to the board base. After all tiles are cemented in place, add the grout, following the manufacturer's instructions. You'll need a rubber trowel or squeegee to work the grout into the joints. Wash off excess grout with a wet sponge.

**4.** Attach quarter-round molding to the edges of the chipboard, mitering the corners for a neat finished look. Stain or leave natural, then varnish.

## PATCHWORK PATTERNS

Here's a practical, do-it-yourself way to dress a floor with a custom design—at the same cost as a plain vinyl tile floor. And you don't have to be either an artist or a tile expert to copy this patchwork-style floor. All you need is a straightedge, a sharp linoleum knife, and a steady hand to cut all the pieces that are necessary for this bright, vinyl tile "rug."

The brightly colored pattern shown here incorporates an assortment of 12-inch-square vinyl tiles in white, green, red, yellow, and orange.

To make the pieces you need for patchwork patterns, start by cutting each of the large floor tiles into four 6-inch squares.

Then cut these smaller squares into thirds, forming two right-angle triangles and one isosceles triangle. (Your cutting job should be much easier if you warm the tile for a few minutes in the oven.)

The next step is to arrange the colored "patches" and background pieces to create an octagonal star design. Finally, form a solid-color border around your new "area rug." Install the tiles with an adhesive, just as you would install any vinyl tile floor.

To create your own pattern, start by drawing the patchwork design on some graph paper, then cut tiles into the geometric shapes that you need to execute your one-of-a-kind patchwork-style design.

# FLOORS
## MAKE YOUR OWN

**1** A tight budget needn't prevent you from creating an unusual, eye-catching floor treatment. Here inexpensive vinyl tile squares were combined with colorful vinyl feature strips to give an ordinary entryway decorative panache. The strips are available by the yard through resilient flooring dealers. What you get with this do-it-yourself tile and feature strip technique is an expensive custom look—in any color combination you choose—at a fraction of the cost. Note how the horizontal placement of the feature strips makes the entry look wider than it really is. A reflective Mylar wall covering behind the chrome-and-glass étagère amplifies the widening effect. If you decide to try a similar floor treatment, make sure the tile squares and the feature strips are the same thickness.

**2** A plebian building material takes on a smart, sophisticated new guise as a floor covering in this tract-home hallway. The bold geometric effect was created by teaming inexpensive particleboard, cut into 23-inch squares, with 2-inch strips of plain pine lumber. To produce this two-toned natural pattern, the squares of particleboard were stained a deep chocolate brown. Common nails and mastic hold the squares and the unstained pine spacers in place on the floor. Two coats of exterior-strength polyurethane varnish went on as a sealer. Without this protection, the unsealed flooring would be quite porous and susceptible to stains. The use of pine molding for the baseboards and simple frame around the door adds to the natural contemporary look.

228

**Stencils, insets, and resilient strips offer wonderfully decorative solutions for floors in need of something new.**

**3** Long ago, stenciled floors were the poor man's answer to the rugs he couldn't afford. Today, however, stenciled floors are a flooring favorite for different reasons. The look is unique and especially à propos for period settings like the Colonial dining room shown here. The simple geometric pattern on the floor emulates the look of marble and slate, but a bold choice of colors livens the look for today. If you'd like to make your own stenciled floor, look to art stores and specialty paint shops for precut stencil designs. Materials needed include acrylic paints, a special short-bristled brush, plus polyurethane varnish to protect the finished floor.

When stenciling your floor, follow these tips for best results.
• Use masking tape to keep the stencil from slipping as you work.
• "Pounce" the brush on newspaper to remove excess paint that will overload the stencil.
• Hold the brush straight up and down, and dab on the paint from the edges of the stencil to the middle.
• Remove the stencil very carefully after each application to avoid smears.
• Before you tape it down for the next repeat, check to make sure no paint has run under the back edge of the stencil. Both standard paper stencils and clear plastic ones can stand up to repeated use and wipings.

3

# LIGHTING

If you haven't familiarized yourself in a while with the latest in lighting—products and techniques —you're in for a pleasant surprise. Advances in product design and technology now make it possible for all of us to become lighting magicians— enhancing our homes not just with lamps and light to see by, but with truly dramatic effect. By a mere flick of a switch or push of a button, you can manipulate light in myriad ways. With the right application of light, you can make an average room look spectacular, hide flaws, and emphasize assets. The proper lighting balance can enhance color. It can make small rooms suddenly look spacious and make overly large rooms take on an air of intimacy. But besides its various decorative applications, lighting has its practical side, too. Today the selection of versatile, convenient, and highly flexible lighting products on the market is greater than ever before.

# LIGHTING
## THE BASICS

In all too many homes, lighting is an afterthought in the decorating plans—and it shows. People often buy lamps and other lighting fixtures primarily for their appearance, giving little regard to their lighting capabilities and effects. As a result, many otherwise well-designed rooms fall flat when it comes to lighting.

Poorly lighted rooms are generally lacking in variety. Although a single light source technically provides enough illumination for an average-size room, it's the light from a number of sources (and how it's distributed around the room) that creates the most interesting and pleasant effect. Nothing is duller than the shadow-free look of an evenly lit space.

Lighting has three basic roles—general, task, and accent (or purely decorative). As a rule, a house's main living areas benefit from a flexible combination of all three types of lighting.

*General lighting* provides comfortable background illumination. It is glare-free indirect lighting that bounces off walls and ceilings, and comes closest to approximating daylight. General lighting fixtures should have dimmers (easy-to-install controls that let you vary the intensity of light) for those times when you want a softer, mood-enhancing glow.

*Task lighting* provides much needed illumination for specific activities such as writing, reading, and cooking. Directed at the task at hand, this localized light is shadow-free and easy on the eyes.

*Accent lighting* can add sparkle and drama from a number of sources. Use recessed lights or track lights on the ceiling to wash a wall with soft colors, spotlight a painting, or highlight textures. Uplights on the floor, shining through foliage, cast intriguing shadows on the wall or ceiling. Other lighting well suited for enhancing space, creating a mood, or showing off objects include well-placed wall fixtures, hanging lamps, and portable lamps.

You might want to experiment with the effects of accent lighting before purchasing major fixtures. To do this, try placing inexpensive hardware store clamp-on lamps in unexpected places. Fit these lamps with different bulbs (clear, pink, silvered reflector, and different wattages, for example) to help you see how a mixture of intensities and colors can add new drama and interest to your surroundings.

*Lighting is a major contributor to the exciting look of this contemporary living room. Uplights, placed on the floor, dramatize two tall plants and cast interesting shadows on the ceiling. Two chrome canister lights show off the colors of the large painting and emphasize its importance in the decorating scheme. The unusual "egg" lamp in the fireplace is as much a piece of sculpture as it is a source of light. A floor lamp and a table lamp provide specific light for reading.*

# LIGHTING
## WHAT TO USE WHERE

**H**ow you use a room should also determine the type and the placement of your light sources. First, decide what you want lighting to do, then look for fixtures that will suit your specific needs.

Once you've worked out the floor plans, furniture arrangements, and color schemes, make a room-by-room lighting plan, keeping in mind comfort, safety, and aesthetics.

### LIGHT FOR MANY MOODS

The living room often is the most interesting room in the house to plan because it requires an assortment of flexible lighting. For relaxing, entertaining, sitting and talking, or watching television, use soft general lighting from indirect sources, such as wall washers, uplights, portable lamps, or cove, cornice, or valance lighting.

For reading or other close work you will want good direct light from downlights, spotlights, or lamps.

This is also the room for some dramatic accent lighting focused on collections of glass, sculpture, paintings, and even plants. Light your treasures with spotlights fixed to the ceiling or walls, or with tiny portable spotlights that stand on a shelf or that are part of a mini-track screwed into a shelf. If you have a wall of paintings, wash it with a clear soft light, or highlight each piece of art with its own precise beam of light to make the grouping a focal point of the room.

As a safety measure, be sure some of the lighting units are on switch controls at the doorways to all rooms.

1

The family room, recreation room, or den calls for almost the same type of lighting as is used in the living room. However, these rooms should have more emphasis on direct lighting for game tables and hobby areas.

Table tennis, billiard, and pool tables must have enough light to cover the wide area. You'll need at least two recessed fixtures with 150-watt bulbs, or two shielded fluorescent fixtures.

### DRAMATIC DINING

In the dining room, the table itself is the focus and thus, deserves proper lighting.

Dining room chandeliers are decorative and elegant, but if they have bright bulbs, the light will be glaring. Instead, use a dimmer on a chandelier, and supplement with other sources, such as valance or cove lighting, or well-placed recessed lighting that will bathe the ta-

bletop or a nearby serving counter in soft light.

The dining room is another place where dramatic accent lighting very often can be extremely effective. Beam a spotlight or a wash of light on a cabinet filled with glass for a truly sparkling effect. Or you can place uplights beneath plants or sculpture to cast interesting shadows. With a glass-top table, an uplight beneath gives an interesting effect.

## SPECIAL LIGHTING FOR BEDROOMS

General lighting in a bedroom should be both soft for relaxing, and bright for cleaning and other tasks. Again, dimmers are the answer.

If the room is shared, have separate bed lights for each person. Small adjustable spotlights or miniature track lights attached to the wall, above the headboard, will beam the light where you want it.

Lighting at a dressing table should be at each side of the mirror, rather than above it. And here, as well as at full-length dressing mirrors, light should shine on the person, rather than on the glass.

An older child's room needs almost the same type of lighting as the master bedroom. Include a glare-free desk light; a fluorescent light is suitable, it it's properly shielded.

It's wise to take a few special safety precautions in a younger child's room. All outlets should be childproof, and lighting fixtures should be out of reach. Ceiling or wall fixtures are a better choice than portable lamps, which can be easily broken during play.

### LIGHT WHERE YOU NEED IT

For general lighting in the kitchen you have a wide choice of fixtures—anything from a luminous ceiling or lighted ceiling panels to cove lighting, recessed ceiling lights, track lights, or a pendant fixture. But general ceiling lights will force you to work in your own shadow,

unless they are teamed with other lights under wall cabinets and over cooking units.

For a small bathroom, the mirror lights may serve both for general and direct lighting. But if the room is large, you will need added general lighting.

To light the mirror, use soft white bulbs or fluorescent tubes in "natural white" or "deluxe warm" white; they are the most flattering to skin tones.

A light above the mirror will cast misleading shadows, so place lights at each side of the mirror, or frame it with strips of light bulbs (clear or frosted).

### PASSAGEWAYS

The front hallway should be a dramatic and welcoming entry to your home. And, with a little help from proper lighting, it will be. Actually, any hallway in the house can be beautifully transformed with light.

If the hallway is large, consider using a series of downlights, with spots and wall washers to light up a picture wall, a collection, plants, or beautiful paneling. A sparkling chandelier can add elegance to a small formal entryway or hall.

Stairways must be properly lighted for safety. Recessed fixtures, such as louvered theater-type "aisle lights" at the sides of the stairs or downlights from the ceiling will light the steps safely, and provide drama, too.

If the stairs turn a corner, be sure the landing is well lighted. Also be sure switches are at top and bottom of stairs, so you won't have to ascend or descend in the dark.

2

**1** Standard picture lights brighten this dining room and serve as accent lights over the "art," which is actually the changing reflections framed in mirrors hung above the buffet. Shades on the lights are slim cylinders, which can be rotated full circle to give a choice of lighting effects. When shade openings are turned to the wall, they create a halolike spread of light. When food is arranged on the buffet, the shade openings are turned downward so the light will focus on the food.

**2** Turn a dark hallway into an interesting picture gallery with one long run of track lights. When you change the items on display, simply reposition the canisters for the best effect. In this hallway, two lamps spotlight the wall-hung art, and a third focuses on the closet. The unusual effect at the end of the hall is achieved with a pinup light. Attached to the wall behind a cluster of eucalyptus leaves, the light casts interesting shadows on the wall and ceiling.

**D**espite the rising popularity of other types of lighting, classic table and floor lamps will always be popular. Their simple lines and pleasing shapes make them right at home in both traditional and contemporary decors.

Because lamps are decorative accessories as well as sources of light, they should be chosen with special care. Size and proportion are especially important in choosing a table lamp. The most common mistake is to buy a lamp that is too big and too tall for the table it rests on. Ornate, statuesque lamps may be fine for a high-ceiling room in a mansion, but they're out of place in the average home. A small, squat lamp will look equally absurd if placed on a large table. And overly ornate lamps are out of place, regardless of their size.

It's also necessary to consider good proportion when you choose a lamp shade. One that is too big or too small, too deep or shallow, for the base will make the lamp look top heavy and out of scale. Choose a lamp with a shade that doesn't overpower the base.

Numerous good-looking floor lamps are available today, ranging in style from old-fashioned classics to sleekly contemporary concepts. Small-scale pharmacy lamps, torchères, and swing-arm styles are ideal for use in today's small spaces. Some floor lamps are adjustable in height and have movable fixtures to shed light exactly where you need it.

A floor lamp should have a sturdy base that doesn't wobble, and, as with table lamps, the lines should be simple and well proportioned.

## CLEANING SHADES

Cleaning a lamp shade is a simple task that doesn't take long. Most are washable, but some high-quality shades must be dry cleaned.

Many of the less expensive shades, however, are not washable, as they are put together with glue or staples. Water will dissolve the glue and rust the staples. Water also will damage painted surfaces or glued-on trim.

If the fabric shade is stitched to the frame, you probably can wash it. Brush off any dust, then swish the shade in a deep bath of lukewarm suds. Rinse in clear lukewarm water, then blot off any excess water with a clean towel. Dry fast, but not in sunlight.

For shades made of cloth, paper, or other materials pressed between two layers of plastic, sponge off lightly with detergent and water to clean them.

To clean a fiber glass or plastic shade, just dip the shade in soapy water, rinse, and hang to dry.

If you have a parchment shade, do not try to clean it in a water bath. Parchment shades are fine-quality paper that has oil rubbed into it, then coloring added. Wipe the surface gently with wallpaper cleaner, a damp cloth, or art gum eraser.

If a high-quality lamp shade becomes badly soiled or stained, consult a professional dry cleaner.

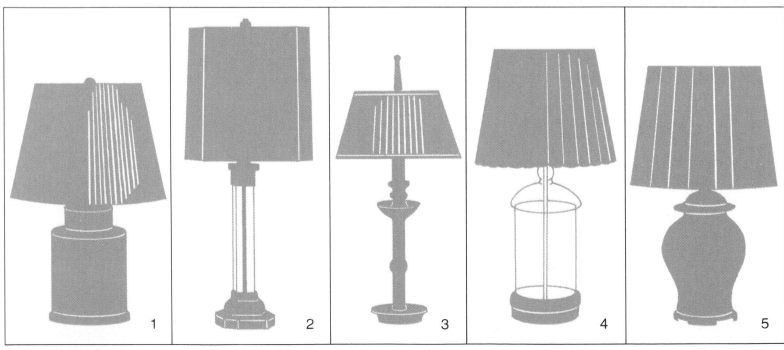

**1** Many classic lamp designs are fashioned after ordinary objects. Such is the case of the **canister** lamp. The bases were originally containers for coffee, tea, and tobacco.

**2** The stately **column base** lamp can vary in height, and is usually brass or glass.

**3** Today, topped with a light bulb instead of a taper, the **candlestick** lamp is a cherished classic in traditional homes.

**4** Today's versions of **apothecary jars** make attractive lamp bases. The jars were originally used by pharmacists to store medicines.

**5** Widely popular **ginger jar** lamps are decorated with many varied designs to enhance all styles of decor.

**6** A **swing-arm** lamp—also called a bridge lamp—is an excellent choice for a game table because light can be focused over a wide surface.

**7** A **torchère** (torch-shaped) lamp is an elegant uplight designed to bounce light off the ceiling for decorative effect.

**8** When space is too limited for a lamp table, a **table/floor lamp** with its own attached table surface is a practical solution.

**9** **Akari lanterns** are hand-crafted of paper and bamboo. These light sculptures emit a soft glow.

**10** The goose-necked **pharmacy lamp** offers great lighting flexibility for reading or conversation.

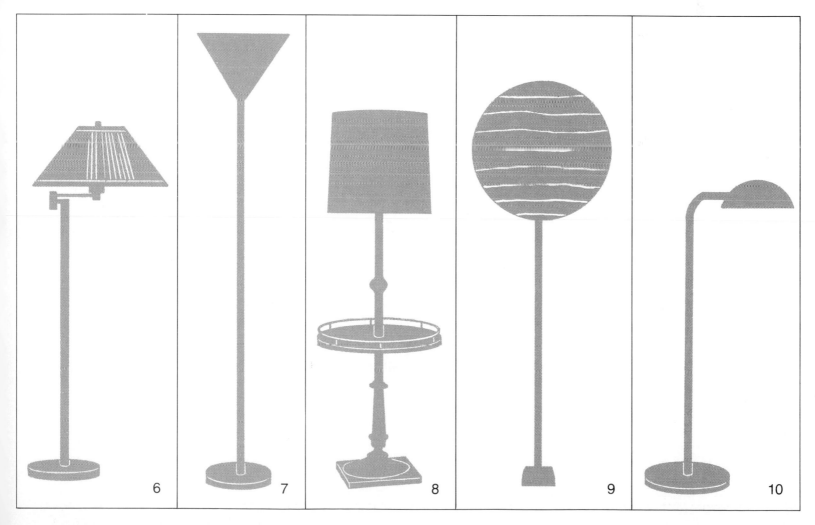

6    7    8    9    10

# LIGHTING/BULBS AND FIXTURES

How do you select efficient lighting from the bewildering array of bulbs and tubes on the market? Actually, the basics of lighting efficiency are simple.

The amount of light a bulb or fluorescent tube produces is measured in lumens. Watts are the units of power needed to make the bulb or tube work properly.

The wattage is marked on the light bulb and on the fluorescent tube. Information about the average lumens and the life of the bulb also is on the incandescent bulb package, but it may not be on fluorescent lighting packages.

Bulbs or tubes that give the greatest number of lumens per watt, or the most light for the least power, are most efficient.

## INCANDESCENT BULBS

Today's incandescent light bulb operates on the same principle it did when Thomas Edison introduced it. When electrical current goes through a small filament wire, the filament heats up enough to become incandescent, that is, light emitting.

Although the basic principle remains the same, almost everything else about the light bulb has changed. Today, there are low-voltage bulbs, as well as new shapes—streamlined tubes, flame shapes, and bowls that look like sculpture.

The filaments may be straight, corrugated, coiled or double-coiled, or in flat ribbon shapes, making the light look like a candle flame, flickering firelight, or bright daylight.

The various types and shapes of bulbs (also called lamps by the industry) are indicated by letters. The "A-bulb" is the common round light bulb that has been used for years. A cone-shaped bulb is a "C-bulb," and a flame-shaped one is an "F-bulb."

The "R-lamps" are reflector lamps; the most familiar in this category are R-20, R-30, and R-40. The numbers indicate not the wattage, but the degrees of beam spread. "PAR-lamps" (parabolic aluminized reflector) have an enclosure of heavy glass and originally were designed for outdoor use. Both R- and PAR-lamps have built-in reflecting surfaces, which throw the light out in a definite direction, and in beams ranging from very narrow spots to wide floods of light.

Ordinary incandescent light bulbs (from 60 to 150 watts) should last from 750 to 2,500 hours. Generally, the low wattage sizes have longer lives than high wattage ones.

Long-life bulbs that last from 2,500 to 3,500 hours are good for hard-to-reach places, but they cost more and deliver less light than standard bulbs for the amount of electricity used.

## FLUORESCENT LIGHTS

A fluorescent tube will give three to four times as much light per watt as an incandescent bulb. It also will last longer.

The number of times a fluorescent light is turned on and off affects its life. The longer the light burns each time you turn it on, the longer the tube will last. Your initial cost for fluorescent lights will include the price of the fixture.

**1** A fluorescent light is a tubular electrical discharge bulb, in which light results when a stream of electrons acts on mercury vapor in the tube.

Fluorescent tubes are available in lengths ranging from 6 to 96 inches and in several colors. Most flattering to the complexion is the "deluxe warm white" fluorescent. In addition to straight tubes are circular and U-shaped ones.

**2** Here are some of the different bulbs available in lighting shops. *Back row from left to right:* standard incandescent light bulb, exterior PAR flood lamp (sealed to be weather-resistant), an interior reflector flood lamp, and a decorative 40-watt globe bulb (frequently used in striplights). *Front row from left to right:* Glare-free silvered-bowl bulb, clear bulb, mini reflector spotlight for small fixtures, regular-size reflector bulb. (The amount of silvering on reflector bulbs determines the width of the beam spread. Thus, you can create a wider or narrower beam by your choice of bulb.)

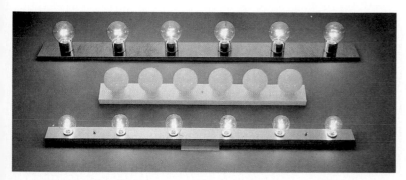

1 Striplights got their start in movie stars' dressing rooms. These lights still are great for wrapping around three sides of a dressing room mirror. However, striplighting can go in other areas in the home, too. The strips come in painted colors and in chrome and brass, and are attachable to ceiling or wall, either out in plain sight or behind baffles to give reflected light.

2 If your room is looking dreary, try some uplights to give it a lift. You can buy several types of plug-in canister lights that will spread light upward to dramatize sculpture, paintings, or the texture of the wall. Cans come in various sizes, and some are angled to flood light in directions other than up. For glare-free lighting, direct the light away from the line of sight.

3 Portable spotlights are versatile and practical; many are moderately priced. The three in the back row can attach to a ceiling or wall, or be placed on a flat surface to light plants. Use the tiny circular spots in front to accent art work. For a dictionary that needs lighting, the long-legged spot would be a good choice.

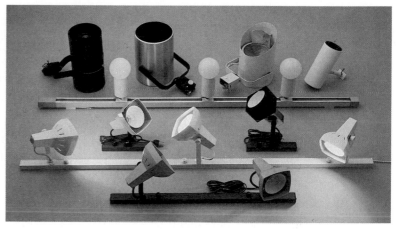

4 Track lighting's greatest asset is its versatility. It is similar to recessed lighting on wall or ceiling, but more economical and easier to install, since a strip of pre-wired track affixed to the ceiling either is connected to existing wiring there or is simply plugged into a wall outlet.

Some of the modules for track lighting are pictured above. Also called lamp holders, canisters, or cans (though they're not all can-shaped now), the modules can join to the track in seconds. The spheres, cylinders, squares and spotlights are available in several sizes and colors. The lights can pivot up and down or can rotate from side to side to put the light where you want it.

Some tracks may be on one circuit, which means all the lights have to be used at once, unless you climb on a stepladder and switch a lamp off. More sophisticated systems give you a choice of circuits, so you can turn on different sets of lights independently using only the wall switches.

You can use regular light bulbs in a track system, but this won't project light on a specific area.

For special effects, consider wide-beam floodlights, narrower-beam spotlights, or some of the newer low-voltage pinspots, which produce an even narrower beam of very intense light to highlight small objects. Many track systems also include energy-saving low-voltage wall washers for general illumination, add-on colored filters, perforated metal filters that create "light paintings" on a wall, and framing projectors with adjustable louvers to precisely control the size and shape of the light beam.

# LIGHTING
## SPECIAL EFFECTS

Dramatic and mood-setting lighting has come out of the theater and into the home. Decorative lighting is as important today as the selection of colors and furnishings.

For many years, theater electricians have created illusions and made settings romantic, eerie, or more exciting simply by manipulating the lighting. And in disco's heyday, lighting achieved its hypnotic, mood-making effects through combinations of color and motion.

Now, all these special lighting techniques are moving into residential lighting, and are creating changeable, exciting home environments.

Although the average home may not be quite ready for nightclub lighting; there are many places where you can use special effects.

The most practical way to add this type of lighting is with a well-placed mixture of uplights and downlights, spotlights, and floodlights all used to highlight the architecture or the furnishings and help create the mood you want.

### DOWNLIGHTS

Downlights are installed on the ceiling or wall to cast pools of light below. The lighting fixtures may be recessed into the ceiling or in tracks. The light itself, depending on the choice of fixture and bulb, can be diffused over a large area or pinpointed to a tiny circle.

Recessed lights give a spacious, uncluttered look, and work well on extra-low ceilings, where surface-mounted lights might be obtrusive. Recessed lights, however, are more expensive to install and use. It takes twice as many recessed units to do the same job as surface-mounted fixtures.

Plug-mold strips, a variation of track lights, come in several lengths. The strips can run around the edge of a room behind a concealing baffle. They will take any type of bulb, with the use of a socket adapter, and are good for flooding a wall with light.

For help in determining your recessed or track lighting needs, go to an electrical store, which probably has a lighting engineer on its staff. Explain what you want to the expert, who will help you decide on the placement and the number of lights needed.

### UPLIGHTS

Uplights are downlights in reverse. Canisters that stand on the floor, behind a piece of furniture, or on a table are available in round or square shapes and in different sizes. The uplights produce dramatic patterns of light and shadows. These versatile fixtures can be beamed up at a sculpture or can be focused on a painting.

Placed on the floor in a corner, an uplight bounces reflected light off the ceiling and into the room for restful general lighting.

### SPOTLIGHTS AND FLOODLIGHTS

Spots and floods both work on the same principle—to throw circles of light on a wall or object. They can be freestanding,

1

fitted into ceilings or track systems, or attached to the wall.

Mounted on the ceiling, a wall-washing floodlight will provide a large expanse of light, literally bathing an entire wall or window evenly from top to bottom. This is a good way to light a large display of paintings.

Some spotlights simply give strong direct light. Others, internally silvered or with built-in reflectors, throw the light exactly where you want it.

One specialized device, called a "framing projector," is a precise spotlighting unit that has adjustable louvers to cut

**Special lighting effects can add new dimensions to your decor by high-lighting and accenting your treasures.**

the light beams to the exact size and shape of a painting, tapestry, or other object. These are costly, but extremely effective for dramatic results.

You can shine a spotlight on almost any object to cast enchanting shadows on the wall. A floor-based rotating wheel of colored lenses or a colored filter fitted over a floor canister or track light module can wash a room or a wall with light.

Remember that incandescent lights convert more energy to heat than to light, so they can damage a painting or the finish on fine furniture (if placed too close or used too long). To lessen the likelihood of damage, you can equip a spotlight with a low-voltage transformer that will let it cast a narrow beam, while using far less electricity. This requires low-voltage bulbs available at most lighting stores. You will get the same amount of light, with less heat.

## LIGHTS BEHIND BAFFLES

Shielding lights behind baffles is an effective way of introducing indirect lighting.

A cornice often runs from wall to wall and is attached to the ceiling, allowing the light to flow downward only.

The cornice idea can be used lower on the wall, as a shelf. Add a translucent glass top to the shelf for a luminous effect.

Cove lighting, also attached to the ceiling, is open at the top and directs light upward onto the ceiling.

Valance lighting, often used over draped windows or on window walls, lets light flow up on the ceiling, as well as shine

2

down the wall or windows. You can buy inexpensive prefabricated systems with prewired fixtures for cove, cornice, or valance lighting.

Or, make your own valance out of plywood and simply attach ordinary fluorescent tube fixtures to the back.

**1** To create your own shadowy original art on an empty wall, buy a large piece of canvas, stretched on a frame. Hang it up and arrange feathery greenery in front of it. Place two uplights on the floor behind the sofa to shine on the leaves and throw light and shadows onto the canvas.

**2** Theatrical lighting adds drama to this small bedroom. Daytime sunshine from the skylight is replaced at night by starlike sparkles from clear globes on a track. The bed seems to float above lights beneath the platform. Built-in lighting on the headboard can be brightened or dimmed.

241

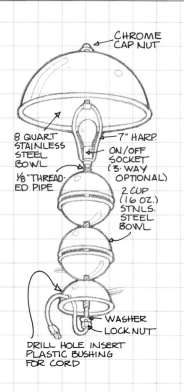

CHROME CAP NUT

8 QUART STAINLESS STEEL BOWL

7" HARP.

ON/OFF SOCKET (3-WAY OPTIONAL)

⅛" THREADED PIPE

2 CUP (16 OZ.) STNLS. STEEL BOWL

WASHER
LOCK NUT

DRILL HOLE INSERT PLASTIC BUSHING FOR CORD

**1** Lamps made from items found in the attic, basement, kitchen, or even a potting shed can provide good lighting, as well as add a whimsical, decorative touch to your home. You can make a lamp from just about anything simply by linking objects together on a threaded pipe (purchased at a hardware store), then attaching a harp and socket at the top. The cord goes through the hollow pipe and comes out at the bottom.

Here a stack of stainless steel bowls creates a shiny contemporary lamp. To make a lamp like this, set the bowls right side up on a piece of scrap wood, then drill a hole in the bottom of each bowl, using an electric drill with a ⅜-inch bit. To keep the drill point in place, make a little dent in the bottom of the bowl with a center punch and hammer. Also drill a hole near the bottom of one bowl for the cord to exit. Cut the rod to the right length, and slip it through the holes in the bowls. Screw parts together; wire.

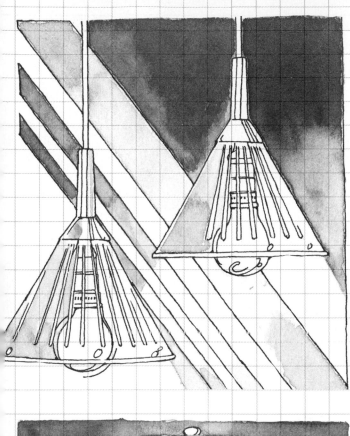

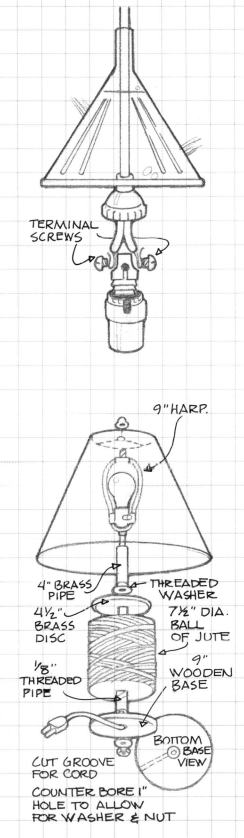

**2** These classy-looking glass hang-ups are nothing more than ordinary kitchen funnels, plus standard glass hardware. You can find such funnels in several sizes at hardware or cookware shops. If you don't want glass, pick a shiny tin funnel, or lacquer the tin in a favorite color.

Choose a lamp cord to match the lamp, and use a colored bulb for an unusual effect.

To make the lamps, simply string all the pieces together, as shown at right, attaching the wires to the terminal screws of the socket. Then wire the lamps to a ceiling fixture, or add a plug and light switch, and run the cord from the ceiling to a nearby wall outlet.

TERMINAL SCREWS

**3** This lamp went together on the same type of threaded pipe as the lamp made with the silvery bowls. The pipe was wrapped with jute macrame cord, purchased at a craft store. A round wooden plaque is the base. Everything is stacked and screwed on the length of threaded pipe.

To make the base sit flat, use an electric drill with a 1-inch spade bit to counterbore a depression in the bottom of the wood disc. Then, drill a hole clear through with a ⅜-inch bit. This way, the nut and washer at the bottom of the rod nestle right into the base. Cut the groove for the wire with a knife.

Look for the Underwriters Laboratory (UL) seal on all fixtures you buy to be sure they meet the National Electrical Code for safety, materials, wiring, and fabrication.

9" HARP.

4" BRASS PIPE

THREADED WASHER

4½" BRASS DISC

7½" DIA. BALL OF JUTE

⅛" THREADED PIPE

9" WOODEN BASE

BOTTOM BASE VIEW

CUT GROOVE FOR CORD

COUNTER BORE 1" HOLE TO ALLOW FOR WASHER & NUT

243

# LIGHTING/DO-IT-YOURSELF IDEAS

With a few basic tools and some do-it-yourself skills, you can create your own ingenious lighting. You can even build recessed and track lighting at a fraction of the cost of conventional models.

Put your imagination to work and scour your house for items to convert to lighting use. Visit your neighborhood hardware store, lumberyard, tile works, or business supply company. The number of items available for only a few dollars will surprise you.

Galvanized pails and stovepipe elbows, old rooftop ventilators, food graters, cans of all sizes, flowerpots and baskets are only a few of the things you can use as decorative lighting fixtures.

If the lights will be some distance from electrical outlets, buy long electrical cords. An extension cord may not be strong enough, especially if you attach the wire to the wall or ceiling or thread it through a hole in the wall.

Don't twist wires or pull them too tight. Fixtures should never hang from the electrical wiring, but from a chain or other support.

Always use low-wattage bulbs under do-it-yourself shades, unless you line the interiors with asbestos. And remember to paint interiors of pails, tiles, stovepipes and such items white, so they will reflect light efficiently. For ceiling fixtures, wiring will be less conspicuous if it is painted to match the walls, run from the fixture to the ceiling molding, and then down to the wall outlet.

**1** Ready-made lighting fixtures may be beyond your budget, but with a little work and imagination, you can create clever lighting effects that cost very little.

This versatile accent light is simple and inexpensive to make. Buy a terra-cotta drainage tile from a building supply store. Then cut a plywood disc to fit inside the tile and nail the disc to a larger disc that will form the lamp's base. Route the wire through a hole in the base, attach a line switch and plug. Screw in a mini spot bulb, plug in the light and presto: You have an instant accent light.

You can use the same basic idea with clay half tiles and turn them into reflector lights for the yard. Simply bury the flared end in the ground, so the opening faces the area you want to light. Use outdoor stake-type fixtures and landscape around the tiles with pebbles.

TERRA COTTA DRAINAGE TILE

SPOT BULB

PLYWOOD BASE

LINE SWITCH

**2** Make this louvered light column to brighten up a dreary corner of a room. The louvers let you angle the light any way you wish. Form the column by nailing together four shutter panels with movable louvers. Then cut a piece of lumber to fit the top and enclose the base. Wire the sockets in series and route the wire through a hole cut in the base. Attach a line switch and plug to the cord, then screw in low-wattage bulbs. For variation of the idea, substitute latticework or panels of pressed wood grillwork you find at the lumberyard. Shine colored lights through the open-worked panels for a festive effect.

**3** Downlights are ideal for tabletop illumination, especially if the table doubles as a work surface for homework or sewing. Store-bought recessed downlights often are costly to install, but you can create a similar, less-expensive, effect with this facsimile. Simply build a plywood box to fit around mini spots. First cut a ½-inch plywood top to the desired size. Space, attach, and wire porcelain sockets to this piece. Cut a second piece the same size to serve as the lower surface. Cut circular holes in this piece to correspond to the position of the sockets on the top board. Cut side pieces. Glue and nail pieces together. Line the interior with foil and asbestos to dissipate heat. Wire unit to ceiling outlet and attach it to the ceiling. Drill vent holes in end panels and attach them.

LINE SWITCH

VENT HOLES

ALUMINUM FOIL & ASBESTOS SHEETING

CEILING

½" PLYWOOD

MINI-SPOT

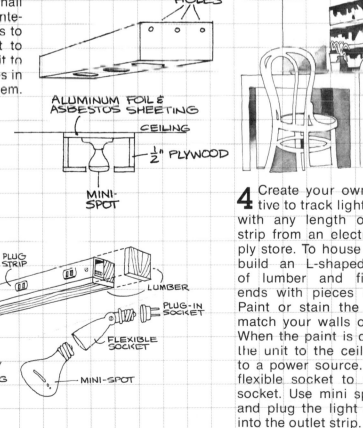

PLUG STRIP

6"

LUMBER

PLUG-IN SOCKET

FLEXIBLE SOCKET

SCREW TO CEILING

TO POWER

MINI-SPOT

**4** Create your own alternative to track lighting. Start with any length of plug-in strip from an electrical supply store. To house the strip, build an L-shaped bracket of lumber and finish the ends with pieces of wood. Paint or stain the wood to match your walls or ceiling. When the paint is dry, screw the unit to the ceiling close to a power source. Attach a flexible socket to a plug-in socket. Use mini spot bulbs and plug the light assembly into the outlet strip.

# STORAGE

It's a rare homeowner who isn't plagued with the where-to-put-it problem. Despite our best efforts to clear our surroundings of unnecessary clutter and confusion, our possessions—like rabbits—continue to proliferate. Often, we delude ourselves by thinking the only solution to an overstuffed house is buying a bigger one. But if you've ever moved from a smallish house to a larger one, you know it's only a matter of time (usually a short time) before the new place is bulging at the seams. So what is the solution to the seemingly ever-present storage squeeze? Generally, it's not a matter of finding more space, but making better use of the space you already have. This requires analyzing every room in the house for its particular storage needs. On the next pages, we'll offer you sensible solutions to help you hide, disguise, display, or (if you're an incurable pack rat) conveniently stash away your myriad belongings.

# STORAGE
## STORAGE PARADE

**A**t its very simplest, storage means a place to put all those items of various sizes, shapes, and uses that embellish our lives. But anyone who has lived with a current-day version of "Fibber McGee's closet" realizes the storage situation is anything but simple. The one good thing about the storage dilemma is there are nearly as many different types of storage available as there are categories of items that need housing.

To arrive at the best storage for your home, start by inventorying everything that will need to be stored in each "living center." Kitchens and baths present obvious storage needs. But also look closely at the family room or living room. Check the bedrooms. Where do you keep books, records, games, camera equipment, sports gear—all those things that are no good if you can't find them when you want them?

Next, figure out *why* you want to store them. Naturally, storage protects the item itself and makes it easier to find (usually). But are there other reasons? Do you need to free up floor space, unclutter the room, even add a decorating focal point to the area? The right type of storage can do all those things while still organizing the oddments in your life.

If you're still thinking storage means a cabinet or bookshelves, then you need to check some of your other storage options: modular pieces, bunching or stacking units, freestanding storage systems, multi-functional units, and open storage, to name a few.

Next, match what you have to store with the type of storage that best suits your needs, taste, and budget.

### MODULAR STORAGE GROWS WITH NEEDS

A single storage unit or a whole wall—you have your choice when you're dealing with a modular storage system. Modulars offer you add-on convenience, perfect for a family with growing needs and a limited budget. In addition to the opportunity for expansion, a modular system lets you rearrange your storage furniture from room to room or from home to home. Most lines of modular furniture offer a wide selection of pieces including doored cabinets, open units with or without shelves, and, often, special-function pieces, such as a desk, bar, or storage case for a stereo system or TV.

Often modular storage systems feature finished-on-the-back units that let you use your storage pieces perpendicular to the wall or as a freestanding room divider. This arrangement often improves your traffic pattern, saves wall space, and organizes your storage all at the same time.

*Storage wall systems such as this Scandinavian-inspired one offer unlimited opportunities to add on, rearrange, and store nearly anything. With total systems like this, you can create a bookcase, a display or storage cabinet (with or without drawers and glass inserts), a stereo center, an office, a bar—even a wardrobe.*

# STORAGE
## STORAGE PARADE

How you go about consolidating your belongings is a matter of personal choice. Here are more options.

### FURNITURE ALTERNATIVES

Most furniture stores display a large selection of single pieces, in every design style, that can help ease your storage squeeze.

Check out a hutch or Welsh dresser for additional dining room or kitchen storage. Bakers' racks are versatile storage pieces that can handle everything from books to plants. And, spacious, attractive armoires can relieve the pressure in bulging clothes closets.

### OPEN OR CLOSED

Americans usually think what's stored should be practical and, therefore, hidden, and what's displayed should be decorative. Europeans, on the other hand, tend to store everything —no matter how pedestrian— on open shelves where items are easily reachable. There's a strong following for both open and closed storage; the decision is yours. But you should keep some things in mind when making the choice.

If what's stored behind closed doors is never used because it's "out of sight, out of mind," then open storage could put those little-used games or vacation photos back into circulation. Still, if open storage of infrequently used items is going to turn them into dust collectors, then a closed cabinet is a better idea after all.

**1** This kitchen with its European accent on storage puts items at their point of use and recruits open shelves to store what most kitchens stash away behind doors. Notice how the wall-hung shelf unit even spans the recessed window, letting cookware and serving pieces function as a window treatment. A small shelf stores spices just above the baking center and food preparation area. Cooking utensils hang beside the range; pots and pans over the work counter. If you can avoid it, don't hang cookware over the range where it will accumulate cooking grease.

**2** Metal shelf units and plastic vegetable bins form practical, colorful storage as well as a room divider in this combination nursery and home office. By facing the vegetable bins in two directions, the unit serves both areas with at-your-fingertips storage of everyday needs.

**3** Two closets at the end of this family room provide all the storage space needed for tableware, serving pieces, glassware, even some books and toys. There's plenty of shelf space for items that need to be reached quickly and easily or that are attractive enough to serve as decorative accessories. Less glamorous items are discreetly filed away in attractive wooden boxes or woven baskets, so the whole area looks good enough to become the focal point of the room. The original closet lights help draw attention to this functionally decorative (or decoratively functional) storage wall.

# STORAGE
## SPACE STRETCHERS

**S**pace, like storage itself, is never in excess. So when planning storage, one big challenge is cramming as much storing capacity as possible into whatever spareable space you have. For space-stretching storage, try these suggestions.

If it's floor space that's at a premium, find what is available and build on it. Use stacking, ready-made storage units that go up the wall to use formerly wasted space. Or construct a slim, to-the-ceiling storage wall. To avoid using any floor space at all, try wall-mounting storage cabinets or shelves.

In a bedroom, you can gain plenty of extra storage space by replacing bedside tables with shelving units that flank the bed or span the entire headboard area.

### PUT WASTED SPACE TO WORK

A room with odd niches or jogs in the wall is a natural for a storage addition. Turn this unused space into an area of shelves or a built-in wall unit.

Another place to add built-in storage is the space that surrounds a window or fireplace. With the proper design, what is basically a functioning storage piece can become a decorative focal point in the room.

When planning built-in storage units, make sure the design is compatible with the rest of your decor. The addition of similar molding or wood trim, for instance, can give what normally is a utilitarian storage unit an architectural look and meld it into your room's overall decorating scheme.

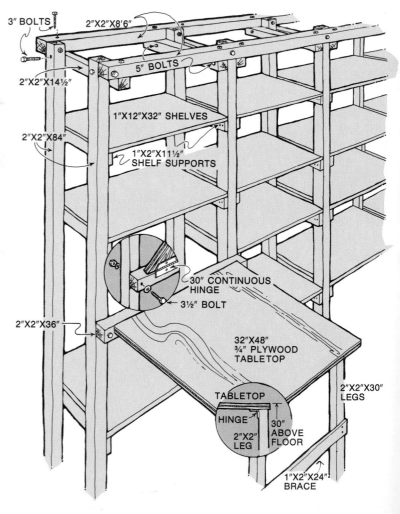

3" BOLTS

2"X2"X8'6"

5" BOLTS

2"X2"X14½"

1"X12"X32" SHELVES

2"X2"X84"

1"X2"X11½" SHELF SUPPORTS

30" CONTINUOUS HINGE

3½" BOLT

2"X2"X36"

32"X48" ¾" PLYWOOD TABLETOP

2"X2"X30" LEGS

TABLETOP

HINGE

2"X2" LEG

30" ABOVE FLOOR

1"X2"X24" BRACE

Storage is meant to con-
serve space, not waste it.
Here are some solutions
for maximum storage in
minimum space.

2

**1** This build-it-yourself wall unit
not only stores books, tapes,
magazines, and serving pieces,
but provides a fold-down, space-
saving dining table as well.

To build this unit, bolt together
the four uprights (7-foot 2x2s and
14½-inch 2x2 crosspieces). Clamp
the pieces in position, drill through
both at once, and bolt them
together before removing the
clamps. Then bolt on lengthwise
6½-foot 2x2s.

Stand the whole unit in place
and nail on the 1x2 shelf supports,
spacing the shelves at the best
height for your belongings.

Make the table legs and hinge
them to the tabletop. Bolt the 2x2
crosspieces on the front of the unit.
Use a continuous hinge to attach
the table. Screw a cabinet catch
under one of the shelves to keep
the tabletop folded up. Cover the
top with plastic laminate (attach it
with contact cement) or paint.

**2,3** Attic space provides hard-
working storage areas,
but this attic offers both stashing
space *and* work surface in this
sewing-storage center. Here,
a wall of cabinets houses
a 64x35-inch table that flips forward to hold a portable sewing
machine. When not in use the table
tucks neatly into its storage niche
behind the interestingly planked
doors. Behind the table is a roomy
shelf for sewing notions.

3

# STORAGE
## BOOKS AND RECORDS

**B**ooks and records, besides the obvious pleasure they bring readers and listeners, offer decorative appeal, too. Books, with their colorful jackets, are particularly attractive and add life and warmth to any room setting.

### PLANNING THE LIBRARY

Estimating shelf space is the first step in housing a book collection. You can figure eight to 10 hardbound books per running foot of shelf space. Paperbacks, of course, will take much less room.

When planning book storage, allow space for books that will be added. Unless you're an incurable bibliophile, remember: Wall-to-wall books are less attractive than groups of books interspersed with decorative accessories or collectibles.

### ON THE SHELF

The size of your present (or anticipated) book collection will help you determine the type of shelving system you need. If you can't bear to part with books, even after you've read them, plan for as large a book storage place as space will allow. Use a wall at one end of a room and build permanent shelves. Or use wall space for shelf standards and brackets that let you add additional sections as your library grows.

If you're an occasional reader with only a few favorite books, a piece of storage furniture may meet your needs. You'll find bookcases in a variety of furniture styles, sizes, and price ranges.

All books should be stored above floor level and away from heat ducts. Really valuable books should be kept in glass-fronted bookcases for extra protection.

### RECORD STORAGE

Records should be stored vertically to prevent warping. With a large collection, plan a rigid vertical divider between every group of 50 or so records. This lets you flip through a manageable size selection without having to handle an entire collection in one row. Make sure records and tapes are kept well away from heat sources and, if possible, store them near your stereo or tape deck.

Book and record collections are never static, so planning for their storage means designing with an eye to expansion. These ideas may help you plan your own library.

**1** Designed to showcase art objects and travel mementos as well as books, this natural pine shelf unit is as handsome as it is functional. To obtain a stunning semi-gloss finish, the shelves were sanded and sealed 10 times. A trio of ceiling lights are angled to dramatize the shelf system and the objects within.

**2** When looking for space to put your books, don't forget to exercise "air rights." Here, bookshelves hang high on the walls to open up the area below and define the space-saving arrangement of day beds. Painted brown, purple, and black, the shelves are a decorative as well as serviceable addition to the room. Adjustable lamps provide good illumination.

**3** Tapes and records, along with a tape recorder and an amplifier, are all within easy reach in this built-in unit made from ¾-inch plywood. The unit is housed in a once-wasted niche at the foot of a stair landing. Shelves are faced with 1x2s. The turntable is secured in the base of the unit.

**4** This sturdy storage unit is designed to take heavy loads. It's made up of a series of shelves and "fins" fabricated of ½x1½-inch spacers covered with ½ inch particleboard. Fins attach directly to wall studs for extra strength.

The design of the "fins" gives this heavy-duty unit a light, up-off-the-floor look and at the same time avoids obstructing the sight line to the clerestory windows above it. Painting the unit the same color as the walls also tends to minimize its size and massiveness.

# STORAGE
## SAVE-MONEY IDEAS

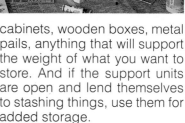

**1** **2**

**T**he need for storage is no respector of financial status. So if you find yourself with a skimpy budget and a bulging closet, here's help.

Saving money starts with preventing waste, which in turn starts with having a good storage plan in mind. After you've tossed out everything you don't need, survey what's left to store. Then keep these basic facts in mind: Everything you store has to be put some*place, on* something or *in* something.

### INEXPENSIVE SPACE

Look for tag ends of space that aren't already used for something else. In your search, look under beds, under furniture, and on the back of doors. Think about shelves that span windows (either above or in front of them). Figure out ways to use space between top cabinets

and the kitchen counter. Several handy storage units that attach under cabinets are available in discount or hardware stores.

Don't forget the space up around the ceiling of a room. Engineer a high-up shelf and store items in decorated cardboard cartons, wooden boxes, baskets, ice cream containers, even attractive shopping bags.

### STORAGE: A PUT-UP JOB

Hanging items that need storing often solves two problems: where to put an item and how to get at it easily. Good old-fashioned pegboard is still a reliable and inexpensive way to hang anything hangable. But other "hang-ups" can also aid in storage. A trip to the hardware store can produce everything from cup hooks for hanging

small items to bicycle hangers for larger things. Garden departments stock wall-mounted hangers for hose and outdoor items. These are versatile helpers for inside storage, too. Even some hangers designed for plants can convert to holders for a variety of non-gardening paraphernalia. Just because a piece of hardware was planned for installation in a ceiling, don't let that stop you from using it on a wall, or vice versa.

If you plan to store your possessions in containers of some sort, you still need to solve the "put-up" problem. Low-cost metal shelving is usually your best bet for housing storage containers. Shelf standards and brackets run a close second in popularity. Existing shelves are great, but if your home doesn't have them, improvise some by laying long boards on bricks, tiles, file

cabinets, wooden boxes, metal pails, anything that will support the weight of what you want to store. And if the support units are open and lend themselves to stashing things, use them for added storage.

### CONTAINERS

Storage containers run from the fancy (and costly) to the standard (and less expensive). But you can find some extremely decorative and imaginative containers that cost you next to nothing. For starters, try hunting down caches such as ice cream cartons (usually giveaways), milk carriers (get dairy rejects), and sturdy cardboard boxes (liquor stores are good sources). Check the housewares department of grocery or discount stores for plastic items such as vegetable bins, laundry baskets, and dishpans.

**1** This storage desk is every bit as efficient as it's stacked up to be. It's an assemblage of a 24-inch-wide door and six flue liners. Your building supply dealer is the source for both components.

The flue liners used here are 13x24x8½-inches high, so a stack of three brings the desk top to a comfortable height. If you want the desk surface higher, simply insert wooden spacers between or below the flue liners.

Each flue liner becomes a convenient cubbyhole in which to store anything you'd normally store in a desk drawer. Just outfit the liners with shallow baskets or trays to keep contents in order.

No fancy finishing is needed for this storage desk. The clay of the flue liners and the natural wood of the door are both perfectly in keeping with the relaxed, informal look of today's most popular decorating trends.

**2** Here's the scoop on a storage unit that's free. It's a simple-to-assemble pyramid of ice cream containers, available at your local ice cream parlor. No fastening, gluing, or building is involved in creating this unit. All you do is place two bricks on the floor to keep the end cartons from rolling, then stack as many containers as you need.

For all-round versatility in inexpensive storage, few things are as effective as these sturdy cardboard cartons. You can use them just about anywhere in your home to hold tools, garden equipment, cleaning supplies, toys, and sewing equipment.

**3** Pegboard can transform an empty wall into a fully functioning storage unit. And depending on what you're hanging on the pegboard, you may very well be creating a focal point wall at the same time.

Here, a pegboard wall in the dining room becomes a display place and storage area for attractive trivets, serving pieces, cookware, and molds.

To create a wall like this, frame the area with 1x2s then attach the pegboard to the framing strips. This technique holds the pegboard out away from the base wall so hanging hooks can be inserted. Paint your storage wall the color of the background wall to make it nearly invisible. Or, if you prefer your storage area as a decorative accent, paint the pegboard a contrasting color.

**4** Metal shelving units, once categorized as "industrial," now are perfectly at home anywhere, including the family room. Here, a striking focal point results from placing a white shelf unit between two windows and lighting it dramatically. Books, plants, television, and decorative accessories all find their way onto these heavy-duty, but eminently affordable, shelves.

Shelf units such as this one come in two standard heights and in several decorator colors. However, if your decorating scheme calls for something more unusual, spray paint will produce the exact shade you want. Prices may vary slightly, depending on your retail source, but dollar for dollar, few investments give you more versatile or practical storage. Although these metal shelf units come knocked down, assembly is easy, and all materials except screwdriver and elbow grease are furnished.

# STORAGE
## STORAGE PROJECTS

Customized storage is an excellent way to get precisely what you need where you need it. Depending on your talent, time, and budget, you can design and build storage yourself, or hire a carpenter or contractor to do it for you.

Every inch of available space is usable when you're building specialized storage. Whether customizing existing space in a closet or cabinet, or designing and building a self-contained storage piece for a specific purpose, you can tailor space to meet your exact needs.

A build-it-yourself storage project has another advantage. It lets you combine a variety of functions into one piece. Maybe you'd like to include a bar within a wine storage area, or a desk in a bookshelf unit. Space for a record player or tape deck is a good addition to a storage area for your music library. Providing this extra convenience is no problem at all when you build your own storage.

### BUILD INTO UNUSED SPACE

Only storage you build yourself can make use of all those little bits of unused space every house has. If you're handy with a hammer and saw, look for space between studs, at the top of stair landings, between top cabinets and counter tops, and around doors, windows, fireplaces, beds, or sinks. Another advantage of customized storage is you can use space all the way to the ceiling—an asset that ready-made storage pieces generally don't offer.

### FREESTANDING STORAGE

Freestanding storage units can do more than stash things. They can serve as room dividers and directors of traffic patterns. Freestanding units also can be used to create living spaces that didn't exist previously.

For instance, an out-into-the-room storage unit can let enough square footage secede from the living room to be turned into a full-fledged dining area with space to store table linen, serving pieces, and flatware. To create a home office in a family room, you can build a freestanding unit that separates the two spaces and stores your office gear. Or try the same thing in a bedroom where you want to create a sewing or crafts center, or gain more space for clothes.

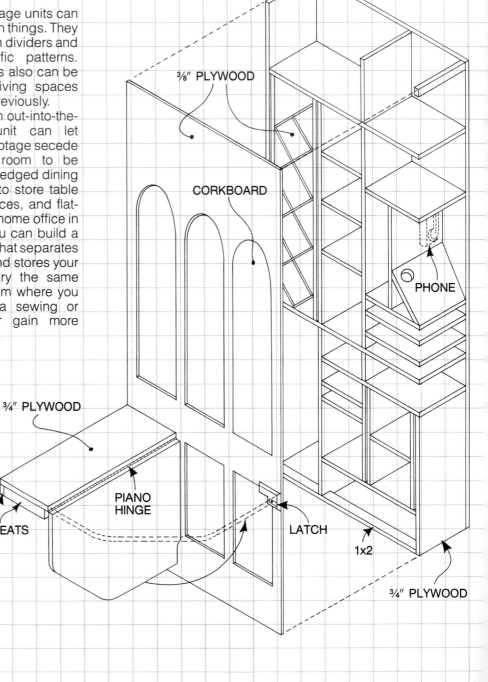

³⁄₈" PLYWOOD

CORKBOARD

PHONE

¾" PLYWOOD

PIANO HINGE

CLEATS

LATCH

1x2

¾" PLYWOOD

When you have specific storage needs, nothing outdoes customized units you can design and build yourself. Here are ideas to get you started.

## MULTIPURPOSE KITCHEN STORAGE

A corner of your kitchen may give you that extra storage space you need. Our storage unit illustrated here puts unused space to work as a wine rack, telephone and message center, cook book library, even a flip-up table that serves as a home office, snack counter, or additional work surface. This handy swing-up-and-swing-down tabletop also can be part of an off-season radiator cover-up. During the heating season, the table stays in its "up" position, secured by a latch at the corner of the main unit. In summer months, the table can swing down to cover the dormant radiator. A piano hinge joins the tabletop to the shelf which rests on cleats and bridges the space between the big storage unit and adjacent counter tops.

Most of this unit is built from ¾-inch plywood. However, you'll need only ⅜-inch plywood for the arched cut-out side and for the slats that outfit the wine rack. Plan to trim your built in unit with ceiling and baseboard molding that matches the rest of the room. That's the difference between an intentional, architectural look and a storage unit that looks like an afterthought.

Our illustration is meant only as a starting place for your storage-design ideas. Each area requires specific dimensions and each family has specific storage requirements. So use our storage tower as inspiration, then alter it to suit your own needs and your kitchen's space.

# STORAGE
## STORAGE PROJECTS

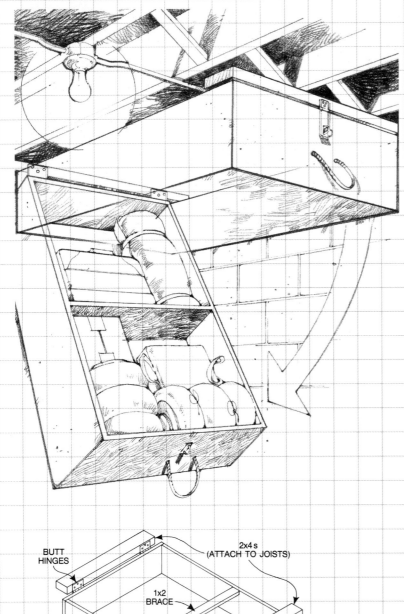

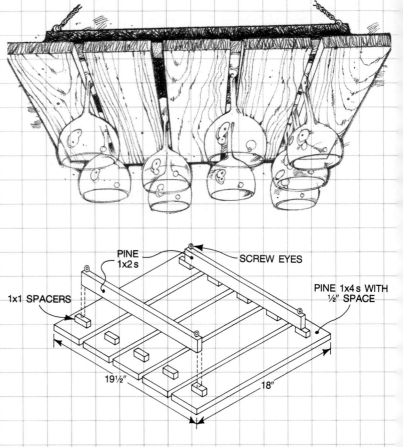

PINE 1x2s — SCREW EYES

1x1 SPACERS

PINE 1x4s WITH ½" SPACE

19½"

18"

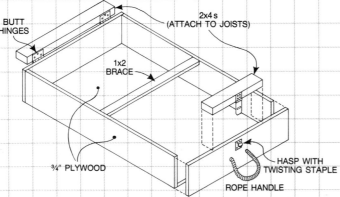

BUTT HINGES

2x4s (ATTACH TO JOISTS)

1x2 BRACE

¾" PLYWOOD

HASP WITH TWISTING STAPLE

ROPE HANDLE

## DROP-DOWN STORAGE BOX

Your garage or basement can net you an extra allotment of storage space if you're handy enough to build a box. A simple plywood box and some elementary engineering outfits an unfinished ceiling area with this swing-down storage box, perfect for sleeping bags, luggage, or other bulky, but lightweight, seasonal items you use only occasionally.

Following the exploded-view illustration at left, build a basic box out of ¾-inch plywood and nail a 1x2 across the middle for stability. Drill holes in one end panel and then insert a piece of sturdy rope to form a handle for the unit.

Next, nail 2x4 anchor boards to the ceiling joists, then hang the box by installing a pair of 3-inch butt hinges at one end and a hasp closure with a twisting staple at the opposite end. This convenient storage locker fits snug to the ceiling joists and up out of the way, making use of space good for very little else. It's a simple matter to undo the latch and let the box swing down so you can retrieve the stored item you need.

With a little workshop experience, you can create customized storage that accommodates exactly what you have to store, the amount of space you have, and your budget.

PINE 1x8s
¾" PLYWOOD
4"
4"R. 24"
2½"R.
8"
PINE 1x4
¾" PLYWOOD
30"
3"
15"R.
20"
18"

## STEMWARE STORAGE

A ceiling-hung rack not only attractively stores stemware but also conveniently puts goblets and wineglasses within easy reach at serving time.

Our stemware rack is 18x19½ inches, designed to accommodate 16 wineglasses, but you can easily adapt these measurements to fit however many (or few) glasses you have to store. The construction is the same, regardless of the overall size of the unit.

Cut the unit's runners from pine 1x4s. The crosspieces are 1x2s with 1x1 spacers used to separate the runners from the crosspieces, allowing space for the stemware's bases to slip easily along the runners.

Use easy screw-and-glue construction to assemble the stemware rack, spacing the runners ½ inch apart. Finish the unit with a coat of satin varnish. Or, if you prefer, stain the unit to match existing wood in your room, then finish with at least two coats of varnish.

To install your stemware rack, use eye screws in the crosspieces, then use a decorative chain to suspend the rack from the ceiling. For more rigidity, screw one end of the rack into a wall, then suspend the opposite end by a chain.

## STUDY CENTER

A desk-and-book unit is a welcome addition to nearly any room of your home. In a kitchen, the study center's shelves, pigeonholes, and work surface provide plenty of room for storing cook books, keeping track of household bills, and planning menus. In a youngster's room, a unit like this may even improve study habits. At least it would organize study materials.

These units, made of ¾-inch plywood and pine boards, measure 30 inches wide. The desk is 20 inches high and 18 inches deep, and the top shelving unit is 24 inches high and 8 inches deep. If you can't spare 30 inches in width, slim down the dimensions to your available space.

Cut plywood to form the desk surfaces and the shaped ends of both units. Saw and sand the remaining pieces from pine 1x4s and 1x8s. Assemble each section with simple butt joints, glued and nailed. Countersink the nailheads and fill before finishing. Prime and paint the plywood parts. Brush clear varnish on the rest, or paint the shelves to match or contrast with the uprights.

Attach the desk and book storage units to the wall, using cleats. For an adult, the desk surface should be 30 inches above the floor. If you're installing the work center in a child's room, make the necessary adjustment in the height of the units to suit the child.

# STORAGE
## STORAGE PROJECTS

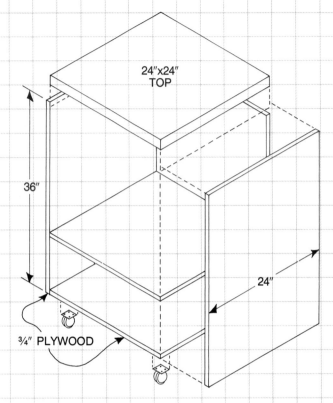

24"x24"
TOP

36"

24"

¾" PLYWOOD

### ROLL-AROUND MICROWAVE CART

This microwave storage cart gives you two bonuses: additional work surface and roll-around convenience. Build the 2x2x3-foot cart from ¾-inch plywood, leaving a 1-inch vent opening along the back of the microwave shelf. Paint the sides and shelves of the cart. Then fashion an easy-clean work surface by adhering plastic laminate to the top shelf, using contact cement. If you want a butcher-block type work surface, substitute a block top for the plywood one.

The knife holder is a sandwich of ⅛-inch hardboard strips

⅛" HARDBOARD STRIPS

5½"

9"

PINE
1x6 s

5"

clamped and glued between lengths of pine 1x6s. Leave spaces between hardboard strips to act as knife slots. Screw a pine base onto the 5½x5x9-inch unit.

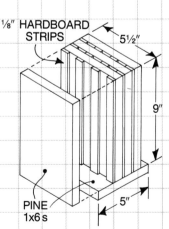

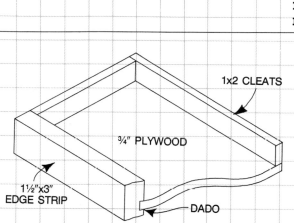

1x2 CLEATS

¾" PLYWOOD

1½"x3" EDGE STRIP

DADO

## OVERHEAD CATCHALL

This handy unit makes use of that last foot or so of space up near the ceiling. It's space that, in most rooms, goes unused; yet it can be converted into a shelf for storing a lot of bulky, lightweight items.

To build this storage tray, nail 1x2 cleats to the wall. Preassemble the edge strip and plywood shelf, then screw the plywood to the bottoms of the cleats. Nail both ends of the edge strip into the ends of the side cleats.

If your shelf is going to span more than 10 feet of wall, support it at the midpoint by attaching a decorative chain to the edgestrip and the ceiling.

Treat this catchall storage unit as part of the wall or as a decorative feature. To make it less conspicuous, finish it the same as the surrounding walls. If walls are papered, paper your shelf as well. To make the shelf a decorative accent, paint it a contrasting color. Or stain and varnish it for a warm wood finish.

To organize your conglomeration of odds and ends, stash them inside good-looking baskets or boxes. For a colorful contemporary look, use plastic bins to consolidate items.

# FINISHING TOUCHES

It's the small touches that have the most effect on a decorating scheme. Accessories, art, and objects of all kinds are what give a room its essential character and élan. Since accessories are the most personal part of decorating, they should be chosen with care and displayed to advantage. The point is not to fill up empty wall and table spaces with a haphazard mélange of "things," but rather to choose accent items that will reflect your personality and give you pleasure for years to come. And accessories needn't be equated with one-of-a-kind antiques. Something as simple as a colorful unframed poster, a bunch of daisies in a bowl, or a display of children's art work can add character to a room at little cost.

# FINISHING TOUCHES
## ACCESSORIES

**B**ecause accessories reflect so much of their owners' personalities, they become doubly important as decorating elements. Room accents deserve the same care in selection as any other furnishings.

To best understand the importance of accessories, look carefully at the homes you most admire and the rooms you feel most comfortable in. Mentally strip away the accents and visualize how bare and bland these rooms would look. Without accessories of some kind, nothing humanizes a room and gives it warmth.

Because choosing accessories is such a personal matter, no one can really do the job for you. Certainly, you can get ideas from others—friends, retail stores, magazines—but in the long run, it's best to rely on your own judgment. Pick and choose your accessories carefully to achieve your own special look.

## COMPATABILITY COUNTS

Unless you are one of those rare people who can artfully combine seemingly unrelated objects, it's best to strive for some degree of visual unity. If, for instance, your living room is formal, you'll be wise to steer clear of rustic collectibles that will make the room look discordant. Beautiful, delicate porcelains would be equally ill at ease in a casual family room.

But let us hasten to add, design unity doesn't require that accents be all of a kind or period. A room that looks too pat, too contrived is boring at best. Don't be afraid to intro-

duce an element of surprise; several antiques in an otherwise contemporary scheme, for example, will add the kind of counterpoint that memorable rooms are made of.

Some accessories—such as lamps, clocks, mirrors, pillows, vases, and ashtrays—serve a practical purpose. Others—such as art, sculpture, pottery, plants and many collections—are strictly decorative. Still other objects cross the line and function in both roles. Lavish the same care on choosing each type.

All accessories, whether they are personal treasures or objects chosen for special effect, should fit compatibly into your decorating scheme. The items should relate in some way to your color plan and the overall mood of the room.

## GETTING PERSONAL

Just where does one find all the mementos and treasures that give a room its special stamp? Books, music, and art are logical starters. Then look to the things you are fondest of (but may not have considered as "accessories"). An old crockery pitcher, a gift from a friend, a favorite scarf (framed), fresh flowers from your garden—all can lend a personal quality to your home when they hold a special meaning for you.

A grouping of family photographs, framed similarly for unity, or memorabilia from your vacations are other ways to add your signature to a room. Put personal collections that you have lovingly gathered through the years on display, so they

can be appreciated and enjoyed by others as well.

## PLACEMENT IS PARAMOUNT

As in all other areas of decorating, scale, balance, and proper proportion are important in arranging accessories. And, accessories can help bring the proportions of an entire room into balance. Large pieces can contribute visual weight to a decorating scheme. You can use a large painting, poster, or an indoor tree, for instance, to balance a weighty piece of furniture or big window elsewhere in the room.

A first consideration in placing accessories is deciding between "clutter versus clean." (And the more clutter, the more maintenance.) If your room is small, this may influence your decision. You'll probably want to use a minimum of accents, preferably small in scale. Another alternative is to choose only one or two large pieces for dramatic effect.

If you opt to surround yourself with collectibles for a cozy, cluttered look, remember that even clutter (or perhaps *especially* clutter) needs to be controlled. Arranging objects in a single grouping is almost mandatory because one major arrangement is about all a small room can take.

Shelves or wall storage allow you to combine many and diverse accessories to form a focal point. If the objects are arranged with an eye to balance and unity, you can create this focal point in a small room without giving it an overcrowded

look. Color and theme coordination are helpful in any arrangement. This can keep accessories from competing with each other, even when they are quite different in design.

## TABLETOP TREATMENTS

First of all, decide whether your tabletop accessories will be seen in the round or from one side, and group them accordingly. Your arrangement should be attractive from every angle.

And, practically speaking, if the same tabletop is to be used for dropping off a coffee cup, an ashtray, or plate of fruit and cheese, leave room to accommodate these extras without destroying your design.

Try combining a lonely single item with a flattering companion or two, such as a small statue with a leafy green plant or a book. Generally, odd numbers of accessories make a more interesting group than even numbers do.

*Here's a classic example of accessories that blend perfectly into the room setting. The bare window frames a collection of colorful antique glass bottles. Perfect complements on the old drop-leaf table are a lamp made from a piece of old pottery, a pitcher filled with garden flowers, and some Shaker boxes, all set on a small antique rug.*

2

3

**1** An entire wall devoted to art
and accessories can be
especially effective. Planning is
the key to an eye-catching display
wall like this one. Note that all
prints are grouped by subject
matter and that each group is
matted and framed differently.
Smaller accessory items, like the
collection of seashells placed
under the pictures of shells, add
interest and variety. Larger objects
nest on the lower shelves to form a
visual anchor for the display. A
subtle gray background color
enhances the pieces individually
and unifies the entire wall into a
cohesive grouping. Shelves are
set on adjustable brackets,
making it possible to accommodate new accessories or art work
of varying sizes.

**2** Patience pays off when you
want to accessorize a room in
a particular period or style. This
Early American setting gets its
appeal from a few special objects
carefully chosen to enhance the
country theme. The old rocking
horse and antique weathervane
took time to find, but the wait was
worth the whimsy these accessories bring to the room. At
the same time, these pieces
provide needed height to balance
the tall bookcase. The mellow
old trunk and the clusters of
collectibles radiate a charm and
character most often found only in
rooms that have evolved slowly
with time.

**3** When it comes to adding
sparkle to a scheme, glass
is a beautiful cut above other
accessories. Clear glass has a
fire-and-ice beauty impossible to
duplicate. Collections of it are
ideal for small spaces because,
like glass-top tables, they visually
take up less space. This display of
crystal—each piece a work of art
in its own right—illustrates the
charm of juxtaposition: mixing old
heirlooms with up-to-the-minute
designs. Here, the effect is
enhanced by the presence of an
old-fashioned lamp set on a
contemporary glass table.

# FINISHING TOUCHES
## ACCESSORIES

1

2

3

**1** If you have a penchant for provincial, then indulge it in a way both pretty and practical. Here, a pine cupboard displays accessories meant to be used as well as admired. A clay cooker, copper pans, and other accents add warmth to the blue-and-white china and glassware.

**2** With a little help from you, down-to-earth objects can make delightfully decorative accents. Here, a cluster of old daisy-filled milk bottles becomes a refreshing centerpiece. Much more at home than a contrived floral arrangement, the grouping complements the antique table. A collection of old Mason jars adds extra color and interest to the built-in sideboard.

**3** Restraint is the key to accessorizing a contemporary setting like this one. The simplicity of the all-white scheme has been carefully punctuated with a few well-chosen items of interest—an elephant sculpture, a round glass bowl filled with irises, and a colorful quilt that is actually a mattress pad to which seaming and iron-on tape have been artfully applied. Stacked pillows provide extra seating.

Accessorizing any room means living with the things you love and displaying them to best advantage. Here are some thought-starting suggestions on how to show off your favorite things with style, once you've gathered them together.

• To help you in your selections, first ask yourself what your room needs most: color, texture, drama, or something to augment other furnishings and help fill in bare spots.

• If you have a potpourri of collectibles and don't know what to do with them, try picking a theme to pull them together. Unlikely objects can be completely compatible when they have a common denominator such as color, shape, style, or function. For added interest, try to vary the texture, shape, and scale of your one-of-a-kind items.

• Some of your treasures may come in such "small packages" that they can get lost, decoratively, when they're scattered around the room. Put them together tastefully and they'll receive the attention they deserve. For instance, colorful seashells gain importance when displayed in a wicker basket or a miniature curio cabinet.

• Consider everything as a potential accessory. Costumes of yesteryear, for instance, can be stuffed, pinned to a fabric mat, shadow boxed, and hung on the wall, museum-fashion. Old magazine covers or menus can form a collage. A collection of marbles becomes a centerpiece when placed in a clear glass bowl. Old hats can be

4

hung on the wall, or scarves beautifully framed.

• A classic way to handle a group of inexpensive and unrelated prints is to mat them all in the same distinctive color and frame them in inexpensive matching frames.

• Be adventurous in your groupings (and don't be afraid to inject a touch of humor). Some of the most unexpected combinations prove the most effective. And when you need fill-in items to complete an arrangement, look to accents that

blend compatibly with almost anything—for example, bowls, boxes, books, and both fresh and dried flowers.

• Living, growing plants, besides being a joy to have around, can make substantial contributions to any decorating scheme. Leafy foliage helps soften the linear lines of walls and furniture shapes. Give green plants the status they deserve and just watch them form a living screen or divider, spark an uninteresting window, or fill a bare corner with greenery.

4 Sometimes, it's not what you do, but what you don't do that puts a special stamp on a room. This window, instead of being covered with curtains, has been used, shadow-box fashion, as a showcase for two antique weathervanes and a bushy plant. Shelves hold a collection of books and bibelots. On the floor, an Oriental rug underscores the beauty of old plank flooring.

# FINISHING TOUCHES
## ACCESSORIES ON A SHOESTRING

**1** Hang your hat on a hockey stick? Certainly. But in this case it's eight inexpensive hockey sticks that form the unusual coat and hat rack. The sticks are nailed together in pairs then attached to a 2×2-inch center core with glue.

**2** Even chairs become accessories (space-saving ones at that) when hung on the wall, Shaker style.

**3** A sense of humor and a little imagination can create an off-beat accessory. Here, a little lamb, lovingly tied with a lime-colored ribbon, grazes in a field of parsley planted in a lined basket, and touched with an occasional daisy. The armoire holds other collectibles for future arrangements.

**4** Any small items hung in an artistic manner can make interesting accessories. Here, jewelry is stored and displayed on a wall studded with nails. Ordinary keys, cookie cutters, or old household tools also would make a fine collection.

**5** Exaggeration is a simple and often inexpensive way to add excitement to a decor. One striking poster of a giant-size geranium, cleverly cued to a live geranium plant below, sets the scheme in this small dining room.

**6** For the price of one big poster you can have artwork for two walls. Simply wrap the poster around a corner, as shown here. If you can't afford all the accessories you want right now, pinch-hit with vegetables or fruit, grouped in baskets or used individually. Later, your edible accessories can go directly to the dinner table!

Accessories can be anything you want them to be as long as they are used in a decorative fashion. All you need is a little imagination and a sense of humor.

3

4

5

6

# FINISHING TOUCHES
## AFFORDABLE ART

1 **When one large painting is a** focal point, keep furnishings simple. In this living room, the background and the modular seating pieces (with one dazzling exception) are in soothing white, chosen to enhance, not compete with, the bold colors of the painting.

2 **Colored canvas, stretched and** tacked to wooden frames, provides a subtle yet sophisticated treatment for this small living room. Mirrors on the window wall reflect the canvas creations.

3 **A long, narrow hallway** became a small gallery when stock molding was used to make a 10-inch-deep recessed "frame" for this collection of prints.

4 **When it's impossible to devote** an entire wall to artwork, a good alternative is to group a cluster of posters and prints over a major piece of furniture. To keep the arrangement cohesive, hang the art with bottom edges even just above the furniture.

**P**rices at an art auction can easily convince people that original art is lovely to look at, but almost impossible to own.

True, most families will never own an original Renoir or Rembrandt, but good-quality art is available—in the form of original prints. Works of many contemporary print-makers are modestly priced and may even appreciate in value (although art as an investment is risky for the amateur).

For original prints, the artist alone produces the master image, just as is done for an original oil painting. But unlike the oil, signed and numbered prints enable many collectors to enjoy the same work of art.

Reproductions, on the other hand, are usually photographic or mechanical copies of an original piece, or silk-screened copies of another artist's work. Reproductions have less clarity of color than originals.

## HOW PRINTS ARE MADE

The artist uses a metal or plastic plate, a stone, a wood block, or a silk screen to create the master image. The image then is transferred to paper by a printer using a hand-operated press. Each print issued is considered an "original."

The most popular types of prints are: *relief, intaglio, lithograph,* and *serigraph.*

A *lithograph* is a print that most closely resembles a brush or crayon drawing. To make a lithograph, the artist uses grease ink (tusche) or crayon to draw on a specially prepared limestone block or zinc plate. The block or plate then is chemically treated so the greased or crayoned areas of the stone attract printer's ink and the blank areas repel the ink. The final step in the process occurs when the inked stone and damp paper (rag) are passed through a litho press where the ink is squeezed onto the paper.

A *serigraph* is the most expensive of the print-making processes. A fine mesh cloth is stretched taut over a wood frame, and then the design is painted on by using the same grease ink as for a lithograph. The grease ink (or crayon) makes parts of the mesh opaque and leaves the design areas open. A squeegee forces ink or paint through the pores not blocked out and onto the paper. Unlike the other types of original prints, the image of the serigraph is not reversed.

An *intaglio print* also is called an engraving or an etching. The design is etched with acid or cut by hand into a plastic or metal plate. With this process, the indented areas, rather than the raised areas, hold the ink, allowing for designs of an intricate nature.

A *relief print* is often called a woodcut or linocut. The areas around the design are cut away, making the design stand out like the letters on a rubber stamp. It is this raised area that is inked for printing.

Each type of print can be produced in multiple colors if several plates, stones, blocks, or screens are used to put down each color on paper.

The artist determines the number of prints to be made from the master image. After the specified number (often fewer than 500) has been printed, the master is destroyed.

A print can be signed by the artist or left unsigned. And, the work may or may not be numbered. The number, usually written as a fraction (76/100) in a lower corner of a print, indicates the size of the edition (in this case 100) and the number of the print (the 76th).

Signatures or numbers do not prove a print's authenticity. The practice of numbering prints just started about 75 years ago. Many of the old masters as well as some modern artists omitted pencil signatures.

## HOW TO BUY ORIGINAL PRINTS

Several factors determine the price of an original print. A smaller edition frequently will cost more initially (and may be worth more later) than a large-edition print. Also, well-known and currently popular artists command more for their work than do new artists on the scene.

Black-and-white is a less expensive production method than color, and the more colors, the more costly the procedure and the print. The condition and rarity of the print also will influence its price. Even dimensions may be a factor in the cost, with the larger graphic carrying a larger price tag.

## WHERE TO BUY PRINTS

You can purchase fine-art prints at galleries, museum shops, and art shows, as well as from art dealers and artists themselves. You'll also find good quality prints in some department stores. If sources are limited in your area, you can buy artworks by mail from galleries and museums in other cities or through art clubs.

## POSTERS

Posters are one of the most inexpensive forms of original art. Many posters are created by famous artists, usually as lithographs or silk-screen prints. Instead of being printed in limited editions, however, the posters often are run off in the thousands. Unsigned ones are the least expensive. Those with the signature in the printing impression are more costly, and a limited number, pencil signed by the artist, cost the most.

## ART APPRECIATION

As you begin to build your collection, remember that the value of art is based primarily on how much you like it. It's always best to buy art for your own pleasure and not simply as an investment.

Pursue one art form at a time until you become familiar with its fine points and can distinguish good-quality work from the mediocre. Whether you choose original prints, oils, watercolors, sculpture—or any other art form—first study and observe. Visit museums, galleries, art shows, and exhibits. Ask for information and advice from dealers, curators, and the artists themselves.

# FINISHING TOUCHES
## OFFBEAT ART

1

2

**A**rt is more than paintings, sculpture, posters, and prints. Actually, just about anything you can think of can classify as "art." It all depends on the context in which the objects are displayed. So if you run across something that pleases your fancy, don't be shy about showing it off. By unleashing your imagination (and sense of humor) you can easily create an offbeat art collection of your own.

And while you're at it, consider being a bit offbeat about where you place your art work. Rather than relegate your art work to a typical living room or dining room location, try expanding your collection to include other rooms in the house.

Here are a few ideas for getting your offbeat collection off the ground:

● Divide one large poster and multiply its effect by framing each piece separately.

● Sandwich boldly patterned shopping bags from fashionable stores between mat board and clear acrylic for a great look at next-to-no-cost.

● Place small heirlooms such as grandmother's lace doilies in ready-made frames, then put them on display in a hallway or guest room.

● Turn a rug into a tapestry by hanging it on the wall.

3

4

**1** If a single work of art appeals to your aesthetic sensibilities but falls short of the effect you want, then why not repeat your favorite? Molded, lightweight plastic shapes such as these serene countenances are inexpensive enough to use in multiples. Although you're not likely to find them in a gallery, you might find them in a display store along with an array of other interesting, offbeat objects.

**2** If you're ready for the big time, then use the art of exaggeration to pep up a dull wall. To make this oversize clock, attach some tiny picture hangers to the backs of wooden numbers purchased at a hardware store. Spray paint the numbers and then mount them on the wall in a 5-foot circle. Cut extra-long hands from hobby-shop balsa wood and glue them on top a metal clock's hands. Before you hang the hands and motor, spray paint them and attach a conspicuous curly extension cord.

**3** Here, folk-art in the form of a handcrafted quilt makes a spectacular wall piece. Placing the quilt against paprika-toned walls highlights its stylized sunburst design and creates a "headboard" for the bed.

To hang a quilt without damaging it, hand-stitch a casing made of twill or muslin across the top edge of the quilt on the wrong side. Then insert a sturdy curtain rod and hang it from concealed hooks behind the top edge.

**4** Art belongs everywhere, not just in the "public" rooms of the house. An assortment of paintings and prints can add personality to any room—even the kitchen or bath. This display of favorite prints adds flavor to a cozy kitchen. To balance the visual weight of an old Welsh cupboard, the homeowner hung a pair of whimsical prints on the wall above the kitchen table. Nearby, a soft-sculpture chair (a contemporary art form) offers both color and textural contrast. Completing the decorative display is a painting that rests on a slim shelf near the window.

P roperly displayed, art can create a mood, inspire a color scheme, serve as a decorative accent, and direct the eye toward architectural detail. One of the keys to an effective art display is well-chosen framework.

Keep in mind that a frame should never be more important than the picture it surrounds. The frame should complement the subject matter, tonal value, and size of a picture, and help blend it into the background decor.

How you frame your art affects not only how it looks, but also how long it lasts. A frame's major function is to protect the art from soil and damage.

When you're ready to frame your artwork, you have a basic decision to make: to have it custom framed, use ready-made frames, or do the framing job yourself.

## CUSTOM FRAMING

Custom framing is the easiest option, but also the costliest. It takes a special blend of craftsmanship and creativity to see and bring out the best in a piece of art. It also takes a lot of time, skill, and patience. These are what you pay for when you go to a professional framer.

A professional frame shop probably will have a larger selection of frames, matting, and materials than you will find anywhere else. Your frame will be made to the desired measurements and your matting cut by hand to fit. Frame corners will be glued, nailed, and hand finished, and mitered corners will be sealed.

Select your framer with care. Ask other collectors for recommendations. A good framer will be well known in art circles.

## READY-MADE FRAMES

Frames such as those in variety stores are adequate for many purposes and cost much less than any other type of framing.

A ready-made frame comes complete with glass, stapled fitting devices, backing, and hanger. All you have to do is pry up the brads in back, insert your picture, and press the brads back into place. Some ready-mades have backing that slides out of channels in the frame to make the job even easier.

Your choice in ready-made frames will be limited to about a dozen standard sizes, ranging from 5 × 7 inches to 24 × 30 inches.

Inexpensive "fast frames" are available, also. They have four small clamp-on corners or strips for the top and bottom of the art. Plastic clips hold glass and backing board together. These frames are for non-valuable art only, as they provide no real protection from dirt.

The metal section frame is a variation of the ready-made. Two equal sides are packaged as a unit with hardware for joining the corners. The sections are available in lengths from 8 to 50 inches. You mix the various parts to build a frame. Glass, backing, and matting are purchased separately. These frames come in several finishes, including silver, gold, pewter, and black.

Secondhand and antique frames can be interesting

choices if they are in good condition, fit the art that is to be framed, and are reasonably priced.

## MAKING YOUR OWN FRAME

If you have steady hands, lots of patience, and the proper tools, you can make a handsome frame in your workshop. Molding is available at lumberyards and art supply stores, and from some custom-framing establishments. Acrylic framing materials are sold in craft and plastic stores.

The tools and materials you will need range from a miter box to assorted brads and finishing nails. In recent years, do-it-yourself frame shops have sprung up. Essentially, you buy materials and the use of tools and work space from these establishments. The shop's staff are available to give technical help and advice.

Don't start your framing project with a large or valuable piece of art. Practice on something small and easily replaceable. Even the wrong type of adhesive or mat board can destroy a valuable print.

If you do decide to tackle the task, here are some tips. Never mount (permanently attach) an original print, drawing, or watercolor on a backing board; that would decrease the value of the art.

The more room fine art has to "breathe," the better. If it is stretched down tightly, dry weather will make the paper taut and it might tear. Attach the art to the backing board at the top with two small hinges of

linen or rice paper. Use only wheat, rice, or starch paste to attach the hinges. Cellophane or masking tape can stain a print beyond restoration.

If you prize a print, don't trim it down to fit a frame. Cutting off the signature or the plate mark will markedly reduce the value of the print. Even if it's a small picture printed on a large sheet of paper, you will be devaluing it if you cut part of it away.

## MATTING A PRINT

The function of the mat is to prevent fine paper art from touching the glass.

Condensation inside the glass will harm the print if it touches it. Glass also can burnish some art surfaces, destroying colors irreparably. In other cases, the glass and the print can become inseparably fused.

If you are "floating" a picture, be sure to use fillets (little wedges of extra-thick mat board) as spacers to keep the art and glass apart.

Use only 100-percent acid-free rag board for both backing and matting. The acid content of regular cardboard matting will literally poison the print. Eventually dull rusty splotches called "foxing" will appear over the surface.

Rag board matting comes only in white and off-white. If you want a colored mat for your original art, other paper or fabric can be adhered to the rag board mat. The colored matting, however, must not overlap the safety mat or touch the print.

Once, there were exact rules about the proper proportion of a mat. It was supposed to be from

3 to 5 inches in width and wider at the bottom than at the top. Today, typically the spaces at the top and bottom of the mat are the same width.

## TIPS ON FRAMING

Original watercolors and prints, as a rule, are framed simply, with shallow, narrow frames, glass, and soft off-white mats.

Traditional oils usually have heavier frames, sometimes in a style that matches the period of the painting. Mats and glass are not used. However, a liner in the form of a narrow fabric-covered insert is used to separate the frame from the painting.

Modern oils and acrylics often are unframed, with the canvas wrapped around the edges of the stretcher. A strip frame may cover the edges.

An unframed canvas draws attention to the pure shape and size of the painting field, as well as to the image.

When framing a reproduction, treat it as you would the original. If the original was an oil painting, mount the reproduction and frame it without glass. If the original was a watercolor, frame it with glass.

The main function of the glass is to protect art from the damaging effects of dirt, grease, moths, and other enemies.

Glass is needed on all art you want to preserve, except on oils protected by varnish or on photographs coated with spray lacquer.

You can buy nonreflective glass that is glare-free, but this special gass does tend to distort colors and deaden black and white. It may make an origi-

nal piece of art—particularly a watercolor or old etching or engraving—look like a poor reproduction.

Plexiglas, like nonreflective glass, is more expensive than regular glass, but it is light in weight. This can be an asset when you are framing a large picture. It won't break as easily and you can drill holes in it.

However, Plexiglas does scratch easily. Do not use it over pastel chalk or charcoal drawings, as it generates static electricity that will attract the chalk or charcoal dust.

## DISPLAY IDEAS

• Groupings are most effective if they are the focal point in a room, and not forced to compete for attention.

• Small pictures, matted in large frames can be used for balance in an arrangement, or alone for special effect.

• Two- or three-dimensional art, such as carved wood or soft sculptures, interspersed among a wall grouping can add interest to the arrangement.

• Last but not least, proper lighting is important for showing your art work to best advantage. Lights that attach to frames are still available and are used mostly for important oil paintings. More popular today are flexible and easy-to-install track lighting systems. Individual canisters can be focused separately to highlight each piece of art, as well as to achieve overall illumination for the grouping. Recessed swivel-dome lighting installations, though expensive, are also good choices.

# HOW TO HANG ART

If you've ever pounded a nail in the wall and watched the plaster come crumbling down, you know picture hanging can be a tricky business. To reduce the risk of damaging the wall, make a cross with masking tape over the spot where you want to drive the nail. The tape will help keep the paint and plaster from crumbling.

What if you muster the courage to nail into the wall, and then decide the picture would look better elsewhere? Simply dab the hole with white toothpaste, let it dry, then apply touch-up paint.

An alternative to the standard nail and metal hanger is wall-mounting tape available at art stores and framing shops. The double-sided adhesive strip or square is applied to the back of the picture, then the picture is pressed to the wall.

A disadvantage of this type of hanger is that the tape won't hold heavy pictures, nor will it work well on porous or textured walls. Humidity also may cause stickers to slip.

## PICTURE-HANGING POINTERS

Putting pictures together in a pleasing arrangement is like piecing together a puzzle: If one piece is out of place, the grouping won't work.

To tie your pictures together, have at least one straight line running through the grouping. For instance, align the bottoms of the prints at the base of the

collection to visually anchor the composition. Other prints might hang pyramid-style around a key piece.

## PREPLAN ON PAPER

What's the *real* secret of achieving a picture-perfect art grouping? Select and arrange your pictures first before you ever pound a nail into the wall.

To preplan a grouping, piece together sections of paper until you have a mock-up the same size as the wall space you want to cover. Lay the paper on the floor and arrange the frames so the grouping is balanced in size, shape, and color strength. Trace around the pictures and mark where the nails will go. (Note: Be sure to check the location of the wire and hanger on the back of each picture. Mark the spot where the top of the picture will be; then measure down to the hanger to determine precisely where the nail should go.)

Tape the paper to the wall, making sure the center is at eye level, and pound nails into the spots marked.

To showcase a single piece of art, you'll want to tie it in with the furnishings, rather than letting it "float" on the wall. You can achieve this integration simply by placing the picture directly above a piece of furniture. A good art-arranging rule of thumb to remember is that the picture should be no wider than the furniture piece below it or narrower than half its length.

# LIVING ROOMS

**P**robably the most important room in any home is the living room. Here's where we greet guests and gather family. Of all the rooms under our roofs, this is the one that most means "home." It is also the room that commands most of our decorating attention. For unlike other rooms, living room space is abstract and flexible, decoratively defined only by how we choose to use it. Although we automatically know what kinds of furniture must be included in a dining or bedroom, we can furnish the living room to suit as many purposes as we like. In the process, the room can (and should) become a highly individual space that both lives up to the name—living room—and still maintains its company manners.

# LIVING ROOMS
## LIVABLE LIVING ROOMS

L et's begin this discussion of living rooms with a close look at what you want the room to do in your household. The living room can be a place for receiving visitors and entertaining guests, almost in the formal "front parlor" tradition of earlier times. Or it can be a room your family actually *lives* in, on a day-into-night basis. You'll want comfortable furniture and all the extras for entertaining yourselves as well as guests: television, reading lamps, perhaps even a dining area. Deciding what you want from your living room space is the important first step in achieving it. Here are some questions you should consider:

• Is your living room immediately on view to callers and guests, or does a hall or foyer handle this role?

• What is the traffic flow into and through your living room? Is it in the mainstream, or easy to avoid *en route* to other rooms?

• How do you like to entertain? In large, fairly formal gatherings, or in a more easygoing manner with small, intimate groups?

• Is the living room *the* central gathering spot for family members? Or do they head instead for the family room or kitchen?

• What does your family like to do together at home? Are they inclined to converge on a central fireplace or television, or does each member prefer a private spot for reading and relaxing?

• Are you fussy about your living room, tending to keep it company ready at all times? Or do you actively encourage comfortable conviviality there?

Analyzing your answers should help you determine the personality you want your living room decor to express. In simplest terms, are you a formal or an informal family?

*Formal* doesn't mean stiff and uncomfortable, filled with stilted antiques and touch-me-not accessories. Nor is *informal* synonymous with "anything goes" decorating. With today's relaxed furnishings and fabrics, the most formal living room still can be comfortable and livable. And the most informal room can be as soothing to the eye as it is to the soul. The difference is essentially in the overall attitude of the room, the immediate ambience you're aware of when you enter.

The room's basic architecture is a major contributor to its mood. Symmetrically balanced windows, built-in bookcases, and an elegant fireplace make a room architecturally formal. The architecture may also dictate the furniture arrangement. Again, symmetrically balanced arrangements, in which the furniture comes in matched pairs are just naturally more classic and formal than random furniture placements. Certain styles and materials, such as mahogany furniture and swagged window dress, silk, damask, and crystal, are also inherently more formal than pine pieces and rough-textured fabrics.

*For all its formal elegance and impressive art objects, this is a room that invites family living. Credit the infusion of comfortable furniture, and the cheerful open-air atmosphere.*

# LIVING ROOMS
## LIVABLE LIVING ROOMS

The special personality expressed in a living room is the sum of its many individual parts. Walls, floor, windows, and furniture are the major ingredients that combine to create a formal or informal mood.

And, though decorating rules are becoming increasingly flexible, simple guidelines exist to help create whichever mood you are out to achieve.

**Formal walls.** Painting in gentle pastels is a failsafe way to "formalize" almost any wall. If you are a true traditionalist, you can find modern-day paints that duplicate the hues found on the walls in historic old homes and restorations.

You'll be equally on the right track with quietly patterned fabrics or wallpapers, such as crewel designs, documentary prints, garden florals, and stencil-like patterns. Certain styles of wood paneling can also help create a traditional look: For instance, those that reproduce the chair rail and wainscoting of earlier days or the moldings and cornices used in Colonial homes.

**Formal flooring.** In a formal living room, beautiful polished wood is almost always a good choice. So are wide expanses of broadloom carpet, particularly if it has a plush pile surface. Elegant Oriental rugs, of course, have long been the quintessence of dress for floors (although they're now equally at home in modern settings).

**Informal walls and floors.** Homey textures, bright colors, and anything that has a handmade look is appropriate for walls and floors in informal living rooms. Translated spe-

cifically onto walls, this means bare bricks, rugged textures in stucco and plaster, and paneling with lots of wood grain: knotty pine, pecky cyprus, rough-sawn cedar. Wallcoverings in informal living rooms run the gamut from strong, touch-me textures to cheerful prints and small-scale geometrics.

Wood is just as at home underfoot in an informal living room as it is in more formal areas. Here, the wood can be painted as well as polished. Informal floors can also be carpeted, but in more extroverted textures and patterns than suit formal-feeling rooms. Some floor covering possibilities include carpet with a textured "made-by-hand" look (Berbers, for example), sisal, grass matting, dhurrie rugs, or colorful, boldly patterned area rugs.

**Formal window wear.** Treatments can vary from nothing at all to elaborate, traditional swag-jabot treatments. Opting to leave a window bare calls for both courage and the right architecture, inside and out.

Truly traditional formal windows also take to shaped cornices, shutters, gathered and pleated draperies, and both modern vertical and time-honored venetian blinds (like the wooden ones in Colonial Williamsburg). More innovative window ideas can work here as well, such as Austrian and Roman shades.

**Informal windows.** These know few bounds: Blinds, shutters, shades, curtains and cafes, both long and short, will all suit the mood—again, depending on the fabric you choose.

**Whether the overall atmosphere is formal or relaxed, a successful living room should make people feel welcome.**

**1** Elegant in its simplicity, this fireplace has a classic charm that's echoed in the basically 18th-century flavor of the room's other furnishings. As background, the fireplace wall is warmed with vibrant coral, a strong color elsewhere confined to accents in the patterned fabric, rug border, and seat on the graceful settee in the bay window.

**2** With all the drama going on overhead, both the furniture and the colors have been kept quietly out of competition for attention. Even though the furniture pieces are large scale in keeping with the room's size, they are low and comfortably livable.

**3** Wide-open spaces can be both invigorating and intimidating to decorate. Furnishings in skimpy scale just won't work in a room this large. Two full-sized sofas, both backed by tables of their own, embrace a generous cocktail table. The massive breakfront along the far wall provides essential balance to the broad windows, left beautifully bare.

**4** Small personal touches, carefully acquired over the years, more than remove any formal chill from this classically balanced room. From the elegant area rug to the collection of precious porcelains, this serene, richly Oriental interior scene is perfect counterpoint to the quiet landscape outside the unencumbered window wall.

# LIVING ROOMS
## LIVABLE LIVING ROOMS

Unlike other rooms in your home, a living room is all free-floating space, waiting for you to define it in terms of your family activities. How well the space functions for you depends on your choice of furniture and its placement.

Every living room requires certain pieces of furniture to make it function. Start with the upholstered seating pieces. A sofa (or more) is standard, but no longer an absolute necessity. Depending on the space you face, a loveseat (or two) may provide a better fit. Or perhaps one of the new modular seating groups will maximize the room size. Whichever major upholstered seating you pick, plan at least two companion lounge chairs as part of the primary furniture group, and then move on to the satellites you'll need to make the arrangement work: tables (no seating piece should ever be far removed from one), lamps, ottomans, and other comfort essentials.

You now have the basics for a livable living room. But where to settle this central arrangement? It may not be centrally located at all, if that would interfere with traffic flow or ignore the room's obvious focal point, such as a fireplace. Every living room needs such a central point to focus the furniture around. Find (or create) yours, and place the largest seating pieces comfortably nearby. Bring up the lounge chairs to complete the arrangement, then add tables in proportion to the upholstered pieces.

In a living room of any size, you'll need a secondary activity area to balance the major one.

It's not hard to make your living room truly livable. First step is to clearly define just what you want this important room to do. Then choose specific furniture pieces to carry out your goal.

It, too, can contain seating pieces, but more likely you'll feature another function here. For example, a work center is a logical idea, and the desk or secretary it requires is usually large enough to provide visual balance. All-in-one living rooms can count on the dining area to play counterpoint to the central seating arrangement. And, if space is particularly precious, you can "weight" the other end of the room with a wall of art that won't eat up your square footage.

Vertical interest is another essential dimension in a successful living room scheme. A tall bookcase or étagère can supply it; so can windows with eye-arresting treatments.

Intangible and too often overlooked, lighting is another major factor in a room's good looks and livability. A living room needs two kinds of light: one for visual comfort when you're reading, writing, or playing games; a second type to contribute to the mood of the room.

If you still think of lighting only in terms of table lamps or ceiling fixtures, you're still in the dark ages of decorating. A center-ceiling fixture is useful only until you can reach and turn on area lighting. Table lamps are an obvious source for this specialized type of lighting—but one we're too apt to rely on completely. Floor lamps are another option; they can be as dramatic as they are practical, providing good lighting without requiring space-encumbering tables to rest upon. Track lighting also fills a range of needs without taking up floor or table space.

3

1 Furnishings in this room are as sleekly contemporary as the architecture. Deftly chosen colors in the art and accessories only serve to call attention to the dramatic scheme. Flexible furnishings like these modular pieces can be rearranged with ease.

2 Here's an example of a symmetrically balanced arrangement that looks anything but staid and static. The major secret of the room's success lies in the simple, classic lines of the eclectic furniture mix.

3 Serenely restful, this on-flowing space serves as a quiet haven for conversation, with seating centered at the room's natural focal point, the fireplace.

4 A small space doesn't have to be downplayed. Bold color accents this multi-function living room which has ample space for relaxing and entertaining.

4

# LIVING ROOMS
## IMPROVING WHAT YOU HAVE

**1** For our redo, we chose this room that had become a bit timeworn over the years. The color scheme was bland to the point of boredom, and the furniture arrangement made convivial conversation almost impossible. Upholstery on the still stylish sofa and chairs had seen better days, as had the carpet. And as the children in the family grew older, furniture needs had changed.

**W**e'd like to make a case for creative living room *redecorating*. Speaking realistically, that's where most of us really begin—by reusing and rethinking our space and the furnishings we've been living with all along. Few of us can afford to start over from scratch. And, even if yours is a first-home situation, you've probably been bestowed with hand-me-downs that have a way of looking, well, like hand-me-downs.

Over the next four pages, we'll show how to move from an uninspired beginning to the updated and exciting room pictured on page 291. Along the way, you'll find a collection of ideas you can apply to your own redecorating.

### STEP ONE: A PLAN

Although your redecorating will be implemented gradually as time and money allow, you must have a start-to-finish plan in hand right from the beginning of the things you want to accomplish with your redo. This way, you'll always know just where you're heading and how to get there in manageable increments. But, although such patience is a virtue, so is a little instant gratification to whet your motivation.

### STEP TWO: IMMEDIATE CHANGES

Analyze your eyesores and select the ones you most want to change. Perhaps it's the wall color or an old upholstered piece that's casting a pall. If so, replace it as quickly as you can.

Even if you can't proceed with the rest of your redo for a while, these first changes will buoy up your spirits and your room's appearance. Oftentimes, an infusion of color or a new room arrangement is enough to spark the room revolution, visually speaking, without a major outlay of either money or energy.

### STEP THREE: THINKING NEW

Once you've rid your room of its most obvious flaws, don't rush blindly into the next stages. Before you start filling in gaps with new purchases, give some thought to the following: Consider how your lifestyle may have changed since you last redecorated. If, for instance, the children have gone off to college (or if you're at the other end of the child-rearing cycle and have a new baby), you may want your room to function differently from what it did a few years ago.

Also, are you knowledgeable about today's new furniture styles and color possibilities? Lots of exciting products and ideas give you plenty to choose from. Look around before you add or replace.

### FINAL STEP: ACCESSORIZING

The finishing—and most fun—touches in any room remake include the little things that add a lot of personality: works of art, collectible treasures, plants, and books. Take plenty of time rounding out this final phase of your redecorating project.

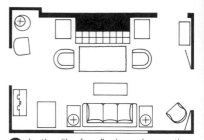

**2** In the "before" plan above, the arrangement of the furniture led people right through the center of the conversation area. Other pieces squared off almost in isolation against all four walls. Simply by pulling the sofa away from the windows and adding the two occasional chairs, a new path through the room was created. (See plan below.) Now seating is placed to make conversation more comfortable.

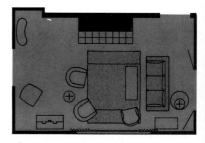

**3** Next step in the plan was reupholstering the sofa in a dramatic new fabric. Enough of the floral print was purchased at the same time to recover the lounge chairs at a later date. (It's a good idea to buy matching fabric all at once, since later dye lots may not be the same, and patterns, like books, can go out of print.)

The nondescript picture window also got a new look with smart gray draperies and light-filtering matchstick blinds.

The area rug, another addition, defines the conversation area and covers much of the well-worn carpet—without requiring purchase of a complete new floor covering.

# LIVING ROOMS
## IMPROVING WHAT YOU HAVE

**1** Rethinking your current room arrangement often can free up old space for important new purposes. Here, the secretary that was once only for show assumes a new working role in "found" space.

**2** Taking a long look at your current activities also can affect your living-room lifestyle. In this case, underdeveloped space by the bookshelves now works as a game center, adding a pleasant new dimension to this living room's livability.

The other major change is a dramatic new paint color for the walls. The soft gray hue provides a refreshing backdrop for the rich wood tones and the vibrant upholstery colors.

A room that sees a lot of living ends up looking the worse for wear. But by rethinking, rearranging, and redoing, you can refit a time-worn room for many years of comfortable living.

**3** The final touch to any decorating or redecorating project is adding the accessories, the small things that make a room spring to life. Lamps, plants, and art works play a major part.

Pieces should be carefully selected over a period of time so they express personality, without depressing the budget. The only major addition in this final phase is the dropleaf cocktail table that pulls the seating area together. A new tray table floor lamp replaces the old lamp and also provides a handy table surface between the recovered chairs.

Compare the compact, finished floor plan with the original dysfunctional one shown on page 288. With just a bit of rethinking and a few new pieces, there's now a place for comfortable conversation, for family activities around the game table, and for home-office work or letter writing in the secretary-desk area.

# LIVING ROOMS
## SPACE STRETCHERS

**1,2** A rolling, folding dining table offers the ultimate in room service for cramped, small-space living. Waiting against a hall wall between meals, it can be loaded in the kitchen and rolled out for everything from snacks to a full-course dinner for four.

Meantime, dressed in space-making white, this living room seems larger than it really is. The area is swept completely clean of all superfluous clutter. Here that includes window curtains, end tables, everything but the paired sofas set out from the mirrored walls to further enhance the illusion of space. Since there's simply no place else to put them, light fixtures are swung from the ceiling, and wall-washing track lights play up the fireplace. One dramatic poster over the mantel and a generous gathering of large green plants complete the furnishings.

**A** growing problem more and more of us face—because of decreasing sizes of houses and more apartment and condominium living—is how to meet all our living needs in less-than-ample space. Fortunately, help is available.

Increasing numbers of today's manufacturers are making dual-purpose furniture designed to eke the utmost from every inch of space. Combined with decorating ingenuity, such multifunctional furniture helps stretch available space to surprising lengths.

### DINING IN THE LIVING ROOM

It's a fact of modern life: Dining rooms are disappearing at an alarming rate, only to reappear at the end of many living rooms. If you're lucky, you may have a separate dining ell already allocated. If not, let's consider ways to fit this sometime function into your everyday living space. First, make it look special-purpose by setting the dining area aside decoratively with a low divider, an area rug, or a wall treatment that differs from the rest of the room's decor.

No space for such special treatment? When one room must do it all, look for adjustable cocktail tables that rise to dining occasions, for drop-leaf tables that snuggle close to walls till you want them, or for classic gateleg tables that swing into action at the sound of a dinner bell. There's also no reason a desk can't do double duty, or, if you're really pinched for space, no reason why you can't use a serving cart or a roll-away table that spends its off-duty hours elsewhere.

### SLEEPING IN THE LIVING ROOM

Although this may seem to be primarily an apartment-dweller's problem, nearly everyone occasionally faces the prospect of having more guests than beds. The obvious answer is the sleep sofa, the living room centerpiece that works a night job, too. Fortunately, many new sleep sofas offer such good design and comfortable seating that their secret stays well hidden until you need it.

Not-so-obvious solutions to the living-sleeping arrangement can be found in chairs and modular units that pop open into beds, and in the old Murphy bed, the kind that folds up into a closet or cupboard. They're back on the market, the time-honored answer to zero space in the living room.

## CREATING THE ILLUSION OF SPACE

The next best thing to actually expanding your floor space is to create the illusion that you have. Although there's nothing new about their use, mirrors continue to offer one of the best ways to visually relieve a claustrophobic space. Whether you use sheet mirror or less expensive mirror squares, the important thing is to make sure the mirrors reflect something that's visually pleasing. After all, there's no point in duplicating the image of an eyesore.

See-through glass or acrylic furniture—coffee tables, dining tables, end tables, chairs, and lamp bases—are also excellent choices for a small room because they don't have the visual "bulk" that solid pieces have.

Another bit of visual legerdemain is the scenic wallpaper mural. Garden, beach, or forest scenes, to mention only a few of the mural designs available, help create the feeling of limitless space. And, today's murals come in a range of sizes, from single panels to fit a narrow slice of space to multipanel designs that cover a whole wall.

On the other hand, it sometimes pays spatial dividends to strip a small room—windows, walls, and all. Keeping furniture and clutter minimal tends to maximize actual living room; so do light, airy colors, laid on in sweeping strokes over both furniture and all the walls.

3

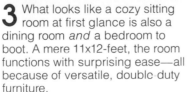

4  5

**3** What looks like a cozy sitting room at first glance is also a dining room *and* a bedroom to boot. A mere 11x12-feet, the room functions with surprising ease—all because of versatile, double-duty furniture.

**4** A dining room hides in the drop-leaf cocktail table. Its ingenious high-low mechanism brings it up to dining height, and the leaves raise to serve four; lowered, it's perfect for cocktails and conversation.

**5** After hours, the room's third personality emerges—from the sleep sofa. To make room for the full-size bed, the caster-mounted cocktail-dining table simply rolls off to another corner.

293

# DINING ROOMS

**T**he very words imply graciousness: dining room. A place apart from the normal noise and bustle of family life, a place to enjoy the good things that come with gathering for even an hour or so each evening. Never mind if your dining "room" isn't really a place apart. A corner, an ell, or even a convenient table will do. The important word here is "dining," not eating on the run or at a counter, but savoring both the food and the family or friends it's shared with. Space planners occasionally predict the demise of the dining room per se. They forget that a dining room nourishes the psyche, too—something as necessary as food itself. For this reason alone, we doubt the dining room as we know it will ever disappear.

# DINING ROOMS
## DINING IN STYLE

**I**t may be a poor pun but it's good decorating advice: Your dining room is a matter of taste. How you furnish it, what colors and accessories you choose, even where you locate it in these days of flexible living are choices as personal as what you serve there. On these pages, we offer you a veritable smorgasbord of dining rooms to inspire you—whether your family lives formally, with gleaming silver and crystal; informally, with earthenware and baskets; or somewhere comfortably between. But inspiration alone often is not enough. Just as with a favorite recipe, there are definite directions to follow in successful dining room decoration.

### AIM FOR AMBIENCE

What kind of *mood* are you out to create in your dining room? Colors, furniture, lighting, everything falls into place more easily once you've established the ambience you're after. If you don't know, think of your favorite restaurant and the mood it puts you in when you're there. Is it sleek, elegant, and formal? Or cozy with bricks and warm wood tones? Early American in mood, with touches of brass and pewter? Or a comfortable amalgamation of personal choices in colors and furniture? Of course, the dining room's overall mood should be in keeping with the rest of your home, especially when it's visible from other rooms.

Once you've set your design direction, consider the practicalities involved in creating a room that's as functional as it is appealing.

### PRACTICAL CHECK-POINTS

Start with the number of people who'll be using the room most often. The table itself should accommodate them comfortably, with generous elbowroom and uncramped leg space. If you're buying unmatched table and chairs, be sure to measure the height of the table bottom and the chair arms so the chairs will fit under the table. Consider also the kind of family yours is. Glass tops may look sleek and space stretching (an elegant one is shown here), but they quickly lose their luster with children around. Give your chairs the same hard scrutiny, and defer your yearning for real suede or brocade till the little ones aren't so.

More practical check points: If your dining room will undergo hard daily wear, look for tabletops with special surface protection, such as plastic laminate, that shrugs off spills, stains, and other assaults. Ditto for chair seats, and for the flooring you choose to underscore your room scheme. If you have very young children, you might consider covering your dining room floor with good looking resilient vinyl.

*Contemporary elegance is reflected in this dining room— through the glass-top table with its acrylic see-through base, the wicker-and-wood chairs designed to look like French antiques, and the impressive arrangement of antique Korean scrolls. A light-color quarry tile floor underscores the eclectic appeal of the setting.*

# DINING ROOMS
## DINING IN STYLE

1 2
3 4

5

**1** A family of collectors gathers around this generous table, homemade from metal plumbing pipes and a laminated maple top. The old bentwood chairs, now slicked with glossy black paint, came from a garage sale, also the source of the very personal collection in the antique cupboard.

**2** Call on the power of pale or neutral colors to "cool" an overly bright room. Here, serene taupe walls, crisped with white woodwork, are mellowed further by the terra-cotta colored floor. Baskets of flowers and a harvest of greenery provide just the right amount of color contrast.

**3** Old or antique furniture is an exciting adjunct to contemporary architecture. Here, visual interest is intensified by the presence of four sleek chrome chairs around an ornate oak table.

**4** Straightforward simplicity is the key to sophistication in this ultra-contemporary dining room. To break up the expanse of space between living and dining areas, a large potted tree serves as a living divider.

**5** In this dining room, a bit of the outdoors comes in, literally, to become the true center of attraction. That really is a living, growing ficus tree smack in the center of the table. The table itself was built around the tree from two half circles of plywood bolted together. The ingenious hostess, who never has to worry about a centerpiece, makes her tablecloths with side zippers.

# DINING ROOMS
## DINING IN STYLE

Once upon a time, dining room furniture tended to come in suites. Everything matched as perfectly as the dishes on the table. No more. And no wonder! All that sameness was as bland as milk toast to the eye. Today's thinking that variety is the spice of visual life has opened the way for very personal dining room furnishings. The basics remain, of course: a comfortably sized table, and chairs enough for guests. After this come your storage needs: for china, crystal, tableware, and linens. But who says these needs have to be met in the same old ways? It's great fun, for example, to mix modern chairs with an antique table. Or try it the other way around. Fresh, too, is the use of serendipitous furniture in the dining room; for example, an antique armoire to hold the china and linens, or bookshelves instead of the traditional breakfront. A French baker's rack can replace a more taken-for-granted buffet, as can a tea cart or rolling warmer stand.

### LIGHT IT RIGHT

One non-variable in any dining decor is proper lighting. Read that, *mood* lighting. Harsh, overly bright light evokes about as much atmosphere as a fast-food spot. The usual source of the soft light you're after is a ceiling-hung fixture, centered over the table. Generally, a hanging fixture looks best (and provides the best light) when suspended no more than 34 to 36 inches from the tabletop. Never use bare overhead bulbs,

except the tiny, decorative kind. Nothing is less flattering—to food, furnishings, or faces—than an overly bright room.

Whatever the overall decorative mood of your dining room, an appropriate lighting fixture for it exists. If you dine in traditional style, multibranched brass or pewter chandeliers are good. Early American rooms take naturally to tin, wood, and wrought-iron fixtures. Crystal is elegant for rather formal dining; however, contemporary rooms spark to more unorthodox illumination overhead: chrome or Lucite fixtures, for example, or track lights, ceiling-mounted and focused downward, discretely and indirectly.

### DIM IS IN

A dimmer switch is an inexpensive additive to ambience in a dining room. The switches are available at hardware and lighting stores, and you can install one yourself using only a screwdriver and the directions on the package. The switch controls the flow of electricity to the fixture, so you can turn the lights up when you need them, then down to a candlelight glow at dinner time.

Larger dining rooms may need more than a central fixture for good overall lighting. Wall sconces are a decorative answer. They, too, should be low wattage, never glaring, and styled to complement the rest of the room's decor.

And don't forget the magic of candlelight! For sheer drama and romantic appeal, nothing can hold a match to this form of lighting.

300

**Surprising pieces of furniture, taken out of context, can be the visual spice of your dining room's life.**

**1** This dining room achieves its country French flavor primarily through the use of color and fabric. Never mind that the "buffet" table is really a dresser gleaned from the heyday of American golden oak furniture. The piece is in perfect keeping with the provincial air of the room.

**2** This delightful dining room/library is filled with antiques and auction finds from the old Southwest. Lending authenticity to the nostalgic decor are brick pavers on the floor, a kerosene lantern from a wild West saloon, old prints in their original frames, and a pine table decked with enamelware—the kind that looks like the tin plates once used on wagon trains.

**3** If storage is the problem, a tall cupboard can be the answer, in a dining room or, just as aptly, in a bedroom. Knotty pine and amply proportioned, the cupboard in this warm, Early American dining room holds everything from linens to liquor.

**4** Nothing much matches here, and that's half the charm of this small (11x13-foot) dining room, with its odd-couple chairs, Welsh cupboard, modern painting, and Oriental-flavored china and carpet.

3

4

# DINING ROOMS
## SMALL-SPACE IDEAS

**1** To solve the problem of the disappearing dining room, one clever homeowner uses a compact console that holds an extendable, 10-seat table inside. During the daytime, the console just sits handsomely in the breezeway/entry serving as a catchall for keys and mail. But when dinner guests arrive, its hidden personality comes out, all 104 inches of it, counting the extra leaves. For parties of six or fewer, the host can set the table ahead of time and still have ample space to welcome guests through the front door (from which the photograph above was taken).

**2** Turning over a new leaf is the time-honored way to gain dining room without sacrificing floor space all day long. This flip-top table gives the old idea a sleek new look: Its yard-square top, made of plastic laminate, literally doubles in size at dinner time. On daytime duty in this airy eating nook (conveniently placed just off the kitchen), the table shrugs off the assaults of the younger members of the family. So, in fact, do the stackable chairs, whose bright covers slip off for easy care.

A dining room is where you find it. Or, perhaps, it's more accurate to say, room for dining is anywhere you *can* find it. Time was when every proper home had a special room set aside just for dining purposes. It made sense then, when whole families were apt to gather there for all three meals a day. Now, a dining room is almost a luxury; one worth fighting for if you have it, but not worth mourning if you don't. The trick is learning to use space in surprising new ways. Apartment dwellers are good at this, through necessity if not native imagination. Apartment people have always known that a foyer could be coaxed into dining room duty, or that a living room could be made to share at mealtimes and still live gracefully the rest of the time.

## DOUBLE-DUTY DINING ROOMS

These same ideas are worth sharing with many of today's homeowners, who are finding that soaring building costs have practically squeezed the separate dining room out of existence. For all of you, we present on these four pages the case for the double-duty dining room.

This is no mystery story, once you understand the plot. It's all about how to get twice the livability from the space you have. The first clue is: Be devisive. Your dining room table must spend most of its time looking as if it were something else. There simply isn't space enough to keep it out in the open, surrounded by chairs. A dining table can be a successful double agent if you disguise it as a game table, a sofa table, even a cocktail table (some come with up-and-down adjustable supports). In order to carry off this secret role, the chairs must be banished elsewhere. Turn them into useful occasional chairs in the living room area, or in the bedroom, or—if their design permits—hang them on the wall.

## TURN THE TABLES

If you're considering a new table, size it to fit your dining situation. Size and shape make a big difference when space is tight. Measure the area carefully, allowing for entertaining, as well as daily meal serving. You'll need to plan a minimum of three feet around the table for seating and serving.

When you shop, you'll find a wide range of table sizes and shapes to choose from. Necessity has long been the mother of clever inventions. Some dining tables fold away, almost Murphy-bed style, into innocent-looking cabinets. Others, such as the homemade version on this page, angle back against a cabinet hung on the wall.

Chairs often can be stashed neatly on the wall beside the table, making decorative strokes of color even the Shakers, who started the chairs-up idea, would applaud.

And that's not the end of space-saving styles. There are also a wide variety of flip-top versions that double their size at mealtime and trim drop-leaf designs that open to provide a spacious surface.

**3**

**3** Mirror, mirror on the wall is a clever idea for this tiny hall. The mirrored facade of the wall-mounted unit hides an entire dining "room" behind its handsome front. A little legerdemain and some stock lumber cut to size are the not-so-secret ingredients. The plywood table is double-hinged to fold down smoothly when it's needed, then snap back up to cover a multitude of odd-size storage needs. The mirror tiles are finished with stock, 2-inch-wide mullion molding, also available from any lumberyard. Another space-thrifty idea: folding chairs hung like wall sculpture.

# DINING ROOMS
## PART-TIME DINING ROOMS

If dining rooms ever were to become an endangered species, it would be because they're sometimes guilty of not earning their keep all day long. The children's doing their homework at the dining room table doesn't count quite enough. A table is a grand, spacious work surface for many activities, but it takes preplanning to bring it into the mainstream of family life.

### ARRANGEMENT IS IMPORTANT

Don't limit your thinking to setting a table smack in the center of the dining room. Often, such a straightforward arrangement inhibits the flow of traffic through the room anyway. Consider off-centering the table to gain more floor space. A drop-leaf table can be pushed against a wall or cozied up to a sofa back. If your family is small, you have only to raise the leaf at mealtime. And when overload company comes, simply pull out the entire table for extra seating.

### EXPANSION PLANS

A separate dining room is easily expendable when the table itself is expandable. If you're short on space, buy a table with extra leaves (they're available even for some glass-topped tables). Between meals, keep the table at its smallest, which is usually just the right size for game playing and desk work.

Where to store leaves when closet space is minimal? A good place to stash them is under a bed, or hang them on hooks behind a door.

### WHERE TO KEEP THE ACCOUTERMENTS?

Part-time dining rooms do pose storage problems: Where do you stash all the accouterments your lovely table settings are made of? The china, glassware, silver, linens, and centerpiece accessories? In a self-contained dining room, the answer often is as simple as a buffet and hutch. But in a room for all reasons, you have to think unconventionally. A dining ell, where the space flows right from the living room, can use a low divider with storage behind sliding doors and ample serving space on top. Where a dining "room" shares the life of a den or study, wall shelves are a handy solution. If your dining is in or near an entryway, be clever about the guest closet you most likely have there, too. A small rolling tea cart (for dishes and silver) can slip right in under your guests' coats.

Think twice about your dining room. Imaginative, double-duty arrangements can provide you with more between-meals living space for all your family's activities.

**1** Why settle for idle walls when you can easily put them to work? Here rough barn siding was used to give this once-dull dining room a rustic air, and to provide space for books, accessories, and plants. And that's not all. The new built-ins created an alcove for an upright piano, and a 14-inch-deep niche for a wine rack.

**2** Awkward space just inside the entry has become the hub of all activities in this compact living room. The teacher who lives—and often works here—had the ell area lined with shelves, creating more than a cozy book-lined nook. When a party is in progress, the host empties some of the shelves and uses them as "buffet" ledges. The table expands when needed (a leaf is stored in the guest closet).

**3** This all-in-one room for entertainment started life as a mere dining room. But that was before the table itself was moved off-center toward the kitchen door, freeing up enough floor space to accommodate a comfortable seating arrangement. Now, guests who come for dinner linger on to chat over cordials. And, best, the hostess never has to leave the room to look after her creations.

3

# DINING ROOMS/TIPS FOR THE TABLE

Setting a handsome table is a fine art, one that requires more than just a talented eye. Today's mix-and-match philosophy leaves you free to set out whatever suits you, mixing the best sterling with unmatching crockery, arranging centerpieces in Ming vases or old bottles, dressing the table itself in anything from lace to time-honored antique quilts. However, grabbing what first comes to hand and handling eclecticism with flair are vastly different. What makes the difference is an understanding of what you are doing, an understanding that begins with good buymanship.

## ALL ABOUT FLATWARE

You have a half dozen different ways to go when you choose your flatware. Let's consider them one by one, beginning at the top of the price and beauty structure with **sterling silver**. Of course, sterling is the costliest way to set your table. But then, it's also the most elegant, luxurious, and valuable. When you buy sterling, law requires that it be almost pure silver (92.5 percent silver). The rest is made up of copper or another alloy that adds necessary strength and durability. Sterling is indeed the stuff that heirlooms are made of; age and use only enrich its elegant gleam and add to its beauty. What the enrichment of sterling will cost you depends on how heavy the pattern is that you choose, and how intricate its design.

**Sterling II** is new-generation silver: sterling coupled with fine-quality stainless steel.

Costing about half as much as all-sterling pieces, Sterling II is an innovative hybrid that combines silver handles with tines, bowls, and blades made of long-wearing stainless steel.

**Silver plate** has graced the best of tables for generations. Here, the silver is only surface-deep, an outer layer of pure silver electroplated over nickel silver (an alloy of copper, nickel, and zinc). With silver plate, you get the beauty of sterling, but at much lower cost. The better quality (that is, the higher priced) plate has a double layer of silver over the most vulnerable areas on the flatware.

**Gold electroplate** employs the same technique as silver electroplating, but 24-karat gold is used instead of silver. You'll also find a choice of sterling or silverplate patterns that are accented or edged with gold electroplate.

**Stainless** used to be standard ware for informal dining; nowadays, it's been styled up enough for fancier fare. Once called **stainless steel**, this flatware is actually a combination of metals, including steel, chrome, and nickel. If your pattern carries the number 18/8, you have flatware made of 18 percent chrome, 8 percent nickel, with the rest steel. The high percentage of chrome and nickel is desirable since it increases the pieces' resistance to wear and washing.

**Pewter** is the perennial favorite of early American *aficionados*. But it's come a long way since colonial days. Today's pewter flatware is free of lead, refuses to tarnish, and takes to the dishwasher with relish.

## BEFORE YOU BUY FLATWARE

When you shop for flatware, handle the individual pieces critically. Test their weight, their balance, their fit in your hand. Pretend to cut food, stir coffee, spear an asparagus. Each piece should feel well balanced and comfortable, or you'll never really enjoy using it.

You can buy flatware by the individual piece, by the complete set, or by the place setting, which can mean three, four, five, or six pieces. Five is fairly standard, and usually consist of a luncheon knife and fork, teaspoon, dessert fork, and soup spoon. The sixth piece to add would be the butter knife.

Often, it makes better sense to buy extra pieces of whatever you'll use the most, for example, dessert forks or teaspoons. You might even want to work up to having two different patterns of flatware, to add daily variety to your table and accommodate large gatherings.

Essential serving pieces? Start with a cold meat fork, pierced vegetable spoon, gravy ladle, and additional serving spoons. And remember as you add to your service that the pieces need *not* all match.

## WHAT'S YOUR DISH?

Like flatware, dishes have a hierarchy all their own, starting with the almost indestructible plastics and ascending to fine china. In between, you'll find a number of nice-to-live-with kinds of dishes: heat-proof, shock-proof, cold-proof pieces that come in an artist's range of colors and patterns.

Starting at the top, from the perspective of price and luxury, we find **fine china**, meaning the delicate looking, translucent kind that glows when you hold it to the light and fairly sings when you tap it gently. Porcelain and bone china are among the offerings here, but don't let their fragile appearances worry you. Both types of china are fired at very high temperatures that leave them strong and chip resistant.

**Vitreous** and **semivitreous** (meaning glasslike) china looks and feels much like porcelain or bone china, but it's less expensive.

**Stoneware**, next in the price hierarchy, also has been fired at high temperatures, but it is decidedly heavy, durable, and tough enough for everyday duty. Stoneware gets its grayish complexion from the clays it's made from, but the versatility of the dishes will brighten a busy cook's life: Some types can go into the freezer or oven with equal aplomb.

**Earthenware** is heavy, also, but it tends to chip more easily than either china or stoneware.

**Glass** and **glass-ceramic** dinnerware are especially good answers to accident-prone households. Some glass and ceramic products are so durable, in fact, they carry guarantees that run from two to three years. And some lead a busy life in the kitchen, as well as on the dining room table: You can bake, broil, and freeze in the same dishes you use for serving.

## HOW TO SELECT STEMWARE

Resist the temptation to call all stemware "crystal." That's a term reserved for high-quality, higher priced glass to which a certain amount of lead has been added. The lead contributes the sparkle and delightful ring we associate with fine crystal stemware; the more lead, the finer the crystal. European-made stemware may obtain up to 35 percent lead; 24 percent is more standard. American manufacturers are not required to disclose lead content, so it may range from 10 to 24 percent.

When you're shopping for crystal, look at how the glass catches light and reflects it—brilliance is an indication of quality. Next, very gently flick the crystal with your fingernail. If you hear a ring and the sound lingers, you're looking at fine crystal. Lead crystal is heavier than ordinary glass, too.

## WHAT THE TERMS MEAN

Because lead softens the glass, lead crystal lends itself to finer and more delicate decorative surface treatments. Fine lead crystal is generally hand-blown into a mold that gives it the shape of a drinking vessel. The hand of the artisan is what gives each piece its individuality, and makes crystal created this way (as opposed to machine blown) more expensive and desirable.

The easiest and least-expensive method of forming glass is by pressing it: Molten glass is poured into a mold and allowed to harden.

To decorate the surface of good crystal, three methods are used. The finest of these is **hand cutting,** where each piece is an individual work of art. **Etching** and **copper-wheel engraving** produce similar results, but the means are quite different. Acid is used to etch off a layer of crystal, leaving a raised design on the surface. In copper-wheel engraving, tiny drills cut the design into the glass. **Frosting,** as in the famous *La lique* glass, uses acids all over the body of the crystal to create a stainy, frosted surface.

**Cased crystal** is a term you should be hearing more often. It describes a method of creating colored stemware by literally encasing a layer of clear glass within a layer of colored glass. When the latter is cut away, the clear layer sparkles through. It's easy to tell expensive cased glass from tinted glass: With the latter, after the glass is cut, color remains the same throughout.

Platinum and gold bands are often applied to crystal stemware. Rings of other colors can be *flashed* or painted onto fine crystal. Keep in mind that all colored bands must be washed with care to avoid rubbing off the color.

## MORE TIPS ON SELECTING STEMWARE

Choose glassware that coordinates with your china and flatware. If you have plain china, you may want decorative crystal. However, if your china and sterling are highly decorated, you may want to use simpler stemware.

Matching the bowls of your goblets to the shapes of your coffee cups adds symmetry to the finished table. But don't be timid about mixing shapes and patterns if you happen to like a less-contrived look.

Your stemware may be of the same design or you might mix and match a colored water goblet with a clear wine glass. (Decorative crystal and delicate heirlooms can get along beautifully with contemporary designs.)

Two crystal manufacturers offer breakage replacement plans. When you send the manufacturers the broken stem and bowl, they'll replace the glass at half the current retail price (plus a nominal fee for postage).

## NEW LOOKS IN LINENS

Linen is another term we cling to tenaciously, even though we're now blessed with blends and man-made pretenders that have all the good looks and texture of fine linens, but almost *none* of the work.

Whatever the material, every well-dressed table needs a basic wardrobe of "linens." First come **tablecloths;** formal or informal depends on your life style. The major difference is in the styling and the fit: A formal cloth drops from 16-to-24 inches all around; for an informal look, allow 10-to-14 inches.

One important tip when you're buying or making a cloth for an expandable round table: The leaf automatically stretches it into an oval shape, which requires an oval cloth.

**Place mats,** once reserved for informal service only, are now acceptable on almost all occasions. They come in sizes ranging from 12-to-14 inches wide and 16-to-18 inches long. And there's virtually no end of styles and materials to spark a table setting.

**Table runners** have returned to fashion after a long banishment. Runners, which are a quick and easy way to dress any shape table, should be about 12 inches wide and have a drop at both ends.

Also back—but with a big difference—are **fabric napkins.** Thanks to today's no-iron care-free materials, fabric napkins are as easy to use as (and, in the long run, actually less expensive than) the paper variety.

## INSTANT MICROWAVE INFORMATION

Microwave ovens, with their space-age approach to food preparation, have really liberated the choice of containers in which you can cook.

Now, you can boil water in a china coffee cup and make hot cereal directly in a bowl. The time in clean-up savings is exciting, but don't get so carried away you overlook the caveats.

Stoneware, casual china, and so-called bake-and-serve dishes are usually safe for microwave cooking. Plus, there are those great heat-proof glass and glass-ceramic casseroles that take to microwaves as if they were made for the role. Indeed, many dishes are, and you'll find them clearly labeled in the china departments of retail stores. Check the bottoms for a stamp that says the piece is microwave worthy.

# KITCHENS

Americans have rediscovered the kitchen as the family focal point. When it last played this role, our homes were small, and the kitchen hearth served both as a source of heat and a place to cook. So it was virtually the only place to gather. Today, the kitchen's rebirth as the gathering spot is born out of our life-styles. Working women and job commuting limit the time families can be together, but the desire is just as keen as ever. What better place to congregate than the kitchen? And, as women and men share in the cooking, the kitchen becomes a natural place for sharing amenities. The result is a kitchen that is now an expanded "living center," truly the heart and hub of the home. At its best the kitchen is the cooking center, a place for dining or snacking, a control center with desk and phone, a hobby area—and most of all, a place where family and friends experience emotional warmth just from being together.

# KITCHENS
## PERSONALITY KITCHENS

**B**efore getting down to the one hundred and one things to consider when planning a new kitchen or updating an old one, reflect a moment on the phrase "Personality Kitchens." Though a kitchen is essentially a work room, to be a truly successful design (and a pleasant place to work in) it must have a personality. So as you collect ideas and begin your plans, be guided by what you see, adapt ideas to suit your own needs, and be sure to put *you* in your kitchen.

### PATIENCE PAYS OFF

Planning a kitchen involves—among other things—your work habits, accurate measurements, electrical wiring, plumbing, storage, and decor preferences. The kitchen is the most complicated room in the house to plan, so no matter how eager you are to complete it, take the time to thoroughly plan it all out on paper before making any decisions. A mistake can be costly to correct, so be sure you're right before you begin. For do-it-yourselfers, some good advice: The best way to avoid costly mistakes or oversights is to consult with a professional kitchen designer or contractor before you embark on a major redo.

### FUNCTIONS FIRST

Start by listing the functions you would like the room to serve. Determine the type of kitchen you want. Is it purely a cooking center? Will you want room for hobbies or for children to play? Will you entertain in it? Will more than one person at a time be cooking in it?

Then, think about what those functions require. Start with the major appliances. They are generally standard in size so planning around them will give you a good idea how much floor space will be left.

### WORK CENTERS

Using your list of ways you want the room to function, start a separate plan for each "work center." For example, at the sink you will need counter space on both sides. Ideally, the waste disposer and dishwasher are part of this area. You also will want to consider storage space for produce, towels, and the like. The point is to consider all the things needed for functioning well in each work area. Think your work processes all the way through from where you will put the groceries down when you come in from shopping, to where you will put the hot pot you take out of the oven. As you begin to fit these work centers into your layout, you will notice that some of them overlap. That's no problem if only one person at a time is working in the kitchen; otherwise you may have to make adjustments.

### THE WORK TRIANGLE

The traditional work triangle is a good guide for laying out your room. Though it is not the *only* formula, it is a reliable yardstick for a step-saving plan. Begin by placing the refrigerator, range, and sink at equidistant triangle points, with each triangle side being no shorter than four and a half feet and no longer than seven and a half feet.

Whether or not you use the triangle system, you should definitely consider the location of each work area in relationship to your work habits.

If possible, start with the sink since that is the busiest area in the kitchen. The ultimate would be to place it where there's a pleasant view. In any case, keeping your work patterns in mind, plot the other work centers in relation to the sink area.

### SYSTEMATIC STORAGE

We will discuss storage in more detail later, but for your initial planning purposes, the basic principle, obviously, is to make storage as convenient as possible. Think about how often you use each item, where you use it, how easy it is to lift, as well as how easy it is to reach. Also, think about storage accessibility to children. Can it save you time and effort if what they want—and can have—is readily available to them? Are "off-limit" items out of their reach?

### TRAFFIC PATTERNS

Although the work triangle may be a perfect work pattern for you, if the children are constantly "in" the refrigerator, you may want to place it where their frequent visits don't interrupt your rhythm. To avoid having people cross your path too often, also consider all other normal traffic and, where possible, reroute it outside the work area.

When laying out your floor plan, remember to leave room for appliances (such as some dishwashers) that you must pull out, and for the oven, refrigerator, and cabinet doors to open. Consider the space chairs need to be comfortably used. Also allow enough room for people to walk around one another easily or to work together at adjacent work centers.

### ILLUMINATING IDEAS

Don't cheat on the lighting for your kitchen. Improper lighting can cause fatigue, aid and abet accidents, and give even the cheeriest room a drab and gloomy appearance.

Use lighting for functional, general, and decorative needs. General lighting, although it creates a pleasant environment, is planned to light the cabinet interiors. Functional lighting, or task lighting as it's sometimes called, is light directly over a work area such as the sink or food preparation centers. The dining area requires a separate decorative fixture to stimulate a sense of relaxation.

When it comes to the decorative aspects, don't pussyfoot around. Whether you use an all-white scheme or pure color, make your kitchen a spirit-lifting environment you'll enjoy being in. To keep it that way, make "easy maintenance" and "durability" watchwords in your selection of materials.

*An all-white color scheme gives this kitchen a timeless appearance. Personalization comes from plants and an assortment of colorful accessories.*

# KITCHENS
## PERSONALITY KITCHENS

1

2

3

**Individuality is the earmark of a room with personality; so strive for uniqueness when decorating your kitchen.**

**1** The combination of exposed brick walls and open shelving gives this kitchen its distinctive charm. Other elements that add appeal are the stained glass window from a wrecking barn, quarry tile flooring, and an old stovepipe used for decorating effect only.

**2** Simple wood shelves and countertops are but two of the ingredients that give this kitchen a country French flavor. White-painted pine decking used to cover the ceiling, one wall, and all cabinet sides also contribute to the European look.

**3** Months of salvaging and recycling brought about the delightfully restored kitchen seen here. Pine lumber salvaged from old houses formed the shelving, walls, ceiling, and flooring. A blend of old and new, modern appliances, and easy-care laminated countertops coexist with antique cabinets found at farm auctions and flea markets.

**4** If your kitchen doesn't measure up to your needs, it may require major surgery to give it the right dimensions. This once dark and narrow room blossomed into a beauty when a wall was removed and a structural beam added. Old floor boards, more in keeping with the 1780 farmhouse character, replaced worn linoleum. Finally, a new multipaned window opens the room to the outdoors.

313

# KITCHENS
## PERSONALITY KITCHENS

1

2

**1** Ingenuity and elbow grease can go a long way if you need to update a kitchen yet can't spend a fortune on it. Here, to avoid the cost of ripping out old walls, wide pine boards (running horizontally) were nailed over existing walls, then painted. Using the same cover-up approach, new brick pavers were put over the old vinyl floor covering. Overhead cabinets would have closed in the small kitchen, so pegboard storage was used and painted silver to blend with stainless steel pots and pans. No space existed for recessed lighting, so the inex-

pensive answer was to surface-mount porcelain sockets. Clear filament bulbs act as the whole lamp. This general lighting is bolstered by fluorescent cove lighting, and the top of the cove acts as a shelf at the same time. A last decorative touch is the use of mattress ticking for the window curtains and place mats for the table.

**2** Designed to be the center of attraction, literally and figuratively, this kitchen is in the center of the home. Wide entryways, rather than doors, open into adjoining rooms, making it easy for family and friends to be part of the action. The color scheme is basically black, contrasting with the natural wood finish on walls, floor, and counters. Center stage is a 4½x7-foot cooking island topped with butcher block. Opposite the gas range with two electric ovens side-by-side underneath, the

countertop overhangs to form a snack bar or a place to sit and watch the cook at work. Low black cabinets hang only on the wall opposite the cooking side of the island. The counters are all 30 inches deep instead of the usual 24. That allows more work space, plus room for open shelves above and space for frequently used appliances to stand on the counter, ready for use.

**3**

**3** To decoratively meld this remodeled kitchen with an adjacent family room, the conventional kitchen "look" was minimized as much as possible. To do this, all functional aspects of the room were given a low profile. The working areas are at waist height with no overhead cabinets screaming "kitchen." (Storage is behind a wall of door-fronted shelves, not shown here.) The eye-level line of vision provides a clean, uncluttered appearance, and shows off to the utmost the graphic effect of the blue and white ceramic tiles and the circular stainless steel hood.

**4**

**4** Pure simplicity from floor to ceiling gives this kitchen its elegant, high-style appeal. The expanse of snowy white surfaces juxtaposed against the warmth of pine wood above and below is arresting to the eye yet soothing to the senses. A protective polyurethane finish covers all cabinets, making them easy to keep clean. Behind the stove, old planks from a discarded Mississippi river barge have been used as a backdrop for liquid measures and a crock of utensils. The serving peninsula and snack bar act as a divider between the kitchen and sit-down dining area.

# KITCHENS
## KITCHEN STORAGE

1 2
3 4

**Shrinking space brought open storage back to the design front, but the hoorays and nays must be weighed by your dislike or love of clutter, ease of accessibility versus depth of storage space, and decorative appeal versus maintenance.**

**1** If you love antiques and your kitchen has wall space to spare, do as these homeowners did and put an old piece to use for both decorative and practical purposes. This lovely pine hutch shows off a collection of china, and neatly stores all kinds of kitchen gear.

**2** This rustic-style kitchen, though small, sports a considerable amount of storage space. A ladder-type frame installed overhead provides easy access to pots and pans, and adds a decorative touch as well.

**3** Be cavalier and remove your cabinet doors if you want storage that's as colorful as it is convenient. The holes left from hinges can easily be filled in, then painted. Here, lining the cabinet walls with silvery reflective Mylar adds an extra decorative effect.

5

6

**4** To gain extra storage space in this one-wall kitchen, simple wood shelves were installed in front of a no-view window, and an extra length of shelving was extended over the range and microwave oven.

**5** A once-wasted wall now holds more than its own! To make a similar system, cut ¾-inch dowels to size and intersect every 6 inches. Drill and screw together at all edge intersections and every 4 or 5 squares in the middle with 1¼-inch screws. Use cup hooks for small items and "S" hooks for larger things.

**6** Here a butcher-block island with a huge iron rack holds a battery of pots, pans, and utensils. One side of the island stores stools and a library of cookbooks; the other side features drawers designed to hold baking equipment.

**S**olving the kitchen storage problem is more than a matter of finding space to stack things. The important thing—whether you're long or short on space—is to effectively organize what space you have. Put kitchen items close to where you're going to use them. For example, store any produce that needs washing or peeling near the sink, cutlery near the chopping board, baking equipment near the oven, and tableware near the dishwasher.

The type of storage you select is largely a matter of whether you like things out in the open or completely hidden from sight (or both). Each kind of storage—open or closed—has special features. Closed or cabinet storage controls clutter and protects the contents from grease and grime. Cabinets do require space for opening the doors, and more than one crack on the noggin has been caused by a door carelessly left open. The standard depth of most cabinets can make it difficult to reach items in the back, whereas open storage is usually shallower with items easily accessible. Open storage is also airier looking and tends to enlarge the room visually. If you opt for open storage, one way to reduce the grime problem is to store in the open only the things you will use every day.

Don't overlook space-expanding extras such as ceiling beams, overhead racks or wall-hung racks that can suspend all kinds of things, racks inside cabinet or closet doors, or even a space-making perforated hardboard wall system with hooks.

# KITCHENS
## KITCHEN DINING

For most people, eating in the kitchen has always had a unique appeal. Perhaps it comes from the pleasant anticipation of wonderful aromas wafting through the air. Or maybe it's the enjoyment of being where the action is, sharing the intimacy and easy informality of family and friends. Whatever the attraction, there's no doubt that dining in the kitchen is, and always will be, a favorite pastime for millions of American families.

What type of kitchen dining you have depends on space, and whether you plan to feed friends as well as family in the room. If your kitchen is your only "dining room," you'll probably want to spruce up the eating area more than you ordinarily would. And although there's certainly no stigma to entertaining guests in the kitchen, you might be more comfortable if you placed a divider between the table and cooking areas. A portable folding screen would do, as would a mini-slat venetian blind (attached to the ceiling) that could be lowered when camouflage was needed. A pierced or semitransparent sliding panel would also do the trick of hiding kitchen clutter from guests.

No room for a standard-size table in the kitchen? Solutions to this problem include a snack bar and stools; a flip-down, wall-mounted table; a pullout counter; or a portable ledge suspended between a doorway and countertops.

2

1

3

**1** One sleek solution to kitchen dining is this 9x3-foot island with an extra-deep 14-inch overhang. Comfortable low chairs slide underneath the overhang. The island is perfect for serving a buffet dinner, too.

**2** This small dining area with its antique drop leaf table, two ladder-back chairs, and Oriental rug, sharply contrasts with the stark simplicity of the architecture. Yet it has a welcome feeling of tradition and warmth.

**3** Not everyone enjoys eating in a kitchen milieu. Here a modular wall system divides a dinette area from the kitchen itself. In addition to providing a backdrop for dining, the unit houses an array of utilitarian items.

**4** Here a handsomely refinished oak table and its chairs beckon you to sit down and enjoy. Adding to the old-time ambience are polished oak floors, a colorful stained glass window, and a collection of memorabilia.

# KITCHENS
## COSMETIC FACE-LIFTS

**I**f your kitchen looks as if it has seen better days, but a major redo is out of the question, give thought to these decorative face-lifting ideas.

• Paint *everything* white—walls, woodwork, cabinets, ceiling, even the floor. Add color and interest with framed posters or prints, a new set of dish towels, and other kitchen accessories. Guaranteed, even the oldest, saddest kitchen will look years younger with the all-white technique.

• Cover damaged or badly worn walls with wood laths placed on the diagonal. Apply a protective coat of polyurethane, then hang utensils, pots, pans, and other kitchen paraphernalia from hooks or nails attached to the strips.

• Cheer up a dark, dreary kitchen by painting wood-grain cabinets with any bright high-gloss enamel, then paint surrounding woodwork white or a color to contrast with the cabinets. Paint the ceiling, too. Flat paint is fine, but it's not as attractive as high-gloss enamel and not as easy to keep clean. While you're at it, remove cabinet hardware and replace with round porcelain knobs or with any of the good-looking contemporary-style wire pulls available in many stores today.

• Ceramic tile can be quite elegant (not to mention expensive). Fortunately, it's possible to achieve a similar look with vinyl-coated wallpaper that's designed to look like ceramic tile. Some "tile" papers are so authentic looking that you have to touch the paper before you realize it's not the real thing.

**1** Nothing has the instant magic that color has—especially when used to cheer up a dreary-looking kitchen. Here plain wood cabinets were treated to molding, then painted daffodil yellow—a perfect choice if you face north or like a sunny look. Plain windows take on personality with stained-glass replacements, and the utilitarian backsplash went colorful with Mexican tiles.

**2** A bold brown-and-white check wallpaper was the beauty secret used to update this corridor kitchen. The pattern is both fresh and sophisticated, and—unlike "kitcheny" wall coverings—not apt to look dated in a short time. Simple, easy-to-clean vinyl blinds replaced grease-collecting curtains.

**3** This 11½-foot-square kitchen had a lot going for it in terms of storage space, but needed a good sprucing up. The inexpensive, yet effective solution was to sand off the crusty old paint on the cabinets and repaint with two coats of blue latex enamel. A washable blue plaid covering on the walls and ceiling adds extra zip to the scheme.

# FAMILY ROOMS

Call it what you want—family room, "rec" room, rumpus room, great room, or den—the point to remember is that this is a space for the family (adults and children alike) to enjoy in put-your-feet-up, let-your-hair-down comfort and ease. As such, you should design your family retreat with relaxing in mind. How you furnish the room (and with what) will depend entirely on the activities you and other family members plan to pursue there. The room needn't (in fact, shouldn't) be fancy or stifling to fun, but neither should it be a catch-all for furniture castoffs. And if your house lacks a specifically designated space for casual, carefree times, then by all means loosen up your living room (or any room, for that matter) to fulfill this very important function.

# FAMILY ROOMS
## FAMILY ROOMS THAT FUNCTION

Those famous bywords of the Bauhaus school of design—"form follows function"—apply to the family room more than to any other room in your house. To paraphrase, what you do in your family room should dictate the way you furnish it. The idea of such deliberate planning may come as a surprise if you'd counted on using hodgepodge hand-me-downs from the rest of the house. But such planning more than pays off in the increased pleasure you'll get from the space. Professional designers call this synergistic approach "space planning," not mere decorating. Whether you intend to furnish a family room from scratch or improve on the room you now have, the first step is to evaluate the way you and your family would like to live there. For one obvious example, will television be the focal point, literally, around which the room will function? If so, certain decorating criteria are already established; for example, you'll need enough comfortable seating space for every family member, plus guests, within convenient viewing distance of the set. You'll also need to consider window treatments that offer light- and glare-control. Even the kind of flooring treatment you choose becomes part of the equation: If you have youngsters who enjoy watching TV lying or sitting on the floor, carpet should be on your list of considerations. And so it goes, as you apply the principle of form-follows-function to each activity pursued by each family member. Perhaps part of the room should remain uncarpeted for dancing. Perhaps the family artist needs work space by a north window. What about the sound system everyone enjoys? Have you allowed the right size shelves for its speakers, for tape storage, and video discs? Acoustics become especially important for music-oriented family rooms and should be considered when you plan ceiling, wall, and floor covering materials.

### COMFORT FIRST

Once you have determined the ways you want your family room to function, you're ready to begin selecting specific furnishings. This is a plan-ahead approach to decorating that leads to a room that both feels and functions at its maximum comfort level. And comfort means much more than over-plush furniture and an ashtray at hand. Comfort has many dimensions, and as many definitions as members in your family. Consider the attitude you want to express in this room, the overall ambience you're out to create. Your living room may express one mood; the family room can convey quite a different one. It can be more intimate, more relaxed. If you put on company airs in your living room, then the family room is the place for unself-conscious, casual decorating that makes closest friends feel like family and your family feel completely "at home."

### GETTING PERSONAL

Another word for ambience is "personality," something you'll hear again and again in any discussion of successful decorating. If you've given careful thought to the way the room will function, you're almost assured of a family room that reflects the personalities of the people who will use it.

If your family includes a collector, plan an area for display. If there's a painter in your midst, or a weaver or photographer, a gallery is in order. If you love Americana, this is the room to give rein to its informal, whimsical side, perhaps a gathering of farm tools that may not fit a more formal living room.

Color is another important tool in imparting personality to a family room. Again, the colors you choose really depend on the kind of life your family will lead in the room. The colors you'd theme into a daytime, playtime area would be livelier than those you'd choose for an evening-oriented room.

### STRIVE FOR EASY CARE

Take the idea of taking it easy quite literally when you lay out your decorating plans. True family-room comfort calls for worry-free living, furnishings that conserve energy—yours. Everything that goes into the family room should be as maintenance-free as can be, shrugging off spills, resisting roughhouse play, whisking clean with minimal effort.

Thanks in large part to today's technology, furnishings now can look as handsome as they function. Many new fabrics have elegant looks that belie their toughness. Some of today's leather-lush suedes, for example, are actually synthetics that come clean almost at the mention of soap and water.

Carpet and wall coverings are also equal to today's leisure living, if you buy wisely. Discuss your application plans with the store salespeople, but also do some homework yourself. Study the hangtags provided by many manufacturers. Look for manufacturers' recommendations and warranties. Opt for fabrics, wall coverings, and floor coverings with surface finishes that repel soil and stains. Vinyl and vinyl-coated wall coverings are good bets for family room use, along with wood paneling specially treated to survive the tough-treatment active homes are heir to. If your family's leisure life-style dictates a hard-working floor, resilient flooring offers ease-of-care underfoot, as well as stylish good looks. The cushioned varieties come with comfort built in, and no-wax surfaces are available to play down upkeep.

*This family room is an extension, quite literally, of an artistic family's interests. Added to the main house, the room is a sun-filled, worry-free place to work and to play. Flooring is easy-care quarry tile. The sofa fabric, in spite of its light color, is sturdy and stain-resistant.*

Entertainment center? Conversation spot? A place to show off a collection? A family room can serve these and many other needs—especially when you plan ahead.

Whatever your hobby, interest, or inclination, feel free to show it off in the family room. In fact, make a point of encouraging all members of your household not only to *work* on projects in the family room, but to display the final results. By doing this—displaying needlework, collections, travel treasures, paintings, pottery, or any number of other hobbies or interests—you're guaranteed to make your family room an inviting place to be.

To promote such use of the room, avoid furnishings that will stifle the creative, do-something spirit. An expensive mahogany table may look beautiful in the family room, but no one will feel comfortable using the table to work on a messy hobby.

Provide your family artist with a spot (be it ever so small) where dripping paint or a glob of wet clay won't damage the floor. This might entail cutting out a square of carpet in one corner of the room and replacing it with resilient tile modules for easy floor care.

If you are a family of avid book readers, by all means let it be known. Books, with their colorful jackets, are decorative objects in themselves and have a marvelous effect when displayed en masse on shelves. But certainly, decoration isn't the only reason for having shelves of some kind in a family room. In addition to the practical purpose of storing books, magazines, stereo equipment, and other electronic apparatus, shelves also are great for storing games that might otherwise get stashed away (and forgotten) in a closet.

2

3

**1** Convivial conversation ranks high on the list of the family that inhabits this open-and-easy room. From the fireplace framed in Dutch tiles to the overstuffed sofas set on a Mexican blanket "rug," the room is made for mellow talk and a free flow of ideas.

**2** Here the emphasis is on entertainment, be it conversation around the U-shaped seating arrangement, or electronic entertainment via the TV and stereo in the shelving unit.

**3** This family room, with its warm Southwestern flavor, is a subtle showoff. The homeowners have indulged their taste for Indian art and artifacts in such treasures as the framed Indian artworks and the San Blas *molas* made into pillows. In keeping with the mood achieved by the Mexican floor pavers, the furniture itself is naturally rough-hewn.

# FAMILY ROOMS
## FAMILY ROOMS THAT FUNCTION

**A**ir conditioning and new building and heating techniques make it possible to convert virtually any area of the house into a comfortable family room. Basements and attics are natural spots and often have wonderfully spacious rooms. However, you may have to make provisions for humidity control or for new heating and cooling units. In an attic, you may need to add more insulation or install windows and a skylight.

An attached garage can be converted into a family room, often with a minimum of remodeling. Although you may have to build a separate garage or a carport later (or forgo a garage altogether), this is still less expensive than building an entire new room.

Even easier to convert into a family room is an enclosed porch or breezeway, a rarely used formal dining room, an extra bedroom, or even a large kitchen. With the availability of versatile, multifunctional furnishings, many of these rooms can do double duty and still retain their original use. Sofa beds, drop-leaf tables, game tables, modular seating units and wall systems, stackable chairs, and occasional tables are ideal for dual-purpose family rooms.

A living room, too, can function beautifully as a family room; so don't overlook this possibility if you have no space to spare in the rest of the house. You needn't forgo a living room look; however, you'd be wise to avoid fragile furnishings, delicate fabrics, and surfaces that are liable to damage.

**1** This English "pub" room began life as a basement garage. Gypsum boards were nailed to the ceiling rafters and to furring strips glued to the concrete blocks at 16-inch intervals.

The diagonal planks, which add to the country tavern look, were nailed through the gypsum boards to the furring strips and toenailed to the beams and planks at the ceiling line. Fabricated box beams cover the ceiling joints.

Wainscoting was simply glued into place, and a plaster-textured paint was swirled on the gypsum boards to give an old-world look. Vinyl tiles cover the concrete floor.

**2** Here a spacious living room became a family room, and a smaller room in the house now is a more formal living area. Rough-sawn cedar panels the walls, and a corner fireplace adds both visual and actual warmth.

**3** A formal dining room with a garden view combines the functions of family room, library, and dining room without sacrificing beauty or dignity. Terra-cotta walls and shelves of books, as colorful as a tapestry, are bright and inviting.

The roll-arm loveseat and upholstered chairs provide ample seating for reading, relaxing, and visiting. For meals the refectory table seats six.

# FAMILY ROOMS
## STORAGE IDEAS

**P**replanned storage is the surest cure for family room congestion. The family that plays together has a wealth of games to put away, plus books, records, hobbies, and other collectibles. Without sufficient storage space, the most well-mannered family room quickly disintegrates to wreck-room status. Here's where some careful space planning can turn a liability into livability. You can supplement meager storage via three different methods:

- Build it in.
- Buy it.
- Recast familiar furniture in a new, stowaway role.

### STORAGE TO BUILD

Built-in storage may be your best choice, especially if you own your own home. Not only will you be adding to your property value, but you (and the contractor or carpenter) can customize every element to suit your family's special needs and make the most of whatever overall space is available. A smashing example of this kind of customization is on these two pages. In this room a wall-wrapping storage and activity center furnishes a family room almost single-handedly.

Totaled up, such custom carpentry may be no more costly than individual, store-bought storage units. A lot depends on the area you live in, whether good craftsmen are available, and what materials you choose for your project. If you decide to take the custom-built route, treat the job as you would any contractual agreement: Have your carpenter spell out the specifications in writing, in advance, covering such items as the kinds of materials that will be used, as well as the starting and completion dates.

### STORAGE TO BUY

The most obvious sources of ready-made storage space are modular shelving units. Modulars come in a cast of thousands: all sizes, suited to all purposes, and made from a choice of materials to blend with any decorating scheme. Since modulars are designed for flexibility, you can arrange and rearrange to your heart's content. Another plus in modulars inherent mobility: You can take them along, if you go on to new living quarters. The units come in finished furniture of all styles, in the unfinished state and in knockdown or "KD" versions you can easily assemble yourself.

By applying the form-follows-function formula to your storage needs, you'll know exactly what you want a storage unit to hold before you ever set foot in a store. Then you'll be able to choose exactly the right modules for your family room tasks. There are adjustable-shelf bookcases, vertically slotted record holders, pigeonholes for cassettes, deep units for TVs, racks for wine bottles, impervious surfaces for desk or bar service. The list stretches to meet a wealth of storage needs.

### STORAGE TO FIND

Another—and novel—solution to family room storage problems is probably hiding somewhere else in your home. At the moment, it may be masquerading as an under-appreciated armoire. Bring it into the family circle to hold a small TV (you may need to drill holes in the back for ventilation and the cord). How about a French baker's rack, those wonderful open-shelf arrangements originally made for cooling breads?

Also consider taking kitchen cabinets out of context and into your family room for hangable storage. Turn an old cast-iron stove into a bar, cast-off school lockers into cabinets, and baskets, camp trunks, and ordinary office file cabinets into highly efficient storage. If you stretch your imagination, it's not hard to stretch your space.

1

**1,2** This wall-to-wall way to end family room clutter began with a detailed plan of everything this family had to "hide." Now, there's a custom-built niche for everything, even the tabletop that drops down for game playing. Between bouts, the table folds up and away, so its diagonal planking plays rich counterpoint to the opposite wall that displays the family photographer's works.

Crafted of rough-sawn redwood planking, the 15-foot-long storage wall stows books, games, stereo, and etceteras on adjustable shelves. The corner television is swivel-mounted so it can face all corners of the room comfortably. Bracketing the wide, wide wall of storage is a built-in bench for seating under a brace of track lights mounted on the ceiling above.

2

# FAMILY ROOMS
## BUDGET IDEAS

Don't let your family room become a receptacle for old furniture or castoffs from elsewhere in your house. But neither be afraid to stray from orthodox furnishings when you decorate the room. Serendipities can be delightfully fresh, funny, *and* functional. If your budget is tight, then this is the perfect strategy for you. Here are some budget ideas aimed at making your family room its very brightest. Borrow some of them now, and, as your bank balance grows, you can trade up to more "serious" furnishings. Even then, however, don't let go of all the whimsical ideas that add up to a distinct personality in a room.

### IDEAS UP FOR GRABS

• Scour your workshop for storage solutions—look for things such as the industrial shelving on duty in the basement family room pictured here. Left *au naturel* or slicked with enamel paint, the "high-tech" shelving is as chic as it is cheap.
• Also borrowable from the basement workshop are perforated metal strip-and-shelf systems. They cost next to nothing and hold almost everything. Paint the strips, brackets, and shelves to blend into the wall behind, and you'll create storage with almost no visible means of support.
• Here's another way to bag handy storage. Buy a trio of sturdy canvas tote bags. Line them up in a row and slip-stitch them together with carpet thread. Hung on colorful hooks, the lineup holds a multitude of paraphernalia.

• Paint is always a penny-pinching means of livening up a room. Use its canned magic in dozens of ways, from the floor up (check out the room-making waves on the opposite page). Stencil-painting and spatter-painting produce low-cost, highly individual decorative effects, and both are options even the untalented can exercise. If you *do* have talent, then the family room's the perfect place to flaunt it. Paint a giant geometric on the wall or floor. Or paint a tree that grows up one corner of the room and spreads out over the ceiling. How about a "zebra rug" on the floor, or floating clouds overhead to lift the looks and spirits of a low basement ceiling?
• It's not news that paint also can perk up has-been furniture so it can make a comeback in the family room. What may be a new idea is painting ordinary pieces so they can play new roles. Again, check out the family room we show here: The folding wood chairs, designed for a gardenlike environment, now bloom quite handsomely under a coat of black enamel.
• And speaking of ordinary things, consider papering a wall with newspapers. Just for laughs, use the color comic sections. If you brush over with a coat or two of clear polyurethane, the news will stay fresh. (The idea works on floors too; there, polyurethane is essential.)
• Be unorthodox in your search for furniture, as well. A comfortable family room couch-cum-guest bed can be created from a folding cot or single bed. Try wrapping it in supple carpeting

(an Oriental rug would be elegant), or cover it with a throw of colorful Indian cotton, tied at the corners with grosgrain ribbon strung through grommets.
• Budget tables can turn up where you least expect them—for example, out behind the garage. That's where we found the wire trash burner on the facing page, now turned table with a topping of plywood. (Any lumber-yard will cut it to fit.) Baskets as tables are basic; add a handsome tray or piece of glass on top to obviate spilled drinks and tipping lamps.
• Lamps, very necessary accessories, needn't necessarily be predictable either. Scout plant supply departments for convertible containers (witness the clay pots made into hanging lights in the family room here). Imagination also can metamorphose ugly dime store lamps into custom creations. Try wrapping a vase-shaped lamp with rough twine coils for an interesting natural texture. Or fill a clear glass lamp base with shells, stones, colorful beads, marbles, or even jelly beans. If the basic shape is classic (ginger jar lamps, for one example), you might add your own custom touch with paint or decoupage.
• While you're in the dime store, case the linen section for the makings of low-cost curtains. Dish towels can be spring-clipped into snappy-looking curtains, as can inexpensive lace-looking tablecloths. Also, you'll often find bedspreads that can double as draperies, and inexpensive roller shades that can be customized with stencils or fabric cutouts.

Once you've set your imagination into motion, you may be surprised at your own ingenuity. Just be certain to step back occasionally to make sure that comfort hasn't gotten lost in the shuffle. And to bind your save-money spruce-ups together, be sure there's a common bond of color.

Come in for a closer look at this inventive family room. In its former life, it was a dingy basement. Now the young family that used to live above it all spend much of their leisure time here.

Paint is the major miracle worker, brightening the concrete block walls and the plywood subfloor laid over the concrete (an inexpensive way to gain underground warmth).

Don't miss the other ideas up for adoption here:
• A coffee table from an overturned washtub topped with glass.
• The end table that was once a wire trash burner.
• The old sawhorse table trick. Topped with a flush door, it's still the most ample, inexpensive dining table and desk around.
• The dramatic "dried arrangements." Plants wouldn't grow underground anyway, so why struggle when you can make a great design statement with a plain wash pail filled with sand and bamboo plant stakes!
• The comfortable sofa backed with a harvest of homemade pillows. Underneath, it's actually a twin bed; the cover is made from colorful kindergarten rugs.
• The over-the-sofa storage ledge. Fashioned from ceiling-hung 2x4s, it also serves as support for lighting to brighten the windowless corner, with fixtures made from coffee cans.

# BEDROOMS

Bedrooms have come full circle in the history of interiors. Time was when they were round-the-clock rooms. Kings, for instance, held court propped among their pillows. And in early American cottages there often was only one room, so all family activities, including sleeping, took place there. Today, the crowd may be somewhat diminished, but the bedroom is back as a room for all reasons. Small wonder, considering the shrinking space we have left for daily living, and considering the ever-increasing pressures of the noisy, hectic world outside. Our bedrooms now are very personal retreats, quiet havens in the mainstream of life, to which we retire, not only to sleep, but to relax and regroup ourselves. In decorative terms, there are innumerable ways to furnish our bedrooms—be they big, small, or in between—so they really do live up to the greater demands we make on them today.

# BEDROOMS
## SLEEP STYLES

We're just now awakening to all the living potential that's hiding behind bedroom doors. No longer need colors always be calm, the scene subdued and somnolent. With today's bedroom available for 24-hour duty as a place to relax, watch television, work, or even dine from time to time, our decorating horizons have expanded accordingly. Even the bed is no longer just a place to sleep, nor is it always the major piece of bedroom furniture. It all depends on how you use your bedroom (and how often) in the course of a day. If you head there only after hours, you may be wasting precious space that could meet myriad living needs. Let's explore a few options.

If you like to watch television, perhaps you should pamper yourself with your own set in the bedroom. How about the stereo? Is good music available only in the "public" areas of the house? Do you ever bring work home and end up at the dining room table? Do you have a convenient place to pursue pet projects: sewing or a handcraft or hobby you'd like to leave out as you go along?

Counting the potentials beats counting sheep, and puts sleep fairly far down on the bedroom activities list (not so far down, of course, that comfort ceases to matter). To help you decide what you want from your bedroom during daytime, read on for some practical suggestions.

### BEGIN WITH THE BED

Aside from their being essential, little else is standard about today's beds Depending on your taste, you can have a dramatic four-poster or an entirely coincidental bed that folds out of sight into a closet or cupboard. In between is a range of sizes and styles planned to suit any sleep style and fit any floor space.

Don't overlook the decorative potential of such bed accessories as headboards and linens. Both are easy to change, and both have an immediate and dramatic decorative effect. Headboards can be almost anything your imagination dictates: Consider a wrought-iron gate, a wall-hung rug, a curlicued-and-carved antique dresser mirror, or a colorful piece of patchwork. You'll see some examples later in this chapter.

Bed linens, as everyone knows, have changed dramatically from the old all-white days. In fact, handsome new sheets are what first inspired the unmade bed idea—the linens were just too pretty to keep under cover.

### OTHER ACCOUTERMENTS

The bed, as we've said, is just the first piece of furniture that goes into the new bedroom. After that, practice as-you-like-it decorating that both meets your living needs and expresses your style. Instead of the usual dresser, consider using an antique corner cupboard. If you're blessed with ample room, trade closet space for a giant armoire and convert the closet to a small study area. Or install a mini-entertainment center in there, with a bar and tiny refrigerator, plus all your stereo gear.

### COMFORT DOES COUNT

Wherever your flights of fancy lead you, don't disregard the basic need for comfort. Of course, we all set our own standards for comfort, but there are a few fundamentals. Good lighting is one. It should match the mood of the room and be ample for the various activities you pursue there. Another important comfort consideration is quiet, especially if you're city bound. Lush carpet and bedclothes contribute to the overall quietude; so will fabric-upholstered walls and multilayered window treatments. Finally, comes the bedding you choose, the major factor in your comfort that's so important we devote several pages to how to buy it (see pages 348–351).

*A delightful combination of colors—hunter green walls, crisp white trim, and warm red accents—infuse this room with winning personality. The wonderful mahogany bed was purchased at a house sale, as were the old wicker chaise and the rocking chair. Adding extra color and interest is a framed stained-glass design hanging in one window.*

# BEDROOMS
## SLEEP STYLES

**A**n idea worth repeating: The things you enjoy most should find their way into your bedroom decor.

On these pages it's nostalgia, all the charm of yesteryear restated in two fairly large bedrooms filled with antiques and approximations. If you, too, define your dream bedroom in terms of brass beds and old quilts, you're quite in step with the times. It seems that the more sophisticated, complicated, and inundated with anxieties our lives become, the more we yearn to turn back the clock, at least in our most private moments and places. For many of us that means our bedrooms. And the step into the past is an easy one these days, even if you haven't fallen heir to an attic full of antiques.

### BUYING NEW NOSTALGIA

Nostalgia has become a big enough trend to inspire good reproductions of all the furnishings you need to carry off a mellow mood. Take brass beds, for example. Look for ones that have been made after the old molds; they have all the rich design heritage of the real thing, but are rescaled to fit today's standardized mattresses and bed linens.

Look also for golden oak oldies, richly grained and often elaborately carved furniture from the turn of the century. Oak is the most honestly American of all furniture materials. A hundred years ago, oak furniture was considered startlingly original—sometimes just startling. It was carved, pressed, bent, veneered, quartered, and distressed. Much old oak furniture—today's full-fledged antiques—was bought by the middle class from mail-order catalogs. When that generation traded up to walnut and mahogany, many of the throwaways were relegated to storage in the attic or barn. Today, these golden beauties are being sold to eager collectors.

There's also a goodly supply of oak reproductions faithful to the quirky originals. You can find the wonderfully ample dressers with triple mirrors that grandma preened in, and the grandly scaled chifforobes in which grandpa kept his celluloid collars. Great old pieces like these are available in brand-new versions, often scaled to suit new space requirements and fitted with modern conveniences.

No nostalgic bedroom would feel right without the proper background. Here, too, modern technology has helped turn back the design clock. You'll find a wealth of period wall coverings to choose from, including some authentic copies of Victorian papers. But these coverings come with convenience that's strictly today: For example, many come pretrimmed and prepasted for easy dip-and-hang installation, and many are vinyl-coated so they literally wipe clean. Still others are strippable.

### FOR THE PURIST

Of course, if you insist on the *real* old thing, your timing is also right today. At nearly every crossroad is a country auction, and tag (or porch or garage) sales are the new national pastime, The furnishings you could not give away 10 to 20 years ago are now highly sought after.

It's no longer news to anyone that wicker has come in off the front porch to high-fashion interiors. In fact, anything that's wicker, brass, marble-topped, or otherwise obviously leftover from the "good old days" is right for a renaissance today. Competition for the real thing is keen—and fun. Furnishing your new "old" bedroom becomes a kind of treasure hunt, one you can enjoy without the fistful of money more venerable antiques would command.

### COLLECTIBLES CONTRIBUTE

Mood is more than the broadbrush statements made by the major furnishings in a bedroom. Often, it's the smaller touches that contribute most of the old-time atmosphere. Bring out your collectibles, antique quilts, leather-bound books, and family photos in antique frames. Perhaps you have a lingering childhood love for dolls or old toys. Maybe you're fascinated with jewelry, paperweights, or needlework. Bits of nostalgia such as these can add personal expression to your bedroom.

**If you sometimes long to escape the press of modern life, consider the nostalgic bedroom furnishings of yesteryear.**

**1** Antiques and collectibles from rural Americana are what stamp this bedroom special. A muted, striped vinyl wall covering, reminiscent of the Victorian era, provides a perfect backdrop for the brass bed and the farm oak furniture. Even with major pieces such as these in place, it's the accessories—the clocks, Tiffany-style glass lamps, and collection of old chests at the foot of the bed—that add the nostalgic charm. But even without pedigreed or expensive pieces, you can create a similar effect. Just use the things you love and group them in close arrangements for dramatic decorating effect.

**2** A beautiful brass bed, covered with a simple chenille spread and fringed throw pillows, is the decorative focal point in this gracious bedroom. The sand-and white color scheme is soothing yet sophisticated. Much more than a place for sleeping, this cozy retreat serves many purposes. A small desk tucked into a window niche provides a place to pay bills and write letters. A wicker *étagère* next to the fireplace functions handily for storage of TV, books, and magazines.

2

# BEDROOMS
## SLEEP STYLES

F our-posters are foremost in the hearts of many romantics, but they needn't be restricted to purely traditional schemes. Today you can find a four-poster bed to fit virtually any decorative style—from authentic old-fashioned to a futuristic contemporary style.

The origin of the four-poster bed goes back to the days when the posts were cozily curtained against "harmful" night airs. Harmful may be exaggeration, but the airs could indeed be chilling, whipping through those drafty old houses. Central heating has stripped away the actual reason for using canopied beds, but certainly not our inherited love for them.

With or without the accompanying curtains, the four-poster is a commanding presence in any bedroom. It's exactly the right piece for a traditional room setting, but also can be taken out of context for contemporary living. Even less than generously proportioned bedrooms can have an adaptation of the four-poster.

If you're a do-it-yourselfer, you can create one of your own. Or, you can achieve a tall-bed effect without actually building posts and frame; use ceiling-mounted wood drapery rods or large dowels to hang the curtains. If your room is too small to handle the scale of a full four-poster, then opt for a small version by draping only the head of the bed area. Use flat panels of fabric for a modern look; choose generous shirring and perhaps a ruffled valance for a traditional scheme. Two of the three beauties on these pages are handsomely homemade.

**1** The reality of owning a four-poster bed may be as near as your local lumberyard. This country-chic canopied bed is entirely homemade (with the exception of the traditional candlewick spread). The bed is a platform with a recessed top that a king-size box spring fits into. The base is made of three horizontal cedar tongue-and-groove 1x8s, capped with a 2x4. Rough-sawn cedar posts (4x4s) at the four corners support the 7-foot-high frame on which sheer cotton draperies are hung from rod-fitted 1x3s. The headboard and chaise longue pillows have been hand-appliquéd with denim and cotton sateen.

**2** Even if you own an elegant authentic four-poster, you need not treat it in the traditional manner. The mood here is decidedly modern, despite the presence of the elaborately turned and polished bed. Credit the calm color scheme, the stylish sheets, and the carefully culled collection of accessories.

**3** This room leaves no doubt about its early American design heritage. At least, not at first glance. But look again and you'll discover a platform bed under the traditional headboard, and a sleek, illuminated storage shelf in the foreground. However, the nicest mood-melding of all is the *faux* four-poster, a successful bit of handiwork that combines 2x2 posts and closet poles, "testered" with calico laced across the top.

341

# BEDROOMS
## HEADBOARD IDEAS

1

2

3

**H**ighly effective in any bedroom decor, headboards can be conjured almost from thin air: You can simply *paint* them on the wall where the real thing would go. Even artistic talent is unnecessary if you use a stencil. Or, consider creating a poster effect by cutting "boards" from wood-grained plastic (the kind you peel and stick on the wall).

Another easy and inexpensive way to head up a bed is by using a width of wall covering applied right up the wall and across the ceiling, canopy-style. Achieve the same effect using fabric. Paste the fabric flat to the wall and cover the edges with glued-down braid. Or, whip out your staple gun and gather the fabric the easy way (stapling into a furring strip nailed on at the ceiling line).

**1** An awkward alcove made bed placement in this small room difficult. To solve the problem, a plywood box was built to fit the slanting space, then covered with fabric to match the spread. The box headboard serves a practical purpose, too: The lid slides off to provide storage for extra linens and blankets inside.

**2** This floral beauty of a headboard is a machine-stitched appliqué, using satin on satin. Batting sandwiched between the front satin and plain backing provides the puff.

**3** Back up your bed to a bookcase if you want a headboard that's as practical as it is good-looking. Here an artful display of framed graphics adds more personality to the scene.

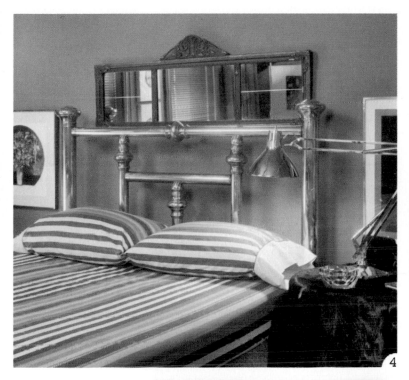

4

5

6

**4** The makings of an interesting headboard are found anywhere, so be on the lookout— especially at flea markets, antique shops, and salvage yards. Here an old, gilded mirror—snatched from a building demolition— brings reflection of things past to a headboard wall.

**5** A colorful Mexican rug enlivens the head of this otherwise featureless bed. To create a similar effect, simply nail a rug (or any banner of fabric you like) to a narrow wood strip, then fasten with hooks or nails to the wall.

**6** Heading up this king-size bed is a pair of iron gates from a salvage yard. Starkly dramatic in their new role, the gates present an open and shut case for what a little imagination can do to wake up a bedroom.

# BEDROOMS
## SPACE-STRETCHING IDEAS

**N**ever, it seems, has there ever been ample room to stow all the essentials of our lives. And in today's multifunctional bedrooms, "essentials" mean much more than yesterday's Spartan bed and dresser; bedrooms now must do more than provide spaces for sleeping and clothes storage. Where do you put the books, television, stereo, and such? Not to mention the sewing machine and exercise equipment?

Tighter spaces and changing needs have brought about a corresponding change in how we use the space we have. More and more of us are thinking of our bedrooms as secondary living areas; we expect them to be just as hard-working and space-efficient as other rooms. Freed from conventions and from conventional furnish-ings, we can use new approaches to eke out every bit of usefulness from every inch of living space. To help do just that, furniture designers are making multifunctional and modular furniture that obligingly shapes (and reshapes) itself to suit our space needs.

① ②

③ ④

**If your bedroom is over-stuffed and under-used, try rethinking your living space to make it more multifunctional.**

**1,2** By giving up a few inches of floor space, you can gain lots of storage in a space-starved bedroom. Here, homemade shelf units hide behind folding screens that flank the bed in this 13x13-foot room. Made of hardboard framed in 1x2 lumber, the screens are covered with grasscloth to provide a decorative front for their practical purpose.

**3** Modular furniture offers a marvelous cure for a cramped bedroom. These clean-lined contemporary modules are all standard in size, so you can stack them if you want, or wrap them around the room as shown. You can buy as many or as few modules as you need to suit your storage and space requirements.

**4** By stealing 2 feet of floor space from this average-size bedroom, the room's occupant gained lots of storage. Curtains are attached to a plywood cornice that extends 2 feet from the wall. Stashed behind the curtains are seasonal clothing items, suitcases, and hobby equipment. Vertical blinds behind the bed can be closed for a shimmery headboard effect, or opened as shown to allow access to books, reading lamp, and radio.

**5** Separate but equal—that describes the "his" and "hers" areas in this 12x15-foot master bedroom. The island bed is backed by a headboard that forms two working and grooming spaces behind it. Even the foot of the bed is functional: A flip-up ledge holds a TV for bedtime viewing.

5

The formal guest room is all but gone, now that "spare" rooms are practically nonexistent in most homes. Today, we disguise the guest room as a den, hide it in a sofa, and use it for many family activities between visitors.

Although our homes may be less spacious than in the past, they still can be gracious and comfortable when company comes to call. Finding room for one or more is a matter of pre-planning. For an easy example, if you choose a convertible instead of a single-purpose sofa, you have an instant guest "room" always at hand. Never mind whether that really means your living room. Sleep sofas have come a long way from the old, rock-hard models you may remember. Today's dual-personality pieces offer real bed comfort by night, and high-style looks by day.

Although sleep sofas are the most obvious way to eliminate guest-work, if you research your favorite furniture store, you'll find others: chairs that flip into single and double beds, innocent-looking cabinets that contain flip-out sleeping space, stacking pillows that pull together for after-hours duty. Search your imagination, too, for all the places that can be coaxed into putting on company manners. Is your attic underdeveloped? Do you have a generous alcove where a fold-away bed could retire behind a freestanding screen? How about a hallway that's out of the way? After all, hospitality is more a matter of *how* than *where* you accommodate your guests' needs.

1 This now-you-see-it, now-you-don't guest room functions as a den most of the time. It's all thanks to a wonderful modular cabinet system that lines one wall of the room. Two of the freestanding, ready-made cabinets hold twin beds inside (only one is pictured here). Two narrower units provide drawer storage and shelf space for stereo speakers. The center unit accommodates books, a stereo, and a television. A plywood lambrequin, upholstered in fabric, frames the window area. Narrow-slat blinds continue the tailored look and offer maximum flexibility for light control.

2 This sleep-sofa has nothing clunky looking about it; its simple, contemporary styling is in step with today. Each section flips out to become a comfortable bed; the cube coffee table is used as a nightstand for stay-over guests.

3 Prefinished hardwood flooring covers one wall of this small, but serviceable, sleep spot. The platform bed, which has built-in storage for linens, doubles as a seating unit. The mattress cover, bolsters, and wall-hung cushions are stitched from synthetic suede. As evidenced by the presence of a sewing machine, the room earns its keep at all times.

347

# BEDROOMS/MATTRESS BUYMANSHIP

A good mattress is a sizable investment that will serve you for a long time. It is not, however, a lifetime investment, as many people mistakenly think.

When do you need a new mattress? If your mattress has been used for a number of years, it's probably time to give it these tests. Strip off the bedding and take a look. Is the surface lumpy? Are there valleys and ridges or a depression in the center? Do the edges sag? Has the mattress lost its resiliency? Can you feel the springs when you press with your hand? Do you feel cramped in your share of sleeping space? If the answer to most of these questions is yes, it's time to start shopping for a new sleep set.

To ensure sleeping comfort and prevent morning backache, test a number of mattresses and buy the best you can afford. A high-quality support system will reward you with many years of good service, but a low-quality mattress will probably sag after just a few years.

## SIZES AND TYPES

The bed size you need depends on your own size, whether you sleep alone or with someone, how much stretching room you want, and the size of your bedroom. Mattresses are made in standard widths from 38 to 76 inches wide and from 75 to 80 inches long. (See chart.)

If you're buying a bed for two, keep in mind that a full size (double) only offers each partner the sleeping space of a baby's crib. Sufficient sleeping space for two adults really requires a queen size; or, for extra stretch-out comfort consider a king. Regardless of the width, a mattress should always be at least 6 inches longer than the person sleeping on it.

There are four basic types of mattresses—innerspring, foam, water-filled, and air-filled.

**Innerspring mattress.** This type of mattress has rows of steel coils sandwiched between layers of insulation, cushioning material, and a fabric cover.

Although the number of coils has often been used as an indication of quality, what counts far more is the thickness of the coil wire, the number of coil convolutions (or turns), and the way the coils work together to support your body while you sleep. Generally, the thicker the wire

and the more convolutions, the firmer the support of the coils. High-quality models usually have coils made of low-gauge (thick) wire with six turns. Coils in medium- and lower-priced mattresses are often made of thinner wire and have fewer convolutions.

The springs are covered with an insulator to prevent the mattress cushioning from working down into the coils. The insulator is made of tough fiber padding, wire, or netting, or some combination of the three.

Mattress cushionings are made generally of polyurethane foam, combined with cotton felt or other fibers. Generous cushioning indicates high quality. The cushioning is secured to the innersprings to keep it in place.

It's best to buy a matching box spring when you purchase a new innerspring mattress. The cost will be about the same as the mattress. The box spring will reinforce support where needed and greatly extend the mattress life.

Like mattresses, box springs also have different coil counts, and the coils themselves may be shaped like a cone or an hourglass. Instead of having coils, some foundations contain metal grids or torsion bars bent in a squared zigzag shape.

Some foundations are not spring systems but combinations of wood and foam. Be sure that the foam layer in this type of foundation is at least a couple of inches thick for resilient support.

**Foam mattress.** A majority of foam mattresses are made of polyurethane, which is manu-

## MATTRESS SIZES

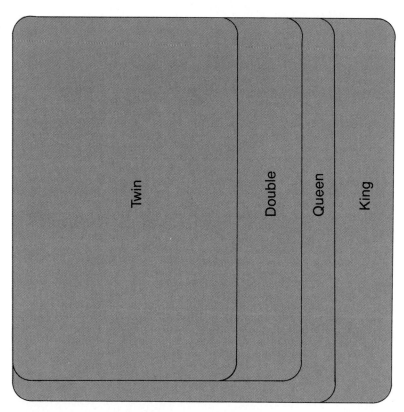

Twin measures 38 inches by 75 or 80 inches
Double (full) measures 53 inches by 75 or 80 inches
Queen measures 60 inches by 80 inches
King measures 76 inches by 80 inches

Note: An extra-long twin, 38 inches by 80 inches, is available as is a California King-size that measures 72 inches by 84 inches.

348

factured in large slabs and cut to size. Mattresses consisting of high resilience polyurethane or polyurethane with embedded thermoplastic beads will give the optimum support and performance.

The most expensive foam mattresses are usually made of latex rubber. A slab of synthetic rubber is molded while in the liquid state, then allowed to harden into a foam core with a dense construction. Because of its scarcity and high cost, latex is used to produce only a limited number of premium-quality mattresses.

Good quality foam has a high "density," which adds weight. Therefore, a very lightweight foam mattress does not usually offer the greatest support and durability.

**Water-filled mattress.** There are two basic kinds of water bed mattresses: a simple bladder filled with water, or a more complex "hybrid" type.

In the simpler type, the bladder is designed to be inserted into a decorative, heavy-duty framing that rests on a pedestal base.

Hybrid flotation systems are made in a variety of ways, but most have an internal water-filled bladder surrounded by a foam shell. The mattress is covered with a heavily quilted ticking and resembles a conventional innerspring mattress. The matching foundation is especially designed to provide the necessary extra heavy-duty support for the water's weight.

The hybrids, however, are lighter and use less water than standard water beds because they're shallower. Most are "waveless" thanks to built-in baffles in serpentine, cone, coil, or cylinder shapes that restrict side-to-side and up-and-down movements. In some mattresses, an added chemical partially solidifies the water and thus reduces wave motion.

When buying any type of water bed system, always make sure there is a vinyl liner that will contain all of the water in case of puncture. Also, be sure to purchase a special water bed heater. This not only provides additional comfort and luxury, but also prevents condensation, which can occur.

**Air-filled mattress.** The new air beds work on the same principle as the collapsible air mattresses used in swimming pools and on camping trips. The core of the mattress is a heavy-duty vinyl bladder, which is enclosed in a foam shell with a cushioned, zip-on cover, much like a hybrid water bed.

Some air beds are filled to a desired firmness with a vacuum cleaner or hair dryer; others are available with a compressor unit and electric controls. The larger mattresses often have dual air chambers with dual controls so couples can choose different firmness.

**Platform beds.** Mattresses specifically designed for use on platform beds have been discontinued by most manufacturers. Today, top-quality foam mattresses are recommended for most platform beds. However, some "island" or "sand box" beds have recessed bases that can be used with a regular box spring and mattress. The base conceals the box spring.

**Adjustable beds.** Specially constructed frames, which allow the head and foot of the bed to be raised and lowered, are now being designed for home use. The electronic controls often feature a built-in massage unit as well. Usually, the mattress designed to accompany the frame is of top-quality construction so it can withstand the extra stress of the regular flexing movement.

## TRY IT OUT

How do you tell whether a mattress is right for you? Test it. Take off your shoes and lie down on the mattress. Almost any mattress will feel comfortable at first, so stay on it for about ten minutes. Stretch and roll around, just as you would when you sleep.

The mattress should support areas of greatest weight, such as the shoulders and hips. Support should be firm, but the mattress also should have enough surface resilience to ensure comfort.

Mattress edges are another indicator of quality. A good mattress will have reinforced sides to prevent sagging when you sit on the bed's edge. The edge may give a little under your weight, but it should spring back when you stand up.

When you shop, ask what's under the cover. If the salesperson can't tell you, ask to see a catalog or brochure from the manufacturer. Also check for a cutaway model to study.

Always read the attached hangtag and label that provide information about the materials and construction.

## IS FIRMNESS FOR YOU?

Although many doctors recommend hard mattresses for patients with back problems, everyone isn't comfortable on a hard mattress, or even a semihard one. Also, manufacturers' definitions of firmness may vary, so don't rely on labels such as "extra-firm" or "ultra-firm" when sizing up a mattress. Determine for yourself whether a mattress feels right.

If you know you want firmness, look for a mattress with thick-wired coils and extra-strong perimeter wires. Also, a box spring with a built-in backboard will increase the firmness.

Or, select an innerspring mattress that has firm support—but beneath an extra-plush top. These soft-top mattresses are usually the highest quality and the highest priced ones available in a line.

## CHECK POINTS

A mattress covering may be tufted, quilted, or smooth-topped (with interior tufting to keep it in place). Check to make sure seams are straight and the stitching even.

Ask about warranties. A good-quality mattress and foundation generally are warranted against defective workmanship by the manufacturer. For premium bedding, a 15-year warranty is common. Lower-quality bedding may be warranted for a shorter period. A good water bed will have a six- to 10-year limited warranty; heaters generally are guaranteed for three to five years.

When selecting a blanket, keep in mind your preferences for warmth, weight, and washability. Blankets are available in wool as well as synthetic blends.

**Wool Blankets.** The *crème de la crème* of blankets, wool blankets are wonderfully warm and invitingly soft. And they come in a wide range of rich colors. Although they cost more than synthetic blankets, a good wool blanket, properly cared for, will last for at least 15 years, and probably much longer. New wool blankets are permanently mothproofed, and some can be laundered instead of dry cleaned. Check the label for cleaning instructions.

**Synthetic Blankets.** Blankets made from synthetic fibers are considerably less expensive than wool, are easy to wash and dry, and are also non-allergenic. Some of the types available are conventional, thermal, nonwoven, flocked, and electric. *Thermal* blankets are good year round. They are comfortable in summer because of their open weave, yet warm in winter when used with a top covering to trap body heat.

Both conventional and thermal blankets are loom-woven; *nonwoven* blankets are made like felt with sheets of fiber layered and "needled" to bind. These blankets are inexpensive, but not nearly as durable or nice to the touch as a woven blanket. *Flocked blankets* are of a velvety nylon bound to a foam base, creating a blanket that is plush, warm, and doesn't mat or pill.

**Electric Blankets.** These are made of light acrylic material on the outside, with flexible heating wires inside. Look for the Underwriters Laboratories Seal, which indicates that samples have been tested to ensure they are shock- and spark-proof when used according to the manufacturer's directions. Twin- and full-size blankets have at least nine thermostats embedded throughout (king- and queen-size have more) so that if a blanket starts to overheat, any one of the thermostats will sense the rising temperature and automatically shut off the flow of heat.

## PILLOW POINTERS

There's really no such thing as a "perfect" bed pillow because everyone has different criteria.

If you're going to shop for others in your family, check out their pillow preferences, too. Quiz them on their choice of soft, medium, or firm, and fat or thin. Although a luxuriously soft pillow is considered a treat by some, others find it annoying to have their heads sink in a sea of feathers.

It's impossible to tell about a pillow simply by looking at it. Pick it up, handle it, and test to see whether it's skimpily or plumply filled.

Here are the most common fillings you'll encounter:

**Down.** Real pillow connoisseurs consider down—from geese and ducks—to be the finest filling that money can buy. It is luxuriously soft and lightweight—and is also the most expensive filling.

**Feathers.** Duck, goose, turkey, and chicken feathers are also used for pillow fillings. Goose feathers are the softest, with duck feathers next. Chicken feathers are considered the least desirable because of their heavier spines and quills.

**Down/Feather Blends.** Various combinations of down and feathers are available. A combination of 20 percent down with 80 percent feathers makes a compact, firm pillow. For medium softness, look for 40 percent down and 60 percent feathers. A 50/50 blend provides a semi-luxurious pillow.

**Polyester Fiberfills.** These include Dacron, Kodel, Vycron, and Fortrel. Such fillings are comfortably soft, lightweight, resilient, mothproof, mildew-proof, and non-allergenic.

**Synthetic/Down Blends.** One of the newest fillings is a blend of polyester fiberfill, plus down and goose feathers. The best features of each filling are combined for comfort and easy care.

**Foam Latex.** These pillows come in varying degrees of firmness and are molded in one piece or shredded. Molded is the best type. Foam is buoyant, mothproof, mildew-resistant, odorless, and non-allergenic.

## SELECTING SHEETS

Today's sheet fashions offer every conceivable color combination and design. But looks alone should not influence your buying decision. Fabric content is an important consideration as well.

The standard fiber content is still 50 percent polyester/50 percent cotton for both muslin and percale sheets, but different blends are now available. A 60 percent cotton/40 percent polyester blend has the practical wash-and-wear features of 50/50, but offers more of the familiar feel and comfort of cotton. There's also a 65 percent cotton/35 percent polyester sheet that offers long wear, fast drying, and softness to the touch.

If you still prefer the luxury of a 100 percent cotton percale sheet, that option is available. Other fiber blends are designed for silky satin-like luxury. One is a 70 percent polyester/30 percent cotton blend; another is a sheet made of 70 percent polyester/30 percent rayon.

## FINISHING TOUCHES

A bedspread, comforter, or duvet will add a special finishing touch to your bed. Sheet manufacturers now are producing comforters and bedspreads that coordinate with sheet patterns and solids.

**Comforters.** When selecting a comforter, you have a choice of several fillings: down, down and feathers, or polyester. Comforters filled with natural materials such as down will keep you toasty warm in the winter and comfortable in the warmer months, but expect to pay top dollar for the luxury of down. Polyester-fill comforters aren't as warm as those filled with down, but they are comfortable when used in combination with blankets or by themselves during the warmer months.

**Duvets.** Long a mainstay in drafty European bedrooms, the

# SEWING PROJECTS

duvet is catching on in America. People like them for their excellent warmth and effortless good looks. When a duvet is used in place of a spread and blankets (as it usually is), all you do is fluff it up, smooth it out, and your bed is made.

Duvets are constructed with a layer of light, bulky filling (down or feather and down) sewn between two layers of fabric so warmth is trapped. They have wall-channeled construction—an inner wall of fabric separates the channels so the down won't shift or bunch up. Because a duvet maintains body temperature without the weight of a blanket, you can sleep comfortably under it in sub-zero or 75-degree weather.

All this comfort and ease doesn't come cheaply, but with proper care a duvet will last much longer than a synthetic filled comforter.

A comfortable alternative to the down duvet is a cotton/polyester comforter filled with 100 percent lamb's wool. Soft, plump, lightweight, and channel-stitched, this comforter resembles the high-priced spread. Because the filling is wool, this type of duvet is much warmer and more resilient than the synthetic kind.

A duvet should always be at least 18 inches wider than the bed. Always keep a duvet in a washable duvet cover that zips, snaps, or buttons on. Linen departments carry these covers in solid and patterned sheeting fabric, or you can make a cover yourself from sheets.

Both down-and-feather duvets and comforters should be professionally cleaned.

With so many colors, designs, and patterns available, sheets are perfect choices for a variety of home sewing projects. Their seamless, larger-than-usual widths and easy-care qualities give them an edge over conventional yard goods. And since sheets are tightly woven, they are durable as well as economical.

Cover your duvet with a perky pattern, then use coordinating sheets for a matching bedside tableskirt and curtains.

## CONSTRUCT A DUVET COVER

You can make a duvet cover with the sheets of your choice. Simply customize solid-colored or patterned sheets to match or complement your bed linens.

To make a comforter cover, you'll need: a duvet (twin, full, queen, or king size); two flat sheets the same size or larger than the duvet; five to 10 Velcro hook-and-loop fastener dots (depending on the size of the duvet), one-inch-wide ribbon or trim, and thread.

Measure the length and width of the duvet. Mark and cut each sheet the same size as the duvet. (When sewn, the cover will be one inch shorter and one inch narrower than the duvet for added fullness.)

Because the cover will resemble an oversize pillowcase when finished, make an opening for the duvet by finishing one end of both sheets. Turn under a half-inch hem on the raw edge of each sheet; press.

Turn the fabric under another half inch and stitch.

Pin trim to the right side of the top sheet; stitch into place.

With right sides facing, pin the two sheets together. Stitch the three unfinished edges, using half-inch seams.

Attach evenly spaced fastener dots (or sew buttons and buttonholes) across open end.

## COVER A BEDSIDE TABLE

To make a circular tablecloth, first measure the diameter of your tabletop. Then add the desired drop to each side. Be sure to add a half-inch hem allowance to each side drop. (See drawing.)

For instance, if you have a table with a diameter of 40 inches and you want a 25-inch drop, add 25 inches plus 40 inches plus 25 inches for a total diameter of 90 inches.

Sheets for round tablecloths

| Diameter of cloth | Flat sheet required |
|---|---|
| Up to 65" | Twin |
| Up to 80" | Full (Double) |
| Up to 89" | Queen |
| Up to 99" | King |

Spread the sheet out on the floor, then fold in quarters to find the center. Tie a string to a pencil, then cut the string to 45 inches—half the desired diameter. Attach the end of the string to a corner on the fold and draw a quarter circle arc. Make a half-inch hem by machine or by hand. (See drawings.)

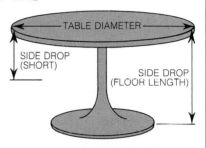

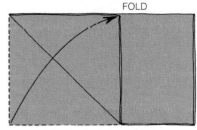

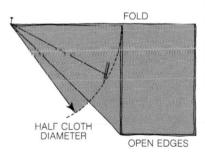

For lightweight sheets you may prefer a narrow rolled hem. First, machine stitch ¼ inch from the edge of the table skirt. Then trim close to the stitching. The fabric will easily turn over this row of machine stitching and your hem will be smoother. Roll the edge a few inches at a time. Slip-stitch the roll into place, catching a single thread of the sheet each time. If a section seems to resist rolling, the machine stitching may be too tight. Correct this by clipping the machine stitching once or twice before continuing.

# CHILDREN'S ROOMS

Like Gulliver in his travels, you enter a completely new world when it comes to decorating children's rooms. All the rules of scale are changed because furnishings must suit a small-scale person who grows bigger every year. Cast back into your own childhood or watch youngsters at play, and you quickly see which furnishings work best for them. A child's room should be a very personal place—a special little world in which to sleep, play, study, and socialize with friends. It goes without saying that furnishings—new, homemade, or hand-me-downs—should be practical, sturdy, and able to withstand child-style misuse. The same is true for floor coverings and walls. But most of all, a child's room should be fun, both for you to decorate and your child to live in.

# CHILDREN'S ROOMS
## YOUTHFUL LIVING

When is a chair a plaything as well as something to sit on? When it is in a child's room, along with the other furnishings that suit a small-fry's needs. Kids use furnishings in ways you might not dream of, so the furniture needs to be extra sturdy and extra safe. Here are some pointers for buying major pieces to suit every use, including creative ones.

### BEDS FOR ALL AGES

From the crib onward, put safety first in buying bedding. Federal standards for new cribs require that slats be no more than 2⅜ inches apart, that rails be an adequate height even when the drop side is lowered, that drop sides cannot be released by a child, and that the mattress fit the crib perfectly so there are no dangerous gaps. Apply the same standards to any crib you might receive as a hand-me-down. If the crib needs sprucing up, be sure to use lead-free paint.

Youth-size beds are popular choices after the baby has outgrown a crib. These small-scale beds generally have guardrails that can be removed when your child announces that he or she is too "grown-up" for such devices. But a youth bed isn't a necessity; you can graduate a child from a crib to a full-size bed. If space is a problem, good choices include trundle and bunk beds. Bunk beds often have a bonus of built-in storage, such as drawers underneath and shelf cubbyholes along the ends. Bunks that can be separated into two single beds are most versatile.

Guest sleeping starts from toddler age onward. Overnight bedding includes sleeping bags, foldaway cots, inflatable mats, and even chairs that fold out to become beds.

Handsome sheets complete the bed dressing and can be used throughout the room for windows, upholstery, and wall coverings.

### FURNITURE WITH A FUTURE

Good furniture carefully chosen will last through the child-rearing years. Flexible modular units are ideal. Landscape them so shelves and drawers are within a toddler's reach. Elevate the stackables when a schoolchild needs the extra floor space for work and study tables. Good basic units will stand the test of time and still look up-to-date.

Apply rigid safety standards to all furniture, including bookcases, cabinets, open shelving, table and worktops, and chairs. None should tip easily or have protruding sharp edges or knobs.

Easy-care surfaces are abundant in children's furniture and regular furniture adapted for kids. Plastic laminates, sealed woods, metals, and easily repainted finishes (including unfinished and home-built pieces) are most indestructible.

A child instinctively makes furniture multipurpose, and some manufacturers have even designed pieces to be used that way. A flat top storage chest makes a wonderful work surface or place to sit, so long as it is a comfortable height.

Many multipurpose pieces are space savers as well. In children's rooms that are small, take advantage of chairs that double as desks, stacking stool and chair sets, and foldaway or adjustable tables.

### FLOOR SHOWS

The floor is an infant's most important furnishing and a favorite spot for many years to come. Both carpet and hard-surface flooring are good choices for backgrounding children's activities. The solution may be to use areas of each.

Wood floors can be painted or stained so the surfaces are practically stain- and waterproof. These are the least expensive solutions. Then add an area rug (nonskid) for warm crawling and cozy sitting.

Resilient flooring is grand for scooting as well as messy activities since it is easily cleaned. Patterns and prints in wonderful colors take the visual edge off the essential coldness of this flooring, but you will want to add a rug to provide a warm and soft sitting space.

Carpet and room-sized rugs provide warmth underfoot but aren't quite as practical as hard-surface flooring. Choose carpet that is stain-resistant. A tight-looped pile will show the least traffic wear. Plaids, prints, or medium tones disguise stains and soiling very well.

*This brightly lacquered bunk bed and two low chests are modular, easy-to-assemble units that can be changed and regrouped to fit the needs of a growing child— from toddler to teen-ager.*

# CHILDREN'S ROOMS
## YOUTHFUL LIVING

### WELL-DRESSED WALLS

Walls in children's rooms can take quite a beating, so keep this in mind when selecting a covering. Good bets include high-gloss paint, scrubbable paper, or paneling.

Avoid patterns your child will quickly outgrow, such as obvious infant scenes. Keep colors bright, warm, and cheerful, but not so garish that they might overwhelm.

### AN OUTSIDE VIEW

Window treatments must monitor light, reduce drafts, and allow for ventilation. The right choice does it all attractively.

Shades provide total darkness but little ventilation. Blinds are a good choice because they can be adjusted to suit various lighting requirements. Curtains and shutters are best for cutting drafts. Often you can combine window treatments.

### GROW LIGHTS

As in any other room of the house, good lighting in a child's room is a must. At the nursery level, avoid harsh overhead lighting, as glare can bother a baby's eyes. Soft, diffused lighting is best for an infant, although you might want a brighter task lamp near the changing area. At the preschool stage, add localized lighting for projects and later for studies.

### ORGANIZERS

A bulletin board of good size is the best organizer for child-works and artworks. For a good-looking wall treatment that's practical, too, consider covering an entire wall with individual squares of cork or sheets of fiber board.

Choose storage units with adjustable shelves that will handily adapt from age to age and hobby to hobby.

**1** Tots and toys go together, and here each treasure has its own space on easy-to-construct open shelves. As the child grows older, shelves will be used for books, model boats, or any other new-found treasures. The old brass bed is a natural with the Americana red, white, and blue color scheme. Bed-making is a snap with polka-dotted sheets and a bright quilt that eliminates the need for a spread.

**2** Any young lady would love the sophisticated charm of this wall covering with lots of heart. The delightful red scheme is continued on a red and white calico bed coverlet. Dolls, stuffed animals, and miniatures displayed in an old printer's drawer act as eye-catching accessories.

**3** Traditional rooms often have wonderful details to delight and charm a child. A case in point is the window treatment here: colonial-styled shutters that slide over the window at night. These and other architectural details, such as the beams, are painted a handsome Williamsburg blue to contrast with the sparkling white walls. Quilts and the bed coverlet give splashes of pattern to the room, a charmer for a child—and adults, too.

**4** Think back to when you were a child. Chances are, you craved a canopy bed. This four-poster canopy was passed down from mother to daughter. The same is true for the handsome old highboy. In the spirit of tradition, blue and white gingham was chosen for the canopy, bedcovers, and perky tieback curtains. A prim print wall covering in soft cornflower blue and white stripes adds to the yesteryear appeal.

3

4

Children's beds can do a lot more than just lie around. Some fold up and out of sight; others spark the color and design ideas for the rest of the room.

**1,2** Talk about a space saver! This fold-up bed takes only 9 inches of floor space when closed. The plywood box holding the mattress is supported by roll-out storage bins and attached to the wall unit by piano hinges.

**3** Striking chevron-patterned sheets decorate the bed and Roman shade in this terrific teen room. Colors pulled from the sheet adorn the walls; high-gloss emerald green enamel with a red border at the ceiling creates a visual molding.

**4** Pick a pretty child's bedspread and paint a patterned window shade to match. Just draw the design on the shade, then fill in with fabric paint that comes in easy-to-use ball-point tubes.

3

2

4

# CHILDREN'S ROOMS
## WHEN THERE IS MORE THAN ONE

**A**lthough there's no denying that furnishing a room for two or more children can be quite a challenge, you can turn to any number of creative solutions. A place for privacy plus lots of space for playing together are the essential ingredients of a room designed for shared living. All space counts, so use it to the limit—floors, walls, closets, even the ceiling.

### PLAN FOR PRIVACY

Children will play together almost anywhere. What's hard to find in a shared room are private places. These are essential for solitary activities, such as reading, studying, or working on hobbies.

Dividers are an excellent solution for the privacy problem, even in the smallest room. You can buy freestanding dividers or make them yourself. Some can be attached to a wall then pushed open or closed, accordion style. A two-sided bulletin board or storage unit is a practical approach, as is a venetian blind attached to the ceiling.

When dividers aren't possible, separate quiet spaces by facing them away from each other, as far away as the room allows. Use the same logic in placing beds. Separate one child's napping place from another's play space.

Use color creatively to cope with shared space, especially if the room is small. For major areas, such as walls and floor, use the visual expanders: neutrals, white, cool colors, and light colors. Keep the general scheme simple, even monochromatic, to stretch every inch.

A toned-down restful background calls for accent colors. Give color the job of identifying each child's personal storage areas and possessions. Be bold, and splash a solid sweep of color on the surface of dressers, cabinets, and bookcases. For a much subtler look, earmark each piece with a small dab of color.

## Happy room sharing starts with clear definition of separate sleep, study, and play areas for each child.

**1** A modular, three-piece wrap-around of laminated plastic defines the sleeping and play area of this two-child room. Storage is tucked into the corner unit. Although intended to function as a complete right-angled unit, the pieces can be unbolted and arranged into other configurations.

**2** Here a storage bunk makes the most of small space. Drawers on one end and under the bottom bunk act as a double dresser.

**3,4** Two active school-age children share this long, narrow room. At one end, beds are placed foot-to-foot along the wall, freeing up space for floor play. A half wall at the head of one bed separates the sleep zone from the study area.

# CHILDREN'S ROOMS
## STORAGE IDEAS

**1** Old school lockers, when fitted with shelves, make perfect stash-aways for clothes and toys. Purge them of their institutional look by painting them in bright, high-gloss colors. Look for lockers in junkyards, or inquire at schools that are slated to be torn down.

**2** Shades of glory, here's found space in an unused upper bunk. A "cage" of horizontal and vertical 1x4s was constructed for the cover-up, then gaily colored window shades were mounted to the uppermost 1x4s along the side and end. A coordinated shade or two can cover windows to pull the look together.

**3** Storage can divide to conquer, as it does in this shared room. Enclosed sections of the divider open to both sides; the younger child using the lower sections, the older the upper sections. The see-through sections give the illusion of space plus privacy.

**4** Plentiful pouches are color-keyed for easy storage organization in this unit to build yourself. Start with a 10-foot ladder supported with a three-sided structure of fir strips. Sew pouches from colorful and washable canvas, attach along the sides, and sling over the ladder rails.

**5** This crisscross wall organizer can adapt to any size wall, any storage problem. Nail lengths of pine 1x3s to the wall to form two-foot squares. Add pegboard and cork inserts, display shelves, blackboards, or what have you to fill each square.

**6** Window-washer bucket totes are handy enough to warrant a custom nightstand to hold them.

**7** Custom designed for both function and good looks, this wall system encourages neatness and organization.

362

# BATHROOMS

Yesterday a stand-in and today a star! Once, for a very long time, the bathroom was relegated to second-class status on the decorating scene. Today, the bath is fast on its way to becoming a center for personal relaxation and grooming that goes far beyond its utilitarian nature. There we retreat to refresh both body and soul, not to mention makeup, hairdo, and even muscle tone. The modern bathroom is a veritable storehouse of personal care implements—everything from exercise equipment to sybaritic saunas, whirlpool baths, and shower massagers. This brings us to the where-to-put-it problem. Finding adequate bathroom storage is only one of the puzzles we'll help you solve in this chapter. If your own bath is cramped for space, poorly planned, or simply lacking in design punch, the solutions may come easier than you think. We'll show you ideas that are guaranteed to get top billing.

# BATHROOMS
## PERSONALITY BATHS

The bathroom is one of the most welcome innovations modern technology has presented to us. After all, it wasn't that long ago that bathrooms as we know them didn't exist.

If you own an older home, your bath may be filled with originals—the antique plumbing fixtures, for instance, that are more or less charming, depending on your interest in nostalgia. On the other hand, if you live in a home or apartment built recently, your bathroom probably has new plumbing, but precious little space, and not a lot of personality.

Big or small, new or old, baths deserve a positive approach. No fixed notions are allowed, even though this is one of the few rooms in your home with fixed "furniture" (the kitchen, of course, is another).

### SHOULD YOU REMODEL?

Although complete remodeling is one possibility, it's intimidatingly expensive. Anytime you start relocating plumbing and replacing major fixtures, you're talking real money, plus prolonged disruption of the room's usefulness. Major remodeling is like major surgery: Sometimes it's the only solution. The important thing is to be practical. Don't leap into a remodeling job before you've discussed ideas with either an architect or a contractor. An architect is an especially good bet if you're planning an addition. Many architects will sell you their time on a consultative basis, charging by the hour to look over your plans for pitfalls. Or, you may want someone to oversee the entire job, from blueprint to ribbon-cutting. You can find the kind of architect you're after in the classified pages of the telephone book; those with "AIA" (American Institute of Architects) listed behind their names belong to a professional association that sets strong standards for membership.

If you don't already know a contractor by reputation, you can track one down through the phone book. Ask for references to other jobs he's done in your area, then check them out. Also, you'd be wise to get estimates from two or three contractors before you make a final choice. You may be surprised at how price quotes for the same job can vary. As with any professional you consider hiring, discuss your expectations and financial arrangements up front, before any money changes hands. A written contract is a sound idea. Make sure it covers specifications for materials to be used, lists a date for starting and approximate completion, and details both the amount and method of payment.

If you're too short of funds or faint of heart to undertake major remodeling, there are myriad other, easier ways to cure a poorly functioning, outdated, or otherwise unlovely bathroom. Let's consider them one at a time.

### THE FIXTURE PICTURE

Without an extensive overhaul, it *is* possible to replace fixtures such as impossibly stained sinks, or tubs and toilets that no longer take their work seriously. Many of the new models on the market not only look new and streamlined, they also do their jobs better and more efficiently than older models. Some of today's water-saving toilets and showers include fixtures that conserve the family hot-water supply, no small consideration in our energy-aware era. Sometimes you can simply update the small fixtures—the faucets and showerheads—with replacement parts any fairly handy person can install.

Ditto for stingy storage areas. You can often install store-bought vanities yourself to add generous under-sink space. New cabinets aren't hard to hang, either. And don't overlook such simple supplementary storage as wall-mounted shelving, freestanding étagères, or fixtures that make the most of the empty wall areas over the toilet or radiator.

More extensive changes in the fixture picture may call for professional plumbing help, but can be accomplished in reasonably short order without major interruption of the bathroom's use.

Don't plan to replace a fixture till you've seen what's new on the bathroom scene, especially in colors. We've gone from white to the brights, and back again, touching all the color bases along the way. Since the fixtures are the bathroom's major furniture, choose what won't tire your eye in the years to come.

Even without major fixture make-overs, you can make a dramatic change in color, using special epoxy paints. Because the paint dries to the kind of slick, brilliant finish you want on your fixtures, it's worth the time it takes to apply it carefully and smoothly. That means priming the original finish to ensure a perfect surface before you roll (or spray) on the epoxy.

### WALLS AND FLOORS

Epoxy paint is a good solution for old tile walls, too. You can redo an awful hue for the cost of the paint, plus patience. Again, priming's important. Epoxy can refresh old bathroom tile better than anything—except *new* bathroom tile.

And that's possible to put up yourself, even if you aren't willing to pull down the old layer. Check your favorite flooring store or tile dealer for new products you can put right over the old.

If you're laying on a brand-new layer, look for ceramic tiles that come in sheets, with flexible grouting already in place. Nowadays, conventional tiles aren't all that impossible, either. Most dealers offer detailed instruction sheets and will lend or rent you all the special tools needed to do the job.

An alternative to tiled bath walls is paneling, with plastic-laminate surfaces that are practically impervious. Panels can go up over most old walls, including tiles. Wood is also a rich way to warm up a bathroom wall; it's practical, too, as our Scandinavian friends have shown in their saunas. For bathroom use, it's a good idea to seal the wood with urethane.

Vinyl and vinyl-coated wall coverings also can get along

**A bath is the most personal room in a house. Let it express your idea of luxury—a place to regather body and soul.**

handsomely in a bath's difficult climate—except in the shower area.

Here's a final wall idea to reflect upon: mirrors. They're especially practical in a dressing or bathroom where they open up cramped-looking quarters.

Moving down to floor level, ceramic and carpet tiles and wood planks take naturally to the bathroom scene. So do resilient tiles and sheet goods.

## THE LIGHTER SIDE

If you have a dim view of the way your bathroom looks, look for a brighter side to the situation. Bathroom lighting is one of the most overlooked aspects of bathroom decorating. But, happily, it's also one of the easiest ills to cure. For shaving or making-up, you need localized bright lights that don't create shadows. This means one on *each* side of the mirror. If your energy conscience twinges at using incandescent lighting, use *deluxe warm white* fluorescents that won't give your morning reflection a greenish glow.

Don't wrap up your bathroom remake without treating yourself to a look, at least, at the luxury items now on the market: saunas, steam baths, heated towel racks, whirlpool massages, hot tubs—the list is luxuriously long.

*Graphic poster artwork adds an invigorating splash of color to this natural-hued bathroom with its luxuriously deep and beautifully tiled tub. The quarry tile floor is unusual for a bath, but elegant.*

# BATHROOMS
## PERSONALITY BATHS

1

2

**Y**our bath can reflect your special interests. It can be a mini-gallery of collectibles or of not-too-valuable artwork. (The room's humidity may damage artwork, so keep your expensive pieces elsewhere.) Or, it can evoke the mood of another time, like the barbershop bath opposite.

Best of all, because bathrooms generally are small, and because you don't spend much time there, you can indulge your love of bold color and pattern. Here, you can get by with stronger design that might be overpowering elsewhere.

**1** A melange of hand mirrors hung on the wall obviously reflects a collector's major interest. But more than that, the mirrors—gleaned from around the world—are apt and attractive accessories for a bathroom. The owner, taking a cue from the collection, papered the room—ceiling and all—with old-fashioned red-and-white gingham wallpaper. Adding to the down-home feeling are the window shutters and vanity, painted barn red to match the wall covering.

**2** Another bathroom that reflects the personality of its owners becomes a minor gallery to show off a collection of colorful Mexican folk graphics. A suede-like fabric, shirred on a rod and hung beneath the sink ledge, conceals plumbing fixtures and gives the petite gallery a more finished appearance.

**3** Only the quartet is missing. Otherwise, the good old days have cheerfully been recaptured in this bath-cum-antiques gallery. Instead of looking past their prime, the old fixtures now are in perfect harmony with the new old-fashioned personality of the room, from the striped wall covering to the swirling barber pole, purloined mantel mirror, and barber shelf, fitted to hold toiletries.

# BATHROOMS
## PERSONALITY BATHS

**1** A mere 24-inch extension was enough to fill this once-dark bathroom with an abundance of natural light. Into the critical 2 feet (the dropped beam marks the original wall) went a sloping skylight roof that now floods the area with sun rays. Eye-level windows set into the tub wall augment the open-air atmosphere, without destroying privacy. The double sinks are a bonus in a busy household. Ditto the cabinet and drawer space beneath the vanity.

**2** Taking another fresh slant on an old bathroom, the owners of this turn-of-the-century Victorian home added greenhouse windows to extend the end of a too-small bathroom about 4½ feet. That's merely the width of the new tile-framed tub and European-style shower, but what a difference it makes in the mood of the room. An old mantel mirror and an Oriental rug are handsome reminders of the room's Victorian heritage.

**3** Just the smallest addition opens up new living potential in this under-the-eaves attic bath. The bump-out skylight makes it possible to lounge in the delightfully different old copper tub (reclaimed by the owner with elbow-grease) and lazily watch the clouds drift by. The sculptured figure next to the tub was fashioned by the homeowner from logs.

# BATHROOMS
## COSMETIC COVER-UPS

1 2

**A**ll of the big, old bathrooms you see here once looked well past their primes. The fixtures were geriatric, set in an over-abundance of space, with too-high ceilings and vast arctic expanses of cold tile. Remodeling might have been most people's response to the problem, but happily, these four homeowners were more far-sighted. They saw beyond the surface problems to the charms inherent in spacious old bathrooms with eccentric fixtures and distinct personalities.

The moral, of course, is look hard and close before you leap into a major remake. You may find, as in the case of this quartet, the plumbing works perfectly, the space is gracious, and the oddities are far more inspiring than the sterile slick-and-shine of contemporary bathrooms. Keep—and capitalize on—the room's *plus* points. Play up its vintage rather than trying to disguise it. Bring in more antiques or collectibles of the same generation. Choose wall coverings, colors, fabrics, and accessories that are appropriate to the room's age. Many of these items can be found at flea markets.

### NEW IS NICE, TOO

At the same time, you can use some up-to-the-moment tricks to cozy up that overvast space and make the room more comfortable by modern standards. Color and pattern are major allies in such sleight-of-hand decorating. To visually lower a too-soaring ceiling, paint it a darker color or run a strongly patterned wall covering overhead. Anything that attracts the eye makes the space "advance," i.e., look closer. The same trick works with floors. If you cover an arid expanse of

aging or ugly tile in a warm-colored carpet, the bathroom will look as cozy to the eye as it feels underfoot.

Large windows are apt to be another problem area in such big, old bathrooms. Actually, you can count the extra size as an extra blessing and dress the windows with an appropriately elaborate hand. Fabrics (even sheets) that match or coordinate with the wall covering are an obvious solution, to both the window and other fabric-hungry areas in the room. Make shower curtains and skirt an old-fashioned sink.

3

4

**1** A peach of a pattern mix tames the soaring space that could have intimidated the new owners of this large old bath. The prints in the wallpaper and curtain, plus the warm peach tones above and below, bring the outsized area into focus. Although you can't see it, the ceiling has been painted the same cozy color as the lush carpet. Both pick up the colors of the prints that enliven the walls and enclose the window in a one-sided swoop of fabric.

**2** To play up the vintage character of this Victorian bath, the original wainscoting and the clawfoot tub were left intact. All new additions have an old-fashioned flair: The calico fabric used to cover the window and walls, the marble-topped side-board now fitted with a wash basin, and the wonderful chandelier used in lieu of a new-fangled light fixture.

**3** The greening of this child-style bath came about by combining a lot of imagination and a little artistic talent. A hand-painted mural depicts favorite animal antics. (The motifs are easy to transfer from greeting cards, children's puzzles and such; simply enlarge the design on graph paper, cut from brown paper, then transfer to the wall, and paint.) Other ideas worth emulating here: the basket used as a light-fixture shade, the skirted sink (the fabric is attached with gripper tape), and grosgrain ribbon used as tiebacks and trim for the simple white curtains.

**4** Patchwork puts an old-fangled bath into a fresh new country mood. For this renovation, no hammer or saw was needed: the redo was accomplished with wall-paper paste, a sewing machine, and a bold blue-and-white patch-work pattern on the walls. The scheme was inspired by the antique quilt now strap-hung as window drapery. To relieve the pressure of so much pattern, solid colors were chosen for the bath rug and the contemporary home-sewn shower curtain.

# BATHROOMS
## EASY UPDATES

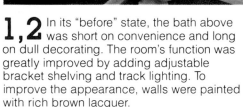

**1,2** In its "before" state, the bath above was short on convenience and long on dull decorating. The room's function was greatly improved by adding adjustable bracket shelving and track lighting. To improve the appearance, walls were painted with rich brown lacquer.

**3,4** The update of this bathroom included the installation of a new tub, toilet, and wash basin in the same locales as the old fixtures. Although not an "easy" project in the literal sense of the word, this same-spot type of installation is infinitely less complex and less expensive than a project that involves moving plumbing—even a few inches. Note that the new basin is set into an easy-to-clean plywood top that features a storage cabinet below. At the windows a cleverly designed louvered panel adds architectural interest to the room; the panel swings out to let in sunshine and fresh air.

**5,6** Here's another example of how you can rejuvenate a dated bathroom without getting involved in a major overhaul. Most of the makeover is, in fact, merely skin-deep: A new wrapping of plastic-coated hardboard protects the badly worn walls within the shower stall, and other surfaces have been given a slicking of vinyl tile to help bring freshness to the once-dreary room.

**Often all it takes to cure the ills of an ailing bath is imagination, a treatment that's easy on the budget.**

If you are stuck with a dated, dismal-looking bathroom, don't automatically assume that major remodeling is the only answer. Perhaps you should consider a minimake-over. You can keep many, if not all, of your existing fixtures and still greatly improve the looks and function of an aging bath with some rather simple updates.

Most outmoded bathrooms suffer from one or all of the following problems: inadequate storage space, poor lighting, difficult-to-clean surfaces, or simply family-worn walls, floors, and ceilings. If you're at all handy, you can correct many of these faults yourself. (You can see the results of such handiwork here and on the following pages.)

Color is your greatest ally when it comes to brightening up a blah bath. Use it lavishly, even in little bathrooms. This is one room where coziness is considered welcome. You can refresh aging walls and cabinetry for only the cost of a quart or two of paint.

And today's rainbow array of wall coverings can take the onus off even the ugliest old tile. You'll also find coordinating or matching fabrics to use in stitching up some new window and shower curtains. Do the labor of love yourself and you'll scarcely dent the budget.

**7** Learning to live with what you have (in the way of old bathroom appointments) may not be as difficult as you might think. Proving the point, this familiar old lavender tile takes on considerable charm when it's topped with a refreshing new wall print.

# BATHROOMS
## POWDER ROOMS

**1** This tiny powder room was given importance beyond its scant square footage by the rich wall covering and companion fabric shirred into a luxurious balloon shade. An antique shaving stand presides over the marble counter and shiny metal basin.

**2** A three-tiered vanity made of travertine marble adds visual interest and defines accessory areas in this remodeled powder room. A wall of mirror brings drama to the small space and shows off the sophisticated gray and beige color scheme.

**3** To update a 6x8-foot powder room, oak flooring strips were used as a surround for the vanity and adjoining walls. The wood gives the room a contemporary touch and provides interesting contrast to antique light fixtures and a vintage beveled mirror.

**4** An old pine chest fitted with a hand-glazed ceramic wash basin replaces the original run-of-the-mill vanity in this builder house bathroom and gives it individuality.

**2** **3**

**4**

**H**aving a "powder room" or half bath near the entry to your home is a definite *plus*, both for your convenience and that of your guests and—according to Realtors—for the resale value of your house. If you're bereft of a powder room, take a creative look for the space to add one. A large closet, a pantry, or even part of a porch or entryway may be good candidates for a half-bath conversion.

The powder room itself can be fairly small since it doesn't accommodate full-sized bathing facilities. To help make the most of limited floor space, many manufacturers offer slightly miniscaled toilets and lavatories, as well as odd-shaped fixtures to fit into corners and niches.

Decorating a powder room can be lots of fun, and you needn't spend much to give the room character and charm. Unlike a full-size bath where there are storage problems and other practicalities to contend with, a powder room can be approached from a purely decorative standpoint. Here you can give free rein to your fantasy with color, pattern, and choice of accoutrements. For instance, you can forget the conventional medicine cabinet and replace it with an antique mirror. And since there's no shower or tub moisture to worry about, you can afford to be less practical than usual with wall coverings, art work, and accessories. To perk up any powder room, fill a bowl with scented soap and put out your favorite towels.

# BATHROOMS
## STORAGE IDEAS FOR SKIMPY BATHS

**M**ost bathrooms have more paraphernalia to house than they have room for. The proliferation of personal-care electronics and anointments alone is enough to make the ordinary bath counter crowded beyond capacity. And even the healthiest among us has long outgrown the so-called "medicine chest" that comes with most standard-issue bathrooms. In addition, the linen closet is becoming an endangered species.

To stow away this spate of bath necessities (and niceties), it's important to look in all possible places—under the sink, for openers. If you've been living with only exposed pipes under there, you've been missing potential storage. You can buy a new vanity, with shelves hidden behind doors, to fit under your existing sink bowl. Any reasonably handy person can install it since there's no real plumbing involved.

The even-less-skilled can curtain off extra undersink storage. A perky cotton skirt is easy to make and gather around your sink. Allow at least double the measurement around the wash bowl. Make a channel at the top of the skirt and run a gathering string through. Glue gripper tape to the bottom of the sink; sew the other half of the tape to the gathered skirt. No one will guess what a multitude of bath supplies are hiding under the hemline.

Look for more unexploited storage space in other unlikely places: in excess head room over the shower, along an undeveloped wall, above a window, or behind a door.

**1** The space race in this tiny bath started with a building products supplier, source for the fiber tubes that have been stacked into a useful sculpture against the window wall. Fiber tubes, by the way, are usually used as forms to hold poured concrete. Made of cardboard, they come in various widths, and can be cut with a handsaw. Sand the raw edges and paint before using small stove bolts to secure the unit.

**2** The shallowest recess in a bathroom wall is all the motivation you need to claim generous storage. Here, a cupboard with sliding doors is set between 1x8 lumber uprights. Dowels set in below make handy towel bars; the basket serves as clothes hamper.

**3** Where there's a wall, there's a way to eke out extra storage areas. These simple wood cabinets turn a wasted corner into catchall shelving. The frames are fashioned from 1x6-inch pine boards, topped with louvered shutters made into doors.

**4** For a variation on over-the-toilet storage, build a plywood unit that boasts cabinet doors and even a rack to keep magazines within easy reach.

**5** Once-wasted wall space over the toilet can be turned into an open linen closet. All it takes is the extremely elementary combination of adjustable metal standards and brackets set with shelves cut from half-inch plywood, and painted.

1

378

2 3

4 5

# BATHROOMS
## LUXURY BATHS

To contradict the old adage: good things also come in *big* packages. Today's self-interest is self-evident in the super-sized, super-deluxe bathrooms on these pages. Actually room for much more than mere bathing, they are the contemporary equivalent of the ancient Roman spa—rich in luxurious fixtures and furnishings. Each room is highly individual and finely tuned to the owner's very personal and private definition of luxury.

Today's master baths add a healthful new dimension to home life. They can serve as an exercise center, sauna, and steam bath to keep fit in, or as a solarium/study to ease tensions in. Soak, relax, read, ride a stationary bike, steam in a sauna: You can enjoy it all within your bathroom walls if your space is large enough.

### SPACE: THE MAJOR LUXURY

If the actual bathroom area is too limited, a devoted sybarite may willingly sacrifice other square footage to gain a bigger one, giving up an ordinary-size bedroom, for instance, to gain a giant-size bath.

If you do go foraging for new bathroom space, try to find it near your present plumbing lines. As we've said before, even when money is no object, drastic plumbing changes can send staggering amounts of it down the drain.

Once you've staked out your generous chunk of space, you'll find almost no end to the wealth of better-living fixtures you can fill it with.

Take lavatories, for instance. Size is an important factor. An extra inch or two is usually well worth a few more dollars. Top-quality lavatories of vitreous china are the most durable; then come enameled cast iron and enameled steel.

As for tubs, the run-of-the-mill variety is a standard 5 feet long: sufficient for bathing, but falling short for luxuriating. Oversized tubs are only one of the variations you'll find. Look for soaking tubs, a treat borrowed from the Orient. They're deep and installed partly above ground.

Then there is the large, sunken bathtub, long the traditional standard for elegant living. More like a small swimming pool than a tub for merely bathing, such sunken splendor accommodates several simultaneous soakers. Often, the area around it is "landscaped" in multilayers, slicked with ceramic tiles or soft with wall-to-wall carpet.

Also on the luxury list are whirlpool baths and hot tubs, boons to both the body and the psyche.

A bath that takes on such social airs demands some special concessions to privacy. The toilet and bidet should be closeted away on their own, leaving the rest of the room centered on the bathing facilities.

If privacy *per se* is no problem, the entire bath can be opened to the outside view. In less-remote settings, the same open-air ambience can be achieved with skylights, illuminated ceilings, or ordinary windows placed so high in the wall the sun can come in, but the neighbor's view can't.

1

2

**1** Everything is sophisticated sleek-and-shine in this almost ascetic master bath. The over-sized tub with its built-in whirlpool faces an open shower stall that needs no curtain in such a water-proof environment of steel, tile, and black glass paneling.

**2** At the other extreme is the sunny open-airiness of this bath/sitting room. To achieve such a sweep of space, the owners combined an ordinary bath and an adjacent bedroom into one expanse that's open to the sky through a row of sun-washed windows. A pair of heat lamps overhead offer warmth on chilly days. Nearby, a glass-enclosed shower stall houses a revitalizing steam chamber.

**3** Here's a nature lover's bath that opens wide to a second-floor sundeck and surrounding treetops. Lush indoor greenery around the tub fosters the feeling of bathing *al fresco*. And if you like the idea, but lack the seclusion, simply use frosted glass panels to protect your privacy.

**4** Elegance, European style, is what this bath is all about. The space-saving shower-in-the-round is self-contained and comes complete with multiple shower heads, heated towel bars, and a soap dish protected by clear sliding panels. The see-through enclosure takes up little visual space and makes the small room seem larger than it is.

# BATHROOMS
## CLASS BATHS

1

2

**1** Interest in more romantic times prompted several manufacturers to bring back an old favorite—the claw-footed tub. Sitting regally in front of a greenery-filled window, the black tub with its gold-colored feet and fittings is the undisputed star of this bathroom. For an extra touch of class, an Oriental rug tops the ceramic tile floor. The windows are at treetop level, so privacy isn't a problem for bathers. Changing seasons dictate what plants go on the window ledge.

**2** This spectacular bath with its wall-to-wall mirrors has all the glitter and gleam of a movie star's dressing room. The backsplash-to-ceiling mirrors bounce light provided by complexion-flattering clear glass bulbs. Several of the mirrors are facades for doors that hide storage behind. Adding to the room's easy elegance are double sinks and a handy makeup niche. Towels and plants offer the only color in this all-white room. Changing the color scheme is as simple as changing the linens. The floor is white-glazed ceramic tile, but resilient vinyl flooring can provide a similar look.

**3** Color and texture combine to give this contemporary bath a warm, inviting look. Cedar paneling, placed horizontally on the walls, weathers well in a bathroom. Sealed oak cabinets are impervious to water spills and provide nice contrast for the handsome hand-glazed pottery wash basins. Graceful hospital-type faucets are set directly into the oak counter.

Reflected in the mirror is a blue-tiled tub and shower area. A double glass Dutch door opens to a small deck where bathers can soak up the sun. For cloudy days, a sun lamp placed high above the tub provides welcome warmth.

**1** Old houses, with large but dated bathrooms, are perfect candidates for major remodeling projects. This 3x16-foot bathroom was updated to today's sybaritic standards with the installation of a new step-up tub, toilet, and a spacious storage-laden vanity. The step-up design allows space for a new, badly needed drain system that features tilted pipes. Cream-colored ceramic tile covers the floor, the extra-deep tub surround, and the lower portion of the wall. Both practical and decorative, the tile visually unifies the many-angled bathing area.

Handsome cherry wood was used for the vanity, which measures a luxurious 8 feet long. Beautiful old cabinets with stained glass doors flank the mirrored area, and add an aura of Victoriana to the room.

**2** Some might call it decadently sybaritic, but a marble tub can't be surpassed for a luxurious way to soak in the suds. Expensive? Yes, but today's market does have less costly products that simulate the look of real marble. This remodeled bathroom was once wasted space at the top of a stair landing.

**3** If a whirlpool or hot tub is part of your remodeling plans, your family and friends are in for a treat. Whether in a bathroom or a family room (as shown), a whirlpool never loses its allure as a place for relaxation and fun. This spa is 84 inches in diameter, and has a bench around the inside, two steps down. A prefabricated whirlpool like this one can go above-ground or below.

# SPECIAL SPACES

Every house has many areas that may be minor in size, but play major roles in how the house functions. Entries, halls, staircases, closets, and attics are more than mere places to pass through or to hide behind closed doors. Although they really aren't "rooms" in the strictest sense, such special spaces do deserve special handling. Preplanning is particularly important here, where every square inch is precious and must be put to good use. Moreover, these small spaces are really satellites of bonafide rooms and usually must follow their decorative leads. An entry hall, for instance, often relates to both living and dining room decors. However, that's not to say the special spaces can't have special personalities of their own.

# SPECIAL SPACES
## ENTRYWAYS

S ince the entry offers the first impression guests have of your home, you'll want to make this impression a memorable one. However small the actual space, it still can extend a warm welcome. Consider the following criteria when planning an entrance area.

*Convenience* translates into a place to put things, and, space permitting, a place to sit. If the entry area has a closet, half your problem vanishes. If not, you may want to provide either a standing rack for hats and coats or a wall-mounted hanger. A small table or shelf provides a handy spot for dropping keys and mail. You may also consider a chest of drawers or a handsome trunk for storing mittens, gloves, and other outdoor paraphernalia. Mirrors in entries are always welcome; you can check your appearance as you go out the door, and guests can check theirs coming in. Also, a mirror makes a small space seem more gracious and spacious.

*Scale* is a second consideration in foyer decorating. Unless you live in a vintage home with an extra-large entry, you're probably dealing with a scant few square feet. Think small scale when dealing with small space. Opt for narrow tables, slim wall-hugging credenzas, or wall-hung shelves that free up floor space.

*Upkeep* is the final entry requirement. Since the first step into your home often brings with it outside mud and dirt, choose durable flooring materials such as wipe-clean vinyl, ceramic tile, or slate. Include, too, a welcome mat or area rug.

1

**1** This spacious entry once was a carport, with a nondescript door leading into the house. Now enclosed, the sun-filled foyer is both good-looking and functional. Guests are greeted with a gallery effect of black and white photographs framed and hung, double-tier, on the wall. (Art is a sure way to enliven any entry without subtracting valuable floor space.) At night, the gallery is dramatized by spotlights positioned on a ceiling track. An Oriental rug makes a colorful accompaniment for the sleek parquet floor.

**2** Step into this gracious entry hall and you step back into an earlier era: 1820, to be exact—the year when this colonial house was built. A six-panel heart pine door leads the way into the wide, stately foyer with its soft colonial colors, period wall covering, and heirloom furnishings. An antique Oriental runner is an elegant cover for the wide-plank wood floor.

**3** Special details add up to give this double-door entry a stunning effect. The bull's-eye window panes over the door are authentic, as is the style of the early American hardware. Hand-painted stencilling neatly frames the door and continues along the ceiling line. Small touches like these don't cost a fortune, yet they add charm and impact to a decorating scheme. You can buy ready-made stencils or design your own.

Even when it's just a few steps wide, a well-planned entryway should bid a warm "welcome home" and serve as a decorative harbinger of what's to come in the rest of the house.

3

2

4

**4** This entry area uses good design rather than walls or partitions to separate it from the living and dining areas. Because it's actually part of the living room, the entry was given focal-point status with the addition of a recycled antique door surrounded by panel inserts of beveled and stained glass.

# SPECIAL SPACES
## HALLWAYS

**I**f you've always thought of hallways as going nowhere, decoratively speaking, take a look at these stylish spaces. Halls can be much more than mere walls and boring doors. Look at them as small art galleries, as major color statements, or as a place to add a touch of decorative whimsey. Try encasing a hallway in a dramatic wall covering—ceiling and all. Or upholster it in fabric. Materials for a comparatively small area like this won't break your budget, and the sound-absorbing fabric will cut down on the noise and echo effect found in many hallways.

Carpet is another good soundproofer that's especially effective in hallways. Buy carpet with a careful eye to durability, since hall traffic is often mercilessly heavy. Flat weaves, twists, and tweeds are your best bets in high-use areas. For safety's sake, tack down hall runners and area rugs so they don't slip and slide underfoot.

Lighting is another safety consideration in a hallway. If you don't have adequate built-in lighting fixtures, consider adding a track of lights overhead (an especially good idea in a hall with a wallful of art work you want to highlight). Or, space permitting, nestle a narrow table or chest of drawers against a hall wall and put a lamp on it. But be sure to avoid furniture that will encroach too far onto traffic lanes. Some other choices for hall pieces are: grandfather clocks, wall-hung shelves and mirrors, or one dramatic work of art that makes the area look furnished without usurping floor space.

2

3

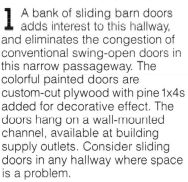

**1** A bank of sliding barn doors adds interest to this hallway, and eliminates the congestion of conventional swing-open doors in this narrow passageway. The colorful painted doors are custom-cut plywood with pine 1x4s added for decorative effect. The doors hang on a wall-mounted channel, available at building supply outlets. Consider sliding doors in any hallway where space is a problem.

**2** A boring succession of walls and doors can be easily enlivened with paint. Here a tunnel-like passage was given pizzazz by applying slick-and-shine enamel—not only on the doors and walls, but on the floor and ceiling as well. Deck enamel works best for wood floors; high-gloss latex is good for woodwork and doors. To keep a painted floor looking good, apply several coats of polyurethane, letting one coat dry completely before applying the next.

**3** Little more than a "crook in the road" between bedroom and staircase, this narrow hallway gained its interest from fabric-covered walls upholstered the easy way: using a store-bought system that consists of long plastic strips, which have "jaws" at the top to hide raw fabric edges, and an adhesive strip to hold it taut against the wall. Available at specialty decorating stores, the system comes with a tineless "fork" tool you use to stuff the fabric into the jaws. Or, you can shirr fabric on the wall. To do this, first frame the entire area with narrow furring strips, then gather the fabric and staple it to them. Use narrow moldings to cover raw edges. Another method is to simply hem the fabric top and bottom and shirr it on two lengths of curtain rod, mounted just below the ceiling line and above the baseboard. (You can special order longer length rods at drapery shops.) With this installation, you can easily take down the fabric for laundering. Either way, a fabric-upholstered wall helps put the quietus on traffic noise, and hides old, unsightly walls in the bargain.

# SPECIAL SPACES
## STAIRWAYS

**1** A climb (or descent) on these carpet-clad open risers leads to an eye-catching art wall at the landing. Carpet tacks attach the heavy rug to a 1x2 wooden brace suspended on ordinary picture hangers.

**2** Music to the eyes, this up-tempo collection of New Orleans Jazz Festival posters is enough to lure even non-jazz buffs up the stairs for a closer look.

**3** An exposed brick wall provides a perfect backdrop for a collection of old-fashioned advertising posters. Note how the posters are arranged in mimicking stair-climbing symmetry.

**4** Poor pun or not, this stairway has had its ups and downs. Previous owners had installed heavy wrought iron railings and flamboyant red-flocked wallpaper. Now the stair has been restored to more traditional decor with a graceful new banister and new wall treatment. To enhance the traditional feeling and add visual interest, compatible wallpaper patterns are set off within frames made from narrow wood molding strips.

**5** What looks like supergraphics on the wall are actually three large canvas paintings. The arrows echo the architecture of the staircase in this turn-of-the-century house.

2

3

4

5

# SPECIAL SPACES
## SEWING AND CRAFTS

Organization is the key to every successful home sewing, hobby, or crafts center. Half the battle is getting all your gear together; the other half is finding a place to put it. Having to rifle drawers, boxes, and closets for a project's paraphernalia is enough to put a damper on any do-it-yourself venture.

Unless you have a spare room where you can close off your projects-in-progress, you'll have to steal a corner for your sewing or hobby area.

Such space may be hidden anywhere: family room, bedroom, laundry room, or even a generous closet. To make the most of it, think in terms of surfaces and storage areas that fold, stack, or stow easily between work sessions. Wherever you find any efficient work space, it should include generous counter space, storage for a sewing machine, and a place to keep small objects. Wall-hung racks, plastic drawers, and wire bins are good storage choices. Put walls to work storing spools, scissors, and yarns. Pegboard is ideal for this purpose. Consider hanging bolts of fabric on wooden dowels. Yarn stores handily in empty ice cream containers.

The final essential for any good sewing or hobby area is excellent lighting. It's great if you can eke out work space within range of natural light, but you'll still need specific task lighting down close to your subject. Any small-based swing-arm lamp will do, but beware of glare. Clip-on lights and draftman's lamps are also good choices for sewing areas.

1

**1** Once a mere walk-through between upstairs bedrooms, this 8x16-foot corridor is now a colorful crafts center. In deference to the narrowness of the area, the generous work surface stores flat, then folds out for crafts projects. With ribbons and paper held at the ready on a pegboard wall, wrapping packages is a breeze. Easy-to-build open shelves hold yarns and organize other stored items. Overhead, a brace of track lights mounted on the wallpapered ceiling sheds a bright light on all activities.

**2** Crisp, clean, and convenient, this multi-purpose laundry room boasts a compact sewing center. Located between a laundry bin and a tall cupboard, the center also houses a drop-down ironing board. A wall of white pegboard holds a colorful collage of thread spools, as well as other sewing needs. Up high are rolls of wrapping paper and glass bottles of buttons.

**3,4** If you can't carve out a sewing center in an existing area, try building one against a mere door's worth of wall space. Hiding behind this louvered door is a complete sewing center. The swing-down tabletop unfolds to a 5-foot-long work surface, and the closet itself is crammed with storage crannies. In it are a rack for two dozen spools of thread, pegboard for sewing accoutrements, a built-in wastebasket, and a rod for hanging projects still under construction. Three large bins on the bottom hold more fabrics and other supplies. Made of ½-inch and ¼-inch plywood and pine moldings, the unit is mirrored at the back.

# SPECIAL SPACES
## HOME OFFICES

1    2

A home office makes excellent sense whether or not you're the type to bring home your briefcase. These days, it's no simple task keeping track of the paperwork our households are heir to. What with bills to be paid, budgets to be balanced, and records to be kept, none of us is immune from "homework." And unless you have a specific spot for taking care of business (we don't mean a dining table dubbed as a desk), disorder is likely to reign. Fortunately, offices can happen anywhere: behind a screen in a living room or bedroom at the top of a stair landing, in a closet or a wall system—any place that has room for a work surface and space for storage.

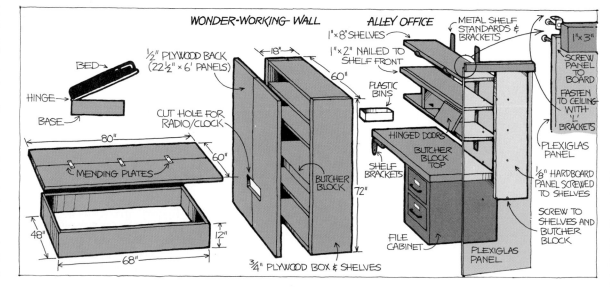

WONDER-WORKING-WALL    ALLEY OFFICE

BED
HINGE
BASE

½" PLYWOOD BACK (22½" × 6' PANELS)

CUT HOLE FOR RADIO/CLOCK

80"
60"
48"
68"
12"

MENDING PLATES

¾" PLYWOOD BOX & SHELVES

18"
60"

BUTCHER BLOCK

72"

1"×8" SHELVES
1"×2" NAILED TO SHELF FRONT

METAL SHELF STANDARDS & BRACKETS

PLASTIC BINS

HINGED DOORS
BUTCHER BLOCK TOP

SHELF BRACKETS

FILE CABINET

PLEXIGLAS PANEL

1"×3"
SCREW PANEL TO BOARD
FASTEN TO CEILING WITH 'L' BRACKETS

PLEXIGLAS PANEL

⅛" HARDBOARD PANEL SCREWED TO SHELVES

SCREW TO SHELVES AND BUTCHER BLOCK

**1** Here an inefficient kitchen alcove became a handy work space. A butcher-block counter fits neatly into the nook, providing ample room for a miscellany of household tasks. Underscoring the butcher-block slab are store-bought plastic drawers. A shelf behind the countertop hangs on wall-mounted cleats with a ready-made spice rack beneath.

**2** Sometimes you can make space function in a bigger way by cutting it down into smaller areas. Livable proof: this all-in-one room, where a bit of clever carpentry carves out specific work areas without actually closing off the space. The wonder-worker is the home-built divider that serves as headboard on one side and an office on the other. The tiny, but storage-laden, work nook, is separated (but not isolated) by a smoked acrylic plastic panel. The diagram shows how it's all done with ½-inch plywood, 8d nails, and glue.

**3** If you're looking for space to stash a home office, study your options from all angles. This tiny, tidy office is a truly new slant on the subject, evolving as it did in the process of an attic restoration. Built of construction-grade 2x4s, the desk top and shelves slip between the exposed rafters to take advantage of their full depth. Add a draftsman's lamp and a fold-away chair, and you have a handy home office that folds up and virtually disappears when the job is done.

3

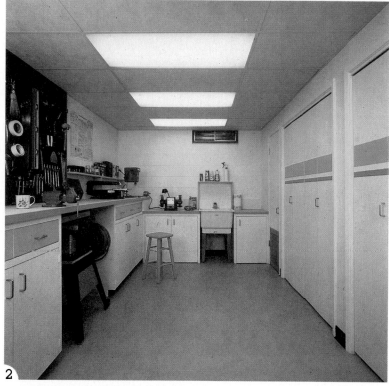

1 2

3 4

5  6

**1** Papered walls and painted cabinets make this all-in-one utility center a pleasant place to do chores. One side of the built-in center features a fold-down ironing board, a hanging rack, and double bins for clothes sorting. To the right is an extra-deep sink, perfect for hand washes, soaking, and potting projects.

**2** This bright and inviting sublevel workshop is anything but substandard in design. It's a magnet for every member of the hobby-loving household, often drawing them at the same time. That's why its 12x16-foot dimensions have been carefully divided into various activity areas. Centered in the rear is the laundry tub. To its right, behind folding doors, is a self-contained booth for spray-painting. Behind the yellow

stripes on the right are two separate work counters. The room-long workbench on the left can handle big projects comfortably.

**3** What once was a breezeway connecting the house to the garage now is a pleasant skylit laundry room. Located near the kitchen, the narrow pass-through features maple shelving above the washer and dryer, and counter tops made of cork board. Mexican paver tiles and a collection of baskets add decorative interest to the functional setting.

**4** A lot goes on in this well-planned room. Besides being a laundry room, the space also functions as a planting center. Efficiency is built into every angle. Plastic laundry baskets—tagged

with each family member's name—contain clean, sorted clothing (it's up to each person to claim his own garments when needed). Permanent press items hang on a tension rod placed over the dryer.

**5** This 5x8 laundry area is actually part of a large country kitchen. Only on washday do the appliances reveal themselves. When it's time to go to work, the black counter lifts for the top-loading washer. Controls for both machines hide behind sliding doors. Above them, one standard wall cabinet conceals the business end of a clothes chute that feeds from the floor above.

**6** An infusion of imagination turned this 6x9-foot sliver of space into a home office/sewing center/ironing room, with storage space to spare. The home office side of the red-and-white room features a desk constructed of 2x4s and Mylar-covered hard-board. The sewing side of the room has a Mylar-covered work surface along with white plastic drawers for threads, patterns, and fabric. An ironing board and two sorting baskets hang from hooks on the wall. A brace of plastic storage boxes serve as bases for the desk and sewing center; their tops are made of 2x4s and plywood covered in Mylar. Every other inch is for storage, with baskets and bins tucked everywhere and overhead rods installed for hanging the ironing.

# SPECIAL SPACES
## CLOSETS

**1** Sacrifice just a dinner plate's width of floor space to create a handy dining room closet like this one. Adjustable shelves in the bright orange interior hold a wallful of table accessories—including linens hung wrinkle-free on rows of dowels. Closed, the sleek white-laminated doors put on a face sophisticated enough for any dinner party.

**2** When is a closet not for storage only? When it becomes a child-sized hideaway, complete with a play loft tucked up over the clothes racks. The compact plastic chests that fit neatly under the clothes eke out every useful inch for the area.

**3** Here's the same generous closet that is in photograph 2, only now the young occupant has outgrown the hideaway loft. The space still serves several purposes, housing the teenager's dressing table/desk (made from modular storage units and a board top).

**4** Functioning as a huge walk-in closet, this garage-to-house passageway serves as a combination mudroom, locker room, and storage area. Removing two closet doors created room for a wine-storage area (made of hexagonal drainage tiles) and an open-shelved spot for sports gear. Two more wood-paneled closets conceal off-season clothing.

**5** Take a cue from kindergartens and include lots of cubby holes in an entry hall closet. You'll appreciate their ability to keep outdoor wearables neatly sorted.

2 3
4 5

# SPECIAL SPACES
## ATTICS

**T**he best treasure you'll ever find in your attic is new space for living. Tucked up under the eaves may be that coveted "room of her own" for a child, a new area for family activities, or a home office up and away from it all. By adding dormers and inserting skylights, you may be able to put this unused space to work.

When assessing your attic's potential, consider these three basic criteria: access, headroom, and structural strength. First off, will the floor stand up to actual use? It would be wise to call in a professional opinion. Now, how will you get there? If you have an existing stairway, you're halfway, steep and narrow though it may be. If you have only a hatch opening, however, you'll have to add a staircase, and that possibility rests on how much space you can find for it on the floor below. A standard stairway takes a rectangle of space 10x3 feet; an average spiral unit should fit into a 5½-foot square. Try to plan the access route away from walls so you won't be bumping into them every time you make the climb.

To determine how much headroom you have in your attic, measure the ceiling height at a point 4 feet out from each side wall. If it's less than 7 feet, you'll need to add a dormer for comfortable headroom. Although this may seem costly, dormers add priceless light and air to attic living.

Heat and sometimes plumbing are other needed features. Frequently you can simply extend them up from the main systems below.

**1** Carved from the attic in a 50-plus-year-old house, this new bedroom/play area combines contemporary spaciousness with old-fashioned practicality. Rugged commercial carpet covers all floor surfaces—a touch of comfort that also comforts the ears of the adults downstairs. With banks of built-ins, cleanup is a breeze. Each child has a special retreat to help keep too much togetherness from posing problems.

**2** Once only old trunks could call this attic "home." But then the architect/owner took a second look at the unappreciated space and decided to turn it into an office. New windows shed needed light; walls are sleeked with plywood over insulation, and low-scaled furniture makes the once-wasted space function beautifully.

**3** To reclaim this attic space, the owners literally had to raise the roof by adding two dormers on either side of the ridgeline. New windows at the gable end more than chase the gloom from the formerly dark room. Low, built-in storage units added around the room's perimeter put once wasted space to work.

**4** This top-flight attic retreat features movable partitions that allow the space to change as family needs and activities change. Although the partitions ensure privacy, they're low enough to let in a free-flow of light and brightness that makes the room a favorite place to be.

3

4

# SPECIAL SPACES
## PORCHES AND GARDEN ROOMS

1
2

The decline from architectural favor of the front porch nearly did away with the sociable pleasures of porch sitting. We tended to move the porch around back and wrap it in a high privacy fence.

Now, the porch is edging back onto the home scene. So are solariums and garden rooms. The recent renaissance of interest in vintage houses gets some of the credit. So does the national preoccupation with fresh air, outdoorsy living—and energy conservation. So popular has the porch-like look become in decorating, even "shut-ins" such as apartment dwellers have adopted many of the trappings: wicker furniture, glossy painted floors, and forests of hanging plants.

If you already have the real thing, you needn't limit its use to summertime only. Moderately inexpensive construction work will winterize an open porch area to extend its life all year round. If you lack even an open porch as a point of departure, consider adding one. Prefabricated doors and windows have put porch building within the skills level of many home do-it-yourselfers. If you are going to do the work yourself, you may still want to get some advice from a reputable architect or builder (you can buy their consulting time by the hour). Especially if you're going to make a dramatic change in the appearance of your home, it's wise to seek the expert help of a professional.

Be energy conscious when you start selecting construction materials. For example, insulated glass panels and sliding glass/screen door combinations will cut down on heat loss in winter and heat gain in summer, without cutting down on the view.

Most windows will need some kind of dressing, if not for privacy, then for protection against winter gusts and summer glare. The simpler, the better in a sun-room. Narrow-slat blinds are carefree and colorful. Vertical louvers offer easy upkeep, contemporary sleekness, and good light control.

In a more traditional porch or sun-room, you might want the tailored look of woven woods, or bamboo roll-up blinds. If you

prefer fabric, consider simple, laminated window shades, or Roman shades made of canvas. Louvered shutters are also a good choice for an enclosed porch or solarium.

If your porch is screened and open to the elements, look to weather-resistant, easy-to-clean vinyl roll-up blinds. They're available in many colors, and some are designed to look like bamboo.

Floors demand special consideration in a porch location. If yours has come in from the cold, chances are you still have outdoor flooring materials such as brick, slate, or concrete. All are acceptable from a decorative standpoint; but come winter, you'll want to add insulating carpet or an area rug.

Sun rooms and porches add greatly to the enjoyment of any home. Decorate these airy spaces with a carefree approach to ensure the utmost in relaxed living.

3 4

**1** Thriving plants, a classic floor patterned from black-and-white vinyl tile squares, and an operable ceiling fan make this former front porch a delightful year-round garden room. Though not heated, the room stays comfortable even in cool weather thanks to windows with double-pane insulating glass.

**2** A sun porch can offer an antidote to winter drearies, especially if you live in a northern climate. Plenty of sun streams through these room-wide windows. Even on gray days, the sun seems to shine here, thanks to the exuberant yellow color scheme. Painted onto the walls and echoed wall-to-wall in the carpet, yellow also serves to solidify the long, narrow space so typical of many sun porches. This one measures only a mere 11 feet wide, but the effect it has on both eye and emotions is expansive.

**3** A welcome addition to a small tract house, this room for all seasons features a slate floor and wall-to-wall windows, shaded with mini-slat blinds on the south. The inviting garden room rests on a concrete slab patio that was poured when the house was built. In the summer, sliding glass doors open to the outside.

**4** Like an old-fashioned gazebo, this open-air garden room is a popular place on hot summer days. Open on three sides, the porch gets plenty of cross ventilation. On sultry days, breezes get a boost from the ceiling fan. The antique wicker furniture is beautifully offset by the patent shine of the wood floor.

# EXTERIOR DECORATING

Exterior decorating? It's a term you may not have heard before, but it's one worth considering. We all care about our home's appearance, but too often we settle for the status quo. The choice of materials and colors and the way they're expressed on the outside of a home can creatively reflect the owners' personality just as much as the furnishings, colors, and accessories assembled inside. Whether your house is small or grand, plain or fancy, traditional or contemporary, you can bring it its best in numerous ways. Whatever your style, way you express it on the exterior of your home d complement the architectural style of the nd be in harmony with the neighborhood le.

# EXTERIOR DECORATING
## FACE-LIFTS FOR OLD FACADES

**F**ace lifting an older house requires more than simply knowing one's way around a paintbrush, hammer, and saw. In fact, the most important aspect of any exterior (or interior) fix-up job is the planning that precedes the work.

That planning can mean the difference between a house that exudes personality and charm, and one that looks just plain dull. And it can mean the difference between a home that concisely expresses a style or period, and one that is merely a confusing hodgepodge.

Whether subtle or dramatic, an exterior face-lift can give a fresh look to a timeworn facade.

### EASY CHANGES WITH PAINT

Sometimes, all it takes to give a house a fresh look is a little paint, judiciously applied to accent architectural details or mask awkward features. Before beginning any paint job, consult with experts at a paint store to be sure you are buying the right type of paint.

Here are some pointers: For wood siding, consider alkyd-base, oil-base, or latex paints. But be careful. You can paint latex over old oil-base paint, but oil-base paint will not adhere properly to latex.

For masonry surfaces, such as brick or concrete block, choose alkali-resistant paints. Exterior latex or special masonry paint are two types; your paint dealer can advise you.

Trim paints offer glossy, enamel-like finishes, which dry to a hard, weather-resistant sheen. Underfoot, deck paint

provides durable protection for wooden surfaces. And special rubber-base paints are made for concrete.

### DRAMA THROUGH RESTYLING

If paint alone won't do the job, a more extensive restyling may be in order. This can range from the redesigning of an old porch to the elimination of it altogether. Or, it may vary from re-siding a home with a new material to extensive construction work that changes the old lines of the home dramatically.

Whatever the extent of the planned face-lift, it's best to proceed cautiously and with an understanding of and respect for any historical or architectural significance your home may have. And, it's a good idea to consult with an architect before attempting any major remodeling. (A lot of well-meaning homeowners have destroyed important and valuable architectural details or have violated the inherent character of their homes in the name of ill-advised "modernizing" or "updating.")

1

2

3

**1,2** Sometimes an exterior face-lift is best accomplished by removing, rather than adding, major elements. Here, elimination of outdated brick-patterned asbestos siding, old-fashioned awnings, and a deteriorating front porch did the trick. The demolition revealed the home's simple, classic lines and permitted sunlight to brighten the once-dreary interior. The newly exposed clapboards were painted

a mellow Colonial Williamsburg green, and the door a lively Chinese red. A rich cream color highlights the trim.

**3,4** Here again, a boxy house received a beauty treatment by starting with a small-scale demolition. Removal of the old green shingles, an unnecessary second-floor window, and a rickety porch cleared the way for a contemporary face-lift. Rough-

hewn cedar siding (applied over new fiber glass insulation) is as good looking as it is maintenance free. Rust-colored paint boldly accents the windows and trim. The only new structural addition is the skylighted vestibule.

The shed-roof, skylighted enclosure around the front door does more than make a boldly contemporary statement; it's an energy-saving air-lock vestibule with a second door inside.

An exterior face-lift can clarify lines or give bold new character to a nondescript home. The transformation of these plain, older houses proves the point beautifully.

# EXTERIOR DECORATING
## FACE-LIFTS FOR OLD FACADES

**1,2** When a home has no
particular historical value
or architectural style, you're free
to make dramatic changes
without inviting the wrath of
~~servationists~~. This exciting
~~c~~ontemporary home is a good
~~...~~ It's hard to believe the
~~...~~ n life as a typical 1940s
~~...~~ w, with a lofty new
~~...~~ shed-roof
~~...~~ the updated
~~...~~ use look
~~...~~ edar
~~...~~ bold
~~...~~ e-
~~...~~ ne

Although the home's restyled
facade sets it apart dramatically
from nearby homes, the house still
blends visually into the older
neighborhood, because of the
emphasis on the steep roofline
and retention of overall proportions
that echo the scale of other houses
in the area.

409

3

**3,4** This home went from dull to distinguished thanks to a well-planned remodeling. As shown in the "before" photo, the exterior styling was boring at best. But the structure had simple lines that the owner emphasized to create a "modern plantation" look. First, the old front porch and the unnecessary and unattractive transom window above were removed. To the right of the front door, a 12-by-12-foot living room addition was built.

To shelter the new living space, and create a pleasant recessed veranda at the same time, the original roofline was extended.

New grooved cedar siding, painted gray, gives important vertical emphasis to the once-squatty facade. Classical touches, including small-pane windows, pillars (which support the new roof) and elegant molding around the front door, reinforce the home's updated look. Other additions include a brick-covered porch and steps, and a wrought-iron entry light.

4

# EXTERIOR DECORATING
## PAINT POSSIBILITIES

A touch of paint can wake up a tired-looking house quicker than any other single treatment. Even if a whole-house paint job is unneeded (or is out of the question financially), just a glossy coat of fresh color on the front door or window shutters can add instant personality.

If a more-extensive paint job is needed, consider all the exterior paint colors on now, as well as those custom mixed. but may not be

at photo-our local quid-take about rea.

**1** Just a touch of painted trim is all it took to set off this clapboard-clad home. In typical, old New England style, the home's wood siding was allowed to weather and is protected only by a coat of linseed oil applied every three years. Against the resulting dark gray patina, pale salmon trim on the eaves, the door, and window frames adds a delightful touch of color.

**2** This charming Cape Cod home gets its handsome good looks from a three-color paint combination. Light eggshell high-lights the windows and beautifully detailed front door against a backdrop of warm beige siding. Charcoal-brown shutters help to visually balance the front door and provide eye-catching contrast.

**3** A house such as this one, with architectural character and natural rustic beauty, needs little more than a touch of painted trim to accent it beautifully. Colonial gray-blue paint subtly sets off the trim around the honey-color door and the handsome small-pane windows. The trim color complements the tones of the weathered silvery-gray siding.

**4** This Georgian-style house has a crisp, yet dignified look thanks to a careful mix of paint hues. The siding and shutters, painted warm brown-tinted gray, are accented with paler gray trim. For drama the stately door is a high-gloss red.

411

**1** The owners of this turn-of-the-century home wanted their paint choice to make a strong statement, but one with warmth and dignity. The successful solution was to paint the old clapboards warm butterscotch, then use white to set off the distinctive trim. Black-painted shutters add crisp contrast, yet blend with the charcoal tones of the scalloped shingles.

**2** Special architecture demands a special treatment. This gingerbread-style house received a subtle but effective combination of three colors to show off its old-fashioned character. Mustard-painted siding provides a good backdrop for the white paint used to highlight the home's ornately framed windows. But what takes the scheme out of the ordinary is the use of deep purple-blue and a shadow line of rusty red to define the architectural lines.

**3** When a roof is clearly visible or prominent as it is on this house, it's important to choose harmonizing paint colors. Here, soft light green blends with the roof tones and adds color without overpowering the home's storybook appeal. White and pale yellow show off the beautifully crafted trim that gives the house its storybook character.

**4** The fanciful ornamentation on this Victorian home is boldly accented with an exuberant paint scheme. Lavish use of white paint sets off the trimwork from the deep purple-blue paint on the clap-boards and ornate shingles. Just a touch of red and purple on remaining trim completes the lively treatment.

415

You can choose from a whole palette of paint colors to enliven an otherwise ordinary house. To glean ideas, take a drive around your neighborhood and surrounding towns.

**1** The charm of this modest Spanish-style bungalow comes from small, but effective, details. Situated in a shady redwood grove, the house still has a sunny disposition because of its yellow painted walls and terra-cotta accents. The earthy color punctuates the deep-set windows and doors. Greenery-filled window boxes give added importance to the small windows to the left of the door. The front steps are painted with bright blue deck enamel.

**2** This ordinary ranch home achieves its distinctive look from a clever paint job.

All details are trimmed in black, then filled in or surrounded with two tones of gold. The garage door's panelled look was accented with simple stock molding, applied by hand and painted black.

**3** This small stucco house was an undistinguished copy of its subdivision neighbors until the owners did some exterior decorating. The effort included a crisp new paint job and the addition of simple black shutters. First, a soft mustard-colored paint went over the stucco. Then black shutters were added to emphasize the small windows. White paint lavished on the front door and on the small-pane windows adds a tailored touch.

# EXTERIOR DECORATING
## DOOR PRIZES

**1** Who says a front door has to be one color only? The door of this Victorian home successfully incorporates three colors. Royal-blue paint on most of the door contrasts beautifully with the light mustard shade on the rest of the house. More of the light shade highlights the center of the special door carvings, which are bordered in mossy brown.

**2** Crisp white-painted trim sets off this distinctive entry. Basic black, highlighted with judiciously applied red and white, makes the entry stylish and inviting.

**3** Here a plain front door easily developed a rustic character. Three roughsawn cedar boards were cut to fit the old door and then glued in place with panel adhesive. Then, carefully whittled dowel ends were glued into predrilled holes in the boards to give the door an old-fashioned pegged look. Rustic old brass and wrought-iron hardware complete the treatment.

**4** This weathered brick town house gets a decorative boost from a blue-painted door and matching shutters. For a hint of urban formality, trim around the small-pane windows, as well as the door's sidelights, is black, repeating the color of the graceful iron work on the stairway balusters.

**5** There's nothing unassertive about this porticoed entry. A bright red door set off by white-painted trim gives the entry a cheerful, welcoming look.

1

2 3

4 5

# CREDITS

# CREDITS

Page 394
  Sharon Landa Design
    Assoc.
Page 395
  Stevenson Projects (2,3)
Page 397
  Philip Tusa Design, Inc.
Page 398
  Linda Elder (1)
  David Ashe (2)
  George Cash (3)
Page 399
  Anthony Moses, The H.
    Chambers Co. (6)
Page 400
  John E. Seals
Page 401
  Antonio F. Torrice (2,3)
  Don Roberts, Roberts Assoc.
    (4)
Page 402
  Amisano & Stegmaier, AIA (1)
  Earling Falck, AIA (2)
Page 403
  Cathy Simon, Marquis
    Assoc., AIA (3)
  Tom Hall (4)
Page 404
  Larry Lambert (1)
  Carol Knott, ASID (2)
Page 405
  Rosalie Gallagher (3)
Page 408
  William H. Lane (1)
Page 409
  Miller/Morris; Urban
    Resources Construction
Page 410
  Gil & Lois Tredwell
Page 411
  David Koontz & Felix
    Campanotta
Page 415
  Margaret D. Woodring (2)
Page 416
  Stephen & Kathy Easley
Page 417
  Marijoan Alioto (2)

**PHOTOGRAPHERS**

We extend our thanks to the following photographers, whose creative talents and technical skills contributed much to this book.

Alderman Studios
Michael Boys
Ernest Braun
Ross Chapple
George de Gennaro
Mike Dieter
Tom Ebenhoh
D. Randolph Foulds
John Gregory
Harry Hartman
Bob Hawks
Bill Hedrich, Hedrich-
  Blessing
Jim Hedrich, Hedrich-
  Blessing
Bill Helms
Thomas Hooper
William N. Hopkins
John Katz
Lisanti
Fred Lyon
Maris/Semel
E. Alan McGee
Clyde May
Bradley Olman
John Rogers
Jessie Walker

**FIELD EDITORS**

We would like to thank the following Better Homes and Gardens Field Editors for their extremely valuable assistance in helping us locate and photograph many of the homes pictured in this book.

Pat Carpenter
Barbara Cathcart
Bonnie Crone
Eileen Deymier
Pauline Graves
Estelle Guralnick
Sharon Haven
Helen Heitkamp
Linda Magazzine
Bonnie Maharam
Ruth L. Reiter
Maxine Schweiker
Barbara Sims
Mary Anne Thomson
Jessie Walker

**ACKNOWLEDGMENTS**

Our appreciation goes to the following museums, foundations, and companies for providing us with photographs of various furniture pieces to be used as artists' reference in the Furniture chapter of this book.

Atelier International, Ltd.: Le Corbusier chaise longue (page 60).
Baker Furniture Museum: French Provincial ladder-back side chair (page 54); Directoire side chair (page 55).
Colonial Williamsburg Foundation, Williamsburg, Virginia: Ladder-back chair (page 47); Chippendale sofa (page 49); Sheraton sofa (page 50).
Collections of Greenfield Village and the Henry Ford Museum, Dearborn, Michigan: William & Mary high chest (page 44–45); Boston rocker (page 47); Queen Anne wing chair, Queen Anne side chair, Queen Anne high chest (page 48); Chippendale side chair (page 49); Federal Pembroke table, Federal armchair, Hepplewhite side chair (page 51).
Habersham Plantation Corporation: Pencil post bed (page 51).
International Contract Furnishings, Inc.: The Pension chair, Alvar Aalto (page 56).
Kenwood Merchandising Corporation: Parsons-style table (page 61).
Kittinger Company. Block front chest (page 49); Sheraton side table (page 50).
Knoll International: Marcel Breuer, Cesca armchair; Marcel Breuer, Wassily lounge chair; Mies van der Rohe, Barcelona chair and table (page 59); Warren Platner table (page 60); Eero Saarinen side chair (page 61).
Herman Miller: Charles Eames lounge chair/ottoman (page 61).
Yale University Art Gallery, Mabel Brady Garvan Collection: Windsor armchair (page 47).

# INDEX

Page numbers in *italics* refer to illustrations or to illustrated text.

## A–B

# INDEX

# G–I

# INDEX

# INDEX

# INDEX